FOUND GUILTY, BUT...

How a legitimate criminal investigation became a political witch hunt, and its aftermath in my life

Joe Kotvas

ISBN 978-1-63525-926-1 (Paperback)
ISBN 978-1-63525-928-5 (Hard Cover)
ISBN 978-1-63525-927-8 (Digital)

Christian Faith Publishing, Inc.
296 Chestnut Street
Meadville, PA 16335
www.christianfaithpublishing.com

Printed in the United States of America

INTRODUCTORY REMARKS

This is an interesting and different type of book to read. Joe Kotvas gives the reader a rare inside look at a dark period in the Hillsborough County Commission. It is written by an actual elected participant on the Board of County Commissioners, rather than a third party writing from past newspaper accounts. From his point of view, you are taken directly into his personal memoirs – his personal experiences. It gives the reader "a different spin" on how we viewed the events as reported on radio, television and newspapers of the time. Kotvas puts the reader in his courtroom chair, sitting next to the co-defendants; in his jail cell; reporting to prison; and the roller coaster ride that followed.

This is the second book that Joe Kotvas has written and self-published. The first was published in 2014 of an often overlooked historical phase of World War II concerning the Japanese invasion and occupation of the outer islands in the Aleutians off of the Alaskan coastline. The title of that first book is "Men of the Invisible War."

But this book is more like his personal diary, written first hand by an actual participant. Our bookshelves and libraries are full of books, novels, articles and documentaries written in the second or third hand by researchers, historians, masters and doctoral thesises, full of citations, footnotes or end notes of their interviews, oral histories, primary and secondary sources. But this is not the case with Joe Kotvas' personal experiences in the crucible of his life. He had been a policeman, later elected to the Tampa City Council, then almost elected Mayor of Tampa, then a one-year appointment on

City Council, then elected to the County Commission…. And then convicted and sent to the federal penitentiary. Where did he come from? Who was he? Joe moved to Tampa from New York City in 1968 and in less than 3 years got elected and took office as a member of Tampa's City Council November 9, 1971 and resigned to run for Mayor in October of 1974 – and came very close to being elected. He again served on Tampa's City Council (October, 1978 – October, 1979) for a year when he was appointed to fill in the vacancy created when Jan K. Platt ran for County Commission. In 1980, Joe joined her when he was elected to the Hillsborough Board of County Commissioners up to his arrest in 1983, conviction and long federal prison term. You also get first-hand experiences of becoming a convicted felon and the many consequences that follow you in life. The opportunities, life's doors and windows that are forever closed. These harsh realities of life and the long lasting consequences are the reason for the admonition: Crime does not pay!

With three vacancies on the Board of County Commission, the governor of Florida appointed three unelected qualified citizens, who had to interrupt their lives to serve the people of Hillsborough County. Local government had to continue. Governor Bob Graham appointed John R. Paulk, from South County, a retired Major General of the U.S. Air Force; Matt Jetton, a very successful real estate developer of Carrollwoood, whose grandfather Matthew Jetton had been one of the early home builders in the Palma Ceia neighborhood where Jetton Street is located; and Dr. E. L. Bing, a noted educator from East County who had been a Principal at Marshall High School in Plant City and leader in the Afro-American community. These three honorable men did such an outstanding job and service to our county, they jointly received the coveted Liberty Bell Award from the Hillsborough County Bar Association.

Since those political dog days of 1983,1984, 1985 smearing reputations of innocent people and their aftermath, Kotvas further documents what was recently published by the University of Florida Press, written by award winning historian James M. Denham in his documentary history of the "Fifty Years of Justice" commissioned by the Federal Judges of Florida's Middle District of Florida; and "the

Witch Hunt" expose written for Cigar City Magazine in its June/July 2012 edition by noted journalist, historian, filmmaker and published author Paul Guzzo, now a reporter with the Tampa Bay Times newspaper. Guzzo's expose was the first of the trilogy saying: "There was a Witch Hunt in Hillsborough County in 1984. It was this community's version of the McCarthy Hearings, as federal prosecutors went to any means necessary to prove that Hillsborough County was corrupt at every level of government..."

Immediately after the Commissioners were convicted, the legal community here experienced a transformational change in the attitude and direction of the U. S. Attorney, an unusual management style not experienced before in this federal district. We assumed that his success had gone to his head. But we were wrong. It wasn't until last year, 2015, that we read with great interest the history of the U. S. District Court for the Middle District of Florida, published by the University Press of Florida, and written by award-winning historian Dr. James M. Denham who had been commissioned by the federal judiciary to document the 50th birthday of the creation by Congress of this "new" federal judicial district in Florida. At page 155, we found this quote from oral history given to Dr. Denham on May 29, 2012 by the Honorable William Terrell Hodges, who became the Chief Judge in the Middle District of Florida upon the retirement of U. S. District Judge Ben Krentzman in 1982: "Soon after Merkle's swearing in, the new U. S. Attorney invited Judge (Ben) Krentzman and Judge Terrell Hodges to lunch and "We were happy to go," as Hodges recalled, but the dining became unpleasant when the prosecutor announced that his main reason for asking us to lunch was so that he could come to an agreement with us that anybody who got convicted, we would give consideration to imposing maximum punishment in every case. That way justice would be served and there was a likelihood that more crime could be prosecuted. I sat there in some wonderment.... In fact, Judge Krentzman just got up and left the table as best I recall. That was the last time we had a conference with Mr. M   don't say that to denigrate the man, he has his idea about w   his function was and he intended to zealously pursue it, which he did. He rubbed a lot of people I think the wrong way in the process."

It is well established in our code of ethics – to respect the judiciary's independence and not try to "influence, mislead or intimidate" the judges. If he did this with the two ranking federal trial judges, who else did he try to influence?

With this information, we can look back with a better understanding. Obviously, the federal prosecutor had come on board with "an established agenda and an enemies hit list of his own." As he unmasked himself, he also threw aside the U. S. Attorney's manual and the long standing principles of sound prosecutorial judgement and standards of performance and accuracy and objective evaluation of the necessary quality and quantity of evidence required in our constitutional system of criminal justice. He closed his eyes and shut his ears to the wise advice Attorney General Robert H. Jackson gave federal prosecutors a long time ago on how to improve their duties as public prosecutors: "The prosecutor has more control over life, liberty, and reputation than any other person in America… at his best is one of the most beneficent forces in our society, when he acts from malice or other base motives, he is one of the worst… because …this immense power to strike at citizens, not with mere individual strength, but with all the force of government itself… a rededication to the spirit of fair play and decency… should animate the federal prosecutor… Reputation has been called the 'shadow cast by one's daily life'… any prosecutor who risks his day to day professional name for fair dealing to build up statistics of success has a perverted sense of practical values, as well as defects of character… he can have no better asset than to have his profession recognize that his attitude toward those who feel his power has been dispassionate, reasonable and just… he is prohibited from engaging in political activities." He went on to say that "the most dangerous power of the prosecutor: that he will pick people that he thinks he should get, rather than pick cases that need to be prosecuted… it is not a question of discovering the commission of a crime and then looking for the man who has committed it is a question of picking the man and then searching the law books, or putting investigators to work, to pin some offense on him… it is in this realm in which the prosecutor picks some person whom he dislikes or desires to embarrass, or selects some group of unpopular persons and then looks for an offense, that the greatest danger of abuse of prosecuting power lies… it is here that law enforcement becomes personal, and the real crime becomes that of being unpopular with the predominant or governing group being attached to the wrong political views, or being personally obnoxious to or in the way of the prosecutor himself." He concluded his legendary remarks by saying: "the qualities of a good prosecutor are… a sensitiveness to fair play and sportsmanship is perhaps the best protection against abuse of power, and the citizen's safety lies in the prosecutor who tempers zeal with human kindness, who seeks truth and not victims, who serve the law and not factional purposes and who approaches his task with humility." Robert H. Jackson is the only man in American history to have held all of these four positions:

U. S. Solicitor General; U. S. Attorney General; Justice of the Supreme Court of the Unite States; Chief Prosecutor for the U. S in the Nuremberg Trial of Nazi War criminals.

Instructors at prosecutors training seminars and conferences refer to Jackson's legendary message as the 10 Commandments to being a good prosecutor. It is required reading and included in the Justice Department's Manual for United States (Prosecuting) Attorneys. It is accessible for all to read…. It is easily found in the internet by googling Robert H. Jackson's the Federal Prosecutor.

In the March 3, 1986 Miami Herald article about Merkle, former Miami defense lawyer Neil R. Sonnett said: Merkle suffers from the Holy War Syndrome " – people imbued with the Holy War Syndrome want so badly to go after corruption and illegal activity that they'll do anything, trample anybody's rights, destroy anybody's reputation. Merkle doesn't understand that a prosecutor has to be concerned with individual rights."

State Attorneys in Jacksonville, Orlando, Tampa – all called for his removal by the U. S. Department of Justice. Governor Bob Martinez joined in that demand and with Bob Graham defeating Paula Hawkins as U. S. Senator – Merkel would not be reappointed. And when he tried to become a U. S. Senator himself, Merkle was defeated by Connie Mack. When he could not control the appointment of a successor in the U. S. Attorney's Office, Merkle lashed out at his boss Attorney General Ed Meese calling him "a liar."

In this trilogy, Kotvas, Guzzo and Dr. Denham document vividly the transformation that occurred from prosecutor to persecutor. Kotvas' memoirs show the prosecutorial overreaching that followed the conviction of the 3 commissioners. The few convictions were overshadowed by 28 losses in rapid succession. The evidence was simply not there. Suspicion, rumor, gossip, speculation, misinformation, innuendo, guilt by association, no corroboration – simply was not enough to meet the established requirements of proof in our American courtrooms for more than 200 years. Twenty-eight defendants were found not guilty by juries, or the judges dismissed the charges or granted a directed verdict of acquittal – and some convictions were vacated in the federal court system. That is simply unheard of in the Middle District of Florida. The lack of creditable proof was so evident that no reprimands, suspensions or disbarment by the Florida Bar occurred. The federal judiciary trying these cases and hearing former commissioner Jerry Bowmer testify – did not believe him. Federal Judge George C. Carr labeled Bowmer "such a liar… He's admitted that time and time again." But where do the individuals found not guilty go to reacquire their stained reputations and how about the humiliation, embarrassment of hauling them into court for trial without the necessary and required proof? One lawyer who was charged and tried 3 different times and found to be "not guilty" 3 different times was quoted as he walked out of the Federal Couurthouse: "Some people have cancer…I have Merkle." After the dust settled, the Mad Dog dragnet – witch hunt – revealed more about the hunters (persecutors) than the hunted (the targets of the persecutors).

Modern day witch hunts should be carefully scrutinized just as closely as the travesty that put the Salem trials and the McCarthy hearings on the books. Are witch hunts a thing of the past? No! Could this type of persecution happen again? Yes, it can! Our front line of defense is a vigilant judiciary and bar associations with courageous leaders that are not afraid to speak up and stand up against injustice and stomping on our Constitutional guarantees. All that has to happen for evil to prevail – is for good men to keep silent and do nothing.

Let's pray that never happens in our country.

E.J. Salcines
Tampa, Florida

*For my children and family, who struggled through this difficult time
To their future generations, who will now
understand what really happened
To all those who fell victim to the government's witch hunts of the 1980s*

CONTENTS

PREFACE

It Could Happen to You

Have you ever been the target of someone who said something about you at work, at a party, or in a group that affected your reputation, something that was not true? Have you ever been accused with no basis in fact, yet people believed the accusations and spread the tales to others, causing you to lose your job or creating other hardships for you? We hear stories like this all the time.

This book is about one such experience—my experience of being charged, tried, and convicted of a crime in which I was never a participant. This all happened because of the lies of one man who committed a crime and, after being caught, sought to save himself from doing hard jail time by implicating others. It's about falsehoods that, over time, became "facts" in the minds of the people, and a jury, who were all denied access to the actual truth in the case.

I was convicted by a jury of my peers. Unfortunately, it was a jury that never heard all the true facts of the case. This is the story of the twisted falsehoods that caused my whole world to come crashing down upon me and changed the course of my life on the morning of February 1, 1983.

The information presented here is documented with names, dates, places, and events, and can be verified in federal court public records and transcripts, news articles, and journals and notes that I kept over the years.

This book details my arrest and persecution on bribery charges as they really happened, as best as I can remember, and elaborates on the missing pieces that never became public during my trial or were never picked up by a biased press bent on sensationalism while wrecking the lives of public servants and well-respected citizens of my community who were on trial with me.

It details how an experienced federal prosecutor was able to manipulate the evidence presented to the court and jury and, in so doing, was able to destroy me, my codefendants, my family, and my friends.

I'll try to show how both the defense and the prosecution did not introduce some information that could have cleared me or would have gotten my case severed from my codefendants. This was information that the jury and the press have not heard or seen until now. Had this information been entered into the record and presented to the jury, the outcome of my trial might have been much different.

My story goes into detail of the odyssey of my life, during and after my trials. It discusses my struggles with prison life and what really goes on behind the barbed wires and gun towers. It tells about minimum security prisons and the pain and suffering experienced by both the defendants who are incarcerated and their families, as well as what one finds when one finally comes home following such a terrible ordeal. Can there be a good life after prison? Yes, there can!

I will give you answers to that question and details of the harsh but successful struggles I went through to regain my dignity and to rebuild my life for myself and my children. I'll try to show all the stumbling blocks, hardships, and failures that confronted me during this arduous rebuilding process.

This is the true story of years of sacrifice and suffering of one person who refused to lie, who didn't give in to requests to untruthfully snitch on others, who refused to give up hope, and who didn't stop fighting when all seemed hopeless. It describes how I was able to keep my faith in God and humanity. It explains the truth about how I emerged from the ashes of disgrace, desperation, and despair to form a new life for myself and my children.

This is my story, told as it happened to me, with the whole truth as I saw it. It doesn't matter what I say or print; there will always be those who refuse to believe the truth. These are the people who look to do what is easiest for them, believing what they've read in the newspapers or have seen on the broadcast news or what they have heard from various sources in the past.

You may ask why this information was not released to the jury. That question could only be answered by the judge who presided over the case and by the ambitious prosecutor who sought impressive conviction statistics to further his political career and who would go to any length to achieve them.

So I leave it up to you to read the untarnished facts and make your own decision regarding my innocence or guilt. Who am I? Am I a criminal, as some would believe, or the victim of a man out to save himself and an overzealous prosecutor who saw an opportunity to use him? I hope when you finish this book, you will be able to decide for yourself.

Nothing will change the fact that I am a convicted felon who was sentenced by the court to do prison time. That chapter of my life will always be with me. However, over time, I was able to write a new chapter. I was able to get a good job, have my civil rights restored, and rebuild my life. Though there are scars, life does go on, and we can make a difference. We can be a testimony to others on how we deal with and overcome adversity.

It is time for the truth of this dark time in my life to be clearly and accurately known. It brings me great satisfaction and closure to tell the truth of my story for all who would care to know.

If asked, even today, I would give up everything I have achieved and all that I possess for the opportunity to be retried as a sole defendant on all the evidence and actual merits of the case, and without all the manipulation. I would gladly accept the outcome, even if it meant I could once again be found guilty and be returned to prison. This is a chance I would be willing to take. For me, it would be worth it to have my legitimate day in court so the people I served and cared about so much could have their faith restored in their friend and public servant.

In this book, I am taking the opportunity I was never afforded by the justice system and never will be. No one can give me back the years of my life that were lost, nor undo the damage that was done.

Nevertheless, this is my story as I remember it. At this point, it's simply a matter of principle and justice.

Joe Kotvas
Tampa, Florida

CHAPTER 1

The Arrest

February 1983

The Hillsborough County Courthouse

It was a bright, clear Monday morning on February 1, 1983, as I walked into my office at the Hillsborough County Board of County Commissioners around seven-thirty and started taking care of the day's business. I had a habit of going in early to get organized on the issues I needed to deal with before any commission or committee meetings.

No sooner did I sit down than I received a call on my private line from Claude Tanner, the owner of Suburban Trash Disposal in the south end of the county and one of my loyal supporters. He would often call and tell me about problems in his area or people who might need help from the commission. But this morning, his call was brief and cryptic.

I picked up the phone and said, "Hello."

All the voice said on the other end was, "Commissioner, watch out for Jerry Bowmer. He's up to something, so be careful when dealing with him. That's all I have to say. Just watch out for Bowmer. I have to go now." Then he hung up.

What a strange call, I thought. I recognized Claude's voice on the other end, but it didn't make any sense to me at the time.

I had lost a bid for congress just a couple of months earlier, but I was still a young rising star in local politics. I knew I would have other chances to move up in politics, for I had a strong following of supporters. I had worked out this plan and had a crazy idea on how to get to the White House in ten years. I might not have made it to the presidency, but I had a plan that would have brought me close if I played my cards right.

The first order of business was a meeting with a group of people from the Brandon Chamber of Commerce concerning a proposed incinerator slated for construction in their area in the eastern part of the county. The meeting did not last long, and I informed them that I would keep an open mind on the matter as they left to meet with fellow commissioner Fred Anderson.

I had been very upset and had not been myself or thinking too clearly after breaking off my engagement with my girlfriend, Debbie, the week before. Although our relationship was no longer working, my feelings for her were still very strong, and I felt I had to keep busy.

I was having a hard time keeping her out of my mind. I was a single dad with three children, two boys and a girl. I had lost my wife, Cathy, to cancer a few years earlier and was struggling to raise my kids alone when Debbie came into my life. She was the first woman who could match my late wife intellectually and in terms of compatibility, besides being an 11 on a scale of 1 to 10 for etiquette and looks! The hurt of caring for someone who could not care for you in the same way can really mess with a person's mind for some time after a parting.

Around eight-forty that morning, fellow Commissioner Jerry Bowmer walked into my office carrying a briefcase. He had just left Commissioner Anderson's office, and he wanted to talk to me.

"Is the commissioner in?" he asked my aide Jane as he walked past her desk into my open office without waiting for an answer. He attempted to close my door to the outer office when I told him, "Don't close it. Please leave it open. I don't wish anyone to think something is going on between us."

Reluctantly, he left it open, walked over, and stood in front of my desk, placing his briefcase on top of it. (Little did I know that the FBI had equipped it with a recorder that would tape any nearby conversations.) Bending over my desk slightly, he started whispering a bunch of nonsense that I could hardly understand; then he started talking loudly and said, "I see you still have that old stuffed eagle in your office that everyone has been wanting to get rid of for some time."

I wasn't paying attention to what he was talking about; I had no interest in what he had to say and had other issues on my mind at the time. I said to him, "Yes, I like the look of strength it gives off. It's our country's national emblem. It should be publicly displayed, not hidden."

He then started telling a joke, and I cut him off, "What is it you want, Jerry? I have a lot of work to do before the meeting, so get to the point." I was getting a little disgusted with his ramblings, and he must have sensed that.

Then he started to whisper again, saying, "Geraci, Geraci." At that moment, unbeknownst to me, he laid a white envelope on my desk to my left. Then he turned and walked out as quickly as he had entered. "What a goofball. What was that all about?" I asked myself.

My phone rang. It was a constituent with a complaint about his drainage ditch not being cleaned. I told him I would take care of the matter. As I hung up the phone and looked across my desk, I noticed for the first time the white envelope that Bowmer had apparently left there. I thought to myself, *What's this clown trying to pull now?* I could see that the envelope was not sealed, and I noted its contents. It looked like a large amount of money, and I had a strange feeling that this might turn out to be one of the bad jokes that he often pulled.

Bowmer had a habit of playing jokes and tricks on his fellow commissioners and staff members, usually in bad taste. Many of us, especially the female employees, did not like it. It never seemed to bother Bowmer, though. He always got his jollies by pulling them.

I had met him years ago. He stopped by my house in South Tampa when he was thinking about running for office the first time. I was then a Tampa City councilman. He met with my late wife and me to ask for advice and help in his campaign.

He seemed like a nice enough fellow at the time. He claimed to be a lay preacher from the Ruskin area, a small community in the south end of the county. I gave him what little information I thought would be helpful but informed him that I could not get involved in his campaign. It's never good for someone in political office to be part of other local campaigns. Doing so would alienate friends and make new enemies.

Over the years, he changed from a shy candidate to a cunning and scheming politician. He won a second term on the county commission when I won my first, defeating his buddy Charlie Bean. I came to dislike Jerry when I saw the way he conducted himself in office, always wheeling and dealing. All he seemed to care about was himself and what was in it for him.

He asked me from time to time to pal around and have drinks after some of our meetings. I brushed him off, making some kind of excuse. He always seemed two-faced, yet we all had to work together for the good of the community. I know for a fact that Commissioner Fred Anderson did not care for him either. He was not the same man I had met at my home a number of years before. His success and influence seemed to have gone to his head. He had become a legend in his own mind.

Holding the envelope, I could feel its thickness, but I fought the urge to take the money out and count it. I picked up the receiver to my intercom and told my aide to get Albert Tosca from the state attorney's office on the phone. If Bowmer wanted to play jokes, two could play the same game just as easily.

I did not like the looks of the envelope, so I put it in my top desk drawer and locked it for safekeeping, never touching its contents. I knew Bowmer would probably come back for it when he didn't get the reaction he wanted, and then I would give him a hard time.

My aide came back on the intercom and informed me that she had Mr. Tosca's secretary on the line. I picked up my phone. "Hello, this is Commissioner Joe Kotvas. I'd like to speak with Mr. Tosca, please." I figured I would ask his advice on handling this kind of situation.

"One moment please while I see if he is in, Commissioner."

After I waited about a minute or two, she came back on. "I'm sorry, Commissioner Kotvas. Mr. Tosca is not in at the moment. Can anyone else help you?"

I told the voice on the other end, "No, no, thank you, but please have Mr. Tosca return my call when he gets in, thank you."

She assured me that she would see that Mr. Tosca received the message and hung up. I figured I'd explain to him what was going on and see what he could advise when he returned my call. I trusted Albert; he was a good person and a good prosecutor.

Tosca was an assistant to EJ Salcines, the state attorney for Hillsborough County, Florida, at that time. I had met him several times at different functions, and over a period, we became somewhat friendly. I trusted him for being an honest man. Both of us were very active in the Latin community.

Whatever Bowmer was up to, I figured I had better let the authorities know about it in case there was a problem. I had heard rumors about Bowmer, had suspicions about him, and didn't care to have anything to do with him. We were not friends, nor did we ever socialize in any way outside the courthouse. We were just political colleagues who worked on the same board.

Since I still had time before my next appointment, I decided to take out my checkbook, go over my bills, and make a few payments since this was the beginning of the month.

As I sat at my desk working on my monthly statement, my aide Jane stuck her head into my office and said, "Commissioner, there are two men outside who said it is very important that they speak with you. They do not have an appointment but asked if you could see them now as it is very important."

I always had an open-door policy and would see anyone at any time, even without an appointment, unlike some other commissioners who would not see anyone unless they had scheduled a meeting ahead of time. So I told Jane to wait a moment before sending them in so I could put my checkbook and statements away.

As the two men entered my office, I stopped what I was doing and rose to greet them as I normally did when someone came to see me. I walked toward the men, and one of them asked if he could close my office door in order to speak to me privately, then proceeded to do so before I had a chance to respond. The other introduced himself as Special Agent Russell Wood, who said, "Mr. Kotvas, we're from the FBI. We're here to talk to you about Jerry Bowmer possibly taking bribes and would appreciate any help you might be able to give us."

I did not get the other's name. Shaking their hands and telling them to have a seat, I proceeded back around my desk to my chair. At the same time, I informed them that I would be happy to give them whatever information and assistance I could.

As I sat down, I noticed one of the agents was adjusting his right sleeve. He was wearing some kind of small microphone attached to the cuff of one of his sleeves under his jacket. As they sat, they once again adjusted their sleeves with the mics so as not to be observed, but I had already seen them. I started to get a bad feeling about this interview. Was this interview being recorded without advising me of the fact? Were they taping our conversation?

I had seen microphones like that before in recording studios and on news reporters. All of a sudden, I had a bad feeling about what was going on in my office. I did not like the sneakiness of these men. If they wanted to record our conversation, why didn't they say so? I had no problem with that; I would have given my permission for them to do so.

At the time, I was unaware that they had vehicles parked at strategic points around the county courthouse, linked with the latest sophisticated tape recorders and equipment in the courthouse itself to catch and tape every word that was being said by anyone in range of their tiny hidden microphones. A total of five high-tech recording devices were working simultaneously, backing each other up in the event one should fail. There was also master recording equipment set up in a small closet off the main lobby.

One of my visitors said, "We're here to ask a few questions about Commissioner Bowmer and some zoning matters, especially about the Geraci zoning." When he mentioned the name *Geraci*, it did not register right away, so then they said the Galleria zoning, the one with the eagle.

As soon as I heard the eagle mentioned, I knew what zoning he was talking about. I said, "Oh yes, we've had a lot of problems with that zoning, an eagle's nest and all that." Then I pointed to the stuffed eagle on the far side of my desk and said, "I like eagles. They are a sign of strength and the emblem of our country."

I informed the detectives that the commissioner had left my office a few minutes before. Then they asked if I could tell them what the meeting with Bowmer was about. I responded that there was no meeting. I told them he just came into my office and started to babble about a lot of nonsense. I hadn't paid much attention because I had a lot on my mind. He then left and walked out of my office toward his, I presumed.

"Yes," one of the agents said and then proceeded to ask again about the zoning I had voted for.

I said, "What? Hold on a moment. If you check the minutes of the board meeting, you will see that I voted against that zoning."

Then they asked me about the Geraci vote at the commission meeting just nights before. I informed them that I had voted against it because it was in my district, and it would affect traffic flow in a negative way, and the community surrounding the property had petitioned the commission to vote against it.

I also informed them that I thought it was strange that Commissioner Jan Platt had voted for it, for I thought I surely had her "no" vote on this one. She had a habit of voting against large developments when there was a lot of community opposition. I told the agents I even tried to get her to change her vote to "no" on the record after the vote count, but she ignored me. So I cast the lone dissenting vote. I could never understand why after all the big developments she voted against in the area, she voted for that one.

Next, they asked me if Bowmer had paid me a bribe for my vote on the Geraci zoning.

That's when it dawned on me what was taking place. Bowmer had come into my office talking all sorts of small talk; then he brought up the Geraci zoning and quickly left my office after leaving an envelope full of money on my desk. I was being had, being used by somebody, and I wasn't sure why.

I knew Jerry had left that envelope on my desk; was that what they were implying? But he did not pay me a bribe. I wouldn't have taken any money from him. He left it on the end of my desk, knowing that he could not give it to me, or I would have thrown him out of my office. Was he trying to set me up for some reason? *Of course, that's it. It must be. Let's see where this discussion is leading,* I thought to myself.

During the few moments they were questioning me, I was hoping to get a return call from Tosca, with whom I felt more comfortable, at the state attorney's office. I hoped he could help in this situation.

Do I tell these agents about the envelope and hand it over to them, or should I wait till they asked the right questions? Why should I tell these guys anything anyway? I thought. *Every time I've tried to give them information in the past on some misconduct within the county or city, they never seemed to do anything about it and only made me look foolish.*

They did not disclose that Bowmer was under arrest or that they were conducting a serious investigation. I knew that these people had been investigating Bowmer for many years, and he always seemed to get away clean with nothing resolved. I can't count the times Jerry bragged about what fools the FBI were. So why tell them anything? After all, I did call my friend at the state attorney's office, whom I hoped would be getting back to me soon.

I would turn the envelope over to him and give him whatever information I could. It could be a feather in his cap instead of for these guys. All this was going through my mind at record speed.

Due to my former police experience, I wanted to see where all this was leading. I would just tell them, "No, he did not pay me a bribe," and that would be the truth. Then I'd just wait for them to ask me the next question (they always have a next question), which should have been, "Did Jerry Bowmer ever give or leave any money with you?" I would then have said he left this envelope on my desk and turned it over to them. Otherwise, I would just give it to Mr. Tosca at the state attorney's office to handle.

So I was getting ready to tell them about the white envelope Bowmer had left on my desk when they asked, "Commissioner, did you take a bribe from Commissioner Bowmer?"

I had not taken a bribe from Bowmer, nor did he mention one to me in my office. So I said, "No, Jerry did not pay me a bribe for the Galleria zoning. Like I said, I did not support it."

At that moment, they stopped asking me questions. To my utter amazement, Agent Woods said, "Commissioner Kotvas, you're under arrest. We know Commissioner Bowmer handed you five thousand dollars for your vote on the Geraci zoning a few minutes ago, and we are charging you with extortion and interfering with interstate commerce, which is part of the Hobbs Act. You have the right to remain silent..."

As Woods droned on, I sat there in shock and disbelief—was this all he was going to ask? He did not wish to go further with the interview before making such a judgment? He continued to read me my rights, but they did not ask any more questions at the moment. I could not believe this was happening to me. I said, "What? Something is wrong here."

It seemed that they were in a big hurry and just wanted to make an arrest. They did not want any more information. I felt I had been had. The whole conversation and interview lasted less than five minutes. My overcautiousness on what I thought I should say caused my arrest, even though I told the truth.

I could not move. I was frozen in my seat in utter shock. I couldn't even speak for a moment. I was in a dissociative stupor, a mental state that remains indescribable to this day.

Then one of them said, "Take everything out of your pockets and put the contents on the desk in front of you, then stand and raise your hands over your head and turn and put them on the wall behind you." However, they did not begin searching me right away.

Fear was starting to overcome me, fear like I had never known before. It was hard to keep my thoughts in order as my mind was going a thousand miles a second with a mixture of confusion, unreality, and uncertainty racing through it. I did manage to realize that, at this point, I had better get some legal advice before going forward. I had already put my foot in my mouth, and I didn't wish to say or do anything more that would get me deeper in trouble until I had a chance to clear the air.

I informed the agents, "Look, I think I need to get some legal advice. I feel I should call my attorney before we continue." As I started to reach for my phone, Agent Woods stretched out his hand and said, "Don't do that," in a forceful voice. "You can contact your attorney later."

I replied, "I really think I need a little legal advice on what I should do here." As a former police officer, I knew I had rights, and one of those was to have legal counsel present during any arrest or questioning if I requested it.

Again, he stated that my call would have to wait, and he asked me once again to empty my pockets, stand up, turn around, place my hands against the wall, and lean forward. At this point, I felt that if I made any attempt to reach for the phone, we would get into a hassle, and additional charges would be filed against me for resisting arrest. So I emptied my pockets on my desk, then stood up and turned around, facing the back wall of my office. He then said to me, "Stretch out your arms and lean forward." I complied, and he began to search me.

When they finished, Agent Woods said, "We would like you to hand over the money Jerry Bowmer gave you."

I was still in shock over everything that was happening and gripped with a near-paralyzing fear of what was going to happen to me and my family. I was unable to respond. He repeated his demand for the money and stated that if I did not turn the money over to them, they were prepared to hold me and seal off my office while they acquired a warrant to search the premises. They clearly repeated that they would come back and tear my office apart piece by piece, leaving it in whatever condition they felt necessary and do whatever it took to embarrass me publicly.

So that was what was in the envelope that Jerry had left on my desk: bribe money. He was setting me up to take a fall, I thought to myself. A deep state of panic came over me, as I expect would happen to anyone under these circumstances. With the forcefulness of these agents, I was having a hard time trying to think straight.

I didn't know what to do or say, and I was having a very hard time responding to them. I did not appreciate the way this matter was being handled. This was not the way a good police officer would conduct an investigation. This was just not happening to me. This was all a bad nightmare, and surely it would be over in a moment. The episode was presenting itself, and I kept wondering, *How could I have let this happen?*

The agent repeated himself with even more force in his voice. I guess he thought I was trying to stall or was playing dumb. At that moment, I tried to get some control of my faculties. The shock of it all had been quite numbing. Again, I thought I would try to contact my attorney, for I felt that if I was going to do anything for them, I should at least have an attorney present to observe what was going on and to ensure that I did not give up any of my rights.

At this point, I stated to them that I would be happy to turn over whatever Bowmer left in my office but would like to have an attorney present when I did. As I said this, I started to reach over for my phone again when Agent Wood said, "That can wait."

I then responded, "Before I do anything, I feel I should have an attorney here to properly advise me." He informed me that I could call an attorney when we got back to his federal building office just two blocks away and that I should turn over the money now. It seemed like they did not wish for me to have an attorney present as they interrogated and pushed for evidence to use against me.

At this point, I made a final protest that I would like to have an attorney present to witness everything and to advise me of my rights. I knew from experience as a former police officer that I had a right to have legal counsel present when information was requested after an arrest. Yet they refused to allow me to call anyone. I felt they were violating my rights, but at that moment, I was in no position to argue. After all, they were the Feds.

I informed them that it would only take a few minutes to get one here, and it should not interfere with their schedule, whatever that might be. They would not hear of it, and I could see that there was no point in trying to discuss this or anything else with them. By now they were getting very irritated with me, and I didn't know what they were prepared to do to me should I make any attempts to try to call for legal assistance. I truly felt, from their strong words and actions against me, that they just wanted to rush through this. I thought I might be in some physical danger if I did not cooperate with them, which most definitely could lead to more charges against me.

Finally, with all hope of legal advice gone, under protest and against my will, I agreed to turn over what Bowmer had left in my office. I told them it was in the top middle drawer of my desk. They asked me to remove it and put it on the desk. I informed them that the drawer was locked. They allowed me to get the keys, so I opened the drawer, took out the envelope, and placed it on the desk. One of the agents picked it up and checked to see if the money was in it. Satisfied, he placed the envelope in his pocket. I was then told to put everything back in my pockets and have a seat while Agent Woods used my phone to get further instructions. The other agent called on his two-way to have a car brought around to the front of the courthouse.

At the time, I could not understand why they were in such a rush for me to turn over the money right then and there. It wasn't until later that I learned that they wanted me to handle the money since they had treated it with a special invisible dye. They wanted evidence on my hands to entrap me. The only problem with that was, they didn't figure Bowmer would place the money in an envelope and leave it on my desk. They had planned for him to hand it to me in cash so the dye would show up on my hands, which it never did, since I never touched the cash.

If I had an attorney present during my interrogation, the situation might have been handled differently. It was obvious that these overzealous agents were in no way going to allow me to get legal assistance that might have interfered with their case.

Since I was helpless, with no idea what would happen to me, I felt the need to do something to get control of my wits. I realized if they were recording all this, the tapes would clearly show that I was not a coconspirator but a victim, with no legal counsel or advice at the time of the arrest.

I asked if I could finish taking care of some personal matters like making out my bills for the month while we were waiting. They did not seem to mind at this point while we all waited for the car to come around the front entrance so we could leave. As we waited, the other agent continued to ask for my cooperation in this matter and repeated that it would help me if I was cooperative.

I was thinking more clearly now and thought about what he had just said, my cooperation. After what these guys had just done to me! Again, from my experience as a former police officer, I knew that the Feds could be dirty in their actions if they wanted to be. I thought they would not treat me that way, but I was wrong. I said, "I would like to get some legal advice before I say anything." I knew now that the best thing to do was to avoid saying anything more, for they would only twist it around to use against me.

We received the call that the car had arrived. As we got up to leave, they did extend one small courtesy. Agent Woods informed me that if I did not give them any reason or cause for alarm, they would not handcuff me; I could just walk out of the building with them to the waiting car. I assured them I would be no problem. They allowed me to put my suit jacket on, and we left my office, passing my aide Jane's office on the way to the side stairwell. I stopped for a moment to tell Jane to cancel all my appointments for the rest of the day as I would be tied up for a while and that I would get back with her.

We left my office and walked down the hall past Fred Anderson's, directly next to mine. As we passed by, I could see two more men who looked like Feds with a plug sticking out of one of the men's ears and a wire running down the inside of his suit. They were standing outside Fred's office, waiting to see him. Anderson already had a group of people from the Brandon area in his office complaining about the proposed new county incinerator that might go in their area. It was the same group that had just left my office before Bowmer and the Feds came in.

We moved quickly down the hall to the corridor past all the other commissioners' offices, continuing to the main lobby and out to the street. As we passed, eyes followed us. A few voices called out, "How are you doing today, Commissioner?"

I would have liked to have said something, but I was still in too much of a daze to even think straight. As we exited the building, I was ushered into a waiting car that was in front of the courthouse, ready to take us to the nearby federal building.

CHAPTER 2

The Interrogation

February 1983

The author

The agent's car stopped at the main lobby entrance of the federal building. We exited and took the elevator to the seventh floor, then entered a room on the right with a numeric keypad lock beside the door. I was rushed into an office with a couple of chairs and a small table. It had no windows.

I was asked to sit down and empty my pockets again, and I complied. One of the agents collected all my belongings in a little basket and left. Two more agents walked into the room and said,

"Mr. Kotvas, we would like your cooperation. We want to know anything you can tell us about Allen Wolfson."

I was now even more dumbfounded. Here I was being arrested for a zoning bribe, and these jokers were asking me about a man named Allen Wolfson. I could not believe what was going on. Where was all this leading? I knew Allen Wolfson; he was considered a wealthy and powerful businessman in our community. I had met him on a number of occasions at social functions. Former Tampa mayor Dick Greco, a friend of Wolfson, had introduced us some time back. But I had never had any dealings with the man. Whenever we met at an event, he would always seem aloof and just walk past me, which gave me the impression he felt I was below him in some way.

I noticed a little recorder in the room with the two agents and assumed they wanted to make sure they got every word I said on tape. I informed them that I would have no problem cooperating with them, but first I wanted to call my attorney and check on my children. I had been told I could do this when I got to their federal building offices.

"I don't have any idea what is really going on here or where you men are coming from with these questions," I said to them. About this time, Bill James, whom I had met a few times at different functions and who was in charge of the federal crime task force in Tampa, came into the room.

He said to me, "Mr. Kotvas, I'm very sorry to see you here."

All I could say was, "I am also sorry to be here under these circumstances."

James stayed in the room and listened as the other agents continued to ask me questions. Again, they said they would appreciate my cooperation in telling them everything I knew about Jerry Bowmer and everything I was aware he was into, as well as information about any other parties that may have been involved in wrongdoing. I was told that Anderson was downstairs in another room and was cooperating and that they would like me to do the same.

I again informed them that I could not help them until I had an opportunity to speak with an attorney. It just seemed like a lot of time had passed since my arrest, and many different agents were continuing to interrogate me without the presence of legal counsel. I felt this was very wrong; how could they keep questioning me without my attorney present? If they wanted help, all they had to do was respect my right to counsel, and I would have been more willing to work with them. Now, however, I was angered by their actions and lack of respect, so I would not tell them anything, nor would I cooperate in any way.

I felt that these were not honorable men. They kept stalling at every turn by forbidding me to make calls or seek legal advice. They could have handled the situation much differently, knowing my background as a former police officer, and I would have given them all the cooperation they wanted. Instead, they insisted on behaving like big shots running the show, treating me like a common street criminal.

After more than an hour of my refusals to cooperate without legal counsel, they finally stopped questioning me. Two new agents entered the room as the others left. One was carrying an ultraviolet light, and he asked me to hold out my hands. He shined the light on my fingers, searching for traces of the dye that had been placed on the money. I assumed they wanted to see if I had touched the marked bills Bowmer left on my desk. It would have been impossible to find traces of dye when I never touched the cash, but they kept looking.

He shined the light all over my hands for some time as both agents kept looking for any traces of contact with the money. I could tell they weren't finding anything. Even I could not see any traces of the dye. The room was warm, and I was beginning to sweat. Soon they called another agent in to examine my hands, while one of them whispered he could see no sign of contact with the money.

The three continued looking. By now, my hands were starting to perspire. After a moment, one of them said, "Yes, now I can see some little specks on his hand." Still, my hands did not look any different to me except for the light shining on the sweat beads that had developed from the warm temperature in the room. Nor did it look like they themselves believed they were seeing anything. They hurried out of the office after that comment.

When the three agents left the room, another agent came in to ask for my assistance. He told me that Anderson was cooperating fully with them, and they hoped I would do the same. They must have thought I was a dunce, that I would not see what they were trying to do. They forgot I used to be a police officer, and I knew how the game was played, good cop and bad cop.

I informed this agent for the umpteenth time that I could not do anything without first talking to my attorney for some advice and direction. He made a face and sighed, then finally stopped all questioning and allowed me to come out into the outer office and use the phone. I had to ask them for a phone book as they had confiscated my book of telephone numbers, along with all my other personal belongings.

Tired, nervous, and very upset, I opened the large phone book and flipped to the number I was looking for. This attorney was a very good friend of mine, Joe Barrs of Barrs, Williamson, and Levens. Joe was not there, but Bill Levens, also a good friend and partner of Joe's, was in.

A short time later, he arrived, and I explained what had happened. He advised me not to say anything to anyone until I had good counsel to advise me. He explained that he was unable to help me because he did not handle criminal cases like mine. Bill was a civil and claims attorney but said he would help me find a lawyer. He said, "Try and stay calm until someone gets back with you and do not, I repeat, do not talk with anyone here." He then left.

I knew it must be well after 1:00 p.m., and I couldn't help but wonder what was next. I had been sitting there for a while when an agent came by. He asked me to stand and said that I was being taken to the magistrate's court for arraignment along with Anderson and that they had to put handcuffs on me. The agent also said that the media had been informed of our arrest and that there were a lot of reporters in the downstairs lobby. He said that they would try and get us through them as quickly as possible and that, if I would like, I could put my jacket over the cuffs so that they would not be visible.

We then left the office and stepped into the elevator. We stopped on one of the lower floors, where Anderson and two more agents joined us. We just looked at each other for a moment as we continued down to the main lobby.

When the elevator doors opened and we stepped out, I could see an army of newspeople gathered out front. As we walked outside, we were swamped by reporters, microphones, TV news cameras, and photographers, all walking backward as we proceeded forward. I looked around and could see passersby on the street stopping to stare at us, wondering what was going on. It's amazing how fast bad news travels, and like vultures, the media preys on it. I knew that news of the arrests would spread like wildfire throughout the city and county and be blown out of proportion. I wondered how my kids would react. What would my family think about all this? I was especially concerned for my mother, who was not well.

We entered a side door of the federal courthouse and walked through the ground floor where the US Post Office was, then turned and stepped into a special elevator that took us upstairs to the US Marshal's office for processing prior to arraignment.

Once we were upstairs, the reporters who were left behind congregated in the lobby. We had a little peace as we were taken to the processing room, where they removed our handcuffs, searched us once more, and placed us in a holding cell to await processing. We were taken out one at a time, fingerprinted, photographed, and asked a lot of personal questions. We signed a number of papers.

Fred Arthur Anderson, a 57-

As Anderson and I sat in our cell, we did not say much to each other except for some small talk. He motioned to me not to say anything there. "These cells are bugged. Be careful what you say." Neither of us could believe what was going on. Anderson, to begin with, was in poor health. A heart attack a few weeks earlier had slowed him down, and he was on medication. He had not been attending the county commission meetings on a regular basis because of his poor health, which made me acting chairman of the commission in his absences.

I was assistant chairman of the commission in line for the chairmanship the following year. It was amazing that he just happened to be in his office on that day. If the Brandon people had not made an appointment to see him, he would have been at home, resting.

I asked Anderson how he was doing, and he said not too well and that they had taken his medication away. He then lay down on the steel bench in the cell as I stood looking out through the bars of the cell door. I asked him how long they interviewed him before he was arrested. He said about twenty minutes or more. I said, "Wow, they must have been in a real hurry to arrest me. They only talked to me for about five minutes."

I told Anderson that while they were trying to interrogate me, they informed me he was downstairs cooperating with them, and they wanted me to do the same. Fred cursed angrily. "They told me the same thing about you."

"I never said a word about anything. I wouldn't even know what to say. I really don't know anything and just wanted to see a lawyer before I would talk to them," I told him.

"The same here," he answered. "That Bowmer is a no-good ——," Fred swore again, then fell silent as he tried to get some rest.

The cell was not very large; it couldn't have been more than six by twelve feet. It had a stainless steel commode with a small sink attached as one unit behind a half so-called partition wall open about midheight without any door or covering for privacy. There were two long metal benches attached to the walls on either side of the cell. I figured the lack of privacy was so the marshals could see what was going on inside the cell area. Other than that, the cell was quite bare and dingy-looking, with a variety of not-so-colorful graffiti written all over the walls and the names of so-called snitches with warnings to beware of them.

The place definitely needed a good paint job and cleaning; plus, the ventilation was not good, with no windows to open or look out. It looked like a big room where someone had put a jail cell in one half and an office with a desk, some chairs, and file cabinets in the other half.

After what felt like an eternity, an attorney named Bennie Lazzara came by to talk to Fred. I figured his wife must have called him when she heard what had happened. After a brief conversation, he told Fred that he would be downstairs in the magistrate's court waiting for him when he came down.

No one had come to see me by this point, as I guess Bill or whoever he was sending was still trying to find out what was going on. A little while later, a lawyer stopped in. His name was Jim Caltagirone, sent by a friend of mine, Dave Webster, my daughter Julie, and her boyfriend, Kevin Bennington. I thought maybe Bill Levens had gotten in touch with my daughter and made these arrangements. I asked Jim if he was a good lawyer and had much success in federal matters. He told me he was good and that he had handled a number of federal cases with both good and bad results. You can't win them all, but he said he had a good track record.

At that point, I didn't care if he was Mickey Mouse coming to represent me; I just wanted out of there. I asked him if he would like to represent me and filled him in on what had happened so far. I let him know that I thought my conversation with Bowmer and the FBI may have been recorded, and if so, the tapes would clear me. I knew the tapes would clearly show that I had nothing to do with this situation.

Caltagirone stated that he was informed that the government did have tapes of what went on in our offices and that he would be getting a copy of them so we would have an opportunity to review what was said. After taking a few notes, he said he would be downstairs when they brought me down for arraignment. He then left, and Anderson and I were alone once more.

CHAPTER 3

The Charges

February 1983

After a short time, we were taken from our cells, cuffed, and escorted to US Magistrate Paul Game Jr.'s courtroom. The charges were read to us by the magistrate, "Mr. Kotvas, you are charged with conspiracy to interfere with interstate commerce by extortion and interference with commerce by extortion."

I knew that extortion was getting money by threats or misuse of authority. The conspiracy charge was little more than planning to extort and is always used by federal prosecutors when possible in a variety of cases to deprive the defendants of much of the protection against the use of mere hearsay as evidence. Prosecutors like it because it is a catch-22 for the defendant and is extremely hard to refute, giving the prosecutors high success ratios. Federal attorneys have been abusing this statute for many years. Placed in the hands of an ambitious, overzealous prosecutor, it becomes very dangerous to our system of justice and our society as a whole.

Many innocent parties are destroyed by such misuse of the law. One day, I pray that Congress will amend it to offer more protection to the American public, or it will continue to drag this country's justice system through the mud and destroy everything we as Americans believe in.

Anderson faced identical charges. As we stood with our respective attorneys, the magistrate asked, "How do you plead to the charges?" First to Anderson, whose attorney Bennie Lazzara said,

"My client pleads not guilty to the charges." Then he began to tell the court what a good citizen Anderson was and all the things he had done for the community. He also described his health issues.

He requested that Anderson be released on his own recognizance pending trial. At that point, the prosecutor Joe Magri said, "Because of the nature and seriousness of the crime and violation of the public trust, the court should place a very high bond on the defendant to set an example for others who might think of committing such crimes." The magistrate then set the bond for Anderson at $100,000.

When my turn came, I also entered a not-guilty plea, and Caltagirone made similar statements on my behalf, and the prosecutor repeated the same things as before about wanting us to be an example to others. So my bond was also set at $100,000, and we both returned to our holding cell upstairs until we could post bond or be transferred to the county jail to be held until trial.

After returning to the holding cell, we both waited for word on our bond and wondered who would put up the money for our release. I knew I did not have the $10,000 that was needed for my bail. For a $100,000 bail in federal courts, you only have to put up 10 percent in cash, which the courts retain as a premium, like an insurance policy. If an individual puts up the 10 percent in cash, it's returned in full when the trial is over as long as that person makes all the required court appearances through the final outcome. If I could get out, I knew I could raise the money, but that would not be possible to do from a jail cell.

I remembered back to my days as a bail bondsman, working for the late Eddy Callahan at Callahan's Bail Bonds across the street from the old Tampa police station back in the midseventies. (Eddy, in his younger years, was an up-and-coming prizefighter who never made it to the top.) I now knew how the families felt and what they went through to get their loved ones bonded out. The shoe was now on the other foot. I sure wish Eddy would have been alive back then. He would have had me free and out in a heartbeat.

After about another hour, it must have been 4:30 or 5:00 p.m. Anderson's attorney came back into the holding cell area with his release papers. He had been bonded out and could go home. We said our good-byes and wished each other good luck. As we shook hands, he leaned over and whispered in my ear, "Don't say anything in here. These cells are bugged." He then left.

Now I was alone in the holding cell, waiting to see what would happen next. Then an attorney came by to see me, one sent by Bill Levens. I told him that I had already retained an attorney and thanked him for his trouble. I told him I had thought that the other attorney was the one Bill had sent and apologized for the mix-up. He said he could understand under the circumstances and wished me well.

Again, I was alone in that cell room, for the courts were now closed, and the marshals were clearing up things for the day. One of them informed me that if someone did not come to bail me out soon, I would be transferred to the county jail and would have to spend the night there, pending securing of bail.

As I sat in that cell, I tried to go over the events of the day that had led to my arrest and imagine what I might have done to avoid the whole mess. Over and over, my mind kept analyzing one detail after another, reliving the entire nightmare. Then I remembered the call I received early this morning from Claude Tanner. Was this the situation he was trying to warn me about? Had he known something was going to happen and tried to warn me? Had I not had other matters on my mind at the time of his call, I might have been more alert to what Bowmer was up to.

Then one of the marshals came in and walked over to my cell, interrupting my thoughts. He said, "Mr. Kotvas, we just got word that your daughter was making arrangements for your bail, so we're not going to transfer you just yet, but they better come through soon, or it will be too late, and you will have to wait till tomorrow."

Being in solitude, I felt totally ashamed of what was happening to me. At that moment, I had no idea how I was going to prove my innocence. It was just bing, bang, thank you, ma'am—and off to jail. I felt if they heard the tapes and listened to the minutes of the county commission meeting, they would know I had no dealings of any kind with Jerry Bowmer. Why was I here? Why was this happening to me? My mind was spinning, with all sorts of thoughts flashing through my head. I was scared, nervous, and all alone. I'm sure most people who are falsely accused and arrested for the first time must feel the same way as I did then. It was a total nightmare.

I was unaware at the time that Bowmer was being kept in a motel somewhere in the city for his protection and making a deal with the government for his cooperation. He was giving them all sorts of information about everyone he knew whom he could implicate in some type of crime to promote his chances of looking good and staying out of jail.

I had been sitting in that cell all afternoon, watching the marshals who were on duty going to and from their office. I hadn't eaten all day, and it seemed everyone had forgotten about me, just sitting in that cell.

I thought it was ironic that just a few years earlier, when I was on the Tampa city council, a good friend Bill Poole had taken me to St. Petersburg to the downtown Hilton Hotel for a private audience with the president of the United States, Gerald Ford. The state Republican Party for the area was having a thousand-dollar-a-plate luncheon for the president, and I was the only one getting a private audience with the chief executive. I don't know how Bill pulled this off, but he was very powerful in local and state Republican circles. He also owned his own company, Poole Engineering Inc.

While sitting in this cell, the scene replayed in my mind. I remember there was Bill, me, the Secret Service detail, and the president in the room. Bill wanted me to meet the president before the luncheon started, and I was allowed a half hour with him all to myself. An average guy like me, just think of it, meeting with the president of the United States. What an honor.

You can imagine how nervous I was. For security reasons, Bill Poole had not mentioned a word to me about the appointment till we arrived at the hotel. All he had told me before we left my office was that he wanted me to meet someone, and it was very important that we go.

I think the president could see I was nervous, and he made me feel welcome. He even offered me a cocktail and had one himself so I would feel more comfortable. He could tell I was young and new to this. After all, my last job was as a police officer for the city of Tampa. He was such a down-to-earth person who was easy to talk to. The meeting was one of the biggest highlights of my life, one that I will always remember.

We sat and talked about my family, local politics, and the city of Tampa's needs. He seemed proud and impressed that I was the first and youngest Republican ever to be elected and serve on the Tampa city council in over a hundred years, if ever, and had defeated an entrenched Democrat incumbent. At the time, there were only two elected Republicans in Tampa and Hillsborough County: myself as the first Republican city councilman ever and a state senator named David McClain, who had been in office a few terms and was popular with many of the voters in his district.

There was a reason for this visit with the president, though I did not realize it at the time. I was being groomed for the position of United States Marshal for the Middle District of Florida. We talked about my years on the New York Transit Police Department and the Tampa Police Department. Then I asked him if he could help me find a fireboat for the city of Tampa, which he said he would look into. We really needed one badly to protect the interests of the Port of Tampa and the city.

After our session was over, we had to leave. I had to get back to my office; plus, I did not have the money to pay a thousand dollars for a seat at the table. What an honor! I was on cloud nine.

When we got back into Bill's car and started heading back to Tampa, he informed me of the real reason for the meeting. The president was going to appoint a new marshal for the Middle District of Florida, and he wanted to see if I would like the job.

Meeting President Gerald Ford

This was an opportunity of a lifetime, a dream come true, but I could not accept the position. I had only been a city councilman for a short time; I felt I would be letting down all the people who worked so hard to get me elected. I told Bill I could not take the position, and he dropped me off back at my office. When I got home that evening, I told my wife and my children about the meeting with the president; they were all excited. I then told my wife about the position that was offered me, and she agreed with me that I had made the right decision (although I hated myself for it because that was one of my lifelong dreams). I later found out that the appointment went to Mickey Newberger.

All these thoughts were coming back—now look at me, sitting in this cell. Unless I could prove my innocence, I knew this would be the end of my ten-year plan to the White House and possibly my political career as a whole.

Late in the afternoon, one of the marshals came in and handed me a brown paper bag containing a dry baloney sandwich and an orange, plus a plastic bottle of water to drink that had been left over from the jail run they made earlier.

This was going to be my only meal for a while. Even though hungry, I couldn't eat much of the sandwich because it was so stale, but I did eat the orange. I was too worried not knowing what was happening to my children or how all of this was affecting my mother and sister. Where was my daughter getting the bail money? My mind was spinning with all the unanswered questions.

When one is sitting in a cell all alone, with nothing to do and no one to talk to, the stress, loneliness, and fear threaten to overwhelm. You begin to imagine all kinds of things. The only thing to do is to control your emotions and focus on the real issues.

CHAPTER 4

The Bail

February 1983

Sometime after 7:00 p.m., just as the marshals were getting me prepared for transfer to the county jail, I was finally bonded out. Jim sent his assistant Jeff Blau to pick me up and try to get me away from the courthouse without too much publicity since there was still an army of reporters waiting outside to see if I was going to get bonded out. There will always be some of them who will wait to get that first interview or comment for an exclusive story.

I knew Jeff from the county commission meetings. He had been an assistant county attorney for some time, and I discovered he was now working with Jim Caltagirone. He informed me that I had been bailed out and that he was taking me to meet Jim at his home office in the business district of Tampa's Davis Islands.

We left the Federal courthouse by a side door without much attention or fanfare. I got in his car, and we drove to Jim's. When we arrived, Jim was waiting for us and greeted me as we walked in. "Mr. Kotvas, how are you doing?" he asked with a smile on his face.

I was still numb from the happenings of the day and could not think straight. I just said, "I'm exhausted from all this. Why is this happening to me? I never took a bribe from Jerry Bowmer."

"I can understand it must be a very frightening experience you're going through," Jim said. He went on to explain that he was working from home temporarily while his primary office was being remodeled. I asked about my car, which he advised was still in my parking space at the county courthouse. He told me to leave it there; it would be safe for the night.

Jim and I then went over the case against me, and he reminded me not to make any statements regarding it to anyone. We finished talking, and he advised to me to go home and try to get some rest as it would be very busy for us the next day. I told him that tomorrow was a county commission meeting day and that I needed to be at work. Of course, he advised me against attending, for he was afraid that I might say something to injure our case. I assured him that I would not discuss the matter with anyone, nor would I give any statements to the attending press. I knew how all this worked from that point on and felt I could handle it.

Again he repeated, "I don't think this is a good idea. The press may try and come over for an interview or call you about what happened. I just don't want you to be giving out any statements till we have a chance to go over all the facts in this case." He seemed very concerned for me.

It sounds funny, but Jim looked and talked a lot like that guy on the TV show *Moonlighting*, Bruce Willis. He laughed about it when I told him. Then I said, "Look, Jim, I am very, very tired, and I promise you I will not open my door to anyone nor talk to any reporters on the phone if they call. I just want to go home and get this stench off my body and rest in my own bed before I get ready for the commission meeting."

After some discussion on the matter, I finally convinced him that this was something I had to do. I knew I was not guilty of these charges; I was not going to hide my head in the sand like a beaten criminal. I was going to work, and if anyone wanted to accuse me of anything, I was ready to face them head-on.

Mr. Caltagirone reluctantly agreed and told Mr. Blau to take me home so I could get some rest and be more alert in the morning. Blau was to pick me up the next morning and stay with me at the commission meeting so I would not talk to reporters about the case. He also advised me that I should start keeping a journal and make notes of everything that I could remember about what happened during my arrest and processing. He wanted to make sure Jeff would be there in case I needed any legal assistance and to get me out of the courthouse and to his office as soon as the meeting was over.

He said I could pick up my car in the morning after the meeting, for he did not want reporters to see it at my house and stop by unannounced. Neither did he want me to answer my phone but have one of my kids do it to screen calls. I told him my answering machine could do that.

I asked about my children, Julie and Steven (who was the youngest, age nine, at the time). My other son Joseph was in navy boot camp in San Diego, and I did not know if he had heard about what happened. I also wanted to know who put up the money to bail me out since I didn't have that kind of cash floating around.

Jim informed me that my daughter, her boyfriend, and my sister, Rose Soriano, and her husband supplied the bail money. My children would be staying with her and my mother, Angelina, for the night to keep them away from all the press people who might try to hound them.

We shook hands as I left Jim's home office, and I got back into his car so he could drive me home. By then, it was about 11:00 p.m., and I was totally exhausted. I was looking forward to a good night's sleep and a very busy day when I got up.

The drive home was uneventful. I was silent most of the way and was in no mood for talking to anyone. When we arrived at my house on North Church Street, Jeff dropped me off and reminded me he would be by in the morning to pick me up and take me to the courthouse for the morning meeting. I thanked him, and he drove off.

As I walked slowly to my house, I looked down the street. Except for a few porch lights still on, most of the houses were dark. I lived on the northeast corner at the dead end of the 7800 block. My home was a two-story house with two bedrooms, a master bedroom for me and a smaller one for my daughter. It also had a kitchen and dining area, a bathroom, and living room upstairs.

On the lower level were two more bedrooms, where my two boys slept, a family room, bathroom, laundry room, and utility room. There was a spiral staircase in the inside middle of the house to move up and down floors without having to go outside. The front entrance was on the north side of the second level of the house with a wooden staircase leading up to it. There also was a side entrance to the first level on the south side of the house.

The place was dark and silent as I walked up the stairs to the front door. I could hear a dog barking in the distance as I opened my front door and turned on the lights. I was exhausted but wide awake. Nobody was home. My children were at my sister's place, and the only thing moving in the house was my dog, Molly. Molly the collie, we would call her. She was a very loving dog, getting up in age but always totally devoted to my late wife and children. She had even saved my wife's life a few months before Cathy passed away.

My wife was a smoker, at least three packs a day, and I could not get her to quit, even after she found out she had cancer. She had been smoking since she was eleven years old in the Bronx. When I first met her, she was fourteen, and I was seventeen. We both looked older than our age and acted it. We were married when she was sixteen and I was nineteen, and our love for each other grew as time went on. All of our friends were betting the marriage would not last six months, but it lasted sixteen years.

Like all marriages, we had our ups and downs, but we managed to work through them. I never liked her smoking and asked her to quit a number of times. But all she would say is, she enjoyed it and we all have to die of something sometime. It was no joke to me or our kids. I guess that's why, to this very day, none of my children smoke. She had to have cigarettes and coffee every morning before she could start her day.

When my wife found out she had cancer—that there was nothing anyone could do and she was only given six months to a year to live—she continued to smoke; it didn't make any difference to her. The drugs the doctors put her on kept her drowsy and sleeping most of the time, for her pain could be so unbearable. Molly would never leave her side. Whenever she was in the living room, sitting on the couch, or in the bedroom lying down, Molly would be right next to her. She knew something was wrong and would not leave my wife's side.

We lived on South Wallace Avenue in Tampa at that time. Because the house carried too many memories for me to bear, both happy and sad, I moved my small family to the two-story residence a little over a year after her passing.

One day in the late afternoon, a few months before Cathy passed away, I was on our patio working. My son Joseph was watching TV in the living room, and Julie and Steven were walking around outside. My wife was resting in our bedroom when I heard Molly barking from the bedroom like she was trying to tell us something. I told my son Joseph to go see what was bothering Molly and keep her quiet because his mother was trying to rest.

All of a sudden, I heard my son screaming, "Dad, Dad, Mom's bed is on fire!" The dog was calling for help and would not leave my wife's side. When I ran into the room, my son was beating out the fire that was on top of her bedspread, which had been covering her. He got it out, and we pulled it off. I could see Molly barking and nudging my wife to wake her up.

My wife was still out of it but unharmed. She had fallen asleep from her medications with a cigarette in her hand, and the bedspread had caught fire. At that moment, I took all her cigarettes and gave them to my son and told him to throw them in the garbage. I told her from here on out, there would be no more smoking; it was too dangerous in her condition.

My daughter, Julie, came running into the house with little Steven when she heard all the commotion. Julie hadn't realized what had happened, but she saw the results of the large burnt hole on the quilt, then asked if Mom was all right. My wife was still dazed from her medications, so she agreed after seeing the burnt quilt that she would not smoke anymore. At this point, it really did not matter. With all the chemo, her meds, and the loss of her hair, everything was making her sick. I told my children to make sure their mother did not have any more cigarettes.

I told them, "No matter what happens in this family, that dog will always have a special place here. She and your brother Joey saved your mother's life. We will never get rid of Molly."

I was so proud of my oldest son for thinking fast and taking action, with a good deal of help from our dog.

These thoughts were now all coming back to me as I walked into my bedroom and collapsed on the bed after taking off my tie and jacket and tossing them on a chair. I still had most of my clothes on when I kicked off my shoes and dropped down on the bed. Molly came over and sat, resting her head on the side of the bed, as I fell asleep.

CHAPTER 5

The Next Day

February 1983

I woke up around 7:00 a.m. Molly was still lying next to my bed as I got up, undressed, showered, shaved, and dried off. I smelled a lot better afterward and was starting to feel better. I took a gray suit out of my closet and got dressed for the meeting.

The phone rang. I was a little hesitant to answer but lifted the receiver anyway. It was Jeff telling me he would be by in a few minutes to pick me up. While waiting for him to arrive, I let Molly out the front door to run around for a while and do her thing; then I had a glass of juice and a few cookies. I remembered that I had left my car in my parking space at the courthouse the day before. Now I would be able to get it and drive it home after my meeting with the county and Jim Caltagirone.

After a short while, I let Molly back inside the house. Jeff came by around 8:00 a.m. I left with him, and we headed downtown to the county courthouse. "I brought you some coffee, Commissioner," he said. "I thought you could use it." Cuban coffee—boy, how I love good Cuban coffee.

When we arrived at the courthouse, we parked in an open space in front. We walked in the front entrance where a number of news reporters spotted us, ran over to take our pictures, and tried to get a scoop on my story. All I said to them was, "I have nothing to say. You need to talk to my attorney."

As we walked through the main lobby, people stopped and turned from all the commotion. Many of them began whispering to one another as they looked at us and could not believe that I would come into the courthouse. I looked at Jeff and said, "This will give them something to talk about."

We walked up the two flights of stairs to my office, which was at the south side of the building, followed by the press. We passed the receptionist and went on to my office with all the other aides and staff members looking on curiously. The press was asked to stay out and move to the reception area or the commission chambers.

I asked my aide if Commissioner Anderson had come in. She informed me that no one had seen him or Bowmer. Then I informed her that since we still had a quorum, she should let the county administrator know I was ready to start the meeting. I was now the acting chairman of the commission. She then left and went down the hall to inform the administrator to get the meeting started.

Jeff and I went into my office, and I told him to take a seat while I went behind my desk and started looking over the agenda for the day's meeting. A few moments later, my aide came back and said there would be a delay in starting the meeting, and we would be informed when it was time.

I was unaware that Commissioner Jan Platt had contacted the governor's office to have me suspended from office till this arrest matter was settled and was waiting for an answer.

Jeff and I sat in my office talking about his days with the county attorney's office. After almost an hour, the county administrator Norman Hickky walked in and informed me that the governor had just suspended me, Anderson, and Bowmer pending the outcome of our situation. He said there would be no commission meeting since there was no quorum. On hearing this, I became very upset, but I thanked the administrator as he left.

I told Jeff we might as well see Jim at his office since there was nothing more we could do at mine. I was extremely upset by that time. As we were leaving, a number of staff members in the hallway said they were very sorry for my troubles. One of the other commissioners' aides came over and informed me in a low voice that it was Platt who had come in early and called the governor.

Many of the staff did not like Platt. She was a do-nothing commissioner who always liked to complain about everything but wanted someone else to fix whatever it was she picked to gripe about at the moment. She had a habit of taking the easy way out and voted no on a majority of the hard issues, which is a matter of public record. Platt came to the courthouse to attend commission meetings but spent very little time in her office planning, supervising her aides, or meeting with constituents.

I was really pissed off as we walked out of the building. Platt could not wait to get rid of us so she could be the one in charge of the board. I knew that with Fred and me out of the picture, she would be the next chairman of the county commission, something she always wanted. We picked up my car, and I followed Jeff back to Davis Islands.

On the way, a strange thought came to me as I was driving. What about Jan Platt? She had a habit of voting no for most major developments even when they had all the county planning staff's approval. But on this Geraci zoning, she voted yes. I was so sure that she would have been a no vote because of all the impact it would have in the area. Yet I was the one arrested for voting no.

Was there some connection between her or her family and the Geracis? Who knows? Why the sudden change in her style of voting? As far as the media and public were concerned, she always came across as Miss Clean. But at the moment, I had other things to worry about, so I just kept driving.

We arrived at Jim's office on East Davis Boulevard around 10:30 a.m. Jim was in, but he wasn't expecting us until much later in the day. He greeted me, told me to have a seat, and asked Jeff to get us some coffee. He also requested a writing pad.

Jim handed the pad to me and said, "I want you to keep notes on everything you can remember. Write everything down no matter how insignificant it may have seemed at the time. I want to know everything that happened in detail to the best of your recollection." The three of us sat in his office as I explained what had happened the day before while Jim and Jeff took notes.

First he informed me that Robert Merkle, the US attorney for the Middle District of Florida, was going to prosecute this case personally with his chief assistant Joe Magri. Then we talked about his fee. He agreed to take my case for a nominal fee since I did not have much money, and my only income was from my county commission salary. I had little savings and no real assets. Jim was aware that the publicity from this case would bring him a great deal of notoriety, so that was why I think he took the case for such a discounted fee.

Jim also told me that Merkle was known in legal circles as "Mad Dog Merkle." He had a reputation of going after a conviction like a mad dog and would stop at nothing to win. I would not fully realize this meaning until my trial was over.

He said the charge was bribery in a zoning case and violating the public trust. Jim also informed me that an attorney named Michael Sierra had been implicated for having dealings with Bowmer and had also been arrested. He said Bowmer was giving the Feds the names of everyone he claimed he had dealings with, and the FBI would soon be making even more arrests.

I knew Michael Sierra; he was a great attorney and somewhat of a political powerhouse in the community. He was one of a number of people whom you would see and try to seek help from if you were going to run for political office. Over the years, he had helped a good number of local- and state-level officials get elected.

He even helped me with some of my campaigns. In all the years that I knew him and all the people he had helped, I never knew or heard of him asking anyone to do anything inappropriate. It seemed ludicrous that he would be arrested or even be involved with a guy like Bowmer. *As far as I know, he never liked Bowmer, and I don't believe he ever gave him any political support. Can this possibly be a form of payback for Bowmer?* I thought to myself since I was now in the same situation.

Jim also informed me that a businessman named John DeCarlucci had also been implicated in our case. I had no idea who this man was. I had never heard of him nor had any dealings to my knowledge with this man. I was at a loss about this.

I thought maybe Bowmer was using his arrest to get back at all those who had given him a hard time in the past and was putting the innocent with the guilty just to look good for Merkle. He knew how the system worked and was very good at manipulating it: he often bragged about his ability to manipulate the Feds.

But for now, I had other things to worry about, and I started to tell Jim what happened the morning the FBI walked into my office and how I saw their microphones hidden in the sleeves of their shirt cuffs; how I felt they were recording everything I was saying; that I felt the recordings should prove I had nothing to do with Bowmer; why I could not vote for the zoning I was accused of taking the bribe for; that I had over a month before informing Steve Reynolds, the attorney for the Geracis, that I would not be voting for this zoning; that Steve and I were friends, and I could not help him on this zoning, for there was too much pressure on me from the community. After all, this was my district, and I did not want to anger my constituents.

Jim said this was good. He indicated we would get back to that later and asked me to continue with my recollection. I also said that Steve had called me to have lunch with him and Nick Geraci that same month. I told him I could not and I could not discuss the zoning with the two of them. I told them I thought doing so would violate the Sunshine Law.

Steve pleaded and begged me as a personal favor just to have lunch, and I would not have to talk about the zoning, just meet the gentleman. I finally agreed, with some reservations, to meet for lunch at a public place so if members of the press showed up, they could sit and listen in on everything that was said and I could not be accused of improprieties. Steve agreed, set up the luncheon, and we met.

After being introduced to Nick Geraci, we sat down and ordered. They did most of the talking between themselves, and I just sat there and listened. I would not go into details about their zoning. When lunch was over and I had to leave to get back to my office, I thanked them for lunch and again informed them that I was obligated to keep an open mind, but in all good conscience, I could not vote for the zoning.

I asked Jim, "Don't you think this will help? This should prove I decided well in advance I was not going to vote for the zoning. My vote was NO the night of the meeting, and no one is going to pay a bribe for a *no* vote."

Jim replied he would contact Steve Reynolds and see what he had to say. He wanted as many of the facts as I could recall and continued taking notes.

After a short while, he put his pencil down and said, "Mr. Kotvas, I'm not going to kid you. The government is trying to build a strong case against you and the others involved. If we can prove what you're telling me and convince a jury, then we have a good shot at this case. It's not going to be easy, so you need to keep taking notes on anything you can remember. We will meet regularly in my office to go over everything. You can call me anytime should you remember something important or if you need anything. I'm here for you. I can't imagine what you must be going through. Just try not to worry too much. You're going to get through this."

For the next few weeks, Jim, Jeff, and I worked together on my case, constantly reviewing the charges and information the government had. No one knew where Bowmer was being kept. It was rumored the government had him in protective custody at an undisclosed location outside of Hillsborough County.

Since I had very limited funds (just enough to get by for a short time), Jim would try and pool the resources of the other two defendants' attorneys in the case and share information between us to strengthen our case. By working together, he felt we would have a better chance. I informed Jim that I wanted to take the stand and tell my side of the story when the time came.

It was understandable that the other attorneys were a little reluctant at first to work with us as their first concern was to their clients. It took a while, but they finally came around, and there existed a mutual sharing of information between the attorneys to everybody's advantage.

The government requested that I turn over my passport to keep me from leaving the country (yeah, fat chance of that happening with three kids to take care of and no money). The FBI also wanted a copy of all my bank accounts and credit accounts and accounts of any stocks or bonds that I might own. I found out later that they went through every account I had with a fine-tooth comb, looking for anything that would link me with any bribes. They were looking for any type of money trail. They believed that if I was taking all these bribes Bowmer said I had taken, there would be a paper trail someplace showing where the money went.

I turned over everything the FBI had asked for to Jim so he could review it first and then turn it in for me. The funny part of it all was, Jim could see I really had no money to speak of. I was like most middle-class Americans: in debt. I had a large mortgage, very little savings, not much in checking, a lot of bills that I paid on time, and a broken-down 1977 Jaguar sitting in my yard that I could not afford to repair. I was getting by on what I made on my commission salary, and that was all I had.

The FBI went through everything I owned and contacted everyone I ever knew for information about me. They even contacted everyone from my personal telephone book that they took from me and copied. Friends would call and say they were contacted by the FBI asking questions about me. It made many of them feel uncomfortable. I just told them to tell the truth; that's all they wanted.

The government was not going to leave any stone unturned in this case. I felt confident about that. What could anyone say? I hadn't broken any laws. This was starting to get stressful for everyone around me, and some people began to distance themselves from me (no one likes being dragged into a federal case if they can help it).

A few thought it was funny to be called by the FBI, but others were afraid of becoming a part of the case. Merkle was putting pressure on everyone I knew, and in some cases, he got very nasty with people. He had his staff looking into every aspect of my personal and professional life as well as that of the other defendants in our case.

Jeff and I went back to my office to retrieve some of my files that I thought might be helpful, only to discover that the FBI had been there just the day before with a warrant to clean out my office. I had no idea what Bowmer was telling these people, but they went into my office and took every file I had and cleaned out all of my drawers of anything of interest to them. They even took the stuffed eagle I had on the credenza.

I was informed by the courthouse security officers who came up to my office when they heard I was in the building that I was not allowed back into my office or in the commission chambers till this matter was resolved. I was told the governor had appointed three new commissioners to take our places, and this was now one of their offices.

I could see they were a little uncomfortable about the whole thing when they escorted us out of the building. One of them had been a friend and was very helpful to me and Fred when we became commissioners. I could tell he was very sorry for my troubles but was helpless to do anything about it. Not to cause a scene, Jeff and I left without incident and went back to Jim's office.

CHAPTER 6

The Pretrial

May 1983

Jim was busy coordinating information with the other attorneys involved in our case. Fred Anderson was being represented by the brothers Richard and Bennie Lazzara, excellent criminal lawyers. Mickey Sierra was represented by Attorney Raymond LaPorte, a criminal lawyer with a superior reputation, and Joseph Ficcarotta, an associate of Mickey Sierra and a good lawyer. Jim felt that, between all of them, we had a good team of legal minds working the case. No one had any idea where the government was hiding Bowmer; it was as if he had totally disappeared.

As time went by, Jim and the other attorneys filed all sorts of motions: some for dismissal of the case, severance from the others, motions for discovery, more time to prepare, and so forth. Most of the motions were denied. We did get a little more time to prepare for trial since the government was still sorting through all the information that Bowmer had provided. The prosecution did supply some of the information that Jim and the other lawyers asked for.

A week or two from the time of my arrest, Jim wanted me to take a polygraph test. It would not be admissible in court, but Jim wanted it for his own records. He asked if I would be willing to take the test. I agreed, and he set it up with a private investigator named Robert Metzgar, a former deputy sheriff for Hillsborough County. I went to see Metzgar at his office one evening for administration of the test. He hooked me up to numerous leads on one of my hands and around my chest. He then proceeded to ask a number of questions as the machine was running. He made little marks on the paper as the polygraph moved forward.

After a while, he stopped the machine and advised me the test was concluded as he unhooked me from all the leads. He told me he would send Mr. Caltagirone my report in about two days. I asked if he could tell me anything, and all he said was that Mr. Caltagirone will let me know.

A couple of days later in Jim's office, he told me that I passed the polygraph test and that it showed I was telling the truth about not taking bribes or being involved with Jerry Bowmer. I was so relieved; I knew I was not guilty of the charges. But Jim reminded me again that the test was not admissible to a jury and could not be entered into the court records.

After a good number of weeks requesting the government to turn over the tape recordings made from my office, it was now March, and I had just turned forty. The government finally turned over a copy of the tape recordings to us. It must have been late April or early May when Jim received his copy of the tapes.

He called me at home and left a message to come to his office the next day to go over them. I was not home at the time, picking up my youngest son from school. When we got back to the house, I checked, and Jim's message was waiting for me. I called his secretary Lora, and she informed me that Jim had a case in court early in the morning and wanted me to come by around 11:00 a.m.

I arrived on time, stopping off in West Tampa first to get us both a cup of Cuban coffee. When I got there, Jim was sitting behind his desk and waiting for me. I sat down in one of the chairs facing his desk. He wasn't his usually smiling self today; he seemed to have a lot on his mind, and that worried me.

"So what's the big urgency, Jim?" I asked. He had been writing something on his notepad ever since I walked in, but he put his pen down and looked at me with a troubled look on his face.

"We have a bit of a problem, Mr. Kotvas," he said. "I received the tapes that the government recorded in your office and listened to them last night, and we have a problem with them."

"What is it, Jim?" I asked.

He said, "I'll let you listen to them, and you tell me."

We both then listened to the tapes using Jim's player. As we listened, I could hear the audio clearly. Then after few minutes into the tapes, I could not believe what I was hearing. The voices were garbled and inaudible and silent with just static in some places. We could only pick up bits and pieces of conversations. It was like that with the rest of the tape right up to the arrest. For some reason, there were no recordings of myself with the arresting FBI agents who entered my office. I thought maybe we would get them later. I know they had microphones on them, and if they went this far to tape Bowmer and I, then surely they must have taped what I said to them in my office.

"This can't be," I said to Jim. "What happened to these tapes?"

Jim just said he did not know. They were what the government sent over. After hearing these tapes, I couldn't even prove what I had said in my office. No one would be able to understand what was being said on the tapes. He looked at me, then smiled and said, "This just might turn out all right for you. If the government can't prove what Bowmer said on these tapes, then it makes for a weak case."

He made a point here, but I still did not trust the government because of the manner they were handling this case. I knew we would be going to trial soon, and we needed to get all our ducks in a row. (We were unaware at this time that Merkle had another little surprise waiting for us when the trial started.)

Then Jim dropped another bomb on me. He told me he received a copy of the minutes of the commission meeting from the night of the Geraci zoning. There was no record of my statements to the other commissioners or to Jan Platt asking them to reconsider their votes. It seems the clerk turned off the recorder right after the vote was taken, and no record was made of any of the comments made after the vote. I could not believe what had happened. How could they stop recording the meeting at that point? They always kept the recorder going a few minutes after the formal meeting concluded.

Jim theorized that the clerks must have thought the meeting was over and stopped the recorder as the commissioners usually just take up time talking with one another when the last vote is taken and waste a lot of recording space. So when they felt the issue was over, they stopped recording.

Now I did not have my objections on the zoning after the vote was recorded. This was great; I couldn't even prove what I said that night because it was not part of the public record.

"It's all right," Jim said. "We'll get through this. We just need to work around it and see how the pieces play. Go home for now, and we will get back together tomorrow."

Jim worked on our case off and on in between other clients (after all, he still had to make a living from the little I was paying him). There was a lot of work involved in my case, plus a lot of research and depositions to be taken. I knew Jim was probably paying for some of them out of his own pocket, but he never said anything to me about it, not to give me more things to be concerned with.

Robert Merkel

About the third week in May, I had my first taste of court and introduction to Robert Merkle, who would be prosecuting my case. I had to appear in court for my pretrial hearing before presiding judge George Carr. This pretrial hearing was held in a small courtroom on the second floor of the federal courthouse. The purpose of the hearing was to determine whether or not the prosecution had enough evidence to take my case to trial. During this hearing, Caltagirone made a number of motions to dismiss my case, have it severed from the others, and request for discovery of information and to have the tape recordings removed from being entered into evidence should the case go to trial.

U.S. District Judge George C. Carr is presiding over the

Then Caltagirone made a motion to suppress the introduction of the money Bowmer left in my office as obtained by an illegal search and seizure. He said, "Mr. Kotvas asked for an attorney to be present when he turned over the money to the government and was denied his right under threat of bodily harm, Your Honor."

Merkle objected to the motion and told the judge, "Your Honor, Mr. Kotvas voluntarily turned over the money to the FBI when they asked him. Do you think the FBI, the greatest law enforcement agency in the country, would use bodily harm against Mr. Kotvas without provocation? No, Your Honor, he was not threatened."

Then the judge turned to me and asked, "Did the agents make any threatening movements on you or show any threatening signs, Mr. Kotvas?"

"No, Your Honor," I replied. "It was just the way the agent said it. That if I did not hand over the money, they would do whatever it took to recover it and tear my office apart if need be. Then I felt afraid for my well-being." (A lot can be implied by the intensity of the way it was said without actually using any physical force.)

The judge thought about what everyone had said for a moment, then declared, "Your motion to exclude the money, Mr. Caltagirone, is denied. Let's move on."

The judge denied most of the motions but allowed for the discovery of evidence to be turned over to the defendant's council. On the matter of the tapes, the judge withheld an opinion until he had ample time to review the matter. After some time, with lengthy discussions by both Caltagirone and Merkle while presenting their case, Jim had me take the stand. He asked me a number of questions about what happened with the zoning vote and about the day of my arrest. I answered to the court my best recollection of the events.

Then it was Merkle's turn to question me, and he came at me with a vengeance, raising his voice and trying to discredit what I had told the court when Caltagirone questioned me. I was very unnerved by his approach, and it was obvious I was becoming anxious on the stand. Jim jumped in and objected a number of times to some of his questions, but the judge overruled him each time.

Then Merkle asked me about my phone call to the state attorney's office. "Mr. Kotvas, you say you were going to call the state attorney's office about the money Mr. Bowmer left in your office?"

"Yes," I replied.

Merkle retorted, "Why didn't you just turn the money to the FBI agents and tell them what Mr. Bowmer had done?"

"Since I had already called the state attorney's office on the matter, I felt more comfortable if they handled it. I had a friend over there that I trusted and wanted him to look into it."

Then in an extremely loud voice that could be heard all over the courtroom, Merkle shouted out, "You're telling me and this court that you preferred to talk to the state attorney's office over the FBI, the greatest law enforcement agency in the country!" He raised his hands over his head and was gesturing as he spoke.

"Yes," I said.

Mr. Caltagirone then jumped up and objected to this line of questioning but was overruled again.

Merkle continued on, "Who where you trying to call at the state attorney's office, Mr. Kotvas?"

By this time, I was so flustered by all the questioning that my mind went blank. I just sat there looking dumbfounded, trying to get control of my thoughts. I could not get my thoughts together. I always had a problem with remembering names when under pressure (and still do to this very day).

He then repeated the question to me and then said, "Was it EJ Salcines whom you were trying to call?"

"No, it was not. It was one of his assistants," I answered but still could not recall him (Albert Tosca) at the time. My hands were starting to shake by now because I felt I had blown my opportunity on the stand. After asking a few more questions, Merkle said to the judge, "I have no further questions of this person."

I left the witness stand and went back to our table and sat down next to Jim. He wasn't looking too happy about the way things had gone. Both sides were finished now, and the judge then made an announcement to everyone in the courtroom. "I feel the government has sufficient evidence to go to trial, and I am putting it on the calendar for a trial start in June. Counselors, make sure everyone is ready by the time the trial starts. Make sure all motions that need to be filed before trial are filed with the court. Court is now dismissed."

We all stood as Judge Carr left the bench, then gathered our things and left the courthouse. On the way out, I said to Jim, "I guess I did not do too well?"

"It wasn't good," he responded. "We'll talk about it when we get back to the office."

I was feeling real depressed about now, and Jim could see that.

"Cheer up, Mr. Kotvas," he said to me. "This is only the first round. I expected that it would go this way. Remember, it's not over till the fat lady sings. We still have a lot of work ahead of us, and we will have another day in court."

We got into Jim's car and drove back to his office. On the way, I said, "Did you hear Merkle? The FBI is the greatest law enforcement agency in the world. They couldn't find their way to the toilet if it wasn't for local law enforcement. We do all the legwork on a case, and then they come on board near the end and take all our information away from us and use it to their advantage so they can get all the glory in the press. If we're lucky, they will mention 'with the assistance of local law enforcement.'"

That really burned me up. The only time any of them get hurt is when they start to believe in their own propaganda and forget to use good police procedures on a dangerous case. I'm not saying the FBI isn't a good agency. I'm just saying they are always looking for headlines first. Ask any local law enforcement agency, and they will tell you the same thing. Local law enforcement will do most of the work, and then the FBI comes along and takes most of the credit, giving local authorities an assist. They think that because they represent the federal government, they can just come in, take charge, and walk all over local law enforcement. My experience in law enforcement and working with other police agencies has taught me that.

I did not say much more after that. We arrived at Jim's office, and he told me not to worry and to go home, that this was only a minor setback. I then left.

We spent the next few weeks putting the case together with the help of the other attorneys. It was now getting close to trial time, and Jim kept filing motions to get certain information suppressed and waiting to hear the judge's discussion on the tapes. He even had private investigator Metzgar check out a number of witnesses who would be testifying.

On Tuesday, May 3, Bowmer was taken to court to appear before Judge Carr on his plea agreement with the government. With his attorney William Lancaster at his side, Bowmer pled guilty, admitting to the judge that he took a bribe for his vote in a zoning case and agreeing to testify against two other ex-commissioners who pleaded innocent to conspiracy and extortion charges.

Judge Carr tentatively accepted the plea agreement that the government had worked out. He then warned Bowmer, "This agreement is not binding. I will make no ruling on it at this time. Your plea is accepted, hinging on the court's final acceptance and ratification pending a presentence investigation."

With the proceedings over, Bowmer and his attorney were escorted out of the courthouse, his attorney going back to his office and Bowmer to an undisclosed location. On the way out, Bowmer was approached by a number of reporters. When asked why he did it by one of the reporters, the only thing he said was, "I was motivated by greed." Then he walked past them to a waiting car and left the area.

CHAPTER 7

The Trial Begins: The Tapes

June 1983

Tampa Federal Courthouse

It was the middle of the first week in June when my trial began. This was going to be the trial of the century as far as Merkle and the news media were concerned.

All the media vultures were drooling for any bits of information they could print or report ahead of their competition. Reporters were looking for an exclusive from anyone connected with the trial who would talk. Members of the media were either on the street in force covering all the courthouse entrances or upstairs hanging around the courtroom.

Merkle knew this trial could catapult his career to new heights, where he would be able to write his own political ticket. He was ready to do whatever it took to get all of us convicted, and he would manipulate the media to his advantage. Merkle was very good at playing this game, and he knew how to leak information to the media at just the right moment, a media that would gobble it up in a way its use would be to his advantage.

The trial was being held in the Middle District Federal Courthouse in downtown Tampa, with Judge George Carr presiding. It was a large courtroom on the third floor on the south side of the courthouse. This room was larger than the one where we had our pretrial hearing.

As you walked into the courtroom, all the walls were covered with dark oakwood paneling, with a long wooden railing separating the large visitor section in the back from the trial area in the front. A jury box was located just to the left of the court on the other side of the railing from the visitors' section. In front of the railing were two sets of long tables with chairs on each side, separating the left and right of the courtroom, for use by the defense attorneys and the prosecution. They were all facing the judge's bench directly in front of the courtroom.

The witness stand was on the right side of the judge's bench, facing forward. Toward the left side of the room next to the prosecution's tables were another couple of long tables with all sorts of boxes and materials of evidence stacked on top, including the eagle from my office.

As we all walked through the courthouse with our attorneys to the waiting courtroom to begin trial, we were bombarded by reporters. None of the attorneys would answer their questions, nor would I or Mr. Sierra. The only one to make a comment was Fred Anderson when one reporter asked, "Were you involved with Mr. Bowmer?"

Fred's only reply was, "I was framed by Jerry Bowmer."

Then the reporter asked, "Why do you think Jerry Bowmer implicated you in this case?"

"Other than the fact that I think he's probably crazy, I don't know," Fred replied and then kept on walking without answering further.

We all entered the courtroom from the front and took our seats at the tables provided. We would be sitting in these same seats throughout the trial. The prosecution would come in with their team of experts and take seats on their side of the courtroom. Everyone was there and ready while family members and friends were sitting in the visitors' section. As soon as the judge entered the courtroom from his chambers, a bailiff called out, "All rise."

Everyone stood until the judge took his seat, and then we all sat down. Before the judge opened the trial, he gave his comments to both the defense and prosecution on how he expected the trial to go and laid down the rules for both sides to follow. Then, on another note, he told everyone in the court that he had reviewed the tapes and made his decision on the tape recordings. He would allow the tapes to be entered into evidence during the trial, and the jury would be allowed to hear them and judge for themselves what took place. With that said, he called for jury selection to begin.

All the defense lawyers raised objections at that moment; the judge denied them and again called for the jury selection. It took most of the week to select the jury of seven men and five women. When jury selection was completed, the trial began.

Both sides began with opening arguments, with the prosecution going first. The jury was not fully seated until late morning, so it took most of the rest of the day and into the next for everyone to complete opening statements.

Merkle opened by claiming that the FBI recorded Bowmer delivering $5,000 each to Mr. Anderson and Mr. Kotvas. Merkle also stated that Bowmer had picked up $15,000 in cash from an agent of the property owners and was arrested before he could split it three ways. Upon his arrest, Mr. Bowmer agreed to give his full cooperation to the government and to wear recording equipment when he delivered the money to his colleagues.

Merkle went on to describe to the jury that Mr. Sierra and Mr. DeCarlucci were brokers of bribes and that the government would prove that all the defendants were involved in criminal activity.

Once the opening statements were completed, the prosecution began to present its case. We all listened to the scenario that Merkle was presenting to the jury. Every now and then, one of the defense attorneys would jump up and object to a particular point Merkle was trying to make. In more instances than not, the judge would rule in the prosecution's favor; and Merkle, with a sinister smirk on his face, would go on with his presentation. Both Merkle and his assistant Joe Magri would take turns presenting evidence and questioning witnesses in front of the jury.

On Monday, June 13, the prosecution introduced the tapes as evidence so the jury could listen to them. Again, objections were raised and overruled. Because of the poor quality of sound and the inaudible sections on the tape, the government had to create a script with its interpretation of what was on the recordings. They had filled in the blanks on the tape with their version of the conversations that went on at the county courthouse so jury members could read along as they listened.

The government would be bringing into the courtroom special equipment and headphones so that everyone involved in the trial could hear the master recorder that would play the tapes. The headphones and script would be given to all the jurors, the judge, the defense councilors and defendants, plus the agents and prosecutors in the room.

Merkle informed the jury that these tapes would document the payoffs made to Anderson and Kotvas by Jerry Bowmer for the down payment of their share of $25,000 each for their vote on the rezoning of a prime 595-acre tract of land set for development in January of that year. On that note, all the defense attorneys requested a sidebar with the judge. He allowed them to come forward, and the prosecutors joined in. They again objected to the tapes and script being introduced; that they would only confuse and mislead the jury. They requested that the agents handling the tapes and creating the transcript be made to testify on how they put all this together.

Judge Carr overruled the motion on the tapes but allowed testimony from the government explaining the situation on the tapes and how they came up with the transcript. Everyone went back to their seats, and the trial went into a short recess while the government had the agents appear for the court.

Also on this Monday morning of the second week of the trial, Jerry Bowmer, who had already pleaded guilty to extortion and made his deal with the government, was sitting in the witness room, possibly getting ready to testify. We had heard rumors that he might be somewhere in the courthouse, but no one had seen him.

About an hour later, the court was ready to reconvene, and everyone went to their seats. The first agent called to testify was Russell Wood, who entered from the witness room and took the stand. Under examination from Merkle, Agent Wood explained how they set up the receiving recording devices in cars parked around the county courthouse and a central receiver recorder in a small room on the main floor of the courthouse. He then explained how he and other agents walked into Commissioners Kotvas's and Anderson's offices and recorded everything that was said.

Under cross-examination, Caltagirone asked Agent Wood, "Did you tell Commissioner Kotvas that you were taping this interview?"

"No," responded agent Wood.

"Why not? Were you hiding the fact that he was under investigation by your agency?" asked Caltagirone.

At that point, Merkle got up and objected, but the judge overruled him.

"At this point, we were putting together a case against Mr. Kotvas and wanted to see if he would come forward with any information about Mr. Bowmer and the money he left with him," Agent Wood answered.

"Did Commissioner Kotvas know you were taping the interview?" Caltagirone asked.

"No, we had our mics hidden from view. The microphones we were using were for communication only, not for recording our conversation with Mr. Kotvas," Agent Wood replied.

Then Jim asked Wood, "How is it that Commissioner Kotvas saw your microphones on your sleeves under your jackets when you came into his office?"

"That would not be possible. We had them well hidden under our jacket sleeves," was Agent Wood's reply.

Jim then said, "Tell us, Agent Wood, did Mr. Kotvas ask to have a lawyer present during his arrest?"

His answer was, "I believe he may have asked for an attorney to be present. But I informed him that he could contact one when we got back to the federal building because we had to leave."

"And how many times did Mr. Kotvas ask you to let him speak to an attorney, Agent Wood?"

"I don't recall. Maybe a time or two, as far as I can remember," Agent Wood replied.

"Don't you think that Mr. Kotvas, being a former law enforcement officer himself, would know his rights under the law to ask for an attorney to be present during his arrest?" Jim questioned Agent Wood.

Again, Merkle got up and objected to the question, but Judge Carr overruled him.

Agent Wood said, "We allowed him to call his lawyer as soon as we processed him back at the federal building."

Next, Jim asked, "Isn't it strange that you had all these recording devices all around the courthouse and on Jerry Bowmer to record everything that was said, yet you did not record any of your conversation with Mr. Kotvas before you arrested him?"

"Objection, Your Honor, the agent already said they were not recording their conversation," Merkle said as he got up from his chair.

"Objection overruled," replied the judge. "You will answer the question."

Agent Wood said, "We felt there was no need to record any further since we had all we needed on the tapes from the defendants when Mr. Bowmer was in their offices."

"Didn't you think it would be wise to record what Mr. Kotvas had to say when you questioned him?" Jim blurted back at Agent Wood.

"Objection," Merkle shouted. "Asked and answered."

"Objection sustained," Judge Carr said.

"I have no further questions from this witness," Jim told the judge.

Jim returned to his seat next to me. I turned to him and said, "These guys are walking all over us. They violated my rights, and this judge is letting them get away with it." By this time, I was very upset the way things were going. Jim stayed cool, though, and told me to be calm, not to allow the jury to see me upset.

I just felt that the court was letting the government have too much say on what went on without us being able to disprove it. So much of what really happened at that zoning hearing and on the day of my arrest was conveniently missing from the evidence for the jury to hear.

Jim had been setting the stage in case I testified to be able to tell my side of the story of what happened in my office. He wanted to get in the part about the microphones, which the agent claimed I could not see.

After a number of agents took the stand, all testifying to the same things Agent Wood had said, Merkle began paving the way for tapes to be introduced. The next agent whom Merkle called to the stand was Agent Dennis Williams. He walked up to the witness box, raised his right hand, and swore to tell the truth, then sat down. This was the "expert" agent who screened the tapes to filter out any background noises. He then went into the mechanics of how it all worked. After Merkle finished questioning this agent, it was the defense's turn. Both Bennie Lazzara (Anderson's attorney) and Jim cross-examined this agent. Lazzara went first. He challenged the agent on the quality of the tapes and their validity. He asked if the agent had found any discrepancies on the tapes.

Agent Williams stated that when he was removing much of the background noise, he found three gaps in the original tape. Two of the gaps were a second or two in length, and the third was a little longer. Lazzara then pressed the agent for what caused these gaps.

At that point, Merkle jumped up and objected. Judge Carr overruled the objection and asked Agent Williams to answer the question. The agent said his field was not authenticating the tapes but to clean them up and remove any unnecessary background noise. Agent Williams then offered three possibilities for the gaps. The first could be an erasure, the second could be a defective portion of the tape, and the third could be failure of the machines to cut off.

After Lazzara finished questioning the agent, it was Jim's turn. Jim questioned the agent for some time regarding the tapes and the gaps. Then he asked the agent if there were any other problems with the tapes or the recording equipment. The agent answered that it seemed that all the tape recorders had malfunctioned at one point or another during the recordings.

I was sitting at my table, taking notes on what the agent had to say. In my mind, I wanted to jump up and say to Merkle, *So this is the FBI, the greatest law enforcement agency in the country, with the best and most sophisticated equipment money can buy, and you mean to tell us that all the equipment malfunctioned at the same time?* I could not believe what I was hearing. How could five separate recording devices, the best the FBI had, all malfunctioned simultaneously?

Jim finished questioning the agent and made his point to the jury, then retook his seat. Then Merkle got up to rebut the testimony.

"Agent Williams," Merkle said, "can you elaborate more on the tapes for the court?"

He then went on to elaborate that he also reviewed four more tapes of the same conversation that were made simultaneously. By doing this, he was able to fill in the missing sections in the transcript that he produced for the government.

"Ladies and gentlemen, as you can see, it's not as mysterious as the defense would have you believe. I have no further questions of this witness, Your Honor," Merkle said.

The judge then said, "If there are no more questions of this witness, he may step down."

The entire day was taken up with FBI agents testifying on how the tapes of the February 1 conversation were recorded at five different locations in and around the courthouse. A total of seven FBI agents testified that day on the tapes. The tapes had been sent to FBI headquarters in Washington, DC, for enhancement by filtering out noise, then returned to the Tampa office.

As the day was coming to an end, federal assistant prosecutor Joe Magri indicated that he would have the jury listen to the best parts of three of the tapes and that the jurors would also be able to read a composite transcript of the three tapes so they could follow along.

Jerry Bowmer never took the stand that day. While everyone was leaving the courthouse for the day, Bowmer was whisked away to a safe house where he would be kept out of sight until needed by the government. He was no longer a codefendant in our case. He had made his deal with the government the moment he was arrested, and he was now the prosecution's chief witness.

Early the next morning, on Tuesday, June 14, the government was ready to play the tapes for the jury. At the request of defense counselors, all the tapes would be heard by the jury and all affected parties. Transcripts and headphones were passed out to everyone who was part of the trial.

Once everything had been distributed, Judge Carr ordered the courtroom to be silent while the tapes were played and to hold all remarks and motions until they were finished. I was sitting next to Jim at our table with a notepad in front of me so I could take notes on what I heard on the tapes. The agent who set up the player asked everyone to put on their headphones so he could start the first tape.

As we all listened to the tape, which had been recorded using the briefcase Jerry was carrying, we could clearly hear Jerry Bowmer walking and talking as he entered the courthouse. Everything was understandable for the first few minutes of the tape right up to the point he entered the commission chambers. Then things started to happen when he got to Commissioner Anderson's office.

We started to hear some kind of static off and on. Bowmer would speak loudly at one point, then whisper at another. You could hear the greetings and the beginning of the conversation between Anderson and Bowmer quite clearly; then everything went into whispers, and it was a little hard to hear what they were saying. You had to follow the script the government provided to know what the conversation was about. When Bowmer was finished and stopped whispering, his voice became loud again as he said good-bye to Anderson.

We could hear him loud and clear as he entered my office and talked to my aide Jane. We could hear them both very clearly as he moved on into my office and started talking to me. But then, all of a sudden, the tape was garbled and inaudible, and it stayed that way until Bowmer began to leave my office. At that time, the sound came back clear, and you could hear everything that was happening after that.

I made some notes for Jim and asked what happened to my conversation with Bowmer? Jim asked me to be patient and listen to the rest of the tapes. Meanwhile, the agent put on the next tape. I looked at the script they had prepared to go along with the tapes. You could see where the government added words where the sentences were not complete or where there was a missing word or two. It looked like one of those fil-in-the-blank forms to fit what they wanted people to hear.

When the next tape was played, you could hear a lot of static and more inaudible statements and very low voices in conversation that they assumed were said in the transcript. Again, when it came to my office, there seemed to be a problem with the tape, which only got bits and pieces of my conversation with Bowmer. At this point, I was asking Jim what was going on here. All he said to me was just, "Be calm. We can talk later. Let's hear the rest of the tapes."

It took most of the day to hear all five tapes, and at times, some parts had to be replayed for everyone. It was unbelievable—the same problems had appeared on every tape. After a number of tapes, you could almost make out most of what was said in Commissioner Anderson's office. But when it came to my office, every tape seemed to malfunction. Most of the conversation in my office was garbled, broken up, and static. What the government did in my case was to write the script by filling in the garble and static of my conversation with Bowmer.

After all the tapes had been played, I was livid, and Jim could see I wanted to say something. He grabbed my arm and said, "Stay cool, Mr. Kotvas. You don't want the jury to see your temper. I'll handle this."

"But, Jim," I said, "this is the FBI. How can all these tapes malfunction when they get to my office?"

"We're about to find out." Then Caltagirone got up from his seat and requested that Agent Williams be recalled to the stand.

Merkle objected, but Judge Carr overruled him.

Then Merkle said it would take a little while to bring back Agent Williams, for he was not in the courthouse at the moment, and he would have to come over from the office in the federal building. The judge called for a short recess until the agent arrived. It was between twenty and thirty minutes before Agent Williams arrived and took the stand. Judge Carr reminded the agent that he was still under oath.

It was very late in the afternoon when Jim was able to question Williams. "Agent Williams, can you elaborate for the court how the tape in the briefcase seemed to go to static and the other four tapes somehow seemed to turn into garble when Mr. Bowmer entered Commissioner Kotvas's office?"

All Agent Williams could say was, "The recorder in the briefcase failed, and the others just malfunctioned."

"No further questions, Your Honor," Jim replied.

Merkle jumped up and asked Williams, "You were able to hear enough from all the tapes to put the conversations in order?"

"Yes," replied Agent Williams; then he was allowed to leave the witness box.

Nowhere on the tapes were there voices of Michel Sierra or John DeCarlucci having any involvement in the Geraci zoning except for the word of Bowmer when he mentioned Sierra's name to Pickens Talley at the beginning of one of the tapes. Everything on the tapes centered on Bowmer, Anderson, and myself. I still could not see why these two men were on trial with us only because Bowmer had said they were.

Again, it was too late in the day to call more witnesses, so Judge Carr recessed court until the next morning at nine and told the government to be ready to call its next witness. All the recording equipment was left in the courtroom in case it was needed again.

CHAPTER 8

Bowmer Takes the Stand

June 1983

Jerry Bowmer was the
government's star witness.

On the morning of June 15, the trial continued. It was warm and sunny, the type of day when you wish you were someplace other than a courtroom.

As soon as Judge Carr resumed the trial, and before the jury was called to sit, DeCarlucci's attorney requested a sidebar. All the attorneys on both sides approached the judge's bench as DeCarlucci's attorney informed the court of a possible conflict of interest in this trial, requiring him to withdraw as attorney. Under a flurry of objections from both the prosecution and defense, Judge Carr allowed him to withdraw.

The judge then declared a mistrial for the part of the trial concerning DeCarlucci and severed DeCarlucci from the proceedings because of the apparent conflict that raised questions about effective legal counsel. This did not alter the conspiracy charge against DeCarlucci; he would have to stand trial at a later time. Now only I, Anderson, and Sierra (who was only charged with conspiracy) would be left to stand trial.

Judge Carr then asked for the jury to come in and take their seats as the trial continued. All the recording equipment was still in the courtroom just as it had been the night before. The judge told the prosecution to call the first witness.

Merkle then called for Jerry Bowmer to take the stand. A door opened from a small room on the side of the courtroom, where witnesses waited to be called to testify, and Jerry Bowmer entered. He was now the prosecution's chief witness.

Bowmer was smiling as I watched him walk to the witness box, raise his right hand, and swear to tell the truth. I could not believe it, but as he took his seat on the witness stand, he winked at us with a sly smile. It appeared that this must seem like fun and games for him. Merkle looked a little peeved at Bowmer as he began his questioning.

Again, the tapes were played for the jury and the court, with Bowmer listening. After the tapes played, Merkle asked Bowmer to explain the conversations on the tapes and to describe in his own words the events leading up to his arrest. Bowmer looked a little more serious now as he began to tell the court how all this came about. He claimed that he had been summoned to Michael Sierra's office late last summer to talk about a rezoning petition coming up regarding the property known as the Galleria project. Everyone in the courtroom was listening very intensely to what he had to say. All the defense lawyers and defendants were taking notes as Bowmer continued with his story.

Bowmer claimed Sierra told him that he had already met with Kotvas and Anderson about the zoning. At that point, I knew he was lying. I turned to Jim and whispered, "He's lying. I never met with Sierra on that zoning. The only person I talked to was Steve Reynolds."

Sierra's attorney jumped up and objected to Bowmer's statement about his client but was overruled.

Jim just squeezed my forearm and said, "Be patient. We'll get our turn."

As Bowmer continued, he alleged that Sierra had told him that he was going to put in for $25,000 apiece (meaning the commissioners), and he was going to ask the representatives of the property for a $100,000 bribe. Bowmer claimed he didn't question the other $25,000, for he assumed it was some overhead, or someone else was getting a cut. To this deal, he told Sierra, "Fine."

Bowmer then told the court it was his understanding that the three of us would vote for the zoning if the $25,000 came through up front. Some time had passed, and it seemed like the money Sierra talked about was not coming through, so he approached Pick Talley, whom he knew and who was working for the Geraci brothers, to meet him in a bar so he could cut a new deal to get the zoning approved. He did not know that Mr. Talley had gone to the FBI with the information and set up a sting on the deal.

Bowmer continued, "Mr. Talley led me to believe he had talked with the property owners and said they would pay something, that they wanted to get this thing done badly enough. There was a lot of money involved in this zoning, so I asked him to give me some figures. I told him I could use around a hundred thousand if a vote needs to be there.

"Then Mr. Talley said to me, 'OK, a hundred thousand. Well, I think that's a lot of money.' Then I told him I would shave the price to seventy-five thousand dollars, and if successful, I would signal him—Talley—by tugging my ear just before the commission meeting on January 27 when the vote on the project would come up."

Bowmer then told the jury that after the tape of him and Talley was played, it was his understanding that Mr. Sierra was the front man on the bribe and that Mr. Kotvas and Anderson had agreed to the deal.

All through his testimony, defense attorneys kept jumping up, objecting to the statements Bowmer was making, only to be overruled by the judge. Nowhere on all the tapes were there any recordings of any conversation with Bowmer and Sierra as to any of the allegations. It was all just Bowmer's "word" on what took place and who was involved. As the trial moved on, all the government had on Sierra was hearsay.

Bowmer continued, explaining that after the zoning was approved, he went back to meet Talley to get the money, not knowing that he was being recorded at the time. "I was given $15,000 in cash as a down payment that night on the $75,000 bribe from Talley. I was then arrested by the FBI as I was leaving the meeting with the money."

Then Merkle asked, "After you were arrested, Mr. Bowmer, did you offer to cooperate and testify for the government to bring the other conspirators to justice?"

"Yes," answered Bowmer. Then he continued to explain to the jury and the court how he wore a wire to implicate the other commissioners in his conspiracy and what was being said on the tapes that was inaudible. After all, Bowmer did have the script in his hand that the government made up for everyone as to what was allegedly said.

When Merkle was finished with Bowmer, it was the defense's turn to cross-examine. Sierra's attorney got up and started asking him questions. "Mr. Bowmer, isn't it true for your testimony here today that you made a plea bargain with the government for a lenient sentence?"

Merkle jumped up and objected, but the judge overruled him.

"Yes," answered Bowmer. "If I testified truthfully and fully, the government said I would receive a lighter sentence."

Ray LaPorte, Sierras' attorney, asked, "You have lied in the past to government officials, haven't you?"

"Yes."

"So who's to say you're not lying now about Mr. Sierra and what happened?"

"Because I have to tell the truth to keep the plea agreement," Bowmer responded.

"To tell the truth, or to tell a story that the government could believe to help you get a lighter sentence?" Mr. LaPorte snapped back.

Again, Merkle jumped up and objected; but this time, the judge sustained the objection, and Mr. LaPorte withdrew the question. It went on like this all day, with Bowmer telling his side of the story and looking quite cocky on the stand while attorneys and prosecutors would jump up from time to time to challenge the questions.

Bowmer would be on the stand for over three days of questioning by both sides. It seemed like he was enjoying all the attention he was getting and this was all a big joke to him. Whatever the deal he made with Merkle, he was going to play it to the hilt. I'm sure the jury must have seen through some of this.

Bennie Lazzara, Fred Anderson's attorney, got up and started to question Bowmer. They discussed Anderson's health, and Lazzara asked Bowmer if he knew that the commissioner was on heavy medication for his heart that day and only came in to talk with the people from the Brandon Chamber of Commerce?

Bowmer replied he was unaware that Anderson had taken any medication. Then Lazzara continued to discredit Bowmer's testimony. "Is it not true that you are a greedy person and it was greed that drove you to taking these bribes?" Lazzara challenged.

"Yes, you can say I was motivated by greed," he responded.

"Isn't it true, because of your greed, you were going to keep all the money for yourself and there was no one else involved with your scheme? Then once you were caught, you needed to make up a story for the FBI to get a deal for yourself?" Lazzara asked in a high voice.

"No," replied Bowmer as assistant prosecutor Magri jumped up to object and was overruled. Bowmer had already answered the question.

"You were going to keep all the money for yourself, weren't you?" Mr. Lazzara shouted at Bowmer as everyone looked up at them at that moment.

A now not-so-cocky Bowmer shouted back, "No," while nervously twiddling his hands on his lap.

Magri again jumped up and said, "Objection, Your Honor. The question has already been answered."

"Objection sustained," replied the judge. "Mr. Lazzara, question asked and answered. Move on with your examination of this witness."

Lazzara made some very good points to the jury that day. I believe the jury could now see Bowmer for what he really was: a greedy, lying, scheming person.

Now it was Jim Caltagirone's turn at Bowmer. He tore right into his testimony trying to discredit the statements Bowmer had made. At this point, Bowmer no longer seemed smug. All through Jim's cross-examination of Bowmer, Merkle or Magri would interrupt, object, and ask Bowmer to clarify his answers.

"Mr. Bowmer," Jim, said, "isn't it true you were trying to give Commissioner Kotvas a hard time the night of the zoning?"

"Not at all," was his answer.

"Isn't it true that Commissioner Kotvas did not want to have anything to do with this zoning?"

"No, he agreed to his share of the zoning payoff."

"A payoff only greedy people like you claim?"

Joe Magri got up and objected to the statement. Judge Carr sustained the objection and told Caltagirone to move on.

"Isn't it true you had numerous conversations with Commissioner Kotvas before the zoning meeting took place trying to get Mr. Kotvas to vote for the zoning?"

"He did not want to vote for it because it was in his district, and it would look bad for him, he told me. I told him we needed his vote. A lot was riding on it," Bowmer replied.

"If you had Mr. Kotvas's vote, then why did you need to talk with him so many times about it?"

"I wanted to reassure him we had a deal."

Jim countered, "In fact, isn't it true that Mr. Kotvas voted NO on the zoning and was the only no vote that night? Do you mean to tell everyone here that someone would pay a bribe for a no vote?"

"He told me he would vote for it if his vote was needed."

"He told you, and did he tell you and did you not see that night that he tried to get the other commissioners to change their votes after the vote was taken?"

"Objection." This time, Merkle shouted.

"I withdraw the question, Your Honor," Jim said before the judge had a chance to respond.

Then Jim asked Bowmer why, when he came into Commissioners Kotvas's office the day of the arrest, he laid the envelope with the money on his desk rather than hand it to him.

Bowmer's only reply was, "We were talking, and he seemed to be distracted by something."

Then Jim asked Bowmer, "Did Commissioner Kotvas pick up the envelope and count the money in front of you to see if it was all there?"

"No, I just left it there on his desk and went to see Commissioner Anderson," was his response.

Jim Caltagirone was trying to demonstrate to the jury that I was not a party to this bribe. He was doing a good job sowing doubt in the minds of the jurors regarding Bowmer's accusations. All the defense attorneys did a good job tearing down Bowmer's claims as lies over the objections of Merkle and Magri.

By this time, it was late Friday afternoon, and Judge Carr continued the trial until early Monday morning. He instructed the jury not to talk to anyone about the case and not to give any interviews to the press. At this point, we adjourned for the weekend to rest and prepare for the next phase of the trial.

CHAPTER 9

The Juror

June 1983

The trial continued early Monday morning on June 20, 1983, with Bowmer temporarily ending his testimony. He would be called back to the witness stand at a later time.

In the audience section of the courtroom was a friend of mine and loyal supporter Joe Pless. He was a retired American Can Company employee and an active member of the company's union. He had been following the trial since the beginning and would stay the whole day so he could hear and see everything that went on. Joe would never miss a single day of the trial and would hang around the corridor outside the courtroom during any short recess.

On this particular day, everyone was coming back from lunch break; Joe noticed one of the male jurors standing in the hallway next to the men's room. He thought it was kind of odd, so he just stood nearby and watched.

A few moments later, Merkle came walking by in the hallway. The juror smiled and winked at him, then walked over and said something to him that Joe said sounded like, "You really did good," and some other things in a low voice that Joe could not make out.

Merkle told the juror that he shouldn't be talking to him out here as he walked into the restroom with the juror following. Then a few moments later, the juror came out by himself and went back into the courtroom. Merkle came out of the restroom a moment later and went into the courtroom.

Joe thought this was very strange and felt the need to tell somebody about it. When he saw Jim Caltagirone and Bennie Lazzara in a corner talking to each other, he walked over and told them what he had seen and heard.

They were very interested in what he had to say and asked if he was sure of what he saw and heard. Joe just said, "I know what I saw and heard, and it was so and so male juror that sits in back of the jury section."

Caltagirone and Lazzara thanked Joe for his alertness and then went back inside the courtroom, discussing the matter.

In the courtroom, all the defense attorneys got into a huddle and started talking about what Joe had told them, and then they all took their seats as the judge entered the courtroom. I asked Jim what was going on, and he just advised me that a problem had come up that we needed to get clarified.

"All rise," the bailiff called out as Judge Carr walked up to his seat on the bench. As the judge was getting ready to sit, Lazzara jumped up and asked to approach the bench before the jury was called in. The judge allowed them all to come forward, and Mr. Lazzara explained the incident that took place outside the men's room with Merkle and the juror.

The judge listened and then questioned Merkle about it. Merkle explained he was going to inform the court of the situation but did not get a chance to, then explained to the judge what happened and what he claimed was said. At this point, the counsels for the defense asked for a mistrial, but the judge said he would hold his decision on that motion until he spoke with the juror in his chambers.

Judge Carr asked that this juror be brought to his chambers while the court held a small recess. After a short while in his office with the juror, the judge returned to the bench and called for the juror to come before him. Standing before the judge outside of the full jury, the juror was told that he was being excused for legal reasons and that he was not to speculate on the reason. The juror was then asked to leave the courtroom.

The judge then informed the defense attorneys that their motion for a mistrial was denied and that we would proceed with the trial. There was a roar of objections by the defense, but as the dismissed juror left the courtroom, the judge denied the objections and called for the jury to return to their seats.

When the jury arrived and sat down, Judge Carr informed them of the dismissal of the juror and that he was being replaced with one of the four alternates to round out the jury to twelve. He did not give any reason for the dismissal and informed the jury that they were not to speculate on the reason.

The four alternate jurors were in the courtroom for the whole trial in case a juror needed to be replaced. They sat at the end of the jury box so they could listen to all testimony and take notes.

Just as the trial was resuming, the ex-juror came back into the courtroom and sat down in the spectator section. He was then noticed by one of the defense attorneys, who brought it to Judge Carr's attention. The judge immediately asked a US marshal to escort the man out of the courtroom and inform him that he was not to return.

As far as Merkle was concerned, nothing more was said, and the trial continued as the prosecution called for the next witness. This time, it was Pickens Talley to verify Bowmer's testimony. He was asked to take the stand and raise his right hand and swear to tell the truth. He gave his full name for the court. "Pickens C. Talley III," he said. Then he took his seat on the stand.

Mr. Talley had been retained by the Geraci family as a consulting engineer for the development of their property. He was a former county engineer and very familiar with many of the county's department heads and members of the planning commission. He knew just about everyone in county government.

Under direct examination by Merkle, Talley stated that allegations of corrupt zoning decisions by the county commission, usually by a 3–2 vote, had been circulating among the area developers for some time. He was brought in to help Stephen Reynolds, the attorney representing the Geracis, on their zoning before the commission.

When he came on board, Talley stated that Reynolds told him that over the course of ten months of negotiations and five commission meetings, and in spite of winning the approval of the county's planning staff, he had been unable to get an answer from the county commission.

"'Here is the cleanest rezoning that I ever had,' Mr. Reynolds said. 'And the commission keeps postponing action.' I told him I would see what I could do on the matter since I knew most of the commissioners personally."

"You were the one who initiated this investigation, were you not?" asked Merkle.

"Yes," replied Talley.

"Would you tell the court what events took place next?" Merkle requested of the witness.

Mr. Talley then continued with his story, stating that about a month before the zoning was to come before the county commission again, he received a call from Bowmer, who asked to meet him in a bar one weekday afternoon.

"I felt this was very odd and grew suspicious, so one morning in the locker room of the racquetball club before the meeting with Bowmer, I told my racquetball buddy, who was a former FBI bureau chief here in Tampa, about the strange call," Talley said.

"He said it sounded strange to him also, and maybe we should talk to someone in the bureau. Together we went to the FBI and told them the situation. They seemed very interested in what Bowmer had to say, so they equipped me with a recording device to tape our meeting."

Mr. Talley was telling the jury what Merkle needed to back up Bowmer's testimony and fill in the blanks on how they came to arrest Jerry Bowmer. As he continued, he told the court that at the next meeting, the FBI gave him $15,000 in marked bills as a down payment for the $75,000 for the approval vote on the zoning. He testified that Bowmer originally wanted $100,000 but settled for $75,000. "After I gave him the marked money, Bowmer left the building we had met in and was arrested outside by the FBI."

Merkle stood up from his chair and said, "Thank you, Mr. Talley. I have no further questions at this time."

Under cross-examination, all the defense attorneys asked the same question. Lazzara went first. "Did you have any contact with Mr. Anderson where he indicated to you that he might want a bribe?"

"No," was the response.

LaPorte asked, "Did Mr. Sierra ever attempted to contact you or meet with you, giving you any indication that he was looking for a bribe?"

Again, "No," was the response.

Then Mr. Caltagirone got up and asked, "Has Mr. Kotvas ever approached you for a bribe?"

Again, "No," was the answer.

Caltagirone hammered the point home. "So Mr. Kotvas never contacted you nor approached you or gave you any indication that he was interested in a bribe?"

"Objection, Your Honor, asked and answered," Merkle called out.

"I'll allow it," the judge replied. "Answer the question."

"No, sir," he replied.

"So for all you really know then, Jerry Bowmer wanted all the money for himself and concocted this story for your benefit and the benefit of the government, and there was no one else involved in this bribe to your knowledge?" Jim blurted out.

"Objection, objection," the prosecutor kept saying.

"Overruled," Judge Carr said.

"He told me they were involved, but I have no direct knowledge of it," Talley answered.

"Do you believe everything Bowmer tells you?" Jim asked.

The prosecutor again objected to the question, which was sustained by the judge, and Jim withdrew the question. He had made his point, and everyone in the court knew it. "I have one last question, Mr. Talley. You know Mr. Kotvas, don't you?"

"Yes, sir."

"Have you ever known Mr. Kotvas to do anything illegal or immoral?"

"No, sir," was his answer.

"I have no further question of this witness, Your Honor," Jim told the judge.

Then Judge Carr told Mr. Talley he could step down and instructed the prosecutor to call the next witness.

Later in his life, in an interview with a reporter, Pickens Talley would say that he ran into Jerry Bowmer in the witness holding area a few times during the trial. The first time he saw him, Jerry gave him a big bear hug and said, "It had to end sooner or later."

The next witness the prosecution called was Stephen Reynolds. I felt good about this witness. I had known Steve since my city council days and considered him a friend. I turned to Jim and said, "Now we will get to the truth of what happened. Steve knows I was not supporting this zoning."

"Stay calm. Let's see what he has to say," Jim said as he squeezed my arm, telling me not to get too emotional.

Once on the stand, Merkle asked Steve to identify himself and his relationship to the Geraci zoning. Steve explained that from the very beginning, he was retained as the attorney representing the property for rezoning for the Geraci family and that, for over ten months, he had been working diligently to get the county to approve the zoning.

Merkle asked, "In all that time, had you any problems with the county or the county planners getting their approval? Please explain."

"No," Steve replied. "I didn't have any problems with any of the staff members. In fact, they were very helpful. The problems started when the zoning petition was to come before the county commission. When I realized that some of the commissioners had concerns about the project, I tried to get an appointment to meet with all the commissioners individually to explain the zoning and answer any concerns they might have."

"And did you?" Merkle asked.

"No, not with all of them. Commissioner Platt would not see me. I was informed by her aide that it was her policy never to talk with anyone about upcoming zonings, that she would hear what we had to say at the zoning meeting. But I was able to meet with the others," he answered.

Merkle's next question was, "What kind of a reception did you get from the other commissioners?"

"Over time, I was able to meet with all the others. Commissioner Rodney Colson seemed very interested in the project and said he would talk with county staff about it and would give it consideration if they saw no problems. I thanked him for his time, then met with the other commissioners, but not all on the same day. Commissioner Bowmer and Anderson were noncommittal. They said they needed more information first. Commissioner Anderson said he would talk with county staff about some concerns he had but would keep an open mind on the matter.

"Commissioner Bowmer said he saw too many problems with the project and that we needed to work some things out, and he would get back with me. I could not understand what problems he was talking about. The county staff had already given the project a green light. He kind of kept stalling the matter every time it came before the commission. I informed Pick Talley about the problem when he was brought on board to assist me with the problem."

"What about Mr. Kotvas?" Merkle asked.

"Commissioner Kotvas told me he could not vote for the zoning, that he was getting a lot of flak from the surrounding neighbors. This zoning was in his district," Steve told the court.

Merkle then asked, "Did it seem to you that they were stalling for a bribe?"

Sitting nervously on the stand at this point, Steve said, "I believe so. They could have been stalling for a bribe. I find no other reason for the long delays."

At this point, Jim turned to me and said, "This guy is supposed to be your friend?"

Startled by Steve's comments, I whispered to Jim, "I can't believe Steve said that. He knew from the beginning I was not going to support this zoning. I told him a number of times long before it ever became an issue."

"No further questions, Your Honor," Merkle said.

Lazzara and LaPorte took turns questioning Reynolds, asking if he was approached by their clients in any way, knowingly asking for a bribe. Steve just replied, "No."

After a while, it was Jim's turn. He got up from his chair very calmly and looked Steve in the face as he walked toward him and said, "Mr. Reynolds, you know Mr. Kotvas, don't you?"

"Yes."

"And you have known Mr. Kotvas for some time, haven't you?"

"Yes, I have."

"You've known Mr. Kotvas ever since he was a city councilman, before he got on the county commission, haven't you?"

"Yes, that's true."

"You've even contributed to Mr. Kotvas's political campaigns in the past, haven't you?"

"Yes, I have."

Jim probed further, "Isn't it a fact that, over the years, you have been before Mr. Kotvas in his official capacity, both on the city council and county commission, on zoning matters and never encountered any problems?"

Steve looked a little unsettled as he looked toward Merkle sitting at his table with a stern look on his face while he answered Jim's question. "Yes, I have never had a problem with Mr. Kotvas in the past."

"Now, Mr. Reynolds, did you not have a meeting with Mr. Kotvas at a restaurant with Mr. Geraci for lunch one day to discuss this zoning matter, where Mr. Kotvas informed you and Mr. Geraci that he could not vote for this zoning at least a month before it came before the commission?"

"Yes, we met with Mr. Kotvas, and he informed us that he could not vote for the zoning and would not talk about it with us, but we could talk about it between ourselves. He would not get involved in the discussion, but at the end of the lunch, he said he would keep an open mind on the matter but don't count on his vote."

"The only reason that Mr. Kotvas met with you both was because of your insistence and long friendship with Mr. Kotvas. Is that not true, Mr. Reynolds?"

"That is correct, sir."

"Was there opposition to the zoning from members of the community in the audience the night of the zoning?"

"Yes, there were people from some of the surrounding neighborhoods."

"So Mr. Kotvas was telling you the truth that he was receiving flak to not support this zoning from the community, was he not?"

Steve hedged, "I guess you could say that."

"No, Mr. Reynolds, you just said that."

Then came the objection from the government, which was overruled by the judge.

"Has Mr. Kotvas always been straightforward and honest in the past with your dealings with him?"

"Yes, he has."

"No further questions, Your Honor," Jim said.

Before Steve Reynolds could leave the stand, Merkle got up and said, "I have a rebuttal question, Your Honor." The judge let him proceed. "Mr. Reynolds, in your opinion, did it seem like Mr. Kotvas was stalling for a bribe?"

Steve couldn't look my way when he answered. "It appeared that way," was all he said. Then he was allowed to leave the witness stand. He never looked my way as he walked out of the courtroom.

I was shattered by Steve's testimony. This was a man whom I had known over the years and who supported me in the past. My late wife and I had socialized with Steve and his wife on a number of occasions. In all that time, there had never been a problem with our professional lives. When Steve came before the city council in the past, he would win some and lose some. Even though I had considered him a friend, I did not always vote his way.

Steve and I had talked some a few months before, just after my arrest. He had told me he would set the record straight on the matter. Today this was a totally different person; I had no idea what happened to change him. It would not be until after the trial that I would find out why he testified the way he did.

Jim turned to me and said, "I don't know what to tell you about your friend, but I hope you don't have too many more like him."

Judge Carr was not feeling well this day, and Mr. Sierra was having a flare-up of back pain that needed attention when the afternoon session began. It was already the thirtieth of June, so the judge recessed the trial early so the jury and everyone could enjoy the Fourth of July weekend.

This made me feel a little better; we would have the holiday weekend off with our families. We picked up all our materials and walked out of the courtroom. I was feeling depressed about the day's events. I just wanted to get home to my kids and rest. Tomorrow would be another busy day for us.

CHAPTER 10

The Trial Continues

July 1983

On Wednesday, July 6, after spending a restful weekend with my family, I returned to court as the trial resumed with the government calling a number of county zoning staff members to the stand. They explained why they gave the zoning a good recommendation and how they tried to explain to the commission the merits of the zoning. Fred Anderson was not looking too well as he sat listening to the testimony. Mr. Anderson's health had been poor for some time. Before our arrests, he had missed a number of commission meetings because of heart problems.

During the trial, Anderson came to court each day not looking poorly; but on this day, he looked very pale and clammy. His breathing was heavy, and he had been complaining to his attorney Bennie Lazzara of chest pains. He seemed very weak to me. Lazzara was getting increasingly concerned for his client.

The trial recessed for lunch, and the judge and jury left the courtroom as all the defendants' visitors and attorneys prepared to exit the courtroom. Fred Anderson slumped over with his head on the defense table and did not stand up with the rest of us.

Mr. Lazzara helped Fred sit up in his chair and was planning to have him checked out by a doctor while on our lunch break when Mr. Anderson began vomiting. His wife, Pat, rushed over to him as his lawyer and a bailiff lowered him to the floor and placed him on his side so he would not choke on his own vomit. Tampa fire rescue paramedics were called and arrived within minutes at the courtroom to begin treating him.

A short time later, the paramedics picked Mr. Anderson up and placed him on a gurney, strapped him down, and wheeled him out of the courthouse with his wife, Patricia, at his side while they administered oxygen to him. He was then rushed to Tampa General Hospital's emergency room.

Judge Carr did not learn of the incident until he got back from lunch to begin the afternoon session. The judge sent Mr. Lazzara, Anderson's attorney, to the hospital to get an update of his condition. It was a while before Mr. Lazzara returned to the courtroom with a report. He informed the judge that Mr. Anderson had a history of heart trouble and that the hospital wanted to keep his client overnight for observation. Judge Carr then said he would recess the trial until he could get a full report on Mr. Anderson's condition.

After all the excitement was over, Judge Carr reconvened and had the jury come back into the courtroom, where he informed them of Mr. Anderson's condition and said there would be a short postponement of the trial. Court would reconvene in the morning with a full report from the hospital to be presented to the court.

As the attorneys were standing around the courtroom, someone overheard Merkle and Magri talking to each other in angry whispers, saying, "This is a fine time for him to pull this stunt. I bet all this is a ploy. He's faking his condition to try and cause a mistrial or gain sympathy from the jury."

They gathered their notes and left the room.

Mr. Caltagirone and I were informed of the statement made by the prosecutors after they had left the courtroom. We were both pissed off at how uncompassionate they could be. But knowing Merkle's reputation, it was no great surprise. I will never forget that statement repeated to us in the courtroom. I was just glad Mrs. Anderson was not present to hear it. Nothing was ever done about it to my knowledge.

The next morning, the judge was informed as to Mr. Anderson's condition by Mr. Lazzara. After running a number of tests, his doctor believed that Mr. Anderson suffered a mild heart attack in the courtroom. He would be released from the hospital later on in the day. The judge delayed the trial for another day until Mr. Anderson could return and continue. Merkle still contended that Anderson was putting on a show for sympathy and was faking his illness. The trial continued the next day.

When we all returned to the court after Fred was released from the hospital, his skin color was looking much better. He no longer looked clammy, and he seemed a little more alert. Judge Carr asked Fred how he was feeling, and Fred told the judge he was feeling much better and could continue with the trial.

The prosecution then called Jan Platt to the stand. Mrs. Platt was now the chairman of the county commission, having been voted upon by the newly appointed members of the commission. She walked in from the witness room and took the stand, raised her right hand, and swore to tell the truth, then took her seat in the witness box.

Jan Platt

Merkle started questioning her by asking, "How would you say your relationship with the defendants on the commission was?"

Mrs. Platt just replied, "There was no relationship between us. We would just try and work together on the board. They would stay in their offices, and I would stay in mine. The only times we would be together was at commission meetings and workshops."

"And how did they behave at these commission meetings?" Merkle asked.

"They always seem to vote as a block, three to two on most matters, especially on zoning matters. Sometimes you could see them in the hallway outside the meeting room laughing or joking around. Other times, you could see them whispering to one another about something, before or after a meeting."

"Mrs. Platt, in your opinion, did you think something was going on between them?" Merkle asked.

Mr. Lazzara objected to the question but was overruled.

"Please answer the question, Mrs. Platt," Merkle said.

"I always had my suspicions that something was going on between the three of them but had no proof. Jerry Bowmer was always up to something and liked making fun of people to everyone around him. He would walk in and out of the other commissioners' offices quite a bit."

When asked about Mickey Sierra, her response was only that she knew him as one of the many attorneys who came before the commission and he was very active in local politics. This type of questioning continued for a while, with defense attorneys getting up and objecting to the way some of the questions were being asked. When Merkle was finished, it was the defense's turn to question Mrs. Platt.

Joe Ficcarotta, the other attorney representing Mickey Sierra, got up and asked Mrs. Platt, "Do you know of, or have any knowledge that, Mr. Sierra offered anyone a bribe or was part of this conspiracy with Mr. Bowmer?"

"No," was her answer.

Mr. Ficcarotta had no further questions and sat down.

Then Mr. Lazzara got up to question the witness. "Mrs. Platt, you said you saw the three commissioners whispering in the hallway and joking and laughing from time to time, is that correct?"

"Yes," she replied.

"Were their offices next to one another, where they could go in and out of each of them together?" Mr. Lazzara asked.

"No," she answered.

"Where is Jerry Bowmer's office in comparison with the other commissioners' offices?" was his next question.

Mrs. Platt stopped to think for a moment then said, "Commissioner Kotvas's office and Commissioner Anderson's office are next to each other at the far end of the hallway. Then there's Commissioner Colson's office, then my office, and Jerry Bowmer's office is at the other end of the hallway right next to the board meeting room."

"So there is some distance between the commission offices?" Mr. Lazzara asked.

"You could say that," was her reply.

"So when these whispers and jokes would take place, were they at the far end of the hall or next to the boardroom?" he asked.

"Usually they took place outside the boardroom just before everyone entered the meeting room, so the meeting could start, or after the meeting was over," Platt answered.

Then Mr. Lazzara said, "So all these whispers and the joking would take place in the hallway in front of the boardroom, with all the county staff walking by and in and out of the boardroom where they could be overheard by anyone nearby?"

Merkle jumped up and objected to the statement, but before the judge had a chance to rule on the objection, Mr. Lazzara withdrew the question. The jury got the point. When Lazzara was finished with Mrs. Platt, it was Mr. Caltagirone's turn to ask the questions.

As Mr. Caltagirone got up to cross-examine Mrs. Platt, he took a moment to scan over some notes he made and then walked over to the witness box, walking past the panel of jurors. He turned and faced Mrs. Platt, then asked, "Did you hear any of the conversation between Mr. Kotvas and Mr. Bowmer on the night of the zoning?"

"No," she answered.

"So you have no idea what they were talking about, do you?" asked Caltagirone.

Again she replied, "No."

"So they could have been talking about anything. Like, 'I don't want to hear what you have to say,' or 'I am not supporting this zoning,'" Caltagirone stated.

"Objection to the statement, Your Honor," Merkle cried out. "It's leading the witness.

"Objection sustained. Rephrase the question, Mr. Caltagirone," Judge Carr said.

"Yes, Your Honor," he replied. "Did it look like Mr. Kotvas did not wish to talk with Mr. Bowmer before the meeting started?"

"I don't know. It seemed something was bothering Mr. Kotvas that night," Platt responded.

"Isn't it a fact that Mr. Kotvas voted against the zoning and that he was the only NO vote that night?" Mr. Caltagirone turned and faced the jury while asking the question.

"Yes, he voted no on the zoning," she answered.

"Did not Mr. Kotvas, after the vote was taken, ask you and the other commissioners to reconsider your vote?" Caltagirone asked.

Merkle and Magri both jumped up to object to the question, but the judge overruled them.

"I'm not sure. He might have said something to that effect. I can't remember. So much went on that night," she said.

"Your record shows you have a habit of voting no on large developments in the county even when they have county staff approval. Yet on this one, you voted for it. Why is that, Mrs. Platt?" Caltagirone asked.

Another objection came from the prosecution side and was overruled by the judge.

"I don't vote no on all zoning matters. I could find nothing wrong with this zoning, and the county staff and planning commission both recommended it for approval."

"Yet Mr. Kotvas felt there was a problem with it and voted no," replied Caltagirone. "No further questions, Your Honor."

As Jim walked back to our table, I still could not help wondering why of all the big developments she voted no on, she would pick this one to vote yes. Was there something more to it that we did not know? Did she have any type of relationship with the Geracis that we did not know? I guess we'll never know. I was the one on trial.

The judge called for a recess until morning. Everyone packed up their notes as we all were looking to get an early start the next day.

It looked like the prosecution was getting ready to wind down their part of the trial. They only had a few more witnesses to present, and then it would be the defense's turn.

Early the next day, the prosecution called their next witness. It was one of the commission secretaries, Mary Davis. Under questioning by Merkle, she told the jury she thought it was odd to hear the three commissioners whispering in the hallways on the night of the zoning in question—so odd that she went home and made some notes on what she saw just before the January 27 zoning meeting was to begin.

Merkle asked her to give a demonstration of what she saw that night. Ms. Davis stepped out of the witness box, sidled up to one of the assistant US attorneys, and whispered.

"They were actually whispering into each other's ears, is that correct?" asked Merkle.

"Yes," Ms. Davis replied as she returned to the witness box. Then she said, "Before the hearing got underway, I saw Bowmer whispering with Kotvas twice in the space of a half hour and also saw Bowmer whispering with Anderson and Anderson whispering with Kotvas. I had observed Jerry going back and forth, and I wondered about it." Ms. Davis then added, "Jerry seemed to be trying to convince Kotvas of something."

Benny Lazzara got up to cross-examine Ms. Davis, asking her if she could hear what they were whispering about.

Ms. Davis response was, "No."

Then he asked her, "Does Bowmer like to play a lot of jokes on the staff and the other commissioners?"

Ms. Davis then told the jury, "Mr. Bowmer played jokes on people all the time, inventing stories that turned out to be sheer fabrication. If Bowmer was to tell me the building was on fire, I would just keep working. I wouldn't believe anything Jerry said."

Then Mr. Caltagirone got up and approached Ms. Davis and asked, "Did Mr. Kotvas seem friendly to Mr. Bowmer that night?"

"No," she answered. "It seemed like Mr. Kotvas was trying to avoid Bowmer and did not wish to talk with him at the time."

"So it's fair to say that Mr. Kotvas did not wish to have anything to do with Bowmer that night and was trying to avoid him, in your opinion?" Caltagirone asked.

Merkle objected to the question, but the judge overruled him and asked Ms. Davis to answer the question.

"Yes, it appeared that way to me," she said.

At this, Mr. Caltagirone said, "No further questions, Your Honor," and then went back to his seat as the judge dismissed the witness.

After a couple more witnesses briefly took the stand, Mr. Merkle rested the government's case against us.

Before dismissing the jury, Judge Carr told the members that he was giving them the day off so the defense could present their motions and prepare their case for presentation to the jury and that the trial would continue on Thursday morning.

That evening at Mr. Caltagirone's office, while discussing our defense strategies, I informed Jim that I still wanted to testify. I felt the jury should hear what I had to say. Jim told me that he felt it would be a bad idea because he believed the government had not proven its case against us, and he would present a good defense for me. He did not want Merkle to have a chance to trip me up in front of the jury and make me look guilty.

I still felt I should say something and told him so. He told me he would consider it and call on me if he felt he needed to.

Next morning, all the defense attorneys presented motions to Judge Carr for a verdict of acquittal for all the defendants in this case. The judge informed the attorneys that he would review the motions and render his verdict in the morning.

For several months, the local radio stations had been having a field day with the trial. A number of them made jokes about trial and the commission. One station, WRBQ, also known as the Q-Zoo, even started a jingle about the three of us and the commission. It seemed like everyone was trying to cash in on our misfortunes one way or another. It was also very hard on our families and my children, who wondered if they were going to lose their father to prison.

When the trial continued, Judge Carr rendered his verdict for denial to all the defense motions for acquittal. The trial would go on for another two weeks as the defense lawyers produced witnesses to rebut the government's case. It was the same with every witness. They all stated Jerry Bowmer was not one to believe; he was a liar who liked to pull pranks on people and could not be trusted.

I didn't find out until after the defense rested that Fred Anderson also wanted to testify in his own behalf and was also talked out of it by his attorney. The entire defense team felt it would be bad for us to testify when all the government had was Bowmer's word and no concrete evidence except for the tapes and money that they felt they could explain away. I had a bad feeling about it, but Jim had been doing a good job on my defense up to this time, so I thought I would see what happened in court in the coming days if I still needed to testify.

Objections and motions and counter-motions were filed with the court as the trial continued. Then on Thursday July 14th, after both the prosecution and the defense rested their case, everyone prepared for closing arguments. The trial was finally coming to an end.

The defense went first. Judge Carr informed all the defense lawyers that they would only be allowed ninety minutes apiece for closing arguments, and the government would be allowed a little more time since they had to address all the closing arguments after all the defense attorneys were finished. Closing arguments were to begin early Friday morning the fifteenth of July.

Michael Sierra, a 42-year-old
disbarred Tampa lawyer was

Joe Ficcarotta and Raymond LaPorte started the morning off, giving the closing arguments for Michael Sierra. They made a number of good points for Sierra, showing the jury that all the government had was circumstantial evidence against his client and Jerry Bowmer's word, which—he reminded the jury—was not trustworthy. Mr. LaPorte stated, "Bowmer has been a con man for a long time." I still could not understand why Sierra was even on trial with us except for Jerry Bowmer's word that he started the arrangements for the bribe. There was nothing really pointing to his involvement.

Then Bennie Lazzara presented his closing arguments for Fred Anderson, stating, "Jerry Bowmer was a bold-faced liar, and nothing he said could be believable."

He explained to the jury that Fred had health issues and was taking a lot of medications even on the night of the zoning. He was on medication the day Bowmer walked into his office and was not fully aware of what was going on. He only came to work that day because of the meeting with the people from the Brandon Chamber of Commerce. He had intended to go home right after the meeting when he was arrested. He also explained to the jury that, except for Bowmer's word, the government could not produce one witness against his client that he did anything wrong. All the government had was hearsay and innuendos.

When Mr. Lazzara finished his closing arguments, it was Jim Caltagirone's turn to give closing arguments on my behalf. Mr. Caltagirone stood up from his chair, walked around to the front of our table, and faced the jury.

In a calm and clear voice, he said, "Ladies and gentlemen of the jury, over the past few weeks, you have heard a number of witnesses testify that they would not believe anything that Mr. Bowmer had to say, that he was a habitual liar who likes to make up stories. I am not going to restate what all the other defense attorneys here had to say about Mr. Bowmer. I am sure you can draw your own conclusion from all the statements made.

"Instead, I am going to tell you about Mr. Kotvas, who is a widower trying to raise his three children by himself. Mr. Kotvas was a former Tampa police officer and city councilman who ran for mayor of Tampa and lost by only a few hundred votes before becoming a county commissioner. In all that time, the government has failed to bring one person forward to state that Mr. Kotvas has done anything wrong. In fact, Mr. Kotvas has an exemplary record as a public official.

"You heard the tapes the government introduced. There was so much static and so many garbled sentences when Mr. Bowmer came into Mr. Kotvas office that the government had to make up words they thought would fit the sentences to fill in the blanks. Yet before all that, and after Mr. Bowmer left Mr. Kotvas's office, the tapes are clear with no static. You have heard the government agents testify that they had a problem with all the recordings at the time Mr. Kotvas was being recorded. The FBI, with the most sophisticated equipment at their disposal, all malfunctioned at the same time.

"You have heard Mary Davis testify that she saw Mr. Kotvas trying to avoid Mr. Bowmer the night of the zoning, that it appeared he did not wish to have anything to do with him when they all went into the boardroom for the meeting. It was Mr. Kotvas that cast the only NO vote and tried to get his colleagues to change their votes."

Then Mr. Caltagirone paused for a moment, looked down at his notepad, then looked up and straight at the jury and said, "Even Steve Reynolds, the attorney for the Geracis' zoning, testified that he knew Mr. Kotvas was going to vote no on the zoning months before the zoning vote. Then there's the five thousand dollars that Bowmer left on Mr. Kotvas's desk. It was concealed in an envelope and placed at the corner of his desk before he walked out of Mr. Kotvas's office. Bowmer did not even hand it to him. Please think about that for a moment.

"Ladies and gentlemen, with everything you have heard in this trial, there is not one piece of evidence to prove that my client is guilty of any wrongdoing."

With all that said, Mr. Caltagirone then thanked the jury for their patience and walked back to our table and took his seat. I was looking at the jury and studying their faces while Jim was making his closing arguments. From what I could see, it appeared that Jim's statements were making an impact on the jury. A few of them kept nodding their heads in agreement from time to time when he made a particular point. Maybe he was right; I should not make any statements. I could see that Merkle had been making all sorts of faces and gestures while Jim was giving his closing arguments.

Now it was Merkle's turn to give the government's closing arguments. This was his opportunity to shine, and he was not going to let one of his assistants take any of the glory away from him. It was apparent throughout the trial that he was out for blood and glory. He was out to get a conviction by any means possible and did not want anyone to steal his thunder.

He began in a loud voice, "I want to thank you for your time and patience, and it's been a long six weeks and a lot of information you have to digest. I wish to point out that Mr. Anderson and Mr. Kotvas were caught red-handed with the bribe money that Jerry Bowmer gave them. Their attorneys are trying to paint a picture of Mr. Bowmer as a liar and jokester, that he concocted this whole thing to save his own skin. Well, ladies and gentlemen, I would like to tell you that Jerry Bowmer is probably the only honest person from this bribery case. You should consider him a hero for coming forward and exposing this triangle of corruption."

Merkle went on and on about what a great person Bowmer was and that they should consider all the facts and evidence in the case. He instructed them that they should not allow their emotions to be swayed by the defense ploy, which was to paint an innocent picture of their clients. Merkle would raise and lower his voice from time to time to get his point across to the jury. The press members in the courtroom were eating all of this up, taking notes and recording everything that was being said. After nearly three hours of his closing arguments, Merkle finally rested his case and went back to his seat.

It was late in the afternoon of Saturday, July 16, when the case was placed in the hands of the jury for deliberation. Judge Carr gave the jury their instructions and what he expected them to consider during deliberation; then he excused them to the jury room.

CHAPTER 11

The Verdict

July 1983

There was nothing more anyone could do. The jury had the case, and we all had to wait around for the verdict. No one knew how long it would take before the jury returned.

Rumors abounded. If the jury came back too soon, it could be good for the prosecution. If they took a long time to come back, it meant that there might be a problem with the case, and it could be good for the defense. Either way, no one really knows what goes through a jury's mind at the time of deliberation. It was getting very late, and the seven men and six women of the jury were sequestered and sent to a hotel for the night to begin deliberation early in the morning.

On Sunday morning, the seventeenth of July, the jury was escorted back into the jury room, where they continued to deliberate. Late in the morning, jury foreman George Rochow, who was an appliance salesman from Bradenton, Florida, sent a note to the judge requesting that the jury hear the tapes and view the transcripts again and to also have dinner sent in to them rather than going out to eat.

I was sitting in Mr. Caltagirone's office as we waited to see when the jury would come back with its verdict. We all had to be ready at any moment so that when the jury made its decision, we could get back to the courthouse as soon as possible. While we waited, Jim got a call from one of the defense attorneys who was on standby at the courthouse, letting him know that the jury had asked to hear the tapes again.

I asked Jim, "What do you think it means?"

All he said to me was, "Not to worry. The government has a weak case. It could mean anything. Remember, there was so much static and distortion on those tapes."

Jim told me to go home but stay by my phone in case he needed to get ahold of me. He would call me if he heard anything. I drove home and tried to relax while waiting for the phone to ring. The passing time kept everyone on edge. My mother had been staying at my house, helping me with my children.

My youngest son, Steven, who was ten at the time, did not really understand what was going on. My daughter, Julie, did not say much, but I could see the worried look on her face. My older son, Joseph, was in San Diego at navy boot camp. Because he was in training, he was unable to attend the trial, and he would call from time to time to get updates.

During dinner, my daughter asked how I thought things were going with the trial. I just told her that I didn't believe the government had a good case and that Mr. Caltagirone thought we had a good chance of winning. I could see the worry on her face, but she did not say too much more, not wanting to worry little Steven or my mother. After dinner, I sat on the couch, watching the news until a movie came on the TV. Then my little son Steven came over and sat next to me as Molly, our collie, followed and sat by our feet.

I put my arm around him and said, "Don't worry, son, things will work out. Remember, we're the good guys, and the good always beats the bad guys. No matter what happens or what you hear about me, know I will always love you and be here for you, no matter what. You and your brother and sister can always be proud. Remember, a lot of people in this town are living better because of some of the things I've done. You can walk around this city and county and see a lot of the improvements that were made because I took the time to fight for them. When someone says Kotvas, always hold your head up. You have nothing to be ashamed of because we cared."

What do you say to a ten-year-old boy who lost his mother to cancer when he was five and might now lose his father to prison if I lost this trial? We could only hope and pray that the jury would come back with a not-guilty verdict.

The next morning, I got up early, showered, and dressed so I would be ready in case Jim called to tell me the jury was back and to come to his office. My mother made breakfast for all of us. She was still in her house robe. After breakfast, I called Lora, Jim's secretary, to find out if there was any news on the jury. She informed me that Jim had stepped out of the office for a moment to talk with one of the other attorneys and would be back soon. She also informed me that Jim had heard that the jury wanted to hear the rest of the tapes today, and she would have Jim give me a call when he got back.

It was almost noon when I got a call from Jim telling me to come to his office right away. He had just been informed that the jury was ready to render their verdict, and everyone had to be back in the courtroom by afternoon.

I called my sister, Rose, that we all needed to be in court this afternoon. My daughter, Julie, would bring my mother and Steven to the courthouse. They wanted to be here for support when the jury came back in. I was really nervous and felt totally helpless as I left the house and drove to Jim's office.

When I got there, Jim was on the phone while sitting behind his desk. He hung up the phone as I walked in and said, "Have a seat, Mr. Kotvas. I did not expect the jury to come back so soon."

I took a seat in front of him and listened to what he had to say.

"Don't ask me what it means because I don't know. It could mean they reheard the tapes and did not believe what Bowmer had to say, or the government made their case. In any event, we will know the outcome soon."

He looked at me with a smile and said, "You look nervous. You have a right to be nervous, but try to relax. No matter what happens, I want you to try to keep your composure. Don't say a word. Just listen to what the jury and the judge have to say. You've come a long way, Mr. Kotvas. I am proud of the way you handled yourself throughout this trial. You've been a perfect gentleman in a very difficult time. Now let's go to the courthouse and see what the jury has to say."

As we left his office, before getting into his car, I said to him, "Jim, I want to let you know, no matter what happens, I appreciate everything you have done for me during this trial. I not only consider you my lawyer but a friend also."

"Well, I appreciate that, Mr. Kotvas, and I too consider you a friend," he replied to me as we got into his car. Not much was said between us as we drove downtown to the courthouse and parked the car. As we got out, Jim reminded me not to say anything and to try to keep calm. As we walked toward the courthouse, reporters were gathering around us, pushing microphones in our faces and trying to get a statement from Jim or me as we walked between them.

"No comment," was all we would say as we entered by the post office entrance to the courthouse. As we walked into the courtroom, some of the other lawyers were already there while Merkle and his staff were standing around by their table, discussing the possible out-comes of the case.

My family had also just arrived and sat behind us. My daughter, Julie, was smiling at me, but I could see the look of concern on her face. My son Steven just sat there and looked around at all that was happening. I could also see the look of worry on my mother's and sister's faces as I turned to give everyone a hug before the judge and jury came back.

We were still waiting for everyone to arrive before we could begin. Fred Anderson, who had not been well throughout the trial, had not yet arrived. He was coming from home with his wife, Patricia, where he had been resting under his doctor's care. About a half hour later, Fred and his wife came into the courtroom, and all the defendants and attorneys were now present.

Judge Carr was informed that we were ready to begin. As he came out of his chambers, we all stood. He then stepped up to his bench and called the court to order. He asked the court, "Is everyone ready to proceed?"

"Yes, Your Honor," was the reply from all the defense attorneys and the prosecution, and then we all sat down. The judge called for the jury to be brought into the courtroom. The bailiff walked to the jury room to bring them out.

I knew something was wrong when I saw the jury enter the courtroom. Some of the women had tears in their eyes, and they did not look our way. They took their seats, waiting for instructions from the judge. You could have heard a pin drop in the room; it was that quiet. You could feel all the tension from the anticipation.

Judge Carr turned to face the jury and said, "Mr. Foreman, has the jury reached a verdict?"

Mr. George Rochow, the jury foreman, got up from his seat and said, "Yes, Your Honor, we have." Then he turned to face the bailiff standing next to the jury box and proceeded to hand a paper note to the bailiff, who then handed it to the judge.

Judge Carr unfolded the note, looked at it, and then asked for the defendants to rise. We all stood up with our attorneys by our side. Then the judge started to read the verdict to the court.

"We the jury find the defendants Anderson and Kotvas guilty of extortion and conspiracy. On defendant Sierra, we find him guilty of conspiracy."

I was devastated when I heard the verdict read. My mother, daughter, and sister started to cry behind me. There were shouts of, "No, this can't be!" from somewhere in the courtroom. Jim grabbed my arm and said, "Stay calm," as we stood there behind our table. Mr. Sierra's wife, Cynthia, cried as she leaned over the railing to hug her husband.

One of the defense lawyers asked the judge to poll the jury on the verdict, which came back unanimously guilty.

The judge called order to the court, thanked the jury for doing a fine job during the trial, and dismissed them. After the jury was dismissed, the judge set a date in September for sentencing to allow the defense attorneys time to file their appeals. He then said all the defendants could remain free on bond till sentencing.

I was in shock, and Jim could see that. He told me to go home and get some rest, and we would talk more back in his office after he had gathered his thoughts for the appeal.

Merkle was in his glory now. The prosecutor and his staff were all smiling and shaking hands and congratulating one another. This trial had made his career, and he was going to push it as far as he could. He was now looked upon as the hero of Hillsborough County.

Everyone gathered up all their materials and belongings. The attorneys were going to meet later to work on the appeal process. Jim was going to take me back to his office so I could get my car and go home. I turned to my sister, Rose, who was behind the railing with my mother, daughter, and son.

I could see they all had been crying. My mother was still crying over the verdict, and my daughter, Julie, was holding her. I told my sister to take Steven and Mom back to her house for the night. I did not want them to be bothered by any reporters who might come around, and I wanted to be alone for a while. My daughter, Julie, thought that would be a good idea, and she would stay with a friend for a while. I hugged and kissed them all good-bye, then turned to little Steven, who looked very troubled. I told him not to worry—things would work out—and gave him a big hug before they all left the courtroom.

Jim had all his papers and notes tucked in his briefcase as he and I were ready to leave the building. We walked out of the courtroom together toward his car while being bombarded by reporters looking for any comments that they could run with. I just wanted to get away from them all, and all I said to them was that I was not guilty of these charges and the truth would come out sooner or later. Finally, we got to his car and drove back to his office.

Upon arriving, Jim let me out and said, "I have some work to do, so why don't you go home and get some rest? Don't talk to any reporters. I'll call you in a day or two and let you know when I want you to come back in so we can go over everything. I know this is a tough break, Mr. Kotvas, but try not to worry. It's not over till the fat lady sings."

"I can't believe this is happening to me," I said to Jim as I left to get into my car, which was parked on the street in front of his office. I just wanted to get out of there and go home.

CHAPTER 12

The Call

July 1983

The trial was over. I just felt like being alone. The last thing I wanted was for people to be around me, even my family. When I arrived at home, I threw my suit jacket on the couch in the living room and walked over to my liquor cabinet. I fixed myself a strong, very strong, highball and turned on the news. The trial ending was on all the news channels, and reporters were getting comments from some of the jurors as they left the courthouse to go home.

I turned up the volume so I wouldn't miss anything that was said and then sat on the couch just watching and listening. My dog, Molly, came over to me and sat in front of me with her head on my lap. I put my hand on her head and started to pet her as I listened to what the jurors had to say.

Then there it was; they said it for everyone to hear. "All we wanted was to hear what they had to say. If they had only testified in their defense, we would have come to a different verdict. We felt that when they did not testify in their own defense, that they had something to hide. All we wanted was to hear their side of things."

I was dumbfounded.

By not testifying and giving my side of the story, I was found guilty. It wasn't the evidence the government presented that convicted me. It wasn't the tapes or the transcript that the government made up that convicted me. It was that I didn't testify and tell my side of the story of what really happened! By listening to the attorneys who said it was not necessary to testify, I had condemned myself in this trial.

I now understood what had happened. How could Jim and the other lawyers make such a big mistake by not letting us take the stand? We had put our trust and lives in their hands. Now we had played right into Merkle's plans. They had felt overconfident that the government had not made their case, that there was no need to testify. What a big mistake. It was too late to go back. The damage was done, and I was convicted. To try and defend myself now would only make me look guiltier. Who would believe me now? I had my chance and blew it!

I just kept getting up and fixing another drink, one after another. I did not care at this point. Molly walked over to her corner of the room and lay down. I walked over and turned the TV off. I did not wish to hear any more comments. After today, I knew my life was ruined, and my children would have to live with the stigma of my shame.

I sat for a moment on the couch in my living room trying to get my thoughts together. My phone kept ringing now and then. I was in no mood to answer it; at that moment, I couldn't have cared less who was calling. I might as well have pulled the phone cord out of the wall outlet. I just sat there drinking one drink after another until my head started to spin. All I kept hearing in my mind was what the juror said: "All we wanted was to hear what they had to say."

After a while, I got up with the last drink I had in my hand, walked into my bedroom, and sat on the end of the bed. The trial had exhausted me both mentally and physically. I put my drink down on the nightstand and just sat there for a few moments, thinking and feeling sorry for myself.

After a few moments of crying and wallowing in self-pity, I opened the top drawer of my nightstand and pulled out a .32-caliber snub-nosed Smith & Wesson revolver that used to be my off-duty weapon when I was on the Tampa Police Department. I kept it in that drawer in case anyone tried to break in or threaten my family.

For a while, I just sat there holding it in my hand, pulling back the hammer, and spinning the cylinder a few times. I was all alone in my house and felt extremely depressed. All I could think was, *Why had this happened to me?*

I slowly raised the gun to my head several times, asking God, *Why, God, why is this happening?* I felt ashamed, exhausted, and confused, and I didn't know where I was going to find the money to continue to pay for my defense. I was out of money, living on a shoestring budget with handouts from family and friends. I held the gun in one hand as I picked up my drink with the other, finished it off, then placed the glass back on the nightstand.

I was not much of a religious person at the time. I had lost interest in God and the church when my wife suffered then died. But sitting on the end of the bed, I cried out in desperation, "Oh God! If you are a God, if you are there, why, why, why is this all happening to me? You took my wife from me. I had to watch her suffer for months from the cancer that was eating her away. She had faith. She believed in you and prayed every night for a healing. She kept her faith till the end, thinking you would heal her. She believed in you. All she wanted was a bit more time to see our little boy Steven as he grew. He was only five when you took her.

"Was that too much to ask? She prayed, I prayed, for you to save her. I took her to different hospitals, to churches where people put hands on her and prayed, and for what? We all have our faults, but she was a good woman. She believed, and you took her anyway. Jesus said in Matthew 17:20, 'If you have faith as a grain of mustard seed...nothing will be impossible to you.' She had that faith, yet you did not heal her. Why didn't you take me instead? You left me alone with three young children to raise. She was everything to me.

"She never asked for much, just a little more time with our children, that's all. If you are God, where are you now? Where is she now? Is she happy? Is she in paradise? What happened to her soul? Why has all this been happening to me?"

I cried out in anger, just lashing out, looking for someone to blame for my shortcomings. I now realized that if I did not win my appeal, I would definitely be going to prison. Then what would happen to my children? What would happen to me in prison? I was extremely angry with God; I guess because I blamed him for taking my wife away from my children and now possibly me as well.

I had always been angry with him since my wife passed away. Since her death, my faith and belief in God and his church was gone. Now my community and my family would see me as a convicted felon.

We are all guilty of one type of sin or another. We all have done things in our lives we wish we could change or that we should be punished for—maybe for not being a good husband or father or a better son to our parents, or for not being more kind to others in need. Being punished for something we did is one thing, but being punished for something we were not involved in is another. Whatever the case, I was going to pay the price, and my children and family would suffer for it.

Forget God, forget everyone. I started to lift the gun to my head again while all the thoughts of what had happened at the trial and what was said after were speeding through my mind. I strongly felt my children would be better off without me. In my heart, I knew my mother and sister would take good care of them.

I had no idea how I was going to prove my innocence, nor did I care at this point. All I wanted to do was escape from it all. I knew that even if I was proven innocent, there would always be those who would not believe it, and the stigma would remain to hound me for the rest of my life. I felt so alone and abandoned, with only the prospect of facing prison ahead of me. As far as I was concerned, my life was over. I felt I would be better off dead; I had nobody I could turn to. I had reached the lowest point in my life; there was nothing left for me but to hit rock bottom.

The bedroom was spinning now, or was it my head? All the alcohol was having its effect on me as I again cried out, "God, if there is a God, you took everything I love away from me. My wife, my job, and now it will be my children. Just show me, show me some sign. Show me some sign so I can believe there is a real God. If you can hear me, what am I to do? What do you want from me? What did you do with my wife?"

All I could think of was, *Is she happy where she is?* I wanted to be with her.

"Is there a heaven? Is this all there is to life? Are we the fools? Did she believe in false hope? She had so much faith, and I have so little. You know I have been haunted every day by this ever since she passed away. Just give me a sign, anything so I can believe, anything to show me you are real. Give me a reason to go on. Anything to believe you are there and can hear me?" I continued to cry out with the gun still in my hand, again raising it to my head and placing the barrel against my temple.

The alcohol was taking over, having a strong effect on me. The room continued to spin, and I was getting extremely dizzy. I pulled back on the hammer on the gun and heard the hammer click. Then I don't remember what happened next; I must have blacked out.

The next thing I knew, my phone was ringing, rousing me from my sleep. I looked over at the clock on my nightstand, and it was around 7:00 a.m. My eyes were a little bleary and bloodshot, I had quite a headache, and I was still a little dizzy from the night before. The lamp sitting on the nightstand was still on.

The sun was shining through the drapes, which were partly open around the windows. I could see my revolver on the floor in front of the bed, with the hammer still cocked. I bent over and nearly vomited as I picked it up, gently lowering the hammer and putting it on safety. I then placed it on the bed next to me. The phone would not stop ringing, so I fumbled to reach it. I figured it must be some nosy reporter trying to get an early scoop.

At first, I was not going to answer it, but a strange feeling came over me that I should. I picked up the receiver and said, "Hello" in a scratchy voice as I flopped back onto my pillow with the receiver to my ear.

The voice on the other end of the phone kept saying, "Joe, Joe, can you hear me?"

The voice sounded familiar. "Yes," I said with a slight slur.

"Joe, this is Robert. Are you all right? Can you hear me? Listen, Joe, I know this is going to sound crazy—I can't explain it—but when I got up this morning, I had a strong feeling that something was very wrong, and I had this strange feeling in my mind that I needed to call you. Don't ask me why. I can't explain it. Just something inside me told me I needed to give you a call. Is everything all right? Are you OK?"

This was my old childhood friend Bob Magana calling from New Jersey. Bob and I had been close friends since high school. We both lived in the South Bronx, and I was the best man at his wedding. He and his wife, Carol, were the best and closest friends my wife and I had. There wasn't anything we wouldn't do for each other.

We would always hang out together. They also were the godfather and godmother of my older son, Joseph, and we were the godparents of their first daughter, Susan. My late wife, Cathy, loved to ride roller coasters and I did not, so Bob would always volunteer to ride with her since his wife also disliked them.

When my wife and I moved to Tampa in 1968, Bob took time off from work to help me move and get settled in. Then as time went on, we would travel back and forth to visit each other or keep in touch by phone. When my wife passed away from cancer in March of 1978, Bob and Carol attended the wake and funeral and stayed with me for a while. After that, things were different for me, and we sort of drifted apart, as many friends do when they are separated by distance and personal situations.

I was not the same person anymore after my Cathy passed away. I was hurt, angry with God for allowing this to happen to my wife. I stopped attending church with my children and worked at whatever I could find until I was reelected to the Tampa city council in a special election late in 1978.

Then one day in 1980, I received a call from Carol, telling me Bob had had a heart attack and was in the hospital in New Jersey being prepped for heart surgery. I flew up to Jersey to be with Bob, who was already in the operating room when I arrived. Carol and Bob's father were in the waiting area. (Bob's mother had passed away a few years earlier.)

It was hours before we knew anything, and things weren't looking good for Bob. All we could do was wait and hope for the best and pray. I wasn't much into praying now, for I had little faith in it.

I did make an attempt at it because I cared for him. I knew Bob was not very religious; you would say he was more of an agnostic most of his life. He, Carol, and their children didn't attend or belong to any church.

Finally, the operation was over, and the doctor came out and talked with the family. He informed us that Bob was resting in recovery. It would be a while before we could see him. The doctor told Carol that it would take time before he would be back to a limited normal life. His heart was very weak, and he only had about 30 percent functioning that was not damaged. From that point on, he would be very limited in what he could do, and he would need to be checked regularly.

I was allowed to see him after he came out of recovery. He was very weak and pale. We talked for a while, but he didn't say much. It seemed that something was on his mind, but he would not say what. I figured he was worried about his condition and his family. I stayed a few days to make sure he, Carol, and his girls were all right and told him that if there was anything they needed, they could just call me, and I would come up. Then I had to get back to Tampa and my own family.

We kept in close touch for the first few months; then as time went on, we would call each other just on the holidays. He had told me something had happened to him after he came out of surgery. By some strange reason, it seemed he had gotten religion. This was not the Bob I knew; this was a completely changed person. He told me that when he came home from work, he and Carol would hold Bible classes in their home with other couples, and they were attending church now. He had transformed into a totally different Bob than the one I grew up with.

At that time, I really did not want to hear about his home ministry. This was probably one of the reasons I did not call him as much as I used to. I was happy for him because he felt God had given him something for which to survive, but I wasn't interested. I was still angry with God for not helping my wife. Besides, I was on the county commission now and trying to lose myself in my career and family.

During these years, I had no trouble finding female companionship, but I wasn't looking for someone to replace my wife. I really didn't care about much more than my family and my job as a commissioner, until Debbie came into my life. We dated for a couple of years, but I guess I was not what she was looking for, and we went our separate ways, just before all this trouble came down on me.

So Bob was in his world now, and I was in mine, and we had not communicated with each other since Christmas of 1982, except to exchange greetings. I never called him nor told him the trouble I was in. My children and my family did not have his number or address, so he was never informed of my situation.

So when his call came the day after my trial ended in July, I was totally surprised. All of a sudden, I sat up on the bed. My head was pounding, but I sobered up quickly. "Oh, Bob," I said with tears in my eyes. I started crying as I told him what had happened.

There was no way Bob could have known what was happening to me. He lived over a thousand miles away from me and never paid any attention to the news. No one had contacted him, for if anyone did, I know he would have been here for me throughout the whole trial. It had never dawned on me to call him or tell him about what was happening.

As we talked on the phone, Bob just listened as I explained about what happened, the trial, the verdict, and my feelings about my wife and God. He did not say anything to me at first. He just listened and let me go on and on. He could tell I was hurt, depressed, and crying. I just needed someone to talk to who could understand what I was feeling and going through.

When I finished talking, there was a long silence on the other end; then Bob said, "Joe, do you remember when I had my operation on my heart and you came up to see me?"

"Of course, I do," I replied.

"Well, just listen to what I am going to tell you," he said. "I've never told this to anyone except my wife." Then he began to explain what had happened to him. He told me that when he went into the operating room and they put him to sleep and then started to operate on him, his condition turned critical. At a certain point during the procedure, the doctors lost him. His heart stopped, and the machines all showed flat lines for several minutes while the doctors and staff attempted to revive him.

Bob told me (this is all in his words, as best as I can remember) that he found himself floating above the operating room looking down at all the people working on a person lying on a table covered with drapes. He could see and hear everything that was going on, and they all seemed worried, talking about the person on the table. He realized it was himself lying there.

Then he told me he saw this beautiful bright light overhead, and he was being drawn to it. A great sense of calm came over him as he was being drawn into a bright tunnel where, at the end, there was bright light. Once he reached the end of the tunnel and was into the light, he could see shadows of hundreds of people coming toward him. They were coming to greet him in a loving way, and some of them he knew. He met relatives and friends who had passed away years before, including his mother, all welcoming him to where he was.

He told me it was a wonderful feeling of love and peace, and the light was so beautiful. Then a beautiful figure with a much brighter light about him came forward and told him that he must go back, that it was not his time yet, and there was still something he needed to do. He could stay if he wanted to, but he needed to go back because his time on earth was not up yet. The urge to stay was very strong, and the people in the shadows wanted him to stay. He told me that the feeling he had at that time was unbelievably beautiful.

Still, he also had a strong feeling that he needed to come back for some unknown reason. So he chose to come back, and he was rushed back through the tunnel into his body, and all the machines started showing signs of life again. It all happened in a matter of minutes, yet he said it seemed he was out of his body for a much longer time. It all seemed like a strange dream to him, until the doctors told him after the operation that they had lost him for a few minutes while he was on the table and that he was considered legally dead until he started breathing again.

I know this all sounds like a fantasy, but Bob was not one for making up stories, especially one of this type. He was the kind of guy who would have made a joke of it if someone had told him they had experienced something like this. Now I could understand why he became very religious after his operation. I hesitated at first, then asked him the question burning within me.

"Bob, did you see Cathy when you were in that light?"

"Joe, I wasn't going to say anything to you about it when you came to visit me in the hospital. I knew how painful and hurt you were when Cathy passed away, and I didn't want you to think I was crazy or making any of this up. I don't think you would have believed me anyway at the time. You've had such an anger and hurt inside of you for a long time."

"But did you see Cathy?" I asked again.

"Yes, Joe, I did. And she wanted me to give you a message. She said to tell you she is happy. You shouldn't worry about her. She is very happy where she is, and everything is all right."

When I heard that, I clenched the phone in my hand, bent over, and wept. My cries during the night had been answered. I knew that God must have heard me that night and that he had sent an answer I could not refute. If anyone other than Bob had told me these things, I would not have believed them. This was the answer I had been looking for, and it transformed my entire outlook on what was going to happen to me.

A great calm came over me as I stopped crying and told Bob how much I needed to hear all that—that his call had come during the darkest time in my life and that I had almost done something very stupid. We talked for a little while longer, and he told me that if I ever needed him, he was there for me.

"I know that, Bob," I told him, and then he asked me to take a moment to pray with him before we hung up.

I cannot describe the feeling of joy and hope that I was experiencing as I hung up the phone. The answers I had cried out for during the night had been given. To me, this was truly a miracle. There really was a God in heaven, and my wife was well and happy.

So if there is a heaven, then there surely must be a hell, but I knew I would not have to face it alone.

Now, don't get me wrong, I did not become any kind of holy roller or Bible-spouting layman evangelist or anything like that. I just felt that my faith had been restored, and I began to have a better outlook on life from then on. I still had many mixed feelings about everything, and you can believe or disbelieve whatever you want, but the one thing I was now sure about was that God does hear our prayers.

I sensed that there must be a reason for all this happening to me, and I would have to wait and see where it would all take me. I now felt I was not in this fight alone, and I could stand up and face whatever was coming my way. Whether God was finished with me or had other plans, only time would tell.

I was regaining control of my faculties now and was ready to face this new day. I can't tell you why, but I felt that somewhere down the line, things would turn around for me—hopefully sooner rather than later! Right now, the thing I had to do was try to win my appeal and stay out of jail.

This was a new day, and I was not going to tell my family or anyone else what had happened to me the night before. I still wasn't sure myself. All I knew is that I seemed to be feeling a little better, and I was going over to my sister's house to get my children and my mother, who would stay with me a few days till I could sort things out.

CHAPTER 13

The Meeting

August 1983

I didn't hear from Jim for a few days, so I called his office and spoke with Lora, his secretary. She informed me that he was out of the office and she would see that he got the message that I had called. Later in the day, I received a call from him telling me to take the rest of that week off and go someplace out of town with my children so I could get away from it all for a while. We would get together the following week.

He felt my kids and I needed a break from all the negative publicity being put out by the newspapers, radio, and TV. He was right; the press was having a field day with all that had happened. They were making Merkle into a superprosecutor, the hero of Hillsborough County. Jerry Bowmer was being held in an undisclosed location out of state, spilling his guts to the Feds about who knows what. That was all anyone knew.

Rumors abounded that there would be a lot more indictments coming down and a lot more arrests made now that the government had won their first major victory in our community. Merkle was on a crusade to make a clean sweep of local government and businesses, trying to get indictments on everyone whom he could get any dirt on.

I took Jim's advice and left town for a few days to visit Disney World with my young son, Steven. My daughter had to stay for work, and my older son, Joseph, was in San Diego at navy boot camp. I needed to get away and spend some time with Steven, who was having trouble understanding what was going on. Ever since his mother had passed away five years before, he had been struggling with a lot of emotional issues. How do you tell a ten-year-old boy that his father might be going to prison soon?

After a few days away, we were back in Tampa. The phone wasn't ringing as much, which gave me some peace and space to breathe. There were a lot of messages, but none from Mr. Caltagirone's office, so I used the time to put out feelers to see if anyone would be interested in hiring me. Money was very tight now; the trial had left me with next to nothing. I needed to find some kind of employment until I could get this mess cleared up. My daughter, Julie, who was just starting her career in real estate, was the only one working in our house at the moment, and her small salary was helping to keep things together.

A few days later, I received a call from my attorney, Mr. Caltagirone. He informed me that he had received a call from the federal prosecutor's office saying that they wanted to set up a meeting to talk with us and asking if I would be willing to meet with them. Jim thought it would be a good idea if we met to see what they had to say, so I told him to set up the meeting. He told me he would give them a call and then let me know when and what time.

As I hung up the phone, I could not help but wonder why they would want to talk with me. They already got what they wanted. They won; they got their conviction. I didn't know what more I could tell them, unless this was some kind of presentencing interview. Anyway, I would just wait until Jim called back.

About an hour later, I received a call from Jim's office. This time, it was his secretary Lora telling me to be in Jim's office the next day around 10:00 am. I asked if Jim was in, and she informed me that he was on his way to court and would not be back until later in the afternoon. I thanked her and told her that I would be there.

The next day, I got up early, showered, and dressed. Then I had breakfast with my mother, who was staying with us for a while to help out with my son Steven. My daughter had already left for work, dropping Steven off at school for me. Just before nine, I left and drove to West Tampa to pick up a couple of cups of Cuban coffee to go. Both Jim and I enjoyed Cuban coffee.

After leaving the coffee shop, I headed over to Jim's office. I wanted to get there before the meeting so I would have a little time to talk with him and enjoy our coffee. Tampa is a uniquely blended community that is proud of its Latin heritage. It was once known for being the cigar capital of the world, as well as for its famous Cuban sandwiches and coffee.

When I arrived at the office, I took a moment to look into Jim's window before entering the building. Jim was sitting at his desk, and I could not see anyone else. *Good*, I thought to myself. *Now we will have a little time to talk before the meeting.*

Jim's office door was open, so I entered, holding the two cups of coffee, and put one on his desk. He looked up and smiled as I took a seat in front of him.

"Do you know what this meeting is all about?" I asked.

"I believe they want to try and make some kind of deal with you," he answered.

"I don't know why. They got their pound of flesh and are wallowing in their victory," I responded.

We just sat there sipping our coffee, waiting for the government to arrive. I asked Jim if I could record the meeting. I told him I had a small tape recorder in my jacket pocket. He informed me that he felt it would not be a good idea and that I shouldn't. *Well, so much for that idea*, I thought. *I'll just wait and see what these guys have to say.*

A little after ten, two men in suits walked into Jim's office. It was Joe Magri and Agent Russell Woods. We all shook hands, and Jim told everyone to have a seat. Mr. Magri and Agent Woods sat on the sofa while I sat in a lounge chair facing them. Jim sat back down behind his desk.

Jim started the conversation with, "So we're all here now. You asked for this meeting, so what is it all about? Mr. Kotvas is here and ready whenever you gentlemen are ready to say what this meeting is all about."

Mr. Magri responded, "Mr. Kotvas, we asked for this meeting to inform you that now that you have been convicted and are awaiting sentencing, more charges and new indictments will be handed down shortly. Our office would like to give you the opportunity to help yourself.

"We know you're a good family man, trying to raise your children by yourself. You're facing a lot of jail time and more to come. We can help you with that. By giving us your help and cooperation, you would be helping yourself and your family. We know of your involvement in all this, and if you would cooperate, we can see that you do as little jail time as possible."

I was stunned at what he was saying. More jail time? New charges? They knew all about my involvement? Where were they getting all this from, Jerry Bowmer? I looked at their faces while Magri was talking. They looked very confident I would buckle under them. Agent Woods just sat there with a little smirk on his face, listening to what was being said. I never liked his attitude toward me after my arrest. I listened and did not say a word as Magri continued.

Jim Caltagirone just sat there in his chair listening. He did not say a word or interrupt the conversation. It was all on me to decide what I wanted to do. If I took their offer, I would have to lie about what I knew. I would have to go along and agree with the government on the statements that Jerry Bowmer had made against others, people whom I did not know or knew only slightly. I would have to make up lies about crimes of corruption of which I had no knowledge and about the people who were supposed to have been involved.

This was all beginning to turn my stomach as he continued to explain that my situation was hopeless unless I cooperated. I could see where they were going with this. In order to save myself from doing any real jail time, I had to sell my soul. These men were not interested in truth or justice. They were looking to get as many convictions as possible, regardless of who got hurt, and they wanted me to be a big part of that.

"Your cooperation will go a long way in cleaning up a lot of corruption in our community," Magri went on. "I assure you, you would be doing the right thing by cooperating with us. Think about your family. Think about your situation."

I was thinking about my family when he said the one thing he should not have said to me. "Why don't you be like Jerry Bowmer, who is giving us his full cooperation, and make it easy on yourself?"

That's all he had to say. My attitude changed from one of being scared to one of being infuriated. Me, be like Jerry Bowmer? Never! At that moment, I was seeing red. I could feel my blood pressure rising as I looked up at the two of them and said, "I'll never be like Jerry Bowmer. I'm not going to lie about things I know nothing about and hurt innocent people when I have no idea if they did anything wrong just so you can get a conviction. No, gentlemen, I'm not going to lie for you."

At that moment, Mr. Magri blurted out, "We don't want you to lie, Mr. Kotvas. All we are asking is that you corroborate the information Jerry Bowmer has given us and share anything more that you could add."

"For me to do what you're asking means I would have to tell lies about people and things I know nothing about. You've already convicted me on lies set up by Bowmer, a conviction that I pray we can overturn."

The two of them were not smiling anymore, nor was their mood friendly any longer. Agent Woods said to me, "We know your involvement in this matter. You're only lying to yourself. You will be going to prison for a long time if you refuse to work with us."

Then Magri interrupted and said, "If you do not cooperate with us and tell us what we need to know, I guarantee you will never see the light of day. We will make things so hard for you that you will be an old man when you get out of prison, and you will never have the opportunity to see your son grow up. You're going to be indicted on so many charges that you will spend years in prison. The decision is up to you. Cooperate or face hard prison time."

After all that was said, the two of them got up to leave the office, saying, "Think about it, Mr. Kotvas. You have until the end of the week to get back with us."

Mr. Caltagirone got up from his seat and told them as they were leaving, "I'll talk with my client, and we will let you know before the week is out."

I did not say another word to them. I just sat there angrily. Who did they think they were that they could come in here and threaten me that I would never see my son grow up, that I would spend years doing hard time? Who were these people that they could threaten me like that?

Jim waited until they had left his office and were out of his building before he turned to me and said, "Well, Mr. Kotvas, I have to hand it to you. You certainly know how to charm people. I want you to know I am proud of the way you handled yourself. Just try to stay a little calmer next time."

"I just didn't like the way they asked me. I will never be anything like Jerry Bowmer, no way. The guy is a rat and a liar, and I'll never be like that. Besides, I don't know what I can tell them. I have no idea what or who Jerry Bowmer had dealings with.

"How could I tell them anything if I don't know? It seems they just want me to agree to sign a blank piece of paper so they can fill in the rest, and then I am to swear to it. I can't do that. I can't hurt innocent people when I have no idea what they did. To save myself, I would have to lie for them. How could I face the people in this town? How could I face my family? Where could I go?

"No, Jim, I just can't do it. It's the principle of the whole thing, to be truthful. Whatever happened to truth and justice? I can't send an innocent person to prison to save myself. I would never be able to live with myself."

Jim went back to sitting behind his desk. He said, "You're an honorable man, Mr. Kotvas, but you need to think about what they said and their offer. Take some time and think it over, then let me know what you decide. But don't take too long. We have to get back to them by the end of the week. That doesn't leave us much time."

"I'll think about it, Jim, and let you know. You should have let me tape this meeting. It might have come in handy for the future. I'm going home now. I'll call you in a day or two." Then I walked out of his office and back to my car. For the moment, there was nothing more either of us could do.

A couple of days later, I called Jim back and told him to let the prosecutor know I had nothing to say, and there was no deal. Yes, I could have seen what kind of deal I could have made with them. But that was not me. I spent my life helping people, believing in the law and justice. All I knew at the time was that these people seem to be only out for glory, out for themselves. It was all a numbers game for them. The more convictions they could get, the better they looked to their bosses, and the better it was for their careers.

I had taken my stand, and now I would have to live with it. The one thing I knew for sure was that if I took whatever deal they offered, I would be admitting guilt to a crime I had nothing to do with, and it would stay with me for the rest of my life.

CHAPTER 14

The Sentencing

September 1983

In September, a couple of weeks after the interview at Jim's office, I received word that on the morning of September 15, we were all to appear in Judge Carr's court for sentencing. It had been nearly two months since we had been convicted in his court.

We all arrived at the courthouse early that morning with our families. Mickey Sierra came with his wife, Cynthia, and family sitting behind him in the courtroom. Fred Anderson and his wife, Patricia, were sitting next to the Sierra's, and my family was sitting up front close to Jim and me. My mother came with my sister, Rose; my daughter, Julie, and my young son, Steven, came later. They all wanted to be there to show support.

My father, who had been divorced from my mother for many years, also appeared in court. I had not been close to my father since he divorced my mother when I was just a child. But on that day, I was glad he came to be with me. I felt I needed all the support I could get as I was extremely nervous. I guess you could say we all were.

On that day, we were in a different courtroom on the second floor of the courthouse. It was smaller than the one we had our trial in. The room was packed with family members, reporters, and spectators, all buzzing about how much time, if any, we would get. Jim and I were seated with the other defendants and their lawyers up front behind some tables facing the judge's bench.

While we all waited for the judge to enter and start the proceedings, we took the time to talk with our families who were standing behind us on the other side of the railing. A few moments later, we heard the bailiff say, "All rise. This court is now in session."

Judge Carr entered the courtroom from his chambers and proceeded to his seat on the bench. He called the court to order as he informed everyone on how the proceeding would go. He then read a memo from Robert Merkle, which he had received earlier. It stated, "The United States respectfully urges this court to impose substantial, meaningful terms of incarceration on each of the defendants, accompanied by significant fines. Anything less would fuel the fire of cynical anger and resentment toward social institutions."

After reading the memo to everyone in the room, he entered it into the record. Then the judge said, "I have read the presentencing reports on all three of the defendants and have entered them into the record. Mr. Anderson, do you have anything to say to this court before I pass sentence on you?"

Anderson, standing in front of the judge with his attorney Bennie Lazzara at his side, did not say a word, but Mr. Lazzara spoke up for him, "Your Honor, I would like to point out to the court as you have read in Mr. Anderson's presentencing report. My client has never been in any type of trouble with the law. Mr. Anderson has been an outstanding member of the community and retired from the Tampa Fire Department as its former chief. He has spent his entire life serving our community and even put his life on the line at times to help others. He also suffers from a heart condition and is in need of good medical attention. We ask this honorable court to take into consideration all he has done for us."

"Mr. Anderson, do you have anything more to add to what I have already received?" The judge asked.

"No, Your Honor," he replied.

"Then I will hear from the next defendant. Mr. Kotvas, do you or your attorney have any additional information you would like to offer this court on your behalf before I pass sentencing?" the judge asked.

Mr. Caltagirone then stated, "Your Honor, I too would like to point out to this court that my client, Mr. Kotvas, has been a model citizen of our community. He was a former New York City Transit police officer and also served on the Tampa Police Department. He is also a former city councilman with an outstanding record of public service.

"For many years, he has dedicated his life to public service, volunteering his time to helping troubled youth. He was the organizer of the Tampa Triton Cadets, an outstanding youth organization in our community. Mr. Kotvas has received numerous awards honoring him for his dedication and service to our community. He is also a single parent, a widower who is trying to raise his children by himself and has a ten-year-old son who needs him and is here in the courtroom today with the rest of his family to see what the outcome will be. I would like this court to take all this into consideration when passing sentence on my client. Also, Your Honor, Mr. Kotvas's daughter is in the courtroom today and would like to say a few words on behalf of her father."

At this point, Judge Carr asked for my daughter, Julie, to approach the bench and read her statement. She came forward holding a paper in her hand that she had prepared to read to the judge. We all could see she was very nervous and had tears in her eyes as she began to read. She read her notes from her heart, explaining how difficult it had been for me and the family since her mother passed away from cancer, what a good father I was to them, and all the good things I had done for our community. She also explained how I was needed at home to help with the difficult task of raising my son Steven, who was having emotional problems as she pleaded for mercy on my behalf.

When she finished, tears were running down her eyes as my family looked on from behind the railing. The judge thanked her and complimented her for the way she presented her statements.

When the judge was finished, Merkle broke into the conversation, stating, "I also ask for mercy. I ask for mercy for a community that has been wracked by scandal, Your Honor."

"Do you have anything to add, Mr. Kotvas, before we move on?" the judge asked.

Nervous and shaking a little, I spoke up in a low tone of voice, "Yes, Your Honor, I would like to say something. In a meeting with Mr. Magri and Agent Woods, they threatened me that if I did not cooperate with them, I would never see the light of day, that I would be in prison so long that I would never see my son grow up."

In a sarcastic tone, Merkle said to the judge, "Your Honor, that's ridiculous. This is just another fabrication on the part of the defendant to discredit our office. Nothing like that ever happened."

Jim did not say a word to the judge either to confirm or deny my statement. He just stood next to me and did not say another word. I guess he did not want to get into it with the government and make things look worse for me.

"If that's all, Mr. Kotvas, we will move on," the judge replied.

He then asked Mr. Sierra and his attorney if they had anything to say, and again, Sierra's attorney Ray LaPorte spoke up for him, informing the court on what an excellent citizen and family man Mr. Sierra was and asked the court for leniency for his client.

We had all made our pleas for leniency before the court, and now it was time for Judge Carr to make his decision. "Does the government have anything to add before I pass sentencing?" Judge Carr asked.

Merkle then spoke up and said, "Your Honor, the government asks this honorable court to impose lengthy prison terms and stiff fines on each of the defendants."

With that being said, the judge then leaned forward a bit in his chair and sat up straight, looking at everyone in his courtroom, and said, "To the families of the defendants, this is a tragic situation. These crimes are a breach of the public trust, in the type that harms not just one or two but harms generally the whole community and the framework of our form of government. I consider prison time the only appropriate sentence for the defendants."

As family members and friends in the courtroom heard the judge's remarks, a number of them began to cry as he began to sentence each of us.

"In the government's case against Fred Anderson, on the first count of conspiracy, I sentence you to eight years in prison. On the second count of extortion, I sentence you to eight years in prison, both counts to run concurrently."

"In the government's case against Joseph Henry Kotvas Jr., on the first count of conspiracy, I sentence you to eight years in prison. On the second count of extortion, I sentence you to eight years in prison, both counts to run concurrently."

At this point, my family started crying and holding and hugging one another behind us.

"In the government's case against Michael Sierra, on the sole count of conspiracy, I sentence you to four years in prison."

He paused for a moment, then said for the record, "I further order that Mr. Anderson will serve his time at the federal facility in Lexington, Kentucky, where Mr. Anderson can receive treatment for his heart condition. I recommend Mr. Kotvas and Mr. Sierra be sent to a prison at Eglin Air Force Base. I am also allowing the defendants to remain free on bond, pending the outcome of their appeals."

You could see that Merkle was angered at the judge's sentences; he wanted us to do much more time and have a heavy fine. It did not happen. I can only speculate that maybe the judge saw some truth in our defense, and maybe he didn't believe everything Bowmer had said.

The judge picked up his gavel and said, "These proceedings are ended." Then he tapped his bench with the gavel, got up, and left the courtroom.

My daughter, mother, and sister came around the railing crying and gave me a big hug. My father stepped forward and said, "I'm sorry, son," as he took my hand and pulled me forward to him so he could hug me; then he started crying as well. I just said to them all, "It will be all right. It will be all right."

Jim walked over to us all and said he would see me later in the week when it would be better to talk and that we all should go home now and get away from this circus. And a circus it was, with reporters mobbing us as we tried to leave the courthouse. We did not have a moment to ourselves until we got into our cars and left for home.

CHAPTER 15

The Public Defender

September 1983

About a day or two after the sentencing, things started to calm down. The phone did not ring as much, but the newspapers were still hammering away at new reforms needed in county government. I needed to figure out what I was going to do now that I did not have a position on the commission. The important thing for me was to find work so I could support my family and pay my bills.

By the evening of the second day, I figured it was time to go out and see a few of my friends who owned businesses and might be able to put me to work until my appeal was ruled on. So early the next morning, I got up, showered, dressed in one of my suits. I had a quick breakfast and left for the day, seeking employment. I started out with business owners whom I had gone out of my way to help when I was both on the city council and county commission over the years. These were people who had told me a number of times that if I ever needed anything or if there was anything they could do for me, I could just ask. I had never asked anyone for any favors for helping them in the past. I was just happy that I could be of service to them. Well, now was the time, and I was going to ask.

It's strange what fear can do to a person. You think you know someone; then you find out that you really don't. What I thought would be a simple thing, acquiring a job with some company, turned out to be a disaster. Everyplace I approached, I got the same reactions. Either the person I needed to see was not in, was busy in a meeting, or did not have any openings. I realized what was going on; I could see they were very nervous and scared with me being in their office. Merkle had done his job well. He had put the fear of his office into them and was looking at anyone who had dealings with me. It was as if I had the plague or some other terrible disease.

For days on end, I tried to see everyone I knew who could help. No one wanted to talk with me, and no one wanted me around. They were all afraid that their names would appear in the papers or that they would be harassed by the government. I was at a low point in my life. I would come home exhausted and drained by all the negative responses I received. Everyone tried to be polite to me. They would say, "You were the best city councilman or county commissioner we ever had, but you screwed up." Or they'd say, "I'd like to help, but I have the government looking over my shoulder."

It seemed strange that when they needed help, no matter what their situation was or who was looking at them, I was there for them. Now the situation was reversed, and it seemed there was no one willing to stand up for me. I wasn't asking for a handout; I was asking for a job to support my children. I was willing to take anything and start at the bottom if only someone would give me a chance. But that was not to be. I started with the Help Wanted ads, but I got the same reactions there.

Two weeks passed before I received a call from Mr. Caltagirone to come to his office so he could talk with me. I made an appointment for the next morning to hear what he had to say. It was around 10:30 a.m., and Jim had just gotten back from court on a new case he was working on. As usual, I came into his office with two hot cups of Cuban coffee to start the meeting off. He always appreciated that and said, "You're a good man, Mr. Kotvas. You never forget." He got up from his chair and smiled at me, taking one of the cups. He then returned to his desk and sat down as I sat down on the other side and sipped my coffee.

"Well, I have to tell you, Mr. Kotvas, it's been one crazy ride handling your case," he started off, then continued, "You realize this trial cost me quite a bit of lost income for what you paid me."

"Believe me, Jim, I know. I know the other lawyers made a lot more money from their clients than I could afford," I told him. "I appreciate all you have done for me."

"It's not just a matter of the money, Mr. Kotvas. I believed in you, and I hope a good friendship developed out of all this. I'm just sorry things turned out the way they did," he responded. "Now what are you doing for money?"

I explained to him what was going on and how I was having trouble finding work. I told him the reactions at the places I tried was and how people were avoiding me. He seemed to understand my predicament as he shook his head.

"I have to tell you, Mr. Kotvas, things are not going to get any easier for you. I hear that Merkle is investigating a number of people who had dealings with Jerry Bowmer, and new indictments will be coming down from the grand jury soon. There is a good possibility that you may be indicted again. How are you fixed for cash?"

I explained to him my situation. "Well, at the moment, I am broke, and if I don't find work soon, I may lose my house. I don't know how I can afford another trial."

"I'm sorry to have to tell you this, Mr. Kotvas, but I'm going to have to withdraw from your case. I can't afford to put any more time in. You will need a public defender for your appeal or any new indictments that may come down. I have to get back into my practice and earn a living also. I hope you can understand our situation," he told me. "You'll need to file a motion of insolvency with the court. I will help you with that and request a public defender take on your appeal."

I had thought I couldn't feel any worse, but when Jim told me this, I hit a new low in my life. I understood where he was coming from, but what was going to happen to me now? At that moment, I felt like an orphan, all alone. What type of public defender would I get? How good would they be? In my experience as a former law enforcement officer, the majority of the people who used public defenders went to jail. They never seemed to have time for their clients and were overworked and bogged down with too many cases to handle, always looking to make a deal rather than take the time to go to trial.

What choice did I have? I was in a catch-22 with nowhere to turn but to the courts. I told Jim I understood and appreciated all he had tried to do for me. He had given his all during my trial, and I truly believed he had proved the government did not have a case against me. But who knew, all the jury wanted was to hear what we had to say. I thanked Jim for all the work he had done for me and said, "I hope we can remain friends when this is all over?"

"Mr. Kotvas, I am honored to have you as my friend, and this office is always open to you. I'll let you know when I have all the papers drawn up and filed and when you have to appear in court again. Now I have to get back to work," he said to me as we both stood up and shook hands before I left.

There was nothing more I could do as I walked out of his office and back to my car. It was all I could do to hold back the tears with the pressure and pain in my chest at that moment as I drove home, wondering what was going to happen to me now.

When I arrived home, it was late in the afternoon, and my daughter, Julie, could see that something was wrong. "Is everything all right, Dad?" she asked. "How did it go with Mr. Caltagirone?"

I explained to her what had happened; she understood but was upset about it too. There was nothing more anyone could do. I was broke, and I had neither assets nor any means to support my children at the time. The prospects of finding a decent job looked bleak. Now that all my prospects had been exhausted, I had nowhere to turn but to the streets to find work.

My daughter, Julie, was working at the time, just starting out in real estate, and she was able to help with some of the bills; plus my sister and mother pitched in with a little help from time to time. My daughter was seeing a fellow by the name of Kevin Bennington at the time, and she was pretty serious about him. He was a kind of wheeler-dealer who had just bought a restaurant in town with some silent associates. It was a steakhouse-cafeteria-style joint. My daughter asked if he would hire me.

Bennington knew of my situation and that I was having trouble finding work, so he hired me at minimum wage. I didn't care—I needed work, and I said I would do anything to generate an income. I didn't like the idea of working for my daughter's boyfriend, for he would throw in our faces every once in a while. But I kept my mouth shut. Basically, I was the dishwasher, floor mopper, and general cleaner, and sometimes one of the food line servers.

A few days later, I received a call from Jim's office informing me that I needed to appear in court with him and that he had the necessary papers to file before Judge Carr. He wanted to meet with me at his office then go to the courthouse together. We met the next morning and headed over to the courthouse. Jim drove. Upon arrival, we went to Judge Carr's courtroom. Jim had filed the motions a few days before, and now we were going to have our hearing. Although the judge had the motions before him explaining our situation, Jim felt he needed to elaborate on them. When called to the bench, Jim explained his situation with my representation and my insolvency to continue with the case.

The judge agreed with Jim's motion and released him from my case. He then accepted my motion of insolvency upon all the documentation I had to present to the court and declared that he would appoint a public defender to represent me on my appeal. He ordered his clerk to pick an independent attorney from the public defenders list to represent me. I would be notified in a few days of who he was.

A couple of days later, I was called back to the federal courthouse, where I received a notice from the clerk's office of who my new attorney would be and his contact information. They had assigned an attorney named Ray Harris, whom I had never heard of. On my way out of the courthouse, I ran into one of the court clerks who knew me. I asked her who Ray Harris was and if he was any good. She assured me that I should not worry, that Mr. Harris was a fine attorney and that I was lucky to have gotten him. He was in private practice and only took on a limited number of appeal cases.

At that point, I felt I might really have a chance with my appeal now that I was given a private attorney over a public one. I felt he would spend more time on my case and really look into what had happened. I left the courthouse and headed over to his office. I knew the area where he was located; it was toward the west end of the city. When I arrived, I could see his office was a small blockhouse situated on a modest corner lot with not much parking available, maybe for two or three cars.

I parked my car in front of the building and walked into his office. There was no receptionist; the office looked bare and a little gloomy. The place was very small, an old house converted into an office with a few small rooms with office furniture. No one was in the front room when I entered, so I called out, "Is anyone home?" A stocky African American man stepped out from one of the rooms dressed in dark trousers and a light-blue long-sleeved shirt with an open collar, looking kind of sleepy. He was just a bit taller than me.

I said, "Hello, I'm Joe Kotvas, and I am looking for Ray Harris."

"I'm Ray Harris, how can I help you?" he answered as I reached out to shake his hand.

I showed him the notice from the court, and he told me that he had been informed by the court that I would be coming by. We talked about my case and my family. He wanted to know all he could about me and about what had happened. He informed me that he would get all the transcripts of the trial and go over them as he prepared my case. He said it would take some time to put it all together and a while to get an answer back from the appellate court.

As time went on and we got to know each other, we would become good friends. I was impressed by his intelligence. I had an interest in history and Japan, and when I found out that he could speak and read Japanese, plus a few other languages, we hit it off from the start. As time went on, we would talk about the case and our families. He was concerned for my young son, Steven, and my daughter, Julie, and how they were handling all of this. He would keep in constant contact with me on my case, and we would get together two or three times a week to go over the transcripts of the trial.

I did not know it at the time, but as we got to know each other better, I learned that he was not a well man. The main reason he did not have much of a practice was that he was suffering from a rare medical condition. He basically was just getting by, taking a limited number of cases that the courts would send him. He was taking medications that slowed him down and would knock him out for a while. There were times when we were together discussing my case, and he would black out on me for a few moments then wake up, not remembering what had happened. A number of years later, his illness would affect his mind and body so much as to put him totally out of work, and he would become bedridden. I guess you could say he was in the early stages of his illness for the time being because he could still function reasonably well and drive his car.

At that moment, I was his only case. He assured me that he was going to do the best he could for me while working full-time on my case since he did not have any other cases to distract him. Despite the limitations of his health, he was still a good appeals lawyer, and I felt I should give him a chance. When I wasn't working at the restaurant, I would be working on my appeal.

CHAPTER 16

From Commissioner to Selling Hot Dogs

October 1983

As people came into the restaurant, some who recognized me would point toward me and stare and whisper while others would just snicker or chuckle under their breath. There were some who felt sorry for my situation and would tell me so. It made me feel a little better knowing that not everyone was against me. Many were surprised to see me out doing what I was doing. It didn't matter to me what they thought; they were not paying my bills.

I did not care for the way Kevin treated my daughter at times, but she was crazy about him, so I tried not to interfere. There was something about him I did not like, and I would just tell Julie to be careful in her relationship with him. The restaurant job only lasted two months. He was making changes and letting people go. Six months later, his eatery went under. He wasn't a very good business-man in my opinion, just a hustler and wheeler-dealer. A few years later, some time after my daughter had broken up with him, he was arrested for some bad business dealings.

In the meantime, I acquired a position with a national paint and body shop, managing one of their locations. It did not matter to the supervisor who hired me that I was a convicted felon. He figured I would be a good fit for the business he was in. That job paid a decent salary and commission. I held on to it for about a year until they closed the location down and started to downsize. Again, I found myself out looking for work, with the same results as before.

I was still too hot to hire with the government coming behind me, asking my previous employers questions about me.

After the end of my trial, you would not believe how many of my acquaintances contacted me to tell me that they had received a visit or a call from the FBI. A good friend at my local bank even told me that the FBI was looking into my accounts. The prosecutor was not leaving any stone unturned. He was trying to establish a money trail, and he must have been looking for anything that he could find to link me with Bowmer. I guess in his reasoning, if I had taken all the money Bowmer claimed he paid me over time, then there must be a money trail someplace.

Mr. Merkle was not going to make things easy for me or anyone. He desperately wanted my cooperation in his ongoing investigation, and he figured I was the weak link that would hand him his case on a silver platter. The more victims or so-called coconspirators he could get to cooperate, the stronger his case would become. He had an agenda, and he was looking into every politician and businessman who could have had any dealings with the county. During this time, he was constantly going before the grand jury seeking indictments. He was hoping he could convince me to cooperate so I would be the cornerstone to his future political career.

Fred Anderson was ill and staying at home while his wife worked to support them. Like me, he was broke after paying all his attorney fees, and he was in no condition to work. No one saw much of them after the trial. Not wanting to be hounded by the media, they sort of kept to themselves, and I understand they rarely left their home except when Patricia went to work or took Fred to the doctors.

Michael Sierra had stopped practicing law, and he was turning over his unfinished cases to other attorneys, waiting to hear from the Florida Bar Association while under appeal. Bowmer had yet to be sentenced on his plea deal with the government. They were holding off on that while he continued to cooperate with them as more indictments were soon to be coming down.

With what little money I was able to save and a loan from a good friend, I was able to put a few hundred dollars together to buy a hot dog cart. I figured if no one was willing to hire me, then I would go into business for myself. At least I wouldn't have to answer to anyone, and I would be on my own. It wasn't easy, waking early every morning to get the cart ready for the day, getting the proper licenses and Health Department approval, and then being spot-inspected occasionally. The hardest part was finding a good location to set up my hot dog shop.

I traveled all over the county and city setting up at different locations, trying to find a spot where I could develop traffic-flow ideal for maximum sales. There was never one good location because I would be asked to leave by the law or some inspector unless I was on private property with permission to be there. I just kept moving from one location to another. Sometimes I would be asked to set up at a specific function or business for the day or night where they needed more vendors. I made a little extra money on those. In the long run, though, I barely made enough to get by.

I drove a worn-out Fury, the only car I could afford, and I would set up my cart at whatever location I was able to get permission. I traded my suits for khaki shorts and a T-shirt while opening my yellow-and-blue Sabrett umbrella over my cart. It afforded me a little shade and helped to keep the hot sun off my head. It had now been well over a year since my conviction. My appeal had been filed, and there was still no news.

When I wasn't selling hot dogs on the weekends, I would get a booth at the old wagon-wheel flea market and sell rock-band T-shirts and different kinds of stuff just to make a few extra bucks. For the moment, I was still out on bail, had a roof over my head, and a loving family standing by me. My oldest son, Joey, was still away on active duty in the navy while my daughter, Julie, was doing everything she could to help out. These were very stressful and difficult times for us.

For the next year and a half, while waiting to hear about my appeal, I continued to sell hot dogs and take whatever job opportunities came along. It was hard for all of us, but especially for Steven, who really did not understand what was happening. At times, other kids could be very cruel when all they knew was what they heard from their parents or the news media.

When Steven was at school, some of the other children whispered and giggled behind his back, or made comments like, "Your dad is going to prison, and he's a crook." Steven would come home and just stay in his room until dinnertime. I tried to tell him that they did not understand what had happened, and they only knew what their parents told them. I told him we had to try and forgive their ignorance and just ignore them. Someday the real truth would be known, and they would think differently.

Toward the end of May 1985, my attorney Ray Harris received word that my appeal was denied and that I would be notified as to when I was to turn myself in and report to prison. Ray called my home and asked me to meet with him in his office the next day.

When we met, he explained what had happened and that I needed to get my affairs in order as soon as possible, for they might be sending me to prison very soon. I was devastated. My heart sank to my stomach, and I had tears in my eyes. I could not understand how they could have denied my appeal. But Mr. Harris just shook his head and said, "Merkle just made a stronger objection, and the judges accepted it based on the information provided by Bowmer and the new indictments that are coming out."

As I left his office and headed home, so many thoughts were running through my mind. *What is going to happen to me now? What is going to happen to my family? Being a former police officer, what is going to happen to me in prison?* I realized there was nothing I could do now. I had to get home and break the news to my family.

After dinner, I broke the bad news to them. My children took it hard. Julie and Steven could not believe we lost the appeal. Not much was said the rest of the night. I could see how upset everyone was, and there was nothing more I could say. The next day, I sat with my daughter, Julie, as we planned how she would have to take care of Steven and our home while I was away. I knew it would not be easy for them, but like her late mother, Julie was of strong character, and I knew she would find a way to manage. I just prayed that someone would see our situation and come forward to help them.

Bowmer was not yet sentenced for his crimes against the community. He was still cooperating and giving names and information to the government on who was involved in additional bribes. To add to the problem, the government also had another former county commissioner, Charles Frank Bean (who liked to be called Charlie Bean), cooperating under a plea agreement for a lenient sentence. His wife was the county attorney Pat Bean. He was also naming names, aiding the testimony of Jerry Bowmer, which now gave Merkle the means to start a witch hunt to go after anyone they mentioned.

It seemed that the two of them had been wheeling and dealing since they were first elected to public office. It was becoming the who's who of Hillsborough County and the State of Florida, with Merkle chomping at the bit. This was going to be his big step-up with the Republican Party and in government circles, and he would not leave one stone unturned.

It was becoming obvious that no one in our community was safe from this witch hunt. Whatever name Bowmer or Bean gave to the government, Merkle would eat it up and go after them with a vengeance. Besides the people Bowmer or Bean worked with, I think they just added names of people whom they did not like, making themselves look good in the prosecutor's eyes. They were doing their best to make others take the fall for their crimes. It did not matter that these people might be innocent. They knew the government would look into them and maybe find something they could use against them, without regard for whose lives they ruined.

The media was having a field day with all the names, and the government quietly leaked information to them to help with their ongoing investigation. They were hoping this would scare more people into coming forward with additional information to help their case.

CHAPTER 17

The New Indictments

June 1985

After I received the news of the denial of my appeal, a couple of weeks passed. Then I received word from Ray Harris that I had been reindicted by the grand jury on multiple counts of corruption, along with a number of prominent people from the community. I was to report to the federal courthouse on the morning of June 8 and appear before US magistrate Thomas Wilson in his courtroom to answer to the new charges. Things were really starting to happen now.

There were over twenty-four civic leaders, businessmen, and attorneys, plus three corporations, being charged. The list looked like the who's who of Tampa and Hillsborough County, and Robert Merkle was going after everyone and anyone who had any dealings with any of them in an attempt to continue the indictments.

The list was long. It included myself, Fred Arthur Anderson, Joseph Henry Anderson Jr., Anderson Contracting Company Inc., Columbia Paving Inc., Lois Bailey, Robert A. Connella, Robert E. Curry, John DeCarlucci, John David Demmi, Marcelino Echevarria, Manuel Fernandez, Leroy R. Gonzalez Jr,. and Laurence I. Goodrich.

Also indicted were Richard D. Guagliardo, Nelson Italiano, Michael T. Novak, Alexander G. Rappaport, Louis Rocha, Cesar Augustus Rodriguez, Harold Leonard Rossiter, Michael Sierra, Suburban Disposal Services Inc., Claude Tanner, Eugene Thomason, and Cullen H. Williams. Many were pillars of the community.

On Friday, June 8, 1985, I arrived at the federal courthouse shortly after 8:15 a.m. and proceeded to Magistrate Wilson's courtroom on the third floor of the courthouse. I was informed that he would be taking everyone in alphabetical order three at a time to move things along because of the long list of names. It was going to be a long morning for us all.

As each group of three were called before Magistrate Wilson's bench, many with their attorneys present, they would plead not guilty. Earlier on Thursday, three of this group had pleaded not guilty. The rest would give their plea today. Because of the complexity of the case, the prosecution expected it would take six months or more to conclude the trial. Many of the defendants told the magistrate they were having trouble finding lawyers who would take on such a long and complex trial.

When Fred Anderson was called to the bench to make his plea, he was still free on bond, as I was. He explained to the magistrate that he needed to have a court-appointed lawyer, that all the lawyers he had spoken with wanted $100,000 to $200,000 to take on this case. Anderson, like myself, was financially depleted from the first trial.

Another defendant, former city council member and building contractor Manuel Fernandez, came before Magistrate Wilson and asked to be represented by a court-appointed lawyer. Wilson responded with, "I sympathize with both of you, but you may have to pay for part of the fees for a court-appointed lawyer." He told Fernandez, "If this were a typical case, you would be able to afford your own attorney. This is not a typical case." He granted the defendants' motion for a court-appointed lawyer and advised them to work it out with the court.

Earlier on Thursday, two other defendants, insurance executive Nelson Italiano and lawyer John Demmi pleaded not guilty to all the charges against them. Scheduling conflicts prevented them from being arraigned with us on Friday. John Demmi and Attorney Laurence Goodrich informed the magistrate that they would be representing themselves.

Attorney Arnold Levine, representing Nelson Italiano, informed the court that trying his client with the members of an alleged racketeering organization would be a conscious effort by the US attorney to prejudice the case against his client, Mr. Italiano, that the idea of being stuck in a massive trial with the emotional and economic burden is more than anyone should be put through. He then submitted a petition to the court to sever his client from the rest of us. It was accepted and would be ruled on at a later date.

Just before the trial was to begin, Cesar Rodriguez informed the court that he was unable to retain an attorney and that he would represent himself during the trial.

Another defendant, Paul Johnson, who was a very prominent Tampa lawyer and a former Hillsborough state attorney, was well respected in both the legal community and the city-county establishment. He asked the court that his case be separated from the other twenty-four defendants and corporations charged in the 166-page indictment. He had been charged with two counts of bribery and two counts of wire fraud in connection with a borrow pit permit he helped obtain for the Hubbard Construction Co. of Orlando, according to the information Bowmer supplied to the federal prosecutors.

Johnson was being accused of charging Hubbard Construction Co. a $50,000 legal fee to represent the company and using part of it to pay $30,000 to former Hillsborough County Commissioners Jerry Bowmer, Fred Anderson, and myself. Bowmer was cooperating with the federal prosecutors, and he and Charlie Bean were not included in our indictment. The Hubbard officials were cooperating with the federal officials and were not accused of taking part in any bribes.

Johnson had as his lawyer Richard Gerstein, the former Dade County state attorney and partner in the law firm with the renowned F. Lee Bailey. Mr. Gerstein also informed the court that Mr. Johnson was not charged with being part of what Merkle had described as "a racketeering enterprise" that had operated from 1976 to 1983. He suggested the "enterprise" bought and sold rezonings, alcoholic beverage permits, borrow pit permits, road paving contracts, garbage rate increases, and cable TV franchises.

Gerstein submitted it would be unfair to try his client, Mr. Johnson, at the same time that a racketeering case was being tried. He then moved that his client be severed from the trial. He was informed that the court would consider the matter and render a decision soon. Paul Johnson and six other defendants were not charged with the "racketeering enterprise" and later were severed from our trial, to be tried at a later date.

When it came my turn to approach the magistrate, I entered a plea of not guilty and informed Magistrate Wilson that I would defend myself in this new upcoming trial. The magistrate shook his head and advised me to get a lawyer. He said, "Mr. Kotvas, I believe it would be in your best interest to be represented by an attorney. Your appeal was recently rejected by the Eleventh Circuit Court of Appeals in Atlanta. Frankly, it may well be that you will be in custody in a very short time," he continued. "It will be very difficult for you, Mr. Kotvas, to prepare for the trial if you are in jail."

I just repeated myself and told Magistrate Wilson, "I don't need a lawyer and plead innocent. I wish to represent myself because of mistakes that were made in my first trial, and if any mistakes are made during this second trial, let it be because of what I did rather than someone else."

"Of course, you have the right to represent yourself," Wilson said to me. "But if I were you, I would reconsider your situation. You will not be given any special consideration on dealing with your defense."

The trial was supposedly set to begin on August 12, but due to the vast number of defendants, many of them still searching for representation that they could afford, the time for the trial was put off until the beginning of 1986, giving all the parties involved time to file whatever motions necessary for the government and court to respond.

On a Saturday evening in July, I was getting ready to take my hot dog cart out to a nightclub on Dale Mabry Highway, where I had been invited for that evening. As I was getting ready to leave my home, a strange feeling came over me to give my good friend Bob Magana a call. It was getting late, and I needed to get set up by 7:00 p.m. It was about 5:30 p.m., so I thought to myself, *I'll just give him a call tomorrow.* I don't know why, but I just could not shake the feeling about calling Bob.

Once I arrived at the nightclub, I started to set up for business; and as time passed, I was busy with the crowd, and the feeling to call Bob passed. I stayed until closing around 2:00 a.m., then packed up everything and headed home. As it turned out, I did not do too badly. I made a small profit for my time that would help with my expenses, but I was beat. All I wanted to do was get home and get some sleep. When I arrived home, it was very late, so I just parked the cart in my yard and decided to clean it in the morning. All I wanted to do was get a good night's sleep.

Around nine-thirty the next morning, the phone rang. I was still in bed sleeping, but I forced myself to answer it. It was Carol, Bob's wife. With a solemn voice that sounded like she had been crying, she said, "Joe, Bob passed way last night."

I woke up fast and sat at the side of my bed and asked her what had happened. She said, "Bob came home from work about 5:00 p.m. last night and said he was very tired and wanted to lie down for a while before dinner. He told me to call him when dinner was ready. Around seven, I sent Suzie in to wake him for dinner. She came back crying, saying that Daddy will not wake up, he is just lying there in bed, not moving. I ran into the bedroom to check on him, and it seems he had passed away in his sleep."

I could hear she was crying on the phone as we talked. She told me she had friends over to help her with all the arrangements. She knew how close we were and wanted me to know right away. I asked her how the girls were taking it, and she informed me that it was very hard for them right now, especially for Suzie, who found him. I told her I would pray for all of them and that, because of my present situation, it would be hard for me to do much. She understood but thought I needed to know.

I told her I was glad she called to let me know. I knew Bob would be in a better place now. We were both crying on the phone. After a little more conversation, we hung up. I sat there on my bed, crying for a while. I had just lost the best friend I ever had, and there was nothing I could do to help his family. I started to remember the feeling I had last night to call Bob. I wondered whether if I had called Bob when I had that feeling, he might have answered the phone and would not have passed away. Or was there a message he had for me, and something was trying to tell me to call? I don't know. A lot of thoughts were going through my mind at the time.

I remembered what he said to me when he called right after I was in all my trouble with the government, how he had died and came back because there was something he needed to do, how he saw my wife and many of his relatives in that light he was in, that he needed to come back to finish something. Was I that something, or was it more? Was the help and encouragement he was trying to give me the unfinished task? Was it because I might have done something to harm myself, and God had other plans for me? I like to believe that.

I'm sure there was more to it, but I like to believe he was sent back to help me stand up and face whatever was coming at me, and realize that I was not alone anymore, that there is a divine purpose in life for all of us, whatever that may be.

I knew Bob was in a better place now; it was his time. I felt good that he passed way in his sleep peacefully, that he did not have to suffer. Maybe it was heaven's way of saying a job well done to Bob. I guess—no, I believe—he is in heaven with my wife now, looking down at us, seeing how we are doing. I lost a good friend, and it hurts like crazy, just like it hurt when I lost my wife. But I feel a part of them will always be with me, to encourage me to go on and face what I have to face and take care of my family the best I can.

I will always have the good memories of our times together. Nothing can take that away from me, I thought as I got out of bed for the day. I did not have anyone that close and personal to me to call anymore. In one sense, I felt more alone than ever. In another, I felt something greater was watching over me. It seems it was now up to me to choose how I faced the future.

Later that day, I told my children and my family that Bob had passed away. I was not able to attend his funeral. As much as I wanted to, I did not have the means nor the permission from the court to make the trip. A lot of things were still going on in Tampa that needed to be worked out, and I would soon be reporting to prison. I guess I will never know why I had that feeling. I should have made that call to Bob to find out. It haunts me to this very day.

CHAPTER 18

Reporting to Prison

August 1985

A few days later, I received the notice to report to Maxwell Federal Prison Camp in Montgomery, Alabama, before the second week in August. The only good thing about it was that I was allowed to travel there on my own, without any US marshal escorts.

At the time, I was unaware that it was the US attorney general's office that runs the Bureau of Prisons and that judges can only make recommendations on where we would go to serve our sentences. This gave Merkle an edge on where we would be sent. With his contacts in the justice system, he made sure we all would be just far enough away from our homes to make it very difficult for any of our families or loved ones to visit us on a regular basis. If any of us were lucky, we might get a visit once a year, if at all. Although there were a number of federal prison camps in Florida, Merkle had us all sent out of state to make it more difficult for us and our families, but close enough to get us back for our second trial. I guess he was thinking that the hardship of being separated from our families would entice us to be more cooperative with his ongoing investigation.

All three of us defendants received notices around the same time to report to whatever facility we were assigned to. Fred Anderson was to report to the prison hospital in Springfield, Missouri, where they could monitor and treat his cardiac condition. This really made it hard on his wife, Pat, and their teenage daughter. The next time Fred would see his family again would be at our second trial.

Unlike Fred and me, Michael Sierra was supposed to go to Eglin Air Force Base Prison in northwest Florida, but at the time, supposedly they had no room for him. So he was to report to a midlevel federal prison in Tallahassee for a while, till room at Eglin became available. His wife, Cynthia, and daughter drove him to Tallahassee so they could spend a little more time with him before he had to report. It would take a few months before he would be sent to his final destination.

About a month into his time at Tallahassee, the prison system prepared to transfer a number of men from Tallahassee to the Eglin prison camp. Unfortunately, the correctional officer handling all the transfer paperwork at Tallahassee was a pig farmer on his off hours and was busy with his pigs and forgot to include Michael Sierra in the transfer orders. When the time came for the prisoners to be transferred to Eglin, Michael inquired why his name was left off the list. All the officer could tell him was he was sorry, but he just didn't get around to it. So now Michael had to wait for the next transfer to happen.

By early December of 1985, Michael Sierra finally got his notice to report to the prison camp in Duluth, Minnesota. They gave him a Greyhound bus ticket and allowed him to report to Duluth on his own, without any US marshals tagging along. When he arrived at the federal compound in Duluth, it too was located on part of an air force base, and it was freezing cold. He was bunked on the second floor of one of the dorms, and the snow was piled high right up to his window. They would use snowplows to move the snow and pile it up in mounds in open areas, for it was so cold that the snow never melted in the winter. He would remain at this freezing camp until he was removed by the marshals for his return to Tampa to face our second trial.

The time finally came for me to leave Tampa and report to Maxwell Federal Prison Camp in Montgomery, Alabama. I packed a few things that I thought I would need to take along on the trip. A good friend, Fred Barksdale (whose great-grandfather was General Barksdale of the Confederate Army and one of the heroes of the Battle of Fredericksburg), offered to drive me to the prison camp since he was already going to the mountains in Tennessee, where he would be staying at his cabin for a few weeks. He told me that Montgomery was not that far out of his way.

Fred had been a longtime friend of mine, whom I met when he was a practicing attorney handling mostly traffic cases. He also happened to be good friends with Bob Johnson, the judge who handled traffic court. We first met in the hallway leading to traffic court when I was a Tampa police officer. He had stopped me just outside of Judge Johnson's court to inform me that a traffic case I was to appear on had already been settled earlier. Over time, we would run into each other and become good friends. Fred was one man who could understand what I was going through since he had had his share of run-ins with the federal government some years back.

When the time came to leave, Fred arrived at my house very early to pick me up. I said my good-byes to my children and family. It was a very emotional time for all of us. My son Steven could not understand why I had to leave, and my daughter, Julie, did her best to hold back her tears as we hugged each other. I told her to just do the best she could to hold everything together until I came home. My mother and sister were both crying as we left. It would be a long time before I would see the inside of my home again.

When I got into his car, Fred handed me a cup of hot Cuban coffee and some Cuban toast that he picked up in West Tampa on his way to my house. He said, "This will have to hold you until we stop for lunch."

The drive to Maxwell was uneventful. We talked some, and Fred offered me some pointers on what to expect when I got to the camp, some of the do's and don'ts. We stopped for lunch on the way at a real good barbecue place in Georgia where Fred had been a number of times on his trips to the mountains. This was going to be a long drive for me and probably the last decent lunch I would have as a free man for a long time. Fred explained to me, "Just try and keep to yourself. Don't say much to anyone, and don't talk about your personal life. Keep your nose clean and do what you're told. Be careful of the company you keep. Don't trust anyone, and you should be all right."

After lunch, we continued on our way. We did not arrive at the security gate to the air force base until late in the afternoon. The prison camp was located inside the base, and the airman on duty gave us directions to the camp. We drove past the offices and housing for the base, past a golf course, and through what seemed like a desolate wooded area, right up to the main compound. Fred stopped at the entrance where there was a sign that read, "Federal Prison Camp, No Trespassing, Authorized Personnel Only, Visitors Please Stop at the Administration Building." He dropped me off in front of what looked like the administration building. We shook hands, said our good-byes, then Fred drove off. I had never felt so alone in my life as I did at that moment.

As I looked around the camp before going into the administration building, I could see that it was well-kept. I entered the administration building and was met by a couple of serious-looking officers. Both were wearing a light-blue shirt and tie with gray pants and black shoes, and one of them also wore a blue blazer with a federal patch on the jacket pocket. Before they took charge of me, I had to wait in a holding area while the evening count was going on. When the count was over, I could hear over the loudspeakers that ran throughout the camp that they were calling the men to chow.

As soon as the count was over, the two officers came back and escorted me to a windowless receiving room just a few feet from a couple of empty steel holding cells with their doors open. They informed me that these cells were the "hole" for prisoners who needed disciplinary action. As I glanced over at them, I could see they had large steel doors with a small almost-square opening that had a steel mesh grille around it. The cells were dark and empty, and the walls were bare, housing only a bench and toilet.

As I entered the receiving room, I looked around and could see in one corner a shower where all new prisoners would be scrubbed down to make sure they did not have any lice on them. A good number of prisoners who come through are loaded with lice that they pick up from county jails. In another part of the room, I saw a Polaroid camera used to take mug shots of all new arrivals before they are fingerprinted, plus a long table onto which I was told to put all my belongings.

As I faced the table, one of the officers walked around to the other side of the table and, in a stern voice, commanded me to place everything I had in my pockets on the table, then strip down and place all my clothes and shoes on the table for inspection. I was then standing naked in front of them. One of them put on a pair of rubber gloves and gave me a thorough inspection, looking into my mouth, ears, running his hands through my hair, asking me to pick up my feet and hold out my hands, then asking me to bend over as one of them gave me a cavity inspection. It was so degrading. They made me feel like I might have been some kind of drug smuggler.

I guess, like all prisons, they might have problems with inmates trying to sneak drugs into the camp. I've heard that all kinds of narcotics smuggling runs rampant in prisons and that inmates know how to use the system to conceal the drugs they are trying to sneak in, using some of the most obscure places on their bodies. (This is still a problem to this very day.)

As I stood there naked and trembling from the cold bare concrete floor, another officer went through all my belongings, separating what I could keep and what I had to send back home. Almost everything I brought with me had to be shipped home. When finished, they boxed everything up, had me address it, and placed it aside to be shipped out the next day.

After they were finished with my processing, I was issued a set of drab green loose-fitting surplus air force work clothes, a clean pair of what looked like old worn socks and underpants, a belt, a handkerchief, and a pair of temporary used deck shoes for use until I would be issued my regular work clothes. This is what all the new inmates were issued when they first reported in. I could not help but wonder how many men had worn these clothes before me. It just left me with a strange unclean feeling. This was all part of the system's way of deindividualizing us, and it was to continue throughout my time in prison. One will find that the system does everything it can to break you down, then rebuild you back to the way they want you to be in the system.

When I arrived, I was given a number that I was required to remember and use on any and all communication and correspondence I sent out. It would also be stenciled on all the clothes I would be issued. From now on, anything that belonged to me was to have this number on it. As far as the system was concerned, I was now 03026-018, assigned to Maxwell Prison Camp, Montgomery, Alabama. The institutions you are sent may change from time to time, but the number will always follow you wherever you go. If anyone wanted to find out anything about any prisoner, they had to use his number to locate the information.

When I finished getting dressed, one of the officers called out to me, "All right, Kotvas, follow me back to the control area."

I was taken back to an area called the control room, where you could look out on to the compound and watch everything that was going on. It had thick glass windows protruding from the building, allowing a view of all corners of the camp. There was an officer sitting at the control, giving out orders over the camp's intercom system while I waited to see where I was going next.

I could see through the glass windows into the prison compound that the camp had two rows of one-story stucco buildings that were used as dormitories and surrounded by grassy areas. Between the buildings were concrete walkways on both sides running down the middle of the compound, ending at a long one-story building used as the mess hall at the far end of the prison. There were ten dorms, five on each side running down the compound. Each dormitory was given a letter from *A* through *J*, which all the inmates were assigned to. The place was built for around two hundred men. At the time I arrived, there were over four hundred being housed there.

The officer in the control room called out over the intercom for the houseman to dormitory G to report. As I waited, I could see how well the men kept the place. It was neatly landscaped with plants and flowers, hedges along the front, sides, and in the back areas, plus tall shade trees throughout the compound. From the outside, it did not look that bad, but looks can be deceiving.

When the houseman from dorm G arrived, he was informed that I was assigned to his dorm, and he was to assign me a bunk and locker. I had not been given a permanent assignment yet; I was told that would come later and that for now I would be called out from time to time to work on different cleanup details around the compound. The houseman then escorted me back to his dorm, which was one of the dorms closest to the control room.

On the way out of the control area, as we walked toward the dorm, I noticed all the men standing around up and down the compound. They all wore green shirts and pants with black work shoes or sneakers. They were allowed to wear sneakers if they had them. Some of them seemed to be drifting aimlessly as they walked slowly around the compound. Some were leaning against the buildings while others sitting in small groups on some of the benches were talking in low tones to one another. It seemed like no one moved too fast around here. The houseman would later tell me that no one was allowed to run on the compound, except in areas designated for jogging. When in the compound area, everyone walked. If you were caught running, you would be written up on an incident report.

As we walked to the dorm, men looked our way and just stared. Some turned to some of the others and said something, then turned back and stared at us some more. It was a strange feeling not knowing anyone there.

While I was being processed, I had missed meal call, and the cafeteria was now closed. The officers gave a baloney sandwich, a peanut butter sandwich, and an apple, which I carried to my new quarters with my sheets, pillow, and blanket, plus whatever other articles I was allowed to have. I ate the baloney and apple, then threw away the bread, which was kind of stale, as well as the peanut butter sandwich. To this day, I can't stand peanut butter.

When we arrived at our dormitory, the houseman showed me where I would sleep. He informed me that I should not get caught with any contraband if I had any, in my area or in the dorm. He also informed me that the "hacks" would pull spot searches to try and catch inmates bringing in and hiding contraband in the dorms. The inmates called all correctional officers *hacks* behind their backs. To their faces, we all said *sir* or *officer* and their name if we knew it.

I came to find out from the houseman that the dorm I was staying in once housed Charles Colson from the Watergate era. This was where he had been sent to do his time when he was convicted back in the seventies. The place had not changed much since then, except that it was more crowded, and the green uniforms all the inmates wore were much better than the hand-me-downs they used to wear a few years before.

The dorm was still a cream-colored stucco building with dark shingles on the roof. The area outside was well-kept, but once you got inside the building, it was a whole different situation. As soon as you walked in, the stench of body odors and the smell of stale tobacco would hit your senses like a brick wall. I could see from the entrance that on my right were two dayrooms. One had a table and chairs for card playing or reading, and the other was a small TV room where the inmates could watch some of the local programs or news. There were a lot of chairs stacked around this room.

The dorm was broken up into rows of small two-man cubicles made up of double iron bunk beds, one atop the other with a small ladder for the guy who slept on top. Attached to the side and head of the bed was a small desk with a small light and some shelf space above the desk. On the opposite partition were two small lockers for personal stuff, one atop the other. There was only one chair per cubicle. The total space for two inmates in each cubicle was about eight by six feet.

The dorm was overcrowded, and even though every two men had a cubicle, space was limited. The desk area was controlled by the senior inmate who had the bottom bunk. The guy on top had to ask his permission to use the desk. Every new inmate was issued a top bunk. How the system worked was, you would eventually be moved to a bottom bunk based on the amount of time you had in the dorm. That was even true when you were moved to a permanent dorm. It did not matter whether you had a bottom bunk where you came from before; if you were new to the dorm, you had to start all over at the top again until a bottom bunk became available. This meant that everyone before you who had a top bunk would rotate down until they got to you. The toilets and showers in each dorm were located toward the front of the dorm before the card room at the front entrance to the dorm. The showers were open stalls so the officers could keep an eye on what was going on in the area as they walked by on their rounds.

There was no real privacy of any type. I also noticed in this dorm that no one really smiled at anyone. Everyone looked at one another with suspicion, especially the new arrivals. It seemed that no one was really friendly in the dorm.

As I settled in that first night, it was the hardest of my life. I had no idea what was going to happen to me, and I missed my children and family. Facing the unknown was going to be a challenge. I did not know anyone, and I felt so alone. I did not sleep well that first night when the lights went out in the dorm around 10:00 p.m. The officers—or hacks, as I would come to call them—came through the dorm at different times during the night for count inspections and to make sure everyone was in their assigned bunk.

I had all kinds of crazy thoughts going through my mind about the kind of men I was sharing this dorm with. Would I be attacked in my bunk or have my throat slit while I slept if anyone found out I was a former police officer? To be truthful, I didn't know what to expect. I know I was very depressed and felt abandoned. The houseman did not say a lot about anything that goes on, for he was busy with his evening chores and told me that he would talk more to me in the morning when everyone left for their work details. Since I had not been assigned to any detail, I would have to hang around the dorm and wait to be called out for different chores, plus help out the houseman.

The lights were turned on in the dorm around 5:30 a.m. Everyone got out of their bunks. Some dressed as others went to the shower area in the dorm to clean up. There was no privacy in the shower area; it was all open for everyone to see as they passed by. Men were showering; others were just washing up at the sinks while others used the commodes or urinals. The houseman had his own cubicle up in front of the dorm where he could get in and out in a hurry when he wanted to. (One of the advantages of being the houseman was that you did not have to share your cubicle with anyone else. This gave them a little extra space and some privacy.)

After everyone was dressed, we all waited inside by the front of the dorm for the hacks to call each dorm out for breakfast. While we all waited, the houseman introduced me around to the other inmates in the dorm. Some introduced themselves, and others just kept to themselves and did not say anything.

This was not a country club or anything like the movies, TV, or news media like to project. Only in looks did it give the appearance of a manicured work camp. It was a minimum-security work camp, and everyone there had to work, or they would be sent to a higher-security institution with gun towers and barbed-wire fences or walls. The purpose of the camp was an honor system, where everyone was on his honor to do his time without causing any trouble.

Everyone there was given a job and paid eleven cents an hour for the time they were working. Some inmates received a little more according to the type of work they had to do and could earn as much as thirty-eight cents an hour. This money went into the inmates' accounts once a month and could be used during canteen sales days, which came around once a week. This was where we were allowed to purchase junk food and ice cream, personal hygiene products, and allowable incidentals like stamps, writing material, etc.

I would later find out that the Federal Bureau of Prisons also had a program called UNICOR, where inmates could work in special types of skilled industry run by UNICOR and where they could earn anywhere from twenty-five cents up to a dollar an hour. The only UNICOR industry on Maxwell Air Force Base was the base laundry. These industries provided a service to the air base and community at large and saved the government millions of dollars in payroll and materials. They were run and staffed by inmates and supervised by civilian-contracted personnel and federal correction officers. To my knowledge, the UNICOR system of operation worked throughout the entire federal prison system on every institutional level were required to fill a need in the prison system.

If a friend or a family member sent us any money, it was deposited into our account, but only ten dollars at a time could be withdrawn. We were not allowed to have more than ten dollars in our possession at any one time, and that had to be in quarters. No paper money was allowed. If an inmate was caught with any type of paper money—one-, five-, or even a ten-dollar bill—they would be sent to the hole for disciplinary action and possible transfer out to a higher-level prison.

The hole was a steel five-by-seven-feet cell with no windows, just a steel bunk attached to the wall and a stainless steel commode and sink all in one attached to the wall. There was a solid iron door with a small slot in the middle of it to pass food trays through.

You were required to pay for everything with quarters. If you needed to do your laundry, the machines in the compound laundry area took quarters. Even the vending machines around the camp and throughout the air base took quarters. To get around the daily quarter quota, you could also use your canteen account to purchase rolls of postage stamps. They were also accepted as currency and payments for favors needed between inmates. There was no limit on the amount of stamps one could have in their possession. As far as the hacks were concerned, they were used for mailing correspondence and legal documents, which sometimes took a lot of stamps. I think the hacks knew what was going on with the stamps and just turned a blind eye to the situation as long as you did not make it look too obvious.

CHAPTER 19

Settling in at Maxwell

August 1985

When our dorm was finally called for chow, we were the last ones to eat. The dorms were called out according to how they passed the night's dorm inspection. Each dorm was graded on how clean and neat the houseman keeps his dorm. The top dorm goes first, then the second, and so on. From my understanding, the interim dorm where I was staying almost always went last, for they kept finding something to be written up. The top dorm gets to keep that position for the week until the next inspection when the points were added up again, and maybe a new dorm got the honor. There was a great deal of competition to get to eat first or second because you got to have a little more free time to do things.

As the men in the dorms who were called first finished their breakfast, the next dorm would be called. When you finished eating, you were to report to the prison bus area or your work assignment to get ready for the day's activity. You had to report to your area on time or go on report. Three write-ups in a month, and you got sent to the hole for disciplinary action. This is why the men in each dorm helped to keep their dorms clean for inspection, trying to get the number one place in the chow line. It gave them extra time before they had to report for work. When the work call went out over the loud speakers, everyone on an assignment had to be at his assigned place, ready to go.

Work call would go out around 6:45 a.m., and you had to report for duty by 7:00 a.m., whether you were finished eating or not. Wherever you were to report, there would be a couple of officers taking a count of all who were present to make sure everyone was accounted for. They would randomly pick out inmates standing in line to work and spot search them to make sure they were not taking any contraband out of the camp. They also searched the inmates when they came back to make sure they weren't bringing in anything forbidden. If you were caught taking away anything not authorized or bringing it in, you were immediately sent to the hole (some of the men would find ways around that).

When our turn to eat came, we had to hurry and be out of the cafeteria by 7:00 a.m. and report back to the dorm for a work count. I have to say, the food they served was not bad for prison food. I was informed that all the preparations and cooking was done by inmates assigned to the kitchen and overseen by a civilian dietician and chef who worked for the prison system. The chef was responsible for ordering all the supplies and food, as well as preparing menus and overseeing the preparation of each meal. The man in charge was a big black man whom all the staff and inmates called *Big Daddy*. He was well-liked by everyone, but he had a few quirks that the inmates had to watch out for.

One of the reasons he was well-liked by the inmates was because he enjoyed teaching them how to cook and prepare meals. Those who got assigned to the kitchen could learn a good trade and use it on the outside when they were released. It was considered one of the best jobs in the camp, and there was a long list of men trying to score that assignment. Also, those inmates who were assigned to the kitchen could prepare and eat what they liked if they did not care for the meal they were serving.

The first day at camp was spent mostly in my dorm helping the houseman clean and listening to what he had to say about the place. When we finished our chores, he walked me around the compound, showing me the boundaries and limits of the camp. Although the prison camp abutted the air force base golf course, we were not allowed to step on to it except to maintain it during work details.

There was a dirt path running from the camp down alongside the golf course that we could use to jog or walk along for exercise, but we were only allowed to go just so far before we had to turn around. There was a marker on the path to show where we had to turn around. Anyone caught going beyond that marker could be charged with escape. The officers were very strict about the camp rules, and some of them enjoyed writing you up for any little infraction, so you had to be on your toes all the time—you never knew who was watching you.

The camp was not very large. The base housed just over four hundred men on just a few acres. There were hedges and shrubbery all around the compound denoting the prison boundaries that we were not allowed to cross without permission. The joke in the place was, "If you want to escape, you have to tunnel under the hedges." It was truly an honor system; one only had to walk right out onto the golf course and continue out to one of the gates of the base to be free. However, if they caught you, you would have five years added to your sentence and be transferred to a higher-level prison to do your time.

The federal prison system contracts with many of our military bases to establish minimum-security prison camps in exchange for a cheap labor force for the military. This saves the military millions of dollars that can be used elsewhere. It's a joint relationship between the two parties that seems to work out well.

As I continued my tour of the camp, the houseman showed me where the commissary was, where everyone went to purchase whatever they were selling on commissary days. Then we walked over to the machine and plumbing shops, where the inmates assigned to the shops fixed everything from small motors to any type of electrical gadgets in the camp, as well as plumbing problems. The one thing I noticed was that most of the inmates here wore clean green pressed work clothes. But they all wore green uniforms, whether pressed or not. The officers, or hacks as we called them, wore shirts and ties, gray dress slacks. and a blue blazer with their badges on the pockets, plus black socks and polished black shoes.

From there, we walked over to the main administration building, where on the side of the building was the infirmary and clinic.

This was where any inmate who was sick or injured would go for treatment. There was also what looked like a drive-through window at the end of the clinic for the dispensing of medications.

The clinic was run by a PA (physician's assistant) who worked for the prison system. Once a week, a dentist would come to give us dental checkups and treat us for any problems we may be having. Most of the time, if work needed to be done on a person's teeth, they would set an appointment. But every new inmate to the camp would have their teeth checked and cleaned within the month of their arrival, plus a complete physical exam to make sure they were not bringing in any disease.

If you were found to have a problem that might be contagious, you would be quarantined and sent to a medical institution. Otherwise, you would get a checkup once a year. Every morning before work, they would announce sick call for those who felt they could not work and needed to see the PA.

From there, we walked over to the weight area, passing a hack or two who just looked our way but did not bother us. I was amazed at the freedom of movement we had around the camp. Inmates were walking to and from dorms or other areas just like they would if they were back home. The place seemed very serene for the moment (that would change as soon as everyone got back from their work details).

We then entered the weight area where inmates could work out and maintain their physical well-being. It was located just adjacent to the bus area behind the dorms. It was not that big, all open with some benches to work out on and racks with dead weights on them and dumbbells neatly stacked alongside. There were a few pieces of workout equipment that you would see in any basic gym. This was one of the busiest areas of the camp and was in use daily by the inmates who had the time to work out.

When we finished walking around the camp and getting oriented to everything, it was almost time for the work crews to come back into the camp. Everyone had to be back in his dorm before the four-o'clock count. If, for some reason, you were not able to be back or were working on an assignment that prevented you from being in your dorm for count, it was your responsibility to inform the supervisor over you and inform the camp.

The prison system takes these counts very seriously. If the count is off, they have to recount everyone again. If it is still off, they are all locked down in their dorms until the count is correct or the problem is corrected. Penalties are severe for missing count, and those who miss are automatically sent to the hold for disciplinary action by the warden. He is the person responsible for everything that happens in the camp, and everyone answers to him. Our warden was a man who did not like anyone who caused problems. He would get rid of them right away and ship them out.

When we got back to our dorm, the houseman went to his cube to lie down for a few moments before things got busy. I walked over to my cubicle and climbed up to my bunk and just sat there, taking in all that I had seen and heard. At that moment, it wasn't as bad as I thought, but it was only my first day.

Men were starting to come into the dorm; they had gotten off from their work details. Some just got on top of their bunks. Others headed for the showers or wash area to clean up. In a matter of moments, the place became crowded and noisy. The guy who had the bottom bunk whom I shared the cubicle with came in and sat at his desk, writing what looked like a letter to someone. He did not say much; most of the men here kept to themselves. They did not like to talk to strangers or new inmates because they did not know if they could trust them. They were always on the alert that someone might be a snitch. The hacks would sometimes assign a snitch or stoolie to a dorm just to find out if anything illegal was going on. You had to earn the men's trust. Until then, everyone kept their distance.

A little while later, the announcement for evening count came over the loud speakers. Everybody had to be back in their dorms and beside their bunks for the camp count. Anyone not at their bunk when the hacks came by had better have a good reason why. Those who were in the shower at the time could not move from it until they were counted. After the count, they started announcing which dorms could move out to eat first.

Once you had eaten, the rest of the evening was pretty much your own. You could walk around the camp or jog to keep in shape, go to the library or recreational dorm to watch TV, work on legal problems using the typewriters, or just work out at the weight area. Some men chose just to stay in their quarters and listen to music or tapes on their Walkmans (these were allowed as long as we used headphones to avoid disturbing the other inmates).

There had been a few changes at Maxwell since the Colson era. The place was kept much cleaner and the buildings were better maintained, but morale among the inmates was still low. No one likes to be locked up and away from loved ones, even in a place like this. You could not leave any personal items out in your bunk area unattended, or they would disappear. Anything you cared about had to be in your locker under lock and key. Commissary was on Wednesdays. If you had any money in your account, it was wise to stock up on the things you needed until the next commissary day.

Compared to upper-level institutions, this was not bad, but it did have its drawbacks. The hardest is your loss of freedom and privacy. The camp was designed for about four hundred men. When I arrived, it had over six hundred. Any new arrivals to the camp who did not have a permanent assignment would be called out to do manual policing of the campgrounds at all hours of the day and night. It was the camp's way of keeping you busy and trying to see how long it would take to break you down so they could institutionalize you.

It did not matter what you did on the outside or who you were before you got here. The hacks seemed to enjoy watching you getting on your knees and picking up cigarette butts or tiny pieces of paper or any type of trash that needed to be picked up. You would have to keep at it till the area was spotless.

The camp had both male and female officers (hacks), and the majority of them were black. At times, it seemed like the female officers would enjoy checking out the showers during count or when they would just walk by anytime during the day. They enjoyed making you feel degraded, and it gave them a sense of power that they did not have on the outside or at home. You must remember, Maxwell was located in the heart of the Deep South. It was once the capital of the Confederacy. Most of the black officers and staff were born into families that were only three generations out of slavery. Most only had a high school education at the time, and this was a great paying job for them, considering the average income for black people on the outside.

Outside the camp and at home, they were just another black person of no particular interest to others. Within the confines of the prison, they were royalty. If you were a person of any importance when you were on the outside and you are white, then some of them would make their presence known to you. You get the message real fast that they are your masters and you are slaves at their mercy. Some of them seem to enjoy getting on your case so they can find any excuse to give you extra work details. Thank God not all were like that. Some of them were pretty decent once they got to know you. I would say the majority of the officers at the camp would not bother you as long as you kept your nose clean and did what you were told.

After a meal, I and a couple of other inmates were called out for a policing of the campgrounds. We were being supervised by a black female officer who told us to walk around and pick up all the cigarette butts around the compound. She looked kind of strange and kept her distance as she watched us. She did not like it when we got too close to her, and she would say, "Just stay where you are and keep busy. You don't need get too close."

I came to find out from one of the other new inmates who heard from some of the men in the camp that she had been transferred to Maxwell from a maximum-security prison a few years ago. There had been a riot, and the inmates had taken her hostage for a while and beat and raped her. She survived the ordeal, but she was never the same after that. She was transferred to a minimum-security facility after she recovered from her trauma.

She still had flashbacks from that incident, so we all tried to stay out of her way as much as we could. No one knew when she might go off on one of us and have that person placed in the hole. You never really know what type of person you might run into in a place like this.

When we finished with our detail and the officer was satisfied with the area, we all walked back to our dorm to clean up. I washed up, and I had just climbed onto my bunk to relax for a few minutes when the houseman hollered out my name.

"Hey, Kotvas, come to the front door. Someone here to see you."

I was confused. Who could it be? Was it a hack? Had I done something wrong? I did not know anyone here, so who would be calling me out? I just jumped down from my bunk and walked to the front of the dorm where I could see a group of inmates standing around outside. As I passed the dayroom, I could see a few of the men from the dorm sitting at one of the tables playing cards. They glanced up at the doorway as I walked by then continued playing.

As I exited the dorm, a tall, muscular inmate with wavy black hair turned to me and said, "Are you Joe Kotvas? My name is Nick. A mutual friend from Tampa told me you would be coming to Maxwell and to keep an eye out for you. I just wanted to see how you were getting along." He was smiling at me as he talked.

"All right, I guess. I just got here yesterday. I'm still trying to get my bearings and all the do's and don'ts about the place," I said. I guess he could see I was down in the dumps as I answered him.

"Well, I just wanted you to know, if you have any problems or you need anything, just look me up. I'm in dorm D. I'm from Tampa also, lived there all my life, and know who you are. I thought you were doing a good job. Sorry for what happened to you, man. Don't worry about anything. You'll be all right. Nobody will bother you here. I'll see what I can do to get you transferred to my dorm when an opening becomes available. You'll like it over there. It's a lot better than this one. Just don't let the system get you down. I'll see you later." Then he turned and walked away.

I could not believe it. Here was a fellow from Tampa doing time at Maxwell, and someone from home told him I would be here and to look out for me. For the first time since I got here, I felt a little relieved. I wasn't a stranger anymore. I now had a friend in this place. Nick knew a lot of the people here and was well-liked. He was a good person to know, and the word would get around that I was an OK guy. I slept a little better that night knowing that I was no longer alone.

The prison camp here was made up of all kinds of inmates. There were some ex–law enforcement officers from around the country, a sheriff or two from the surrounding area, politicians like myself, judges, drug dealers and drug smugglers, bank robbers, lawyers, businessmen, and corporate executives doing time for all sorts of white-collar offenses like tax evasion, and people who just happened to be in the wrong place at the wrong time.

Informants were moved here for their own protection and given a limited sentence. A number of inmates were transferred in from higher prisons to finish out their time in the camps so they could become acclimated back into society. We would call them short-timers because they only had a year to a few months left on their sentences before they were released.

I came to realize that I really didn't have a problem with the inmates here. Many of them were in similar situations as me and just wanted to do their time and get back home to their families. It was from the upper-level prisons that you heard all the horror stories. You kept your nose clean so as not to have cause to be sent to an upper-level institution.

By the end of my first week at Maxwell, I was finally given clean new uniforms, underwear, socks, and a pair of shoes, all with my number stenciled in. By the second week, I was given a permanent work detail. I was assigned to work at the base hospital as a clerk in the radiology department. Talk about strange coincidence. I had started out early in my career as an x-ray technician.

I enjoyed the job even though I was limited to the file room and was not allowed to walk around the department or the hospital. It was a lot better than being tied down to the camp. All the people here treated you like a human being. Although they knew I was an inmate, they did not know what crime I was convicted of, so some of them kept their distance. Overall, everyone was nice to me.

Like many of the men at Maxwell, after breakfast, I would walk over to an area where a number of what looked like old school buses would be parked to pick up the inmates and take them to their work locations. After work, the buses would pick us up at designated stops. You better not miss your pickup, or you would be written up. Sometimes they would spot search you before you left the camp. They always searched a number of the men when we returned.

Time moved slowly for me at Maxwell. Nick was a big help, and his wife and family would come up to visit him once or twice a month. He would always give me the latest news from home and help keep my spirits up. Because of the distance and limited finances my family had, I never had any visitors. When visitor call was announced on the weekends, I would just stay on my bunk as the names of the lucky inmates were announced over the PA system.

Nick was a short-timer who had done a number of years in a higher institution for drug-related charges and had been transferred to Maxwell to finish up his time. He had kept his nose clean and earned the right to be in a minimum-security camp.

The weekends were always the hardest and most depressing for me, not being able to see my children. There were a number of men in similar situations. Because of the open space of the camp on the air base, once in a while, the loneliness and isolation from loved ones caused a man to crack, and he would take off from the camp. When captured these men would never be returned to the camp.. They would be sent elsewhere, with five years added to their sentences. It has happened to short-timers with just a few months left on their sentences who received Dear John letters from their wife or girlfriend. It is so easy to slip up; you had to stay alert.

Except for the mail and an occasional phone call that I had to call collect, I would not have known what was happening to my family. Even here, my phone calls had to be limited because of the cost to my daughter. I know my daughter, Julie, was struggling with trying to take care of my son Steven and our home. I felt so helpless that I could not assist her.

Because of my situation and distance from Tampa, I was forced to ask the court to allow Ray Harris to represent me in the upcoming trial. Ray would work with all the other attorneys on our defense. There was no way I could assist him from where I was. I felt I was in a state of helplessness and was going to get screwed by the government again. I think Merkle's thinking was, if he could keep us all separated and far from our families, one of us would break and make a deal.

After a little over two months at Maxwell, while I was walking around the compound for exercise, I received a call over the loudspeakers to report to the control booth. Upon my reporting, the officer at the booth said I had a couple of visitors from the federal prosecutor's office who wanted to speak with me. Did I wish to speak to them?

I had a choice: I could choose not to speak to them if I did not want to, or I could see what they had to say. At first, I wasn't going to see them. I was still angry from all they had done to me and my family. But then I thought better of it and decided to hear what they had to say. I was escorted to a small visiting room reserved for attorneys who came to Maxwell to see their clients.

Once I was in the room, the escorting officer left and closed the door behind him. In the center was a table with two men sitting at one end and an empty chair at the other end. It was David Runyan, one of Merkle's assistant US attorneys, whom I recognized from my trial, and an FBI agent. As I approached, they introduced themselves then said, "Have a seat, Mr. Kotvas. How are you getting along here?"

I looked at them and said, "It's hard being so far from home."

"Well, maybe we can help you with that," Mr. Runyan said. "You know you have another trial coming up soon. Maybe we can make things a little easier for you. You know if you get convicted on these new charges, you may never see your children again until you're a very old man."

He was making no bones about what was going to happen to me if I went to trial and lost.

"We may even be able to help you with your first conviction," Mr. Runyan went on to say. "If you will just cooperate with us and help us with our case, we can make things a lot easier for you. You won't have to do all this time. You could be out in a short time, enjoying your family and getting on with your life. Think about it, Mr. Kotvas. If you work with us, we will see that the court is made aware of your cooperation, and we will try to get your sentence reduced and have you relocated somewhere near your home and family."

He was making a good argument for me to cooperate. I really wanted to get out of this place, even if it was better than the county jail or a maximum-security prison. But what could I tell them? I was not involved in the crimes charged in my first case, let alone in these new charges. They did not believe me then, so I knew they wouldn't believe me now. To do what they wanted, I would have to lie and make up stories for them. No, this was not me. I couldn't do that. I could not hurt people who have done nothing to me.

I just looked at them then said, "I'm sorry, but I can't help you. I have nothing more to say to you."

"Look, Mr. Kotvas, Jerry Bowmer and Charlie Bean are cooperating with us. Why don't you work with us like they are? It will be so much easier for you and your family," the FBI agent interjected.

"I'm sorry, gentlemen, but there is nothing more we have to discuss. I am not going to lie for you like Bowmer has. As far as I'm concerned, this interview is over."

I then got up to leave as they kept telling me I would regret not cooperating with them, that I was only making matters worse for myself, that I would be old and gray when I got out of prison, that I would miss all the best years of my life with my children—I could tell they were angry with me. They had thought I would be an easy mark for them and that they could bully me into cooperating. As I exited the room, I knew they were telling the truth, and I was already feeling the pain on the inside. I just prayed that some miracle would develop by the time the trial started.

I was to find out later that I was not the only one Merkle had sent his cronies to see. He sent them to see Fred Anderson and Michael Sierra, with the hopes that one of us would buckle under and cooperate. Up to this time, he had built a gigantic case mostly on the words of Jerry Bowmer and Charles Bean. He was now looking for more help to cement the charges in his new case. He needed one of us to crack, but that was not going to happen.

As the months passed, I thought of what Runyan had said. My spirits were down. Things were not looking too good for me at the moment. I was at a loss for information on how the attorneys back home were doing. When I had the chance to call home, all I would get from my daughter was that Ray Harris was working on it.

The camp would show movies once a week in the visiting hall and give out free popcorn. The inmates enjoyed this night. Some would just take the popcorn and return to their dorms while the greater number would stay for the movie. It took our minds off our situations, and we could use our imagination to take us to faraway places.

Once a week, a group from one of the Baptist churches in the area would come and hold fellowship meetings for whoever wanted to attend. They were held in the visiting area, and a good number of inmates would attend. I attended a few of them. It was a good way to talk to someone who was not always watching me. They also served refreshments, which I think was one of the reasons they always got a good turnout.

A good number of pastors from different churches around the state would come on Thursday nights to hold services with us. One of these groups was the Burdettes. They came to hold prayer meetings and fellowship with the inmates. They were a very nice old couple who had a small church near the Alabama-Georgia border. They would travel over a hundred miles round-trip to come and fellowship with the inmates. I would talk with them for a while after the services. Mrs. Burdette would always say, "When the door closes, the Lord will always open a window for you." Over time, we would become friends, and I would look forward to the meetings. It took me away for a short time from the day-to-day drudgery of the place.

On another night during the week, a Jesuit priest would come to Maxwell to hold Catholic services for inmates of that faith. I attended those services as I was brought up Catholic. His name was Father John Krozer, and he was a card. He was always in good spirits, and he always made time to hear what we had to say. He had a lot of empathy for us and would tell stories that some of us heard as children about the apostles who suffered and were imprisoned for their faith. He would hold mass and give us the sacraments. He seemed to enjoy coming to the camp each week in addition to his other priestly duties.

To many of the inmates, these fellowship breaks were a good relief from the day-to-day life we had. There was a time not too long ago when hardly anyone would even bother to come and fellowship with the inmates. If it wasn't for Charles Colson starting the prison ministry program when he got out of Maxwell back in the seventies, none of this would have been possible. I think the work that these volunteers do in the prisons is a great benefit to the system and the community as a whole.

One day in mid-November, as I was hanging out around the recreation hall, I met this one new inmate, a tall, stocky black man who lived there in the city of Montgomery before he was arrested. He wanted to know if I would like to play a game of air hockey with him. I said, "Sure," and we played and talked. He asked me what I did on the outside. I just told him I was a former public official. "What about you?"

He told me that he was a drunk out of work and had no place to stay for the winter. So he pissed on the US Post Office property in Montgomery to get himself arrested.

I said, "What?"

He explained that pissing on a US Post Office was a federal offense, and he would be tried by a federal judge who gave him six months for the offense. There in Montgomery, they sent all federal misdemeanors to the camp, which was better than staying in the county jail or sleeping on the streets. He got detox while waiting for trial in the county jail, then was transferred to the federal marshal's after his trial in federal court. The time he got would carry him through the winter with a roof over his head, three meals a day, a shower, and clean clothes to wear, plus any medical and dental care that he might need.

I just laughed. Here was a fellow who had no place to go, no job, and no money, who needed a place to stay for the winter, and who knew how to manipulate the system to his benefit. Like I said before, the place was made up of all sorts of people working some type of angle.

Thanksgiving was a depressing time for me. Sure, the camp had turkey for us all, but the atmosphere in the place was somewhat depressing. Like myself, many of the men there missed being home with their families. You just had to do your best to keep yourself occupied and not dwell on your former life and move on.

December came, and you could feel the stress in the air with the Christmas holidays approaching. Some of the men would make little gifts for their families in some of the workshops in the compound. The warden would allow certain parts of the camp to be decorated for the holidays, like the visiting area for the benefit of the family and friends who came to visit. The different religious groups who came to fellowship with us would do their best to build up our sprits with inspirational songs and prayers.

For a number of us, these were the first holidays we had spent separated from our families. Some lucky inmates had families who would come visit them on Christmas. I knew my children would not be able to be here nor anyone from my family. My sister, Rose, always had a big family dinner for Christmas, with my brother-in-law dressed as Santa Claus, giving presents to all the kids. I knew my children would enjoy that. They always got a big kick out of it every year. The best I could do was give a reverse-the-charges phone call to the family to let them know I was all right and wish them a happy holiday. Then, like the rest of the inmates, I just hang around the compound playing cards or watching sports on the television sets in the dorms or recreation areas.

A few days later, we were all called together for an emergency count. I came to find out that one of the inmates took off from the camp and was missing. For the next few days, security was tight. It seemed that the inmate took off from the jogging path next to the golf course and had his girlfriend meet him with her car down the road. They then drove off the base together.

The word came from one of the inmate clerks who worked in the administration building that the inmate had been caught hiding at his girlfriend's house and was taken into custody. We never saw that fellow again. They said he was given a hearing and more time was added to his sentence, and he was transferred to a maximum-security prison. Rumor has it that the girlfriend would be charged with aiding and abetting an escape.

It happens from time to time. I guess the temptation gets to be too much for them. Then something happens, and they snap. I felt sorry for the sap. He really messed up his life. For the next few weeks, that's all anyone in the camp would talk about.

CHAPTER 20

The Trip Back to Tampa: The Odyssey Begins

January 1986

The weather got a lot colder after the beginning of October. Everyone was issued old army hand-me-down coats and work gloves that kept us pretty warm. The temperature in Montgomery could get below freezing at times. The men who worked out in the weather, like the lawn crews, would bundle up to stay warm.

During the first or second week of December, I received a letter from my daughter, Julie, with a newspaper clipping about Jerry Bowmer being allowed to move to Tennessee. According to the article, Judge Gorge C. Carr granted a motion by Bowmer's lawyer William Lancaster of Tampa, requesting permission to travel between Tennessee and Florida, in part for security reasons.

Go figure—the guy who was the mastermind of this tragedy and the star witness for the government was still free as a bird and was allowed to buy a farm in Tennessee, plus the freedom to travel back and forth. Merkle was really giving Bowmer all the federal perks for his cooperation while he remained free on bond. He couldn't make out any better than that while others had to suffer at his expense. There were even rumors circulating that Merkle helped Bowmer acquire the mortgage for the farm. But they were just rumors, my daughter said in her letter.

The holidays came and went, and life went on as usual at Maxwell. It was a very lonely time for me without my family. The warden had a big Christmas tree decorated and set up in the cafeteria, but that only made things more depressing and hard for many of us inmates who would not see their families during this time.

During the first week of January, I received a letter from Ray Harris, my attorney, telling me that I would be returning to Tampa sometime soon for my second trial. The trial would be starting soon, and all the attorneys were required to have all their motions filed so that the judge would have time to review them before the trial began.

In a way, this was good news. I would have the opportunity to see my children again and possibly have a chance to be with my family back in Tampa. It had been a long six months since I had seen or held any of them in my arms. The scary part was what I would be facing in this new trial. Since my incarceration, I had been kept out of the loop, and I had no idea what the attorneys were planning or what the government was up to. I figured I would find out soon enough when I got home.

As the days went by, I continued doing my job on the base and returning to the camp with the other inmates on the prison van. The routine was always the same. As the buses and vans returned to camp, spot searches were made as soon as you got out of the vehicle; then you go to your dorm to clean up, with midday count before chow. The rest of the evening belonged to us, but because it was now very cold in Montgomery, most of the men stayed in their dorms hanging out in the dayroom playing cards or watching news or sports on the TV, or just staying around their bunk area. A few would brave the weather and walk around the compound or just go over to the recreation building to hang out with friends from some of the other dorms. Like most crowded places, you had your different ethnic groups that hung out together. Many of the Hispanics would congregate together and keep to their own, speaking in Spanish. The blacks had their little cliques, and the Anglos and others just did their own thing.

When my bunkmate would allow me to use the desk area, I would use the time to write letters home to my family. The fellow in the lower bunk whom I shared the cubicle with was a pretty decent fellow who kept mostly to himself. We never had a problem with sharing the desk area. He was the type of fellow who just wanted to get his time over with and go home like the rest of us. On the whole, I really did not have a problem with anyone at Maxwell. During this time, a good number of the inmates there were ex–law enforcement, former politicians, tax evaders or petty drug dealers, and those charged with a lesser offense.

On Wednesday evening, the fifteenth of January around 6:30 p.m., I was summoned to the control room. The officer on duty informed me to gather all my things together from my dorm because I was scheduled to go out tomorrow morning. This was the news I had been waiting for over a week to hear. He gave me some boxes then told me to make sure I packed everything and returned to the Receiving and Discharge room with all of it.

In a little over an hour, I was back at the control area with my personal belongings and the institutional belongings ready to be packed for storage. I entered the control room and was escorted to a Receiving and Discharge room, where I placed all my belongings on a long table, then was asked to step back.

When I did, I was told to take off everything I was wearing and to strip naked then place it all on the table in front of me. I was then searched thoroughly, bending over and spreading my cheeks as they examined me, making sure I was clean and had no contraband hidden. As for my belongings, they were inventoried and placed in a box to be stored until my return to Maxwell Air Force Base at the end of my trial.

A small box of my toiletries and papers that I would need in court would be traveling to Tampa also, but I would not see them again until I got there. I asked if I could take my Bible and rosary with me to read along the way but was refused the right to have them. I then asked if I could have some religious self-help reading material sent on to Tampa too, but that was refused also. The rosary was given to me by my mother before I left home when I had to report to the prison camp. I could not understand why it could not travel with me.

One of the officers in the room explained that I was not allowed to travel with anything on my person. I was only allowed the clothes on my back. Everything I would need would be sent on ahead to Tampa for me.

I was still naked and shivering from standing in that cold room on the frigid concrete floor. The officer told me to get dressed and report back to my dorm. I would be told when I needed to report back in the morning. I got dressed, left the building, and headed back to my dorm. The houseman said to me as I entered, "So you're to be leaving sometime tomorrow?"

"Yes," I said. "I'll know more in the morning."

"Well, good luck to you, Kotvas. I hope things work out for you," he answered.

Some of the men in the dorm heard the news and wished me well. The news of my leaving got around the compound fast. Some of the men whom I had been working with or had gotten acquainted with while I was here came by to wish me well and say good-bye. I knew some of them would not be there when I returned to Maxwell. Nick would be one of them; he was due to go home in a few weeks. He had served his time and was looking forward to rebuilding his life and being with his family again. He was a big help to me, getting through the transition there.

When it was time for lights-out, I climbed onto my bunk and just stared at the ceiling, thinking. I knew it would not be long before I would be back in Tampa—hopefully, by tomorrow night. After all, it was only about an eight-hour drive from Montgomery to Tampa, Florida. I wondered what type of transportation I would be traveling in, then tried to get some sleep.

The next day, Thursday, January 16, I was awakened at 5:00 a.m. by one of the corrections officers, who told me to get dressed and report to Receiving and Discharge. I got up fast, dressed, and went to the washroom to clean up a bit. I had to borrow some soap and a comb to clean up. All my toiletries had been boxed up to be shipped to Tampa. When I finished, I quickly walked over to the Receiving and Discharge building.

As I entered, one of the officers in the room said, "OK, Kotvas, over here, and strip down to bare skin. Put everything on the table in front of you."

I complied as ordered. Once naked, again they gave me a thorough strip search. I find this type of search filled with indignities, but I guess it is necessary, considering the different types of people who are incarcerated. I was told to lift my arms then run my fingers through my hair, turn around, and bend over. Then I was told to spread the cheeks of my butt and lift my genitals to demonstrate that nothing was concealed. Then I was asked to lift each foot one at a time and then to extend my hands forward and turn my palms upward. When they were satisfied I was clean, they told me to get dressed and sit on the bench in the corner of the room.

By now, it was a little after 6:00 a.m., and the Silver Bullet that would be taking me to Tampa had arrived. I was told to step outside and wait by the doorway. The bus looked like a big Trailways bus, but with bars all around the windows. It pulls into Maxwell once or twice a week. When the bus arrives, there is no movement allowed by any of the inmates on the compound. It is like a temporary lockdown till the bus leaves. The inmates jokingly call it the *Silver Bullet*. A number of US marshals stood around the bus with sawed-off shotguns. It was not yet dawn, and I was very cold standing out there in just a short-sleeved shirt. My guess was that the temperature must have been around thirty-five degrees.

I had to stand out there for about twenty minutes with my teeth chattering until I was told to go back inside the building. What a relief. It was warm inside, and it felt good. After a few moments, the lieutenant from the bus came in and ran a chain around my waist, then a pair of handcuffs through the chains, and the chain was wound around my waist again. The effect was to attach my wrists to my waist in order to negatively affect my balance. Then he attached ankle bracelets around my ankles to make it difficult to run off. It also made it difficult to walk; you had to take short steps. Then, and only then, was I taken on board the bus. The bus was almost full with other prisoners being transferred to different locations. It was a motley bunch of fellows, some clean-shaven, others with beards or unshaven stubble. Some looked like they hadn't had a bath in over a week. I was placed midway on the bus in an empty aisle seat.

We departed Maxwell AFB around 7:00 a.m. The sky was starting to get lighter, and the sun was just starting to come up. It looked like it was going to be a nice cold, clear day. I found myself looking forward to returning to my hometown and seeing my family again. I knew this bus trip should only take eight or nine hours to get to Tampa. So once I was locked into my seat, I just settled back, thinking I'd be in Tampa for supper.

By the middle of the day, we stopped for lunch. The marshals gave us all boxed lunches, which had been packed at one of the institutions along the way. Inside my box were two sandwiches (one with American cheese and the other one with what looked like compressed chicken, both on plain white bread), plus a piece of fruit and a small plastic bottle of water. There were no condiments for the sandwiches. We had to eat them just how they gave them to us—dry.

When we finished, a marshal collected the empty boxes and plastic bottles; then we started to move again, heading south. Our first stop was at the Okaloosa County jail in Crestview, Florida, where we picked up and dropped off another prisoner. After everyone was settled in, we continued to head south.

From Okaloosa, we went on to Eglin Air Force Base, which also had a federal work camp. I was feeling good right about now, for we were now in Florida. Upon arrival at the camp, the marshals got off the bus with their shotguns and circled the bus while they brought out another prisoner to transport somewhere. His name was Robert, and they locked him in the seat next to me. He was formerly a banker from Tennessee and was being taken back to Tennessee to be a witness at the trial of a friend of his.

When we left Eglin, we traveled back to the Okaloosa County Jail to pick up yet another prisoner, who was also in cuffs, chains, and leg shackles. This was how the US Marshal Service transported all its prisoners. From this second Okaloosa stop, we then headed east on US 10 toward Tallahassee.

It was now about 6:30 p.m. when we arrived at the Tallahassee federal prison. Looking at the place, you could see that it was an old prison with high walls and guard towers, surrounded with razor-wire fences. It was a dark-gray and ugly-looking place, much worse than where I had been at Maxwell. I realized then how lucky I had been. Although I was tired from the long day's bus ride, it was a nice feeling to realize that I was only four hours from Tampa.

We were all told to stand up and exit the bus. We would be spending the night here. We were all taken to an intake area where our shackles and cuffs were removed; then the corrections officers at the prison recuffed us as the marshals departed.

It wasn't until sometime around 9:00 p.m. that I was placed in a cell with one other prisoner, who happened to be Robert, the man who sat next to me on the bus. They issued us each two sheets and a pillowcase. It was cold in that cell, but the prison would not give us any blankets. They also issued us a toothbrush and toothpaste. There was no soap, or washcloth or towels, or any shaving gear. That part had some logic to it. There were no showers in the cellblock we were in. The only thing we had in our cell was a couple of iron bunks drilled into the walls, with an all-in-one stainless steel cameoed with a small sink on top that had one spigot you pressed down on for water to drink or wash. I noticed a stale, musty odor of urine along the cellblock.

On Friday morning, January 17, around 3:30 a.m., a prison officers came by with trays holding our breakfast on them. Shortly after we had our breakfast, some officers came to take Robert and me back downstairs for another strip search. After the search, I was informed that I would not be going directly to Tampa, even though it was only four hours away. The officer in charge told me that I was scheduled to go back to Alabama. I was being transferred to Talladega to wait until the marshals from Tampa came to get me. This all seemed crazy to me. It made no sense.

I was placed on another bus with only a few fellow prisoners on it. We left Tallahassee about 5:30 a.m., and the bus drove straight through to Talladega, Alabama. It was still before noon when we arrived at the Talladega prison. The place was a fairly new facility. It had a double razor-wire fence all around the place, with gun towers placed every so many yards apart. It was a chilling sight to see the razor wires all through the fences.

It kind of reminded me of the old WWII POW camps, or concentration camps, that I had seen in the movies, but more modern. I was taken to Alpha Unit, which was built on the plan of a circle, but the cells were arranged like the seats of a theater, in an arc, and stacked two units high, upper cells and lower cells with a catwalk and stairway to the upper level. Here again, it was the same routine: fill out forms, strip naked, be searched, and then be issued clean laundry (undershorts and an orange jumpsuit).

This place was unlike any place I had ever been in, even in all my years as a police officer. The cell doors were solid steel with a small window at eye level and a hatch toward the bottom where the food was passed through. The cell I was placed in was empty, and I was impressed that it was unusually clean. There was no smell of urine in this facility. The walls were cinder block, freshly painted in an off-white, cream color. The cell also had a ceramic toilet and separate sink. The entire cell was no more than the size of a utility closet and designed for two adults. It had a small window in the rear that looked out upon the backside of the prison and the wonderful open fields beyond.

I came to find out that one of the rules was that once a prisoner is assigned to Alpha Unit, he was not allowed out of the cell except to be escorted somewhere or because of sickness. The only sight of other human beings was through the small hole in the door. I felt totally isolated and alone in that cell. There was absolutely nothing to do and nothing to read. I was left to sit or pace the small area. After a while sitting in total isolation, I called out to one of the officers sitting at the control desk in the middle of the cellblock and overlooking all the cells.

When he came over to see what I needed, I informed him that I would like to have, if possible, a Bible, a pencil, and some paper. It was evening before they came back and gave me the Bible to read. I never got the pencil and paper that day. The Bible was some comfort. It triggered memories of all the people and voices of those folks back in Tampa who had prayed with me before coming to prison. With the Bible in my hands, I felt less lonely but still extremely isolated from humanity.

By Saturday, January 18, I was still at Talladega with no news about getting to Tampa. I had been sitting isolated in this cell for two days with no one to talk to and the officers only looking in on me through the peephole to see if I was still alive and in my cell, or passing the food trays to me through the open slot in the steel door when mealtime came around.

After two days of asking for a pencil and paper, I was finally given some writing utensils. This was when I started to keep a chronological record of my experience through this ordeal—partly to pass the time and partly to help keep my sanity. It also helped that I could make notes and scribble thoughts in preparation for my legal defense.

At about six o'clock each morning, the officer came by and opened the little hatch through which the food tray was passed through and kept it open until they closed it around 6:30 p.m. This was the only window that a person in that cell could see out into the main area of the cellblock. Without a watch, without a clock, without a calendar, it was all the more important for me to stay oriented. My only way of telling time was to ask when they brought my food or to watch the dawn and the dark from the little window in the back of my cell. Other than that, there was nothing to do. I just spent my days lying on my bunk, staring up at the celling, or reading different parts of the Bible from time to time, always coming back to the story of Job for some reason, or pacing the little area I was in. The isolation in those cells was enough to drive a sane man crazy after any length of time. The Alpha Unit in that institution was where they housed the most dangerous and violent inmates who were too dangerous to be placed in general population. It was like a solitary-confinement unit where once you're in it, you have no physical contact with anyone else in the institution at any time, except for the officers who watch over you; and even they stay at a distance, only talking to you when it was necessary.

For me to be in this place and treated like this was madness. I was a nonviolent inmate charged with a white-collar crime, no history of violence, a former police officer and politician, sent to a minimum-security prison, yet they were treating me like the most violent and dangerous of criminals.

Why was I brought here when I was only four hours from Tampa just a few days before? Nothing seemed to make sense the way the government did things. You cannot tell me this was cost-effective. Could it be something the prosecutors wanted me to experience in an attempt to break me down? Who knows. The day just passed as slowly and silently as the day before.

By Sunday, January 19, I was looking real raunchy and feeling worse. The small hatch had just been opened for the day, and it was close to 6:00 a.m. It reminded me of how you keep and feed animals in a cage. I could not remember when I had a shower or shave. I just felt so dirty that it made me feel less than human, just another animal in a steel cage. I had not had a change of clothes since I arrived there. A shower would be a blessing; I was beginning to stink and could imagine what my cell must smell like.

I could hear movement outside my cell, so I got on my knees and looked through the open hatch to see what was going on. They had three prisoners shackled in chains and were escorting them out to what they called the recreation area just outside the cellblock. The officer passed me without saying a word. About an hour later, the prisoners were brought back into the cellblock and returned to their cells.

There was no place to sit in this cell except on the bunk, the floor or the commode, with no back support. While lying on the bunk and sitting in odd positions all this time, I had been developing pain in my lower back. *Talladega* will forever be an ugly word for me.

While the prisoners were outside for their rec time, one of the officers came over to my cell and said, "Kotvas, get up, turn around, back up, and put your hands through the open slot. I'm taking you to the shower."

I got up from my bunk, walked over to the steel door, turned and put my back against it, bent down a little, and placed my hands through the slot in the door. The officer proceeded to cuff me, then told me to step back as he opened my cell door. He told me to come out; then he put shackles on my ankles so I could only take small steps while I walked.

With my hands cuffed behind me and my feet shackled, I hobbled over to the shower area that was at the far end of the cellblock. Once at the shower, he removed my leg shackles and told me to stand to the side. The shower stall had a grated steel door that the officer opened for me as I walked into it. He then closed and locked the door, which also had a slot opening in it, and told me to turn around and put my hands through it. I put my back to the door and placed my hands where he could remove my cuffs. I undressed and passed my smelly clothes through the slot in the door. I then began to shower. The water was cold, and I was shivering under it, but it felt good to be clean again. When I finished and dried off, the officer handed me a clean pair of boxer shorts and another jumpsuit, which I immediately put on. There was no privacy in this place; they watched every movement that you made. When I finished, I was told to turn around and put my hands back through the slot; then I was recuffed. He then opened the shower door, asked me to step out, and reshackled my ankles; then I hobbled back to my cell.

Again the same routines here: unshackle, go inside, turn around, and put my hands through the opening to be uncuffed. Now that I felt a little clean again and had been out of my cell for a while, I could smell the faint odor of my body that had been lingering in the cell before my shower. I guess they didn't provide air fresheners.

The Dog Pound

Around noon, for the first time, I was given the opportunity to have some sort of recreation. An officer came by my cell and had me go through the same routine, then escorted me out a side door that led to the outside rec area. I could not believe what I saw: the area had three long totally fenced cages that resembled what looked like dog pounds. If anyone has ever been to an ASPCA animal shelter or a veterinary's holding area or Human Society shelter, you would know what I mean. I was amazed at the comparison.

The officer opened the one at the far end, and I entered it after he removed my shackles. Then he locked it behind me and left. As I stood there, I realized how cold it was outside. My guess was it was in the low forties with a windchill that made it seem colder. A few moments later, they brought out two more prisoners who were placed in the other two cages. None of us had anything warm to wear. The officer at the far end of the compound who was watching us had a nice warm coat and gloves on. But they would not issue us any warm clothing. All we had on were our short-sleeved cotton jumpsuits to try and stay warm in.

Each of the three areas that we were in was long and narrow, about half the size of a handball court. I could picture in my mind a dog running up and down in this area like they do at the pounds. I guess the system thinks that because we are considered criminals, we should be treated like dogs. On the ground at the far end of the cage was a basketball, nothing else. I walked over to it, picked it up, and found out it was half deflated. I don't know what they expected me to do with it since there was no hoop in any of the cages. You could not even bounce the ball; it was so flat. I guess this satisfied the rules of the system by calling this recreational equipment. So all I could do was pace up and down the cage and try and keep warm.

I was a bit elated, for now I had someone I could see and talk to. However, the man in the next cage was from Cuba and spoke no English. The other man on the other side of the Cuban was also a Cuban, but he could speak English and was also desperate for someone to talk to, so we shouted back and forth to each other. It was good to talk to someone, even a stranger, for a little while. We shouted across the cages for a short while, but the cold was getting to us. I kept walking and jumping around in that cage to keep warm as I continued to shout over to the other guy. In a short while, I was getting really chilled, and without pockets, I had no means of warming my hands. I just tucked them under my armpits to try and keep them warm.

I did not realize, nor did anyone tell me, that once we came out, we could not go back inside until our hour was up, so we just walked and shivered out in that cold, hoping not to get hypothermia before our time was up. When it was time for me to go back inside, I couldn't wait to get back into my warm cell.

If they ever wanted me to go out again, I would pass until summer came. Being isolated in my cell was bad, but freezing out there was worse. The food they served us was edible, which is all I could say about it. The food at Maxwell was much better. If I was forced to stay in Alabama, why didn't they just take me back to Maxwell? It wasn't that far away.

I tried to settle in for the night, but the pain in my back was killing me. To take my mind off it, I would read the stories in the Bible. I enjoyed reading about the saints who were unjustly imprisoned, and I tried to relate my own situation to some of theirs.

On Monday morning, January 20, I woke up with severe pain in my lower back. It wasn't just from here. It had started when I was in Tallahassee lying on those cold steel bunks, and it had gotten worse each day. When I tried to get up, I could barely stand or bend over. I slowly made my way to the open hatch on the steel door and called out to the officer who was sitting at his station monitoring the cellblock. I called out that I was in pain and needed to see the physician's assistant. He just looked over to my cell, then continued doing whatever it was he was doing.

Finally, after several pleadings, he came over to my cell to ask me what all the shouting was about. I explained my pain and my situation and that I needed to see a physician's assistant for the pain in my back. He said he would put in a request and notify him when he made his rounds, but for now, there was nothing he could do for me. By late in the afternoon, the physician's assistant came by and gave me some ibuprofen for my pain. It did give me some relief, but my back was still hurting.

Those of us in public office would never have seen or been aware of any of this. All of this was a real eye-opener. The public and the politicians have no real concept of what happens to a person once they enter the prison system. I thanked God for giving me the opportunity to share this burden. As I thought to myself, maybe in some small way, I could help others open their eyes and their hearts to help bring about some changes in this system. Treat a person like an animal, and he will behave like an animal. Treat a person like a human being, and he will behave like a human being.

Now it was Tuesday, January 21, and it was the sixth day of my confinement while still in transit from Montgomery to Tampa. A little after daylight, I was told to come out of my cell. I was being moved. I was taken to a holding area where there were already a few other prisoners waiting to be moved also. I was then told to get out of my jumpsuit and strip naked. Again I spread my legs and bent over as they searched of me. I was given old frayed undergarments (shorts and a T-shirt) and an old pair of pants, but no shirt or coat to wear. I was still wearing the old canvas deck shoes I was given when I started to travel. After I dressed, they shackled my legs, chained, and cuffed me so I could only take small steps at a time.

We were all taken outside into the cold and told to get onto the bus that was waiting for us. Again the bus looked like an old Greyhound or Trailways bus, but the prisoners (depending on where you were) called the bus *Jailways*, or the more common term *the Silver Bullet*. Our destination was the Birmingham, Alabama, airport, going to parts unknown. I wondered if this would be my final move before I got to Tampa. The Feds knew I had a court date coming up, and I needed to be back in Tampa soon.

On this same day back in Tampa, Fred Anderson's attorney Robert Polli filed an emergency motion with the federal court, stating that Mr. Anderson had received abusive treatment at the hands of the US marshals during an attempt to bring Mr. Anderson back to Tampa last week.

He explained to the Judge that Mr. Anderson, who had been confined to the medical facility at the federal prison in Lexington, Kentucky, was subjected to a fourteen-hour travel schedule, causing Mr. Anderson to have an angina attack. He was cuffed to his waist, stuffed in a car with two other prisoners, driven from Lexington to Terra Haute, Indiana, then put on a plane for some city in Virginia. Then he was flown to Birmingham, Alabama, before finally going on to Oklahoma City, Oklahoma.

Mr. Polli also told the Judge that Mr. Anderson was overcome by "excruciating pain in his chest" and was taken to the medical facility at the federal prison in nearby El Reno, Oklahoma, for observation and treatment.

US district judge George C. Carr, acting on Mr. Polli's motion, ordered that doctors examine Mr. Anderson when he arrived back in Tampa to determine if he was medically fit for his upcoming trial.

He also ordered that US marshals take extra care when bringing Mr. Anderson back to Tampa later that week, before his Friday's medical examinations.

CHAPTER 21

The Odyssey Continues:
The Flight to El Reno

January 1986

When the bus arrived at the airport, we all got off and hobbled over to board the big 727 jet that was owned by the Justice Department and flown by the US Marshals Service. The Justice Department owned a few of these planes to transport prisoners all over the country. These planes are known to the inmates who have been transported by them as "Jail-Air" or "Con-Air Airlines." The plane had a number of marshals standing around it with shotguns ready for any type of trouble that might occur.

(Nearly a decade later, I would see a movie starring Nicolas Cage called *Con Air*. Boy, did that bring back a lot of bad memories. I have to say, except for the type of plane used in the movie and some Hollywood theatrics, it was a fairly accurate description of how the US Marshal Service picks up and transports prisoners.)

Once aboard the plane and seated, the marshals chained each of us to the floor of the plane so that we could not leave our seats unless the marshals unlocked us. This kind of gave us the feeling that if anything would happen to this plane, the marshals would have an opportunity to save themselves, and we would go down with the plane. It also brought to mind the old Roman slave galleons, where they chained the prisoners to their seats, and they had to row for the Romans into battle. If the galleon got rammed and was sinking, all the prisoners on board would go down with the ship, chained to their positions.

From Birmingham, we were flown to Richmond, Virginia, to pick up more prisoners, then on to Lewisburg, Pennsylvania, to let off some prisoners and pick up a few more. I wondered if I would ever get to Tampa. This all seemed like an unnecessary way to travel.

After Lewisburg, we set off for Terre Haute, Indiana, to let more of us off and pick more up. We only stayed in each city for an hour or two until all the paperwork was done and the count was correct. Then we took off again, but now our destination was Springfield, Missouri, again to let off and pick up more prisoners. When we left Springfield, the plane headed for Oklahoma. After a long and tiring flight, we finally arrived at Oklahoma City, our last stop. This was nowhere near Tampa, and it was freezing outside the plane.

Some of the marshals got off the plane and secured the perimeter holding their shotguns while a few of the others on the plane started to unshackle us from our seats. We were ordered to get up and hobble over to the bus that was waiting for us outside a little distance from the plane. We all hobbled as quickly as possible in the freezing weather over to the bus that we all hoped would be warm, for none of us had any warm clothing on. It did not matter who we were or what we had done. All we were to them were just convicts on the move. It had snowed this day in Oklahoma, and snow was piled high everywhere around the airport.

Once we were all on the bus and the bus was secured, we left for the prison in El Reno, Oklahoma. We had left Talladega around 7:30 a.m.; it was now around 8:30 p.m. Thank God the bus was warm. It was dark and cold outside as the bus drove toward the prison. The bus seemed to be pretty full with all of us and the marshals who were escorting us. We were not able to see anything out the windows as they were frosted up, but what we could see looked very deserted, flat and desolate.

When we arrived at the El Reno prison, it looked like something out of an old prison movie. It had large dark-gray stone walls with huge gun towers with catwalks around them overlooking both the inside and outside of the prison. Razor wire wrapped all around the ramparts, and floodlights illuminated the inner and outer compound. There was a large solid iron gate that the bus drove through before driving through another gate to the receiving area.

At the receiving area, we were ordered off the bus and told to walk inside the building. We all hobbled off the bus in our chains as the cold air hit us like a sheet of ice penetrating our flimsy clothing. Here in the receiving area, again we were asked to strip out of our clothes till we were all standing there naked as they searched each of us before giving us all some used uniforms to wear. After everyone put on the uniforms, we were all given some clean linen and a blanket and then escorted through a passageway up a stairwell to the third level of the prison, where we entered a large holding cell. The cell was already crowded with men sitting or sleeping three rows high on bunk beds.

The cell had a sort of houseman who looked after the place and assigned bunk space. Due to the overcrowding, a number of us had to sleep on mattresses placed around the floor and hope no one would step on us getting on and off their bunks.

I estimate the cell must have had around twenty-five to forty men in it, give or take a few. Space was very limited as they kept pilling more prisoners into the place as others left. Showers and toilets were off to the far end and open for everyone to see into. No one had any privacy, and some men had to sleep on the floor just beyond the toilets. The place stank of stale air, cigarettes, and body odors, and looked like something out of a Russian gulag.

I found an available mattress and placed it in a corner on the floor before someone else claimed the space. I put my sheet and blanket on it, then sat down and looked the area over. This was a temporary holding area, which housed all sorts of men from all over the country who had been convicted of all sorts of crimes but were not considered a danger to the other inmates in this cellblock. Everyone here were waiting to be moved to other institutions, or going for a court appearance just like I was, or just waiting to be assigned to a cellblock in this institution. The place had an officer in a closed secure partition area off to one end of the cellblock who oversaw the area to make sure there were no problems and to answer any concerns that any of us might have. He also kept the count for the cellblock and announced who would be moving out the next day to catch the Jailways bus.

As I sat on that thin mattress, I tried to get some rest, but the place was noisy, and people were constantly moving about. About 10:00 p.m., right after the count, the officer said lights-out, and everyone went to their bunks or mattresses to turn in.

The next day, Wednesday, January 22, lights came on around 6:00 a.m. as we all got up to take turns using the wash area and toilets. I thought I might see Fred Anderson or Mickey Sierra coming through here, but I did not see anyone I knew. Even here, not much had changed. None of us could leave this holding area or join the general population. We had to stay until our name was called to be shipped out again.

We were totally confined to this area for the duration of our stay. Looking out the huge windows that were covered with large iron bars on the outside, all you could see was the rooftops of the prison and the gun towers. The prison would serve us our food on trays that they would bring into this holding area for us. We were not even allowed to eat in the prison cafeteria. You ate whatever they gave you, or you went without. The food left a lot to be desired, but I ate what I could and always drank the milk and would trade my fruit or dessert for extra milk at times. There was always trading of food or other items going on between the prisoners. In the prison system among the inmates, if you needed or wanted something from another inmate, there was always a tradeoff.

The houseman saw to it that everyone had a place to sleep, and he was also responsible for the cleaning up of the showers and toilets. I noticed someone who looked like an American Indian who was partially paralyzed on one side of his body helping the houseman. His right side from his arm to his leg was paralyzed, and he dragged his right leg when he walked. This was Oklahoma; many Indians lived there and in the surrounding reservations.

I found out later that the poor man had been shot by the police while trying to run from a grocery store after stealing a couple of steaks and putting them down his pants. He was not armed, just trying to get away and back to his family with the food. He was a very poor Indian who owned nothing and was out of work, looking for a way to feed his family, I was told.

The store owner had seen him take the meat while looking at the mirror over the meat section and notified the police officers who were nearby. When they tried to approach him, he ran off; and one of the officers pulled his revolver, called out for him to stop, and then fired one shot that struck the fellow in his back, hitting his spine, and causing him to be partially paralyzed. Seeing he was an American Indian and the robbery took place on Indian land, when he got out of the hospital, he was tried and convicted in federal court. The judge, looking to make an example of him, sentenced him to five to ten years in prison, without regard for his wife, his children, or his injury.

He ended up doing his time here at El Reno, making around fifteen cents an hour and picking up any odd jobs he could find to make a little extra money to send home to help support his family. I could not believe the lack of sensitivity the system has for these people.

None of this made any sense to me. Here we are in the twentieth century, and we still treat these people like animals. Look at what the white race did to the American Indians. I once read in a history book that by 1905, the census for the total population of all the Indian nations in the United States was about five hundred thousand in a country that once had tens of millions of Native Americans. This was a true genocide by all those who came and took these lands from them. By the time the late seventies rolled around, the census had slowly increased to over a million or more.

What we did to these people continues even today; many still treat them as subhumans, without concern for their rights or property. I could feel for what happened to this poor man, which made me feel very ashamed. I wished there was something I could do for him, but I couldn't even help myself at the moment. I would always remember what I saw there, and someday I hoped to try and make some small difference.

By Thursday, January 23, not much had changed, but I was now able to use the phone in the cellblock. Everyone was given a number and time they could use the phones, but we all had to reverse the charges. I was worried I would not catch anyone at home, but as luck would have it, I was able to get word out to my children that I was all right and tell them where I was. I told my daughter to inform Ray Harris about what was happening to me and to ask him to look into why I was not in Tampa yet.

After all this time, it felt good to hear the voices of my children and my mother as each one came to the phone. Then after about ten minutes, I had to relinquish the phone to the next inmate. It was amazing how a week ago, while I was being transported within the system, I was in Tallahassee, only a little over four hours from Tampa. It is difficult for me to understand why the government was spending so much of the taxpayers' money to ship me and other inmates all over the country. I wondered if Fred Anderson or Mickey Sierra were going through the same situation as I was and being transported all over the country like me. Where could they be now? Had they made it to Tampa already, and was I the only one still in transit? I know the prosecutors said they would make it hard for me. Was this part of it? Only time would tell.

On Friday, January 24, I was awakened in the middle of the night by the officer on duty in my cellblock. He told me to get ready because I would be leaving on the plane at 4:00 a.m. After I dressed, I was escorted downstairs to the intake processing center. As I walked into the area and looked around, I saw Fred Anderson for the first time. He was standing in a corner in one of the holding areas next to a number of other prisoners. He was not looking too well. His skin looked clammy, and his color was kind of grayish. His eyes seemed dark and sunken into his skull with a glassy stare.

They placed me in the same holding area that he was in. The place was dark and dingy, with poor lighting and what looked like mildew around the walls. I quickly walked over to him and asked how he was doing. He told me he hadn't been feeling too good, and all this travelling hadn't helped him. He informed me about the angina attack he had a couple of days ago and how they placed him in the infirmary for observation when he arrived there.

It was good to see a friendly face for once, but Fred never smiled the whole time we traveled together. I asked him how long he had been there, and he said a few days now. They had kept him in the infirmary because of his heart condition. I informed him that I also had gotten there a few days ago, and they had kept me in a large holding cell all this time. Before we could finish our conversation, an officer shouted out for all of us to strip down naked and stand in a single line as the officers walked down the line and searched each of us.

It was very chilly in that room, and everyone was shivering standing there on that cold concrete floor. When the search was over, we had to wait a while before they started to issue us clothes to wear. They gave me an old pair of khaki pants and an old khaki shirt, but no undershorts. For Fred, they gave him a pair of khaki pants and only an olive-green T-shirt to wear. We had no socks and only worn-out canvas deck shoes to wear.

At this point, we all lined up again while they chained and cuffed all of us. Then they put the ankle braces on our legs to make it difficult for us to walk. As much as I hated it, I knew this was the standard procedure for all law enforcement agencies when transporting prisoners, and I had to get used to it. This procedure makes it difficult for a person to run and helps deter the urge to escape.

It was freezing cold outside the processing room where our bus was waiting to load all of us on. All the officers and marshals were wearing warm parkas and gloves while holding on to their shotguns. They told all of us to step outside and wait along the wall as they made the bus ready. We could feel the freezing cold wind blowing in from the open door. Many of us asked if we were going to be given coats to wear because it was freezing cold. Of course, the requests were denied. They said we would not need them because it wouldn't be that long before we were on the warm bus.

Once outside, standing next to the wall of the building, many of us tried to huddle together to keep warm. It had to be below freezing out here, and the marshals were nice and warm in their parkas while we were freezing. It seemed like some of them enjoyed watching us freezing as we stood there. We could hear some of them laughing and whispering to one another as they looked us over. It would appear that this was a sadistic game for some of them.

We were forced to stand out there for almost a half hour without any warm clothing, but it seemed like an eternity. We had nothing but the thin shirts on our backs. It seemed like they were having a little problem with our bus and had to drive another bus to the area to take us on. Again we had to wait in the cold until they got that bus warm and ready for the trip.

By now, it was obvious it was going to take a bit longer to get the bus ready, so they told us to go back inside the holding area until they were ready to leave. Thank God, what a relief to be back inside. We were all shaking and shivering from the cold, but we didn't have that icy-cold wind blowing on us anymore. Once the bus was ready, they escorted us out of the building again, and this time, right onto the bus. It was a blessing; the bus was warm. The time was now close to 6:00 a.m. and still dark outside. Fred and I sat next to each other for the ride to the airport. We did not say much to each other as we sat there. I could tell that he was not feeling well. He just stared silently most of the way.

When we arrived at the airport, the bus drove straight to where the plane was and then stopped a little distance from it. We were ordered off the bus as they checked our prison numbers and counted us while we all exited the bus. Then again, we were counted by the marshals from the plane as we hobbled aboard. Fred and I stayed together as we boarded the plane, and luckily, we were assigned seats next to each other as they locked us in.

This was the first time I really got to talk with Fred since he did not wish to say too much when we were back in the holding area or on the bus. Fred always had a fear that Big Brother had ears and eyes everywhere and would be listening in on anything we might say. He informed me how he too was badly treated during his transfer period from Lexington, Kentucky, to Atlanta, Georgia, to here, en route to Tampa with me.

Fred was still not looking well. He looked more like a character out of an old Bela Lugosi movie than anything else. I was hurting inside for the way they were treating him. We had both been feeling the power of the federal government.

Upon leaving Oklahoma City on the Con Air 727 jet, we flew to New Orleans, Louisiana, to pick up a few more prisoners. We stayed at the airport no more than thirty minutes, and when everyone was secured in their seats, we then took off again.

CHAPTER 22

The Odyssey Goes On:
Miami Federal Correctional Center

January 1986

After leaving New Orleans, we were headed for the Miami, Florida, area, where we landed at the Opa Locka Airport in the early afternoon. Here, we all were unlocked from our seats and told to line up outside the plane where a bus was waiting to take us to our next destination. As we exited the plane, it was so exhilarating to smell and feel the clean warm Florida air in my lungs again. My spirits started to pick up, for now I felt it would only be a matter of hours before I would back in Tampa and could contact my family.

Once we all exited the plane and lined up for the count, Fred Anderson was called out and taken away from the rest of us as two marshals who were dressed in suits came forward, signed some papers, and escorted him to a waiting van. The rest of us, including myself, were told to board the waiting bus. Why take Fred and not me also? Even though the final destination for Fred and I was the same place, I had to ride on the bus with the rest of the prisoners to another location. I had no idea where they were taking Fred; they never told us anything. But I was hoping he was headed for Tampa and that my turn would be soon. Again, I could not understand why they would take one of us and not both of us in the same van. They had plenty of room. It appeared to me that this would be more cost-effective. That was the last time I saw Fred until our trial began back in Tampa.

The bus left the airport with the remaining prisoners and me, headed for the Federal Metropolitan Correctional Center (MCC Miami). By 3:00 p.m., we arrived at MCC Miami for processing. As we drove into the center of the facility, I could see a number of large and small buildings clustered together with a courtyard in the center, with a number of outbuildings off to one side. Also, there were large open areas all around the place.

The institution was surrounded by high chain-link fences three rows deep going all around the compound with gun towers on the outside placed every so many yards apart. On top of the fences were razor wires woven all through and traveling the length of the fences. In between two of the fences was a vehicle security road for the officers to drive around the prison, checking for any type of security breach. The area was a far cry from the institutions I had previously been to. I could see inmates walking freely around the main area of the compound, but the bus was going over to one of the large buildings away from the main compound, which looked very secure.

When the bus finally stopped to let us all out, we were on the far side of the institution. We exited the bus then entered the two-story building for processing. By this time, it had been over twelve hours since any of us had anything to eat. We all explained to the processing officer at the facility that we had not eaten all day and were very hungry. The fellow just simply ignored our needs and put us all in holding cells until we could be processed.

No food was forthcoming. By 8:00 p.m., many of the prisoners were starting to holler and make all kinds of noise, saying that they were hungry and had not eaten since early morning. It was not until 8:30 p.m. when an officer escorted a trustee into the processing area with a cart containing sandwiches and juice. We each received two dry bologna sandwiches and a six-ounce can of juice. This was all the food we would get until the morning. Here again, the same routine: they strip-searched us then gave us clean jumpsuits to wear.

I and two other prisoners were then separated from the others who would be sent to general population. I and the other two prisoners were sent to another two-story secure building that had a chain-link fence around it with razor wire all along the top, and you had to walk through a locked gate before you got to the steel front door of the building. The place was off to the side of the general compound. This unit I was entering was a maximum-security unit where they kept dangerous and high-profile inmates. (This is the same unit that, a few years later, would house Manuel Noriega of Panama, after he was arrested by the US government.)

Once we were in the building, I could see the place had a good number of private cells, upper and lower levels with a catwalk for the officers to make sure everyone was in their cells. The place was squeaky clean, and the floor shined as if it had just been waxed. There was no smell of urine or mildew in the place. There were a number of steel tables with four round seats attached to each of them in the center of the cellblock. I could see officers working in the control booth and officers walking out on floors, looking into some of the cells. I was issued a mattress and pillow, clean sheets and a blanket, and also some toiletries. You had to ask for a razor and return it when you were finished using it. They would give you a disposable razor to shave with. I was placed in a cell on the lower level all to myself. *Great, another solitary unit*, I thought to myself as I settled in for the night. The ten-o'clock count was about to begin, and everyone had to be in his cell for lockdown and lights-out. *At least this place is clean*, I thought as I attempted to get some sleep.

Saturday, January 25, lights came on at 6:00 a.m. Then someone opened my cell door and left it open. When I stuck my head out to see what was going on, I noticed most of the cell doors were open, and some of the inmates here were walking in and out of their cells. I came to find out that I did not have to wear cuffs in this unit. I could move around and talk to any of the other inmates in this unit, and I would feel a little more comfortable now that I could finally shower and shave. I was also able to call home from one of the phones that were attached to the wall at the far end of the cellblock next to the control room and let everyone know that I was all right and where I was.

They would bring our food over on carts from the main kitchen and have the trustees dish it out to us on food trays. We would then sit at one of the tables and eat. After the meal, they would collect all the trays and utensils then take them back to the main kitchen for cleaning. I have to say, the food here was a lot better than what they gave us on the road at the other institutions.

Although this was a maximum-security unit, as long as we did not cause any problems, we had freedom of movement inside this unit. If you were a troublemaker or causing problems, you would be sent to the hole, where you would not see daylight until they let you out. No one was allowed out of this building. They had a small recreation area next to our building, fenced in and isolated from the rest of the center, where we could go out to walk around and get some sun, or shoot a few hoops on the small basketball court made for this unit, or work out with some of the weights in our area to try and stay fit. This area was separated from the rest of the population, and one had to have special permission to enter.

Sunday came around, and it was now January 26. Not much was going on in the unit. I talked with some of the other inmates who had been there for a while. They informed me that after they did a thorough check on your background and they didn't find any problems with you, after a few days here, you might be transferred out to the main unit.

It was still morning, so I walked over to the officer monitoring the unit and asked about church services and if some of us Christians could have Bibles so we could fellowship together. The officer informed me that I would have to speak to the chaplain about it later in the day, and those services were to be held around 5:00 p.m. that day.

As five o'clock came around, there was no chaplain and no church service for any of us. During the time I spent in this unit, no chaplain ever came by to see any of the inmates or hold any type of service. As the day grew old, I figured that services in the prison must be over by now, so a few of us got together to pray among ourselves.

Don't get me wrong, I had never been one for praying or religion or anything like that in the past. And this was not some act at playing jailhouse religion that goes on in these places all the time. Only, ever since I received that phone call from my friend Bob up in New Jersey about my wife a few years earlier, it had changed me in some small way, and I found myself praying again that something good would still come from all this.

Late Monday morning, January 27, nothing much was going on when I was informed by the duty officer to get all my things together. I was going to be transferred into the population. As I walked over to my cell, I looked over to one of the few TVs in the unit. A number of the prisoners and officers were watching the *Challenger* shuttle takeoff.

At around 11:35 a.m., as we all watched the shuttle taking off into space, a few moments later, we all saw it explode in the air. There were all kinds of shouts by everyone. Someone said, "Wow."

Another said, "Look at that, can you believe it?"

Another cursed and exclaimed, "They're dead."

Others just said, "Oh my God, I can't believe this."

I could see tears on some of the inmates' and officers' faces as they looked on in disbelief as the news commentator tried to explain what was going on. The compassion these inmates had for those poor souls on that shuttle surprised me. They may be thought of as scum and hard criminals, but they were still human beings with human emotions.

We were all in shock at what was happening on TV. It was all anyone could talk about in the unit. Sometime around noon, I was escorted to the main compound with some of the other prisoners, all carrying what little belongings we had. As we exited our unit, most of us looked up to the sky to see if we could see anything.

Even here in the Miami area, you could look up into the sky toward the northeast where the cape would be, and everyone here could see the smoke plumes high in the sky. Except for us, there was not much movement around the compound. Everyone was glued to any TV set that was available.

As we continued on, I was taken to a large building three stories high and escorted to the second floor, where I was assigned to Unit "B." This unit had over 140 men in it—all crowded together. The area in which I was assigned to sleep was formerly an old TV room. It was small, and there were over ten of us assigned to sleep in it. There was one toilet and one sink nearby that twenty men had to share.

Space was at a premium. Even the TVs in this unit were crowded around, with everyone listening to the news about the disaster.

The building had administrative offices on the first floor, with housing units on the second and third floors. The one good thing I found while settling in was that someone had left a Bible in the unit for anyone who wished to read it. I think it must have come in handy for anyone who wished to pray for the souls on that shuttle.

Once I got settled in, I walked outside the building and looked up. I could still see traces of the plumes of smoke lingering high in the sky. Under my breath, I just said, "God, have mercy on their souls." I knew there was nothing anyone could do. It was in God's hands now.

All that day and into the evening, all anyone could talk about was what was on the news in relation to the *Challenger* disaster. Even there in prison, one could see the sincere compassion that many of these men felt for those astronauts and their families. It kind of took away our troubles for a while. Society may deem these men as heartless criminals, but they are also human beings with feelings. The same way this disaster affected our country, it affected everyone in that institution.

The next day, Tuesday, January 28, I awoke early in the morning to such a joke. There we were, twenty of us trying to use the one toilet and sink, all within the thirty minutes before going to the cafeteria to eat, then being hustled off to our assigned work details to start the day. There were only eight showers in the entire unit for 140 men. I had been assigned as one of the unit's orderlies to sweep the unit and take out the trash and also clean the shower stalls.

Even today, all anyone talked about was the *Challenger* disaster, and they kept most of the TVs on the news networks. This also helped to keep their minds off their problems and focus on something else. They had a chow hall here, where they served halfway decent food to all of us. This place was very spacious and spread out. One could get enough exercise just walking from building to building.

By Wednesday, January 29, the buzz around the compound was not so much centered on the shuttle anymore. Life was getting back to its normal routine. By midafternoon, I was able to see one of the caseworkers and ask about my legal mail and legal papers, which had been taken away from me back in Talladega last Tuesday. These were the legal papers I had been working on for my attorney, which I would need for my pending trial. I had been working on them while I was in solitary confinement there. I had been asking about them ever since I arrived in Miami, and all I got was the runaround.

The mail from Talladega to Miami should not have taken that long, two days tops. I attempted to stress the urgency of finding them since I needed my notes to prepare for my upcoming trial within the next week. The fellow informed me that because of the severe cold weather affecting the telephone lines up north, he could not call Talladega to check on my mail; they were having a winter storm. He said I should come back tomorrow and see him, and he would see if he could get through by phone to Talladega. There was nothing more I could do at this point but wait till tomorrow. It was enough to get me feeling depressed.

The next day, Thursday, January 30, after my chores, I proceeded back downstairs to see the caseworker again. After waiting about a half hour, I was able to see him. He informed me that he had gotten through to the authorities at Talladega that morning, and they had informed him that they had mailed my legal mail to a holding center in Jacksonville. It had gone out on the twenty-eighth in care of the US marshal of the Middle District of Florida.

He then called the marshal of the Middle District and was told that my legal papers and mail had not yet arrived, but when they did, they would be forwarded to Tampa. This was the first bit of help and good news I received in two weeks from this entire traveling nightmare.

Around 12:30 p.m., I was called out to report to the R and D center for processing. When I arrived, again I was told to strip naked so they could search me, then put on clean clothes. They gave me my civilian clothes that I had worn into prison last August. It was amazing. These clothes had followed me all the way here, but everything else that I needed was still in transit.

There were two US marshals waiting for me to finish so they could take charge of me. After I finished dressing, one of them came over to me and put a chain around my waist and then cuffed me and ran the chain through the cuffs. They did not shackle my legs. While I was standing there, another marshal did the same thing to another prisoner who was also going back to Tampa for trial.

The marshals who had come for me were from the Tampa office, and they came in a white van. For the first time in a long time, I was being treated as a real person—a human being. Although the chains had to be on, these marshals tried to make the trip from Miami to Tampa as comfortable as possible for us. We arrived in Tampa about seven hours later, where the marshals then turned us over to the Hillsborough County Sheriff's Office to house me till the duration of my second trial.

The driving distance from Montgomery, Alabama, to Tampa, Florida, is about 450 miles, but that odyssey of fourteen days by bus, airplane, and van covered the equivalent of more than 4,700 road and air miles. What would normally have been just a ten-hour road trip took a total of fourteen days.

To this day, no one can convince me that the shortest distance between those two points was a roundabout trip of nearly five thousand miles. The cost in manpower, fuel, food, and housing has to far surpass the cost of a few hours of overtime for a couple of US marshals driving a van over a normal eight-hour workday.

These two weeks of traveling seemed like a lifetime for me. It had been an unbelievable nightmare that I was glad was over. I am grateful, however, to have been allowed to see these things, these people, to feel these conditions. As much as it was a twilight zone for me, this is a condition that every prisoner lives with constantly. They are in this system every day, undergoing this type of treatment for weeks, and maybe months, of confinement while in transit.

The things that happened to me on that trip were not exceptional. I realized I was not being singled out for any special treatment, better or worse. And this is the frightening fact about it all, that these conditions I have described are enforced every day, right now, and will be tomorrow and the tomorrow after that, until someone makes an effort to deliberately change and improve the system.

Not only were there needless indignities, but there was the sheer terror of knowing that the bus you were on could catch fire or the plane could crash, and we would not be able to move to safety. Our very lives were at the mercy of the marshals who were transporting us. I would always wonder if some accident should befall anyone traveling this way, who would the keepers stop to save first? Would they save one another and run off, or would some stay to help the less fortunate who were chained to their seats? Thank God I never had to find out.

CHAPTER 23

The Hillsborough County Jail

January 1986

While I was still in transit to Tampa, I heard there was a little setback in the government's case. It seemed that by the end of the first week in January, six of the defendants indicted in this massive corruption case had been severed from my second trial that was coming up. US district judge George C. Carr had held a hearing on the matter of the six and ruled in their favor.

Unlike the rest of us who faced racketeering and conspiracy charges, these five men and one company faced lesser charges. The judge said they would be tried at a later date after the upcoming trial ended. Our trial was supposed to start sometime around February 3 and would last about six months.

Judge Carr further explained that each of these separate trials was expected to last no more than a week, with one exception, the trial for Tampa lawyer Paul Johnson. That trial might last two weeks. Mr. Johnson was being represented by the well-known attorney F. Lee Bailey.

This was a major setback for the government. The government knows that when you try a number of defendants in a group, they all get caught up in one another's charges. It's a numbers game with the government, one that is well used even today. When a jury hears the testimony and sees what evidence the government has, even if one of the defendants is innocent, if they think one is guilty, then they assume all must be guilty—and the government wins.

When you're severed and tried by yourself, you have a better chance of winning your case. The government is never happy when this happens.

What I heard was that assistant US attorney Joe Magri argued in front of Judge Carr for the government, saying, "The bottom line is that the evidence in this case will show that there was a corruption train in Hillsborough County. These defendants were part of that train. When they paid that bribe, they knew what they were participating in."

The judge, without challenging the government's evidence, ruled that it would be fundamentally unfair to force the lesser defendants to attend a trial that could last as long as eight months when separate trials for each would last no more than one or two weeks. He said, "A jury at the end of a six- to eight-month trial might have difficulty parsing out the evidence and distinguishing between those defendants charged with racketeering and those charged with lesser offenses."

According to an article I read from the *St. Petersburg Times* about the ruling, Mr. Johnson, standing with his attorney F. Lee Bailey after the judge had ruled, said, "A separate trial means that when I get my trial, I'll be tried on the issues in my case and not the issues in someone else's case."

The other four defendants and one company that also were severed and would have separate trials were Lois Rocha, a Tampa consultant; Lois Bailey of Snellville, Georgia; Nelson Italiano, who owned Italiano Insurance Agency and was a former patronage chief in Tampa for former governor Reubin Askew; Manuel Fernandez, a Tampa contractor and former Tampa city councilman; plus Columbia Paving Inc. of Lakeland, Florida.

When I arrived in Tampa, I was turned over to the deputies at the Hillsborough County Central Jail located in downtown Tampa next to the apex of interstates I-275 and I-4. I was placed in a temporary holding cell and then reprocessed into the county system. After being photographed and fingerprinted and signing more papers, I filled out my visitors list so my family could visit me while I stayed there.

I was then escorted to a room to strip down and was searched and given an orange jumpsuit to wear. I placed all my clothes and my few belongings in a plastic tub. Then I was told to hold my hands out. They cuffed me then gave me a thin mattress, sheet, blanket, and small pillow to carry and escorted me to the second level, down a corridor that had large holding cells at the other end and a few solid private cells along the sides. You could smell the foul odors of urine and cigarette smoke coming from these holding cells. The corridor and cells looked dirty and dingy. I was placed in one of these single solitary cells that had two doors to enter. One door was solid steel with a small window that had a steel cover over it so the guards could look into the cell about eye height, and a tray slot toward the lower part of the door. The other door was made of bars of steel with a tray slot at its lower end. It was basically clean but looked well used.

The cells were maybe six by eight feet, with a stainless steel commode and sink all built into one unit at the far end of the cell and a stand-up open shower stall across from it. Bolted to the wall was a single steel bunk bed where I placed the thin mattress, sheet, blanket, and pillow they gave me. There were no windows in the cell, and the walls were made of steel. It had a fluorescent light sealed on the ceiling at the top center of the cell, plus a large lightbulb on the ceiling between the two steel doors. Down the hallway of the cellblock were the population cells that housed a good number of prisoners in each of them. Those cells were for prisoners who were going to court the next day or waiting to be assigned a permanent cell or would be transferred to another facility. The main cells for those doing time here were on the next two levels.

For some reason, I was not assigned nor placed in the general population. I was placed in this isolation cell away from everyone. Again, this was a cell that was used for the most violent of criminals or prisoners being punished and sent to solitary confinement. I guess they thought I was some kind of dangerous person who needed to be watched.

Once inside the cell, they closed and locked both doors. From where I was, there was nothing to look at but the four walls and steel doors. Every now and then, an officer would open the little window and look in on me to see what I was doing. I had no other human contact. The first night there was a hard one for me. All night long, I could hear the men down the hall in the population cells yelling, laughing, and screaming at the guards and one another. The sound vibrated off the steel walls. All I could do was just lie there. Even when it was lights-out, the noise did not stop. When the large light went out in my cell, the small light between the two steel doors stayed on all night, keeping my cell well lit.

I would just lie there, tossing and turning trying to find a comfortable position. (There was none.) When morning came, the big light came on and a little while later a food tray would be passed through the slot in the first door that I had to walk over to and reach through the slot on the door facing me to reach the food tray at the other slot. They never opened the outer door, just passed everything to me through the slots and looked in on me through the little glass window every so often. The food was not very good, but it was all I was going to get until the next mealtime.

During the day, things seemed to get very quiet along the cellblock. Most of the men housed there were either in court or being transferred. The few who were left were probably sleeping after being up all night. I had no watch; it was removed from me with all my belongings during transit. The only way I knew it was day or night was by all the hollering when the men came back to their cells at the end of the day from court. Then the noise and screams would go on all night long. The only time to rest was during the day when they were all out.

At the time, I had no idea how long I would be in that cell under those conditions. By the looks of things, it was to be my new home for a while. Between the noise going on all night and the total isolation of my cell, it was maddening.

By the second day, I was allowed to make a reverse-charge phone call from the jail. I called my house and tried to reach my daughter. When she answered, her voice seemed so wonderful to me. She told me everyone was worried since no one knew where I was or what had happened to me since my last call. I told her to get a hold of my attorney Ray Harris and let him know where I was and to come and see me, also to tell my sister, Rose, I was all right and that I was in the downtown county jail.

After a couple of days without any more communication with anyone and no visit by my attorney, I was beginning to worry. My legal papers and notes finally caught up to me and were delivered to my cell. This was a big help; now I could start working on my situation. I still had no clue on what was going on with my case and when the trial would start. At night, all the noise and banging on the cell bars and walls made getting any rest difficult. I would dose off from time to time but awaken every time there was a large bang or disturbance. From time to time, I could hear officers outside my cell running down the cellblock to quiet some disturbance in one of the holding cells.

On one particular night, someone in one of those cells set his mattress on fire. I could hear the deputies running back and forth and calling for fire extinguishers to be brought up. They put the fire out before it could do any damage, but you could smell the odor of smoke on the cellblock for a couple of days. Things like that happened every once in a while in the county jail. Those were the cells where they housed drug addicts, alcoholics, and all sorts of characters. This is why no one slept around there in the evening; it was the liveliest place around. When you're in an isolation cell 24-7, it has a way of playing with your mind.

At times, when I did doze off for a while, I would wake up with little red spots on my arms or chest. I would soon find out that they were from roaches that had been crawling on me when I fell asleep. I could see them moving about when I would lie still. Due to the total isolation I was in, they were the only company I had to talk to. I managed to catch one and placed him in an empty Styrofoam cup that I had with a cover to keep him in. I assume it was a him because I had no idea whether it was a male or female. I just needed some company and anything living to talk to. All those days of solitary isolation were starting to get to me.

On Monday, February 3, Ray Harris came to visit me at the county jail. It was a relief to see him again after all that time. We were placed in a special attorney-client visiting area where we could talk without anyone listening in. He finally brought me up to date on everything that was going on. Ray informed me that Claude Tanner had hired a top-notch trial attorney out of Miami by the name of Joe Bealer, supposedly one of the best in the country since this was going to be a long trial, with so many defendants being tried together. He must have been some big attorney, for Mr. Tanner was paying him one million dollars for his time and travel back and forth from Miami to Tampa to represent him throughout the entire trial. The majority of the other attorneys felt that Mr. Bealer, because of his reputation and experience, should be the lead attorney for the group, and Ray seemed to agree.

From what I was told, most of the attorneys representing the other defendants were being paid anywhere from around thirty thousand dollars to a quarter of a million. Mr. Bealer was the highest paid of them all. I, with no money, could only afford a court-appointed attorney. I know that even though Ray was a public defender, he was trying his best for me. But Ray Harris just didn't seem like the same man anymore. He looked tired and not well at all. When I asked him about it, he just said that it was the medications he was on that made him tired, but he was all right. For the time being, I let it go. At that point, there was not much I could do, or so I thought at the time.

I knew from when we first met a couple of years ago that he was suffering from some unknown illness that he picked up in the service when he was stationed in Japan many years ago. He also suffered from diabetes and was taking a lot of strong medications for both of his problems. Some of them would knock him off his feet after he took them, so he would take those at night. Others left him in something of a twilight state and caused him to doze off every now and then. But he was all that I had to help me, so I had to make the best of the situation. At the time, I had no idea what my options were.

He informed me that they had been holding strategy meetings with everyone to make sure they were all on the same page. There was a lot to go over, and Bealer wanted to make sure everyone was willing to work together and would share any information that would help us all.

Ray then asked how I was holding up, and I informed him about my ordeal in arriving. Ray told me he would be filing a motion with the court to see if I could be put on house arrest until the trial was over. Surely, it was obvious that I was not a flight risk or danger to anyone.

He then said that Fred Anderson had arrived back in Tampa a week before, and his attorney had filed a motion with the court for house arrest because of his medical condition. The judge had Fred evaluated by court-appointed doctors to verify his condition. When their report came back, the court granted his motion, and Judge Carr had him placed on medical house arrest over Magri's objections. The prosecution was hoping to use Fred's condition to continue with their intimidation, with the hopes of getting Fred to break and make a deal. Because of the incident that happened during the first trial and because it was obvious that Fred was not a flight risk, the judge was inclined to cut Fred a little slack. He was required to wear an ankle monitor at all times and was limited to court appearances and doctors' visits only.

My heart skipped inside of me at the thought that I might have a chance to be placed on house arrest also. This way, I could be reunited with my children and family, work on my case with Ray and the others, and sleep in my own bed for a while. Now I knew where Fred was taken when they split us up after our flight. I couldn't have been happier for Fred that he was given this opportunity to be home with his wife and daughter. It would be far better than staying in that jail. Knowing his condition, I couldn't say how long he would have been able to last before something bad would happen to him.

Then Ray informed me that Michael Sierra's attorney Ray LaPorte had not heard anything from Sierra and did not know where he was. All he knew was that he was still somewhere in transit and was expected to have arrived in Tampa by then.

We talked about the charges I would be facing, and Ray said he was working on that and that he needed to get all the information he could about what really took place. It would help him if I kept notes on anything I could remember, no matter how small or insignificant it might seem.

When we finished, Ray left, telling me he would be back in a day or two. He had a few motions he needed to work on before the trial. I didn't tell him about my friend the roach, which I was keeping in my cell. When the meeting was over, I was escorted back to my solitary cell.

Back in my cell, time moved very slowly for me. I would pick up the cup with the roach in it and talk to him, asking how his day had been and telling him about what was going on with me. All he would do was just stand there looking at me, wiggling his antennas. I named him Harry for no reason at all. It was the name that just came to me at the time.

Harry was helping me keep my sanity. I would take notes of my situation and surroundings to help pass the time. When they would pass my food tray to me, I would put a little something in the cup for Harry. For the next few days, Harry was the only friend I had in there.

It's funny how your mind works when you're locked up 24-7 with nothing to do in your cell but wait, work on your notes, and talk to a roach. My mind would reach back into my past and work its way forward to how I got here. All the things I had done over the years to help others, it all seemed for nothing since none of that mattered anymore in my situation.

My thoughts traveled ever further back in time, beyond my days of being a city council member, past my days of being a police officer here in Tampa or back in New York. For some strange reason, they took me back to a time in my life when I was a young married man just starting out with my life. Even then, I guess I was kind of a rebel, trying to help people and change the establishment.

I don't know why, but I started remembering back in August of 1963. I was one of those white Freedom Riders people read about in the papers, a white person driving a car full of black people from the Bronx, New York, to Washington, DC, for the civil rights march on Washington. I was around twenty years old then and had only been married for a year. I remember how my wife worried and did not want me to go. She worried about all the stories we would hear on the news about the civil rights movement and what was happening to Freedom Riders in different parts of the country. Like many other young white folks, I believed in the civil rights movement and in equality for all, and I felt I needed to do something to help.

The march on Washington

I remembered the drive down from the Bronx to New Jersey, then through Delaware and Pennsylvania, a car or bus full of other Freedom Riders broken down on the side of the road, waiting for a repair truck. Those of us who came from the north never ran into too much trouble, but some from the South were having a hard time of it. The news media never really talks about it, but in all that crowd that attended that March, a quarter of the people who took part were whites. We all got to hear the Reverend Martin Luther King's speech " I Had a Dream," although our group was situated toward the back of the crowd. It was a scorching hot day, as I remember. The National Guard had trucks with large water tanks situated throughout the area for the large crowd and ambulances for heat exhaustion or medical needs. When our group returned home to the Bronx late that evening, it was without incident.

I remember telling Bob Guilder the story about it here in Tampa years later. He was a friend of mine and former director of the local NAACP. I even showed him the button I had kept all those years that we all wore at the time. Maybe that was one of the reasons why I got along well with most of the people on Main Street in West Tampa, where I used to walk the beat as a Tampa police officer. The area was a predominantly black business district that had supported me on my first run for the Tampa City council. Boy, some of the things that run back into your mind when you're totally isolated from everything. Now look at where I ended up.

It wasn't until a couple of days later that I was finally removed from my cell and given my civilian clothes, which my daughter had brought to the jail a few days earlier for me to wear when I had to go to court. As soon as I got dressed, I was transported to the federal courthouse, where I was placed in a holding cell in the office of the US marshal. Early in the morning, as I sat in that cell, they brought in Michael Sierra and placed him in the cell with me. Boy, was I happy to see a friendly face!

We gave each other a hug and shook hands. After a few moments of asking each other how we were holding up, I told him all about my traveling odyssey and what had happened to Fred Anderson. When I finished, he went on to share with me what his experience had been.

He told me about the conditions he lived in up north. He had been put in a cell on the second floor of a prison in Duluth, Minnesota, and the snow on the ground was as high as his window. It was freezing cold there. He had to jog in the snow whenever they gave him his hour of recreation. Michael went on to explain that getting to Duluth, he was given a bus ticket and was allowed to travel on his own to get there. When it was time to make the trip back to Tampa, he was put on the Silver Bullet bus, and the driver presumed he was a flight risk, so he put a chain around his waist, handcuffed him, and then ran the chain through the handcuffs, allowing him very limited motion (this brought back my own experience).

From Minnesota, the Silver Bullet then traveled to Marianna, Indiana, where he had to stay for a couple of days at a maximum-security prison. From there, he was placed on another Silver Bullet bus and taken to another federal facility somewhere else in Indiana. The weather there was cold as all get out; plus they would not give any of them coats or warm clothing to wear. The only piece of top clothing he had on was a short-sleeved shirt as they traveled.

The bus then traveled from Indiana all the way to some place near Boston, Massachusetts, where there was an airport. The Silver Bullet pulled into a side entrance at the airport and drove down the road a little way to where a plane was waiting for them. They all exited the bus then boarded Con-Air to their next destination. They told him they did not have any room for all his legal papers and that they would be shipped later and catch up with him in Tampa. So all his personal belongings that had traveled with him this far were left on the bus, to be shipped at a later time.

When the plane took off, it flew to someplace in the Carolinas where he said he was picked up by two US marshals as he disembarked the plane. One of the marshals was George Rodriguez, whom he knew from his law practice back in Tampa. They put him in a van, and they drove from the Carolinas to Tallahassee, where they spent the night. Then the next morning, they drove on to Tampa. He told me that he had just arrived there in Tampa late Saturday night just before his court date, with nothing more than the flimsy clothes on his back.

When he finished talking, we just sat in that holding cell waiting to be taken before Judge Carr. We were waiting to hear if the judge would consider our motions for house arrest that Michael's attorney had filed earlier and Ray had just filed on my behalf.

After about two hours of waiting in that cell, the marshals came and escorted us over to the federal courthouse. When we arrived, both our attorneys were standing there in front of the judge's bench, waiting for us. The judge had not arrived in the courtroom yet. I could feel my heart pounding in my chest as we approached them.

We were all talking for a few moments before the door to the judge's chambers opened, and Judge Carr walked out into the courtroom and seated himself behind his bench to begin the hearing. We all stood facing the judge as he informed us that he had received our motions and would be rendering a decision shortly after the government filed their response and he had time to review the matter. With that said, we were returned to the custody of the US marshals and escorted back to our holding cell, waiting for transportation back to the county jail. We stayed in that holding cell most of the day, and they gave us plain dry baloney sandwiches to eat with a piece of fruit and a bottle of water. This was all we had until they transported us back to the county jail late in the afternoon.

When we arrived back at the jail, as soon as we changed back into our jail jumpsuits, Michael Sierra was taken back into the general population, and I was sent back to my solitary cell. When I arrived back at my cell and the deputy opened my cell door, I noticed things in my cell had been moved around, and the cell had an odor of bug spray. I asked the deputy why my things had been moved. He informed me that the exterminator had been by the cellblock spraying the whole area for bugs. He then closed and locked the two doors to my cell, and I was alone again.

I immediately started looking for the cup that I had placed Harry in. I could see a number of roaches lying dead around the corners of the cell, and then I found Harry. The cup was at the side of the box that held some of my legal papers. It was tipped on the side with the cover off. Harry was still in it, but dead. They had done a good job of spraying my cell; I guessed I would not be bothered by roaches for a while.

It is hard to explain to anyone what it was like to be locked in an isolated cell 24-7 with a light on all the time, not seeing or talking to anyone day after day. Unless you have been in a situation to experience it, you can have no real concept of what it was like. My little friend was gone now, and I felt sad and empty inside. Again, I was really all alone, with nothing more than my own mind to entertain me.

CHAPTER 24

Let the Games Begin

February 1986

Throughout the time of my conviction in my first trial and right up to this second trial, Merkle and his staff had been very busy. He was living up to his nickname *Mad Dog Merkle*. Because of the growing popularity in the community that he was receiving after my first trial, through the press and the public, he felt he was invincible and could do whatever he wanted to our community. With Jerry Bowmer and Charles Bean making up whatever stories he needed to hear, Merkle felt he had a blank check to turn the lives of anyone he wanted in Tampa and Hillsborough County upside down.

Like the Joe McCarthy (Republican US senator from Wisconsin) investigations, whose witch hunts of the early '50s fueled the fears of widespread Communist subversion throughout the country, Mr. Merkle felt the need to start his own witch hunt on the words of Bowmer and Bean to spread the fear of widespread corruption within our community, using reckless and unsubstantiated accusations, as well as public attacks on the character of local and state officials, plus our good citizens as a whole.

He used the power of his office to have his staff and agents intimidate and threaten anyone and any business that had dealings with any level of government. He was looking into the dealings of the Tampa city council, the mayor's office, the Hillsborough County Commission, our judges and state attorney, plus some of our state legislators. His agents and assistant prosecutors would pay visits to businessmen at their offices or their homes, or the homes of their employees and relatives.

At the time of my arrest back in 1983, I had a small personal phonebook that I always kept with me, with names and numbers of my family, friends, and frequent contacts. This had been taken from me and copied by members of Merkle's staff to be used to contact those individuals in hopes of trying to get more incriminating evidence on me and others. I'm sure they did the same to the other defendants who were on trial with me. Mr. Merkle was able to manipulate the grand jury. He was a very charismatic person. Apparently, this was the same grand jury that had issued our new indictments this past May. Mr. Merkle was now having them focus on new allegations of corruption in both county government and the state attorney's office.

Merkle felt he was God's gift to the justice system, and he had contempt for EJ Salcines and his office as state attorney. He felt sure if he pushed hard enough, he would find something on EJ (as he is called by his friends and most of the people who know him), or on some members of his staff that would tear apart the state attorney's office.

The Honorable EJ Salcines

In 1983, EJ Salcines, as a courtesy, voluntarily appeared before the federal grand jury not once but twice to answer any questions the jury or federal prosecutor might have. For over two hours, Mr. Salcines answered all the questions asked of him on both occasions; plus he provided files, turned over a number of cases as requested, and made available assistants whom the government could interview. He gave Merkle and the grand jury his full cooperation because he had nothing to hide.

Since Mr. Merkle did not find what he wanted on Mr. Salcines in his first or second visit, in 1984, Merkle invited him back again for a third and fourth visit to the grand jury, in hopes of entrapping Mr. Salcines with his questions. On the third visit, Mr. Merkle started attacking Mr. Salcines and his office with a vengeance. Realizing what Mr. Merkle was up to and refusing to be railroaded, Mr. Salcines invoked his Fifth Amendment rights.

Although Mr. Merkle was unable to get any indictments against Mr. Salcines for lack of any proof or any witnesses of wrongdoing, Merkle got the satisfaction of causing Mr. Salcines to take the Fifth and injure his career as the state attorney. If he could not get EJ Salcines, he would go after members of his staff to further damage the office of the state attorney. By this time, Merkle had been conducting a yearlong witch-hunt investigation into the office of EJ Salcines. He had no direct proof to back any of his claims because they were all bogus, just based on his gut feeling. But in his mind, he truly believed that Mr. Salcines was somehow corrupt. He was going to use all the legal means that he had at his disposal—and allegedly some that were not—in his effort to bring down Mr. Salcines. He had turned this into his personal crusade.

Up to this time, Mr. Salcines had been the state attorney for Hillsborough County for sixteen years and a shining star in our community. But because of the extreme prejudice by the federal prosecutor's office and amid widespread publicity about the investigation and the indictment of his former chief assistant Norman Cannella on charges that he fixed cases for members of an alleged drug ring, Mr. Salcines's star came tumbling down, and he lost his bid for reelection that year to Bill James, another former federal prosecutor. This opened the door for Mr. Merkle to investigate Mr. Salcines on two fronts.

Merkle, in a meeting with Governor Bob Graham, was able to get the governor to request a special investigation into Mr. Salcines. Mr. James, at the request of the governor, ordered a special state probe into Mr. Salcines's affairs. A state grand jury was convened, but after a lengthy investigation lasting over a year, they could find nothing unethical or illegal with Mr. Salcines's conduct.

During this same time, Attorney Barry Cohen, who represented EJ Salcines, said, "Merkle is intent on ruining Salcines. He wants to get EJ, and that's all there is to it. He doesn't care what he has to do. He's been looking, looking all this time for anything, and he is still looking."

Mr. Cohen even took out a full-page ad that read, "Merkle's McCarthyism mentality is a threat to innocent people." He asked the justice department to look into the tactics and conduct of Merkle's office. At the time, the justice department did not find any fault with Merkle. However, as time would prove, Mr. Cohen was right on the money.

Merkle was a man who could not stand criticism, no matter how minor it might be. To criticize him would put you on his "someone to look into" list, and he was looking into a lot of people. He had the power and was using it to his advantage, even if it meant crossing the line to get a conviction. He would invite people to talk with him or the grand jury. They would come in good faith; then he would come at them in bad faith to rattle them and confuse them until they told him what he wanted to hear.

The tactics he was using on witnesses during this time must have been the same tactics he used on the witnesses in my first trial, like Attorney Steve Reynolds, who changed his statement on what really happened to fit Merkle's examination to the jury. Mr. Merkle was not only an expert but a master at intimidating and manipulating the people he interrogated.

Upon the arrest of Norman Cannella, the former chief assistant state attorney under EJ Salcines, Mr. Cannella's good name was dragged through the mud by the media on information from the federal prosecutor's office. He appeared before the Honorable Terrell Hodges, chief justice of the Middle District Court. Merkle had led the grand jury to believe that Mr. Cannella had taken $75,000 in bribes to protect a supposed Tampa drug ring.

Mr. Cannella's trial lasted seven weeks before the government rested its case. Lee Atkinson was the lead assistant US attorney for the trial. Before the judge turned the case over to the jury that Monday morning, Judge Hodges asked Mr. Atkinson if there was anything more he wished to add to the indictment. Mr. Atkinson said, "No, Your Honor."

From what I could gather, the judge recessed the hearing until after lunch to give Mr. Atkinson time to add any additional information to the indictment for the court and the jury to consider.

Mr. Paul Antinori, representing Norman Cannella, made a strong point in his motion to the court to acquit his client based on hearsay evidence. The judge would give his decision on the motions after lunch.

Back from lunch, and before the jury was to be called back in, Judge Hodges quizzed Mr. Atkinson sharply on the government's conclusions based on their evidence against Mr. Cannella. He asked if this was all the government had to present, and Mr. Atkinson said it was. He told the judge that he knew the evidence against Mr. Cannella was circumstantial but felt it was strong enough for a conviction.

At this point, Judge Hodges agreed with the defense and said, "Based on the lack of evidence, hearsay, and circumstantial evidence, I find it is equally consistent with innocence, and I am ordering a directed verdict of acquittal for Mr. Cannella." The court then apologized to the defendant for the way the government handled his case, and he was free to go.

Scenes like this would go on for the next couple of years in Tampa. The agents would come in pairs, with no warrant or concrete evidence, only hearsay, under the ploy of just wanting to talk to someone about one thing or another, asking if they knew or had knowledge of any wrongdoing by the person they were inquiring about. They would sow fear and insinuate threats of possible indictments on conspiracy or obstruction of justice just to try and get someone to give someone else up. All this had been going on for some time now, and the community and press were starting to take a different look at how Mr. Merkle was running his office. With the new trial about to start soon, he was hoping to add some big new indictments to his credits. His list of unindicted coconspirators was growing. While all this was happening, he was starting to alienate a lot of his supporters, including the press.

It was the beginning of February now, and so much was happening. With so many people being indicted and possibly more to come, the motions and countermotions were flooding the court. Looming over the heads of our community, the government so far had a list of well over two dozen unindicted coconspirators, who, through the grapevine, reportedly included prominent members of our political and business community. Who they were and why they were targets, none of our attorneys could find out because a federal judge had sealed the list. Some of the names were expected to come out at our trial. Merkle's office had announced that the grand jury was expected to act again soon. The possibility of more indictments coming out during the trial had the defense attorneys nervous. This was one of the reasons why so many members of both Tampa's legal and political community were anxiously awaiting the start of our trial.

By this time, Norman Hickey, the county administrator whom we had appointed during my first year as county commissioner, had resigned. He had accepted a position as chief administrator for the San Diego County out in California. He was our county administrator during the worst days of the alleged corruption trial.

My attorney Ray Harris informed me that Jan Platt, Pickens Talley, and Rodney Colson had been subpoenaed to testify in my trial again. The government was going to use a lot of the evidence from the first trial to establish the racketeering charges, including the tapes they recorded of Bowmer coming to the commission offices.

While most of the commissioners chose not to say much about the trial or the defendants, Jan Platt had been quite vocal on the stand in my last trial and in the press throughout this time. I still could not understand why she of all people voted for the zoning I was convicted of. There is an old truism that states, "He or she that protests the loudest has something to hide."

Jan Platt

I would like to make it perfectly clear: I am not saying that Mrs. Platt had done anything wrong, nor am I accusing her of anything. To this day, I have no knowledge of any of that. She is what she is, Miss no vote on all major developments. She was always trying to be the darling of the county commission and was one of the key pet witnesses for Robert Merkle's witch hunt. It left a lot of unanswered questions in my mind—why no one would ever take the time to look into her voting record or family affiliations. I guess everyone was too busy looking into everyone else; they wanted bigger fish to fry.

By February 3, the trial was starting to get underway. The process of jury selection was beginning. The courtroom was a circus of lawyers, prosecutors, defendants, reporters, and spectators. The court had moved our trial to one of the larger courtrooms to try and accommodate everyone. Someone from my family would try to come to court every day to give me moral support and bring me some good Cuban coffee and toast early in the mornings before the trial would begin. Whenever possible, my mother would try to be in court every day when she was able to get someone to bring her. I have to say, some of the court bailiffs and marshals were sympathetic to my situation and looked the other way when I drank the coffee. I always had to finish it in a hurry so no one would get into any trouble.

Those few moments were great; it made me feel human again and that people still cared. As a whole, most of the people who worked at the federal courthouse were very decent and kind.

The regiment had begun. In the morning, I would get up and get dressed for court. The US marshals would pick me up very early and transport me to the federal courthouse, then escort me to the courtroom. This was how it would be until the trial was over.

On the evening of February 4, I was told to get my things together, that I was being moved. I was finally transferred from my solitary cell near the noisy main-population holding cells to cellblock 200 c/1 on the third floor of the county jail. Surprisingly, this area of the jail was much quieter than where I had been previously held.

It was a large cellblock with sixteen one-man cells split into two levels, eight on the first level and eight on the second level, with a stairway to the upper cells on both ends of the upper catwalk. There was also a large open area on the first level in front of all the cells, with four metal tables spread out and four metal stools attached to each of the tables, bolted to the floor. In front of all that by the entrance to the area was a desk where an officer sat and could watch all the cells and could press an alarm or call out on his walkie-talkie if he needed any assistance.

They had assigned me to cell F on the second level. The cells ran in alphabetical order. *A* through *H* on the upper level and *I* through *P* on the lower level. The officer escorting me to my new home had to knock on the cellblock door and announce himself over his mic to gain entrance. Any inmates sitting or standing around the open area were told to return to their cells and locked in before we were allowed to enter.

Once inside, I was turned over to the officer in charge of the cellblock, and he escorted me up to my cell, where he closed the steel door and locked me in. As I looked around, I was amazed at how clean and bright everything was. This was a far cry from the dingy cell I came from. Like most cells, there was a stainless steel toilet and sink in one corner of the cell. There was also a steel bunk bed bolted to the side of one of the walls and a little work area where one could sit and read or write. At one of the back corners, a narrow vertical window, no more than six inches wide and about seven feet high from floor to ceiling, provided a view of the outside world. The glass in it was very thick.

As I looked out, I could see the street below and the movement of traffic. I could also see the entrance ramps to I-4 and I-275, with traffic coming off and going on. I also looked straight out. I could see the projects directly across the street from the jail and children playing in the small park across the way. It made me long for my children and family. My sister, Rose, and her family did not live too far from there, but it was too far to see. As narrow as the window was, I still had a pretty good view of the outside.

The cell was painted in light tan colors, as was the whole cellblock. When I turned and looked through the little window in the cell door, I could see that many of the cells were occupied, but there were a few empty ones, also with their doors left open. As I settled in to my new surroundings, I did not feel so isolated any more. The officer would walk around the cellblock from time to time, checking on everyone and taking his count.

When he stopped by my cell, he informed me of the rules of the cellblock and the day when I could order snacks and things from the canteen when they delivered it once a week. They only allowed four inmates out of their cells at a time for recreation and to stretch their legs in the open area. This cellblock was used to house some of the most serious capital offenders while many of them were waiting for trial like myself in state or federal court, or waiting to be sentenced on charges for murder, drugs, larceny, or robbery.

This was the maximum-security holding area for inmates who needed to be watched closely. If they thought one of the inmates was a real threat to anyone or to the system, such as a serial killer who had nothing to lose, that person would be the only one let out of his cell by himself after everyone else was placed back in his cell. This inmate had the whole area to himself and was only allowed out for an hour to stretch his legs or move around while he stayed in shackles. Two officers would be in the area to watch his movements. This was the type of cellmate I shared my time with while I stayed at the county jail. I guess someone thought I would fit in well with them. Over time, we would all get to know each other well.

CHAPTER 25

Justice on Hold

February 1986

Cesar Augustus Rodriguez, a
55-year-old former bar owner

On the morning of Wednesday, February 5, the jury selection came
to a screeching halt. Talk about a comedy of errors and tragedy—the
trial was interrupted by mishap, a misplaced juror, and a missing
defendant.

It all began when one of the potential jurors found out he was in
the wrong courtroom and was sent away. Plus, Mr. Cesar Rodriquez
was not present in the courtroom because of an injury he suffered the
night before. Looking a little annoyed, Judge Carr announced to the
nearly two dozen lawyers and fifteen defendants in the courtroom
what we already knew by way of the media.

Judge Carr stated to the full courtroom, "Mr. Rodriquez had an accident and will be unable to attend the proceedings today and for the next two days. Apparently, he will be able to attend next Tuesday. Of course, we cannot proceed with the jury selection without his presence." With that, the judge rescheduled the jury selection for the next Tuesday morning.

In the previous two days, nine jurors had been seated, and the judge advised them not to discuss the case with anyone, nor read or listen to any news articles about the case, before he dismissed them until Tuesday. He gave the same instructions to the pool of potential jurors.

Mr. Rodriquez, who was fifty-five years old at the time of our trial, had been attacked around four-thirty in the morning while leaving the Act IV Lounge on north Franklin Street in Tampa. According to the information I received from my attorney Mr. Harris, Mr. Rodriquez was hit by an unknown person on the back of his head with a bottle or club. When Mr. Rodriquez turned around to face his assailant, he was then struck in the face from a heavy fist. The assailant took off when a friend came by to assist Mr. Rodriquez. The friend then took Mr. Rodriquez to the hospital, where he received thirty-six stitches above his eye.

At the time, Cesar Rodriquez was a nightclub owner and developer of the Cigar City Truck Stop east of Tampa off US 301. The government was charging him with three counts of mail fraud—one count each of racketeering, racketeering conspiracy, and interference with commerce by extortion. Merkle really liked to get melodramatic with overkill on charges to try and get the majority of convictions in any given case.

So the trial was put on hold, and I was returned to the county jail, where I would have to stay in my cellblock until the next Tuesday. General visiting hours were on the weekends, and I looked forward to the visits from my family but felt sorry that my youngest son, Steven, had to see me like that. It is very hard to explain to a young boy why all this was happening to his father. My daughter, Julie, would bring him to see me once in a while when she came to visit. I could see in his eyes that he didn't understand why all this was happening. He would never say much when he came. I could see that all we went through during the first trial, and now the second one, was starting to have a negative effect on him. It was so difficult only seeing them through a glass window and talking to them through a phone on each side of the window, not being able to hold or comfort them.

When I was back in my cell, I would think of my life before all this happened—how I could have been a better father to my children or a better husband to my wife before she passed away, what I could have done more for them, or my mother, or my sister. How the questions fill your mind when all you have is time on your hands.

When they would let a few of us out of our cells, I would socialize with the other inmates or just walk around the area once in a while, looking into some of the other cells and talking to the men who were still locked in. Over time, we became a close-knit little community, everyone telling one another how their day in court went or what was happening to them, talking about their lives before being arrested, making jokes, or telling stories about things that happened in their lives. They were an interesting lot; it helped keep my mind off my troubles and depression.

When Tuesday came, the trial began again with the selection of the rest of the jurors. It wouldn't be till the middle of the next week late in the afternoon that all twelve of the jurors and six alternate jurors were picked. The next day, Judge Carr gave his instructions to the jurors, and that afternoon, the trial began.

During this time, on Saturday the eighth of February, a secret federal court document had been leaked to the press by some unknown person, possibly from the federal prosecutor's office. Merkle denied he or his office had anything to do with it, saying that his "office acted appropriately in filing the secret court document." This was one of the known tactics that many prosecutors used to injure someone's character or reputation when they don't have enough evidence to get an indictment, similar to what they tried to do to EJ Salcines, Norman Cannella, and others when they could not find anything on them.

While our trial was going on, Merkle was attempting to get this secret document filed for the grand jury to review. The document made allegations against Mayor Bob Martinez for bribery. The document also named city councilmen Tom Vann and Eddie Caballero, alleging that they had all been given a bribe in 1979 to influence the selection of the city's cable television franchise. One must remember that a lot of the information that many of these allegations were based on came from Jerry Bowmer and Charles Bean. The mayor and the two city councilmen denied the charges. Merkle had the document in his possession for quite some time and just happened to pick this time to file it. It also just happened to be around the same time that Mayor Bob Martinez was starting out on his bid for governor within the Republican Party. ("Oh, the webs we weave, when we set out to deceive.")

Merkle stated, "The decision to file the document was taken without regard to considerations political or otherwise extraneous to our official responsibilities. Our office has always and will continue to conduct itself appropriately."

When the information was leaked, Mayor Martinez inquired as to who leaked the contents of the document. He had not yet asked the US Department of Justice to investigate. Many of Martinez's supporters started criticizing Merkle. Mayor Martinez's campaign director John M. "Mac" Stipanovich termed Merkle's handling of the allegation "irresponsible conduct."

Merkle's reply was, "After a judge ordered the documents turned over to the defense attorneys in the ongoing Hillsborough County Commission bribery-corruption case, it was members of his staff that requested the documents be sealed."

The way Merkle and his staff were conducting these secret investigations into the lives of many of Tampa's elite citizens was starting to create waves of contempt for him in many Republican circles. The local and state Republican parties were starting to have second thoughts about Robert Merkle.

A few days later, our trial had begun again, and it was Judge Carr who ordered the documents sealed. He instructed Merkle's assistant prosecutor Joe Magri not to mention any of the names from the sealed documents during his opening statements.

Before the jury was asked to come in and take their seats, the judge dealt with a few written motions that had been submitted by various attorneys a few days before, asking to have their clients severed from the trial. Judge Carr had reviewed the motions and was ready to render his decision. Joe Bealer, the attorney representing Claud Tanner, was one of those requesting the severance. Judge Carr denied the motion and other motions that he had received that past week.

He did, however, grant a few of the motions for severance, for Paul Johnson and Nelson Italiano and a few others, which brought us down to nineteen defendants. Originally, there were a total of thirty of us being indicted. Some of the defendants had their charges dismissed while others were at least lucky enough to be severed from the circus.

Those attorneys who had not filed motions to sever got up and asked, "Your Honor, I would like to ask the court to sever my client from this case," then would give their reasons. One by one, each attorney would stand and ask the same question. Then Judge Carr would just deny the motion.

After about the third or fourth had gotten up, my attorney Ray Harris took his turn, getting up and saying, "Your Honor, I request

Mr. Kotvas be severed from this trial." That was all he said, and his request was also denied. Ray wasn't looking good. He had been ill for a long time, and it seemed his condition was not getting any better. I asked him, "Are you going to follow it with a written motion?"

His response was, "It's OK. We got it on the record." That was all he said about it.

Not knowing much about these kinds of things, I had to put my trust in him to follow through and that he knew what he was doing. It wouldn't be until a few years later, working with a new attorney on my appeal from prison, that I would find out Ray had just made one of the biggest mistakes in my case. At that point, Ray should have filed a written appeal of the judge's ruling to sever. If he had done so, Judge Carr would probably have had to sever me from the trial because once the appeal is filed with the federal appellate court, it would have held up the trial for everyone, and who knows how long that would have taken. Judge Carr could not afford to hold up a trial of this magnitude, and he would have had to sever me from it.

I then would have had my real day in court being tried by myself without any codefendants and mountains of evidence and witnesses that had nothing to do with me. The odds would have been in my favor since the government never did have real concrete evidence against me, just the word of Bowmer and a witness or two who had made deals with the government. It might have called for a possible dismissal of the charges or a not-guilty verdict. But what did I know at the time? I'm not a lawyer.

I was totally unaware that Mr. Harris failed to follow up with a number of written motions during my trial. As the trial progressed, the type of medications he was taking would cause him to doze off quite a bit during the proceedings. I think this accounted for the lack of motions being filed on my behalf.

The government had me where they wanted me. As the only one locked up during the trial, I had no real access to any information, nor could I properly help with my defense. Because I felt sorry for Mr. Harris, who was sick and had a family who needed him to have the income from this case, I just put my trust in him and believed he would do right by me. I did not realize, nor was I informed at the time, that I could have asked for a different attorney to represent me. I only have myself to blame.

After all was said and done, the jury was called in to take their seats, and the trial began with opening statements. The prosecution would begin with assistant US attorney Joe Magri giving the opening statements for the government. Sitting at the same table with Mr. Magri as he rose to give his opening statement were assistant US attorneys John Fitzgibbons and Lee Atkinson, plus US attorney Robert Merkle himself. Mr. Magri was using a train analogy to detail how we former commissioners and others were supposed to have conspired to form a racketeering enterprise from 1976 to 1983.

He stated as he addressed the eighteen jurors, "A corruption train was built in this courtroom, with these nineteen defendants who joined together to build it, operate, sell tickets for it, and ride it. This was a criminal partnership that picked up steam in late 1982 and operated until the FBI and a federal grand jury derailed it in 1983. When you peer through one of those windows on that train, you will see the clear participation of these defendants."

He went on to say, "Former Commissioners Jerry M. Bowmer and Charles F. Bean III"—who were not on trial at this time—"were at the core of this corruption and will testify about the scheme. The bribes were motivated by a desire to build businesses, hurt competition, and make money."

When Mr. Magri finished his opening statements, it was now time for the defense lawyers to present their opening arguments. Attorney Robert Polli got up to give his opening arguments. "Ladies and gentlemen of the jury," he opened, "this train that the government claims to exist is really a two-man handcar." He was referring to Bowmer and Bean. He went on to say, "Jerry Bowmer is the glue the government intends to use to hold this case together."

Then attorney Pat Dougherty got up. He was representing Robert Cannella, who was a Tampa zoning lawyer. I could never understand what Robert Cannella was doing on trial with us. To my knowledge, he was one of the straightest A lawyers you would ever want to meet. His only involvement I could see was that he shared an office with defendant John Demmi, whom Merkle was after with a passion. I figure Merkle was putting the screws to Robert to try and get him to cooperate with them to turn on John and the others, like they tried with me.

At the time of our trial, Mr. Cannella's wife was terminally ill with cancer. I know he had to be out of his mind with worry over all of this, trying to take care of her and his family, plus the pressure of this trial. He did not deserve this. He was a very good man who did not belong there. Knowing what suffering my late wife went through, my heart went out to him.

Mr. Dougherty said, "The evidence will show that Jerry Bowmer was the track, conductor, and engineer of the train—that my client, Robert Cannella, had no involvement and is innocent of these charges."

When Mr. Dougherty finished and sat down, attorney Julianne Holt got up to give her opening statements. She was working closely with Joe Bealer and sat at the same table with him and his client, Mr. Claude Tanner, one of the owners of Suburban Disposal Services Inc.

She opened with, "Ladies and gentlemen, my name is Julianne Holt, and I have one of the most difficult tasks of all these lawyers. Unlike them, I do not represent a person whom I can bring into court to defend himself or whom you could look at every day. I represent Suburban Disposal Services Inc. It happens to be a company, not a person. I am charged with the responsibility to prove beyond a doubt that my client had nothing to do with the charges filed against it. During the course of this trial, I will attempt to show you that my client is innocent of all charges. Thank you." Then she took her seat.

A number of other defense lawyers, when it came to their turn to speak, had harsher words to discredit Bowmer and Bean.

Then John Demmi took his turn to give opening arguments. Mr. Demmi was representing himself. He called Bowmer "the cancer of Hillsborough County." He went on to call him a "bold-faced liar who would do or say anything to make a deal and get special treatment."

It went on like this throughout the day, until my attorney's turn came up. Mr. Harris said to the jury, "I will attempt to show you that Mr. Kotvas was not a participant but a victim of Mr. Bowmer, like so many people whom Bowmer used. Mr. Kotvas was a single parent trying to raise his children by himself when his wife passed away with cancer. He is a former Tampa police officer who served his community well and former Tampa city councilman with a distinguished record. In all that time, Mr. Kotvas has served the needs of our community.

"Only when he became a county commissioner did he ever have to serve with the likes of Jerry Bowmer. Bowmer is a user, and knowing the type of person Mr. Kotvas was—a person with compassion who tries to help anyone he could—Mr. Bowmer used that to his advantage to frame Mr. Kotvas for something he had no involvement in. Thank you." Then Ray came back to our table and sat down.

On February 28, Bowmer was back on the stand as he continued to testify to the so-called bribes. He stated that former commissioner Bob Curry came to him two years into his second term to talk about a petition for a borrow pit on behalf of J. C. Strickland, who was a relative of his daughter. Previously, this project, which was proposed by Strickland and Joseph Anderson, owner of Anderson Construction Co., faced significant opposition from the neighbors. Bowmer claimed he had met with Anderson (no relation to Fred Anderson) before the vote, but Anderson failed to mention a price to guarantee approval for the pit. For this reason, Bowmer testified he and Commissioners Fred Anderson and Joe Kotvas voted against it.

Then Bowmer said he had met with Curry before the vote, and Curry claimed he could get $2,500 for Bowmer's vote on the application.

The trial went on like this, with Bowmer testifying and the government presenting its case and calling one witness after another, trying to explain this so-called railroad before introducing the courthouse recordings from the first trial to give credit to their claims.

CHAPTER 26

A Sentence Is Suspended

March 1986

On the morning of March 4, Tuesday, before the jury was seated, Judge George C. Carr entered the courtroom and took his seat behind the bench and said, "Before we begin the proceedings, there is a matter I need to take up. In the government's case against Michael Sierra, I am suspending his four-year prison term and instead placing him on four years' probation, serving one year at the Goodwill Industries halfway house in St. Petersburg as a special condition. He can only leave the halfway house to attend his present trial and to confer with his lawyer Raymond LaPorte. This order is to take effect immediately."

Ray LaPorte had filed the motion for a sentence reduction on February 14 after exhausting all appeals to overturn his 1983 conviction. In the motion seeking reduction, Mr. LaPorte argued that the sentence caused medical and financial hardships for Michael Sierra and his family and that detaining Mr. Sierra in the county jail was contrary to the court's expressed recommendation.

Tribune photo by AUGUST STAEBLER
A smiling Michael Sierra and his wife, Cynthia, walk out of the
federal courthouse Tuesday after his prison sentence was
suspended. He was placed on probation.

Everyone on the defense side was happy for Mike. I know he and his wife, who was in the courtroom when the judge read the order, were ecstatic. My heart skipped a beat on the news. Maybe there was a chance for me to get my sentence suspended! The only one that did not look too happy was the lead prosecutor, Joe Magri. It appeared that the day before, he had gone before Judge Carr to argue against reducing Sierra's sentence. Now the judge had made his decision, and it was final.

My attorney and Fred Anderson's attorney told us that they would file similar motions. When asked by the media, Ray Harris said, "Mr. Kotvas's appeal will be based on the same arguments as Mr. Sierra's request. There is a devastating effect on his family, especially on his children. Mr. Kotvas lost his wife to cancer in 1978, and he is the only one they have to provide for them."

As for Fred Anderson, his attorney Robert Polli said, "He is compiling evidence for a sentence-reduction request. He has until March 18 to submit his arguments."

After all the congratulations and handshakes, Judge Carr called the court back to order and asked that the jury be sent in as the trial went on. Bowmer had been testifying for the last couple of days, and Magri called him to the stand again. A lot of it was a rehash of the evidence from the first trial. The jury would hear the recordings again, and the government would fill in their version of the blanks from the missing parts on the tapes.

For me, it was like the first trial all over again. Bowmer came into the courtroom smiling and acting like it all meant nothing to him. He and Bean had made their deal with the government, and Merkle was seeing that they were taken good care of. They were Merkle's golden boys who would catapult him up the political ladder.

After Bowmer was seated in the witness box, Magri asked him about an alleged bribe involving an investment banking firm. He alleged that he received a $10,000 bribe arranged by Fred Anderson to approve a St. Petersburg firm of William R. Hough to act as the investment banker for the $200 million solid waste recovery plant. When Magri asked him what Joe Kotvas's part was, he said, "I believe the deal included Joe Kotvas, but I cannot say for certain whether Kotvas received any money."

At that point, I turned to my attorney and said, "He knows I would not take any money or be part of that deal if it really happened. He is just naming names and putting people in situations to protect himself."

Bowmer went on to say that a friend of Anderson was also involved, Harold Rossiter, who was under indictment in our trial facing racketeering charges. Then the commission rescinded its contract with Kidder Peabody, and he voted to solicit bids from other investment companies to make it look better to the general public.

Magri now asked Bowmer about John Demmi. At that point, Bowmer went on to another alleged incident that involved Mr. Demmi. He told the court that Mr. Demmi offered him $25,000 to select Kidder Peabody to be the second investment banker, that Demmi claimed to be representing Kidder Peabody. At this point, John Demmi got up and objected to the question on the basis of hearsay.

Judge Carr overruled it, and Bowmer continued, saying that Mr. Demmi never paid the money and that he, Bowmer, had tried to collect on the payoff until his arrest in February 1983, when he was charged with extortion for accepting a bribe in another case.

Again, Mr. Demmi got up to object and asked the court to strike this testimony from the record, saying, "This testimony is based on hearsay and no evidence of any bribe being paid."

Mr. Magri responded, "Mr. Demmi will have his chance to cross-examine the witness, Your Honor."

Judge Carr then overruled the objection and told Mr. Demmi to take his seat and that he would have his turn to examine the witness.

Bowmer then told of a botched attempt to solicit a $120,000 bribe from landowner and businessman Eugene Thomason. Bowmer explained that Thomason told him in 1981 that he wanted to sell a 586-acre ranch to the state Department of Corrections, which wanted to build a maximum-security prison on the land. During a meeting at the Bush Boulevard Ramada Inn Lounge with Mr. Thomason, Mr. Thomason got up to go to the restroom and handed him a napkin, instructing him to name a figure.

Bowmer then said he wrote $120,000 on the napkin; then Mr. Thomason tore it up and said, "I can handle that."

With that said, Bowmer then claimed that he went to Anderson and Kotvas and told us that he could get us $20,000 apiece and maybe $30,000 each if we would vote for Thomason's property as a prison site.

Then Bowmer said for all to hear that Kotvas and Anderson refused the deal and that he could not get us to go along with it or change our minds. He said that before he could do anything more with the project, he was arrested by the FBI.

When it was John Demmi's turn to question Bowmer, he tore right into him over the objections of Joe Magri. Demmi asked Bowmer, "You never received any money from me, did you?"

"No," answered Bowmer.

"Isn't it a fact that you made this whole thing up to help your situation and get a better deal from the government?"

Again, Bowmer replied, "No," as Magri jumped up and objected.

"Overruled," Judge Carr said.

At that point, John Demmi said, "No further questions at this time, Your Honor."

Robert Polli, representing Anderson, then got up and asked Bowmer a number of questions, "You say Mr. Anderson was part of your conspiracy, and you were taking bribes together?"

"Yes," Bowmer replied.

"Then why would he, Mr. Anderson, and Mr. Kotvas turn down such a lucrative offer even if there was opposition? You all have faced opposition before," Mr. Polli pointed out.

Again, Joe Magri got up to object, but the judge overruled him and told Bowmer to answer the question.

"I don't know why. It was a good deal. I just think they didn't want to take all the heat, it being a prison and all that."

Then Mr. Polli said, "Isn't it true you wanted all the money for yourself and were trying to see if you could get it to pass, and Mr. Anderson and Kotvas had no involvement in your plan?"

"No."

"Objection," Magri shouted out. "I object to this line of questioning."

Again, Judge Carr overruled the objection.

Since the question was already answered, Mr. Polli moved on, "Tell us, Mr. Bowmer, isn't it a fact that you have been making all this up and are just trying to implicate my client, Mr. Anderson, to cover your own guilt?"

"No," Bowmer said.

"Objection, Your Honor. Mr. Polli is trying to badger the witness," Magri stated.

"Objection overruled," the judge answered.

"No further questions, Your Honor." Mr. Polli turned and walked back to his seat.

Now it was my attorney's turn. Ray Harris got up from his chair and walked over to Bowmer then said, "You just testified that Mr. Kotvas didn't want any part of your plan. Isn't that true?"

"Yes," Bowmer replied.

"In fact, you could never get Mr. Kotvas to go along with any of your ongoing enterprises," Ray Harris said to Bowmer.

"No," was the reply. Again, Magri objected, and the judge overruled.

Mr. Harris only asked a few questions at this time then sat down next to me. I asked him why he didn't go after Bowmer, and he said it was only the beginning and there would be time.

It was now growing late in the afternoon. The judge called a recess until the next day. Before I was taken away by the marshals to go back to the county jail, Ray Harris informed me that he would have my motion on Judge Carr's desk by early morning. Everyone was tired and wanted to get home to their families. Joe Bealer told most of the attorneys that they would all meet later that evening at one of the other attorneys' office to go over the day's events.

I was taken back to the county jail in chains. Every morning when I was taken to the federal courthouse, I would be taken in chains. When we would get to the courtroom, the chains and cuffs would be removed out of sight of the jury. Then at the end of the day when court was over and the jury gone, the marshals would recuff and chain me for transport back to the jail.

Now that Michael Sierra had his sentence suspended to probation and could stay at the Goodwill Industries halfway house, he no longer needed to be cuffed or chained. Fred Anderson was on house arrest and had to wear an ankle bracelet to keep track of his movements. I guess I was considered the only real danger who needed to be shackled like an animal and kept locked up. But like Mr. Sierra, if the judge granted the motion that my attorney was filing, hopefully I would be out of that jail and possibly in a halfway house also.

Once back at the jail, I changed back into my prisoner jumpsuit and returned to my new cell area. Inside, I saw that four of the inmates were out of their cells, one walking around the area, two sitting and playing cards, and the other just standing around not doing much of anything. The officer in charge of the cellblock escorted me back to my cell then locked me in. He informed me that I could come out for an hour when this group was back in their cells. It was up to the officer how many times or how many prisoners, up to a max of four, he would allow out of their cells, as long as they did not cause any trouble and kept to the rules.

Back in my cell, one of the cellmates who was out of his cell came by my cell and stopped by my tray slot and started talking to me. I guess being the new fish on the block, everyone was interested in what was going on and wanted to know what happened today. This inmate looked like a young kid. He asked me if I had any smokes. I just told him I don't smoke. Cigarettes are like gold in a place like that. They are used as currency among prisoners in just about every type of institution. It is rumored that you could have someone killed for a couple of cartons of cigarettes in some institutions.

The young man informed me of what was going on within the cellblock. He was very talkative and informative about everything. He wanted to know who I was and what I was in for; then he began to tell me his story and the story of some of the others. That was when I found out what type of a cellblock we were in. Just about everyone there was either waiting for trial or waiting to be transferred to a higher prison to serve out their time. It was also where they kept those who were charged or convicted of murder.

I asked him what his situation was. He informed me he was there for grand larceny and attacking a store owner with a knife. He just went on like that until it was time for him to go back into his cell and the next group would be let out. In the months to follow, I would come to know him and all my other cellmates well.

CHAPTER 27

Defendants Lose Bid for Sentence Reduction

March 1986

On Thursday morning, March 6, we were all back in court, some sitting and going over their notes while others huddled in small groups, talking and joking in whispers. Others just stood around and waited for the proceedings to start. I was sitting next to Mr. Harris, who was looking over his notes, as I drank my Cuban coffee that my sister had brought for me. She was off today and had brought my mother to court with her. Michael Sierra's wife, Cynthia, had brought some breakfast sandwiches to court for Mike, and she handed me one also. I thought that was very nice of her. It was a far cry from jail food.

A lot was going on that morning. Looking around the courtroom, I could see that something was up. The word was that Merkle was asking for a new federal grand jury to convene so he could continue with his ongoing investigation that he claimed was not finished. The grand jury that had been investigating all the so-called corruption for the past three years had been dismissed a couple of days ago. Merkle felt there was a lot more to be investigated and that the grand jury's work was not complete. He was not finished with his witch hunt.

Also, I found out that the day before the grand jury was dismissed, they had indicted state representative Elvin Martinez on charges of lying to the grand jury in response to questions about personal drug use. This was insane. It seemed like Merkle was trying to indict just about anyone whose name ended in a vowel.

Representative Martinez was the head of the Criminal Justice Committee in the Florida House. Representative Martinez maintained he did nothing wrong. He was a man who was well respected both in Tallahassee and Tampa, but he was also a good friend of EJ Salcines. I could see where all this was going—first his chief assistant prosecutor and now his friends. By this time, complaints about Merkle were starting to come in from across the community. It was all anyone in the courthouse was talking about that morning.

State representative Elvin Martinez

All I was concerned about at the time was what the judge would say about our motion. When the bailiff called out, "All rise," Judge Carr entered the room, walked to his bench, and sat down. Everything turned quiet in the courtroom.

He began with, "With regard to the motion for sentence reduction filed by Mr. Robert Polli on behalf of Fred Arthur Anderson, the motion is denied. With regard to the motion for sentence reduction filed by Mr. Ray Harris on behalf of Joseph Henry Kotvas Jr....the motion is denied."

When we all heard the court's decision, my mother and sister had tears in their eyes. I was devastated, but Ray put his hand on my arm and gave it a little squeeze. "Stay focused, Joe," he said to me. "I know this is hard for you, but the decision was at the judge's discretion."

I looked over to where Joe Magri and Robert Merkle were, and they were huddled together, whispering and smiling. I wondered what part they had to play in this decision. I know Fred and his wife were not taking it well either. We were both very depressed that day.

The judge gave his decision without any reason for the denial. He knew Fred was not a well man, and he could have cut him a little slack. I guess he felt that putting Fred on house arrest and letting him stay home with his wife and daughter during these proceedings was a type of sentence reduction. Our time in court also counted toward time served on our sentences.

But it was still hard for me, knowing I could do nothing to help my children. The judge knew my financial and family situation. Of all the defendants in the trial, I was the only one locked up and held in the county jail. It just seemed like the government was really trying to stick it to me. I was not a threat to anyone nor a flight risk. Yet of all the defendants, I was not only kept from being able to defend myself; I was also separated from my family and the general public.

All the defendants had the freedom to meet with their attorneys or the whole group of attorneys any time there was a meeting. I had to sit in my cell and wait until Ray Harris would come to the county jail, which wasn't that often, to bring me up to date or try to catch up in the courtroom for the few minutes we had before court would begin. I never had a chance to really give any input on my defense, seeing I was locked up and excluded from all the evidence.

When that magistrate had told me almost a year ago that I would not be able to work on my defense from prison or a jail cell, he knew what he was talking about. There was no way the government was going to allow me to defend myself or allow me to work with all these attorneys to try and prove my noninvolvement and innocence.

Merkle may have had a gut feeling of my guilt with the limited amount of evidence he had against me. He was making sure that I would feel the full power of his office, and he had me right where he thought he wanted me to be—to be able to torment me, with my family and children so close yet being out of contact with them or anyone, only seeing and talking to them through bars and windows on visiting days or in court. He knew if they could break me into cooperating, this trial and any others that were coming up would be a slam dunk. I was the only one in the trial he had some control over. I guess he thought I was the weakest link and figured it was only a matter of time before I would break under those conditions and squeal like a pig. How wrong he was.

I had no hard feelings against Fred that he could go home each night after court to his family and a good cooked meal. Nor did I have any hard feelings against Michael Sierra because he got his sentence reduced. I was very happy for them. Someone had to be the government's whipping boy, and I guess that left me.

CHAPTER 28

The Witch Hunt Widens

March 1986

Bowmer had been on and off the stand for a number of weeks now, explaining about the tape recordings and the people he claimed to have received bribes from. Then on Tuesday, March 11, around mid-morning, Bowmer was asked by the assistant prosecutor, "Tell the court of some of the other bribes you had with defendant Michael Sierra."

Councilwoman and Mayor Sandy Freedman

Mr. Sierra's attorney objected and was overruled, and Bowmer went on with his testimony. For the first time in our trial, he mentioned Councilwoman Sandy Freedman, who was the chairman of the Tampa city council and was also running for mayor of the city of Tampa during this time since Mayor Bob Martinez was running for governor of Florida and the office of mayor was up for grabs.

The whole courtroom stirred in a buzz of whispers when her name came up, and the judge had to call the room to order before telling Bowmer to continue. Bowmer went on with his testimony regarding Ms. Freedman. He alleged that Michael Sierra said to him that she was on the take on the city council seat and that she worked with him on a bribe that she had doubled-crossed him on. Bowmer also claimed Sierra told him that Freedman would be able to work with them, that she was "one of us."

Ray LaPorte got up on behalf of Sierra and objected to the testimony as merely hearsay. The judge overruled, but when the prospector finished, Mr. LaPorte got up to take his turn at Bowmer. LaPorte asked, "Did you have any conversations with Ms. Freedman?"

Bowmer replied, "No, I didn't."

"Do you have any personal knowledge of this allegation?"

"No, sir, none whatsoever," was his reply.

Throughout his testimony on Ms. Freedman, Bowmer never told of any specific bribes in which she had allegedly participated. It was all a matter of hearsay, with no proof and only his word that all this had occurred. Ms. Freedman, who was attempting to become the first elected woman mayor of Tampa, had not been charged with a crime nor indicted.

It was plain to see that, in spite of Jerry Bowmer and Charlie Bean's accusations and the way Merkle and his office were presenting this information, there was no foundation to these charges. Still, the leaking of information to the press allowed a lot of character assassination to go on. No one was safe from the comments made on the witness stand, and the press was eating it up.

When Ms. Freedman read about this testimony in the press a day or two later, she realized she had been a target in Merkle's ongoing investigation. She was furious with the federal prosecutor's office for not giving her the opportunity to clear her name. On Friday,

March 14, she immediately sent a letter requesting a meeting with Mr. Merkle to clear her name and get the facts right.

Bowmer had given this information to Merkle back in 1982 when he was making out his list of so-called bribes to cut his deal with the government. Bowmer was smart; I guess he figured the more names he could give the government to investigate, the longer he would stay out of jail. He knew that the longer the list, the more time the government would need to look into everyone, regardless if they were guilty or not. It could take years, and he would stay out in protective custody. This is exactly what was happening. He hadn't been sentenced yet, and he had not served a day for his crimes. He knew how to play the government, and Merkle was eating his information up, looking into every person whom Bowmer would mention.

In response to her plea to grant her an opportunity to clear her name from Bowmer's statement, on Monday, March 17, Mr. Merkle sent a reply to Ms. Freedman, stating, "While I here neither question nor endorse the propriety of your conduct as a member of the city council, I assure you that the government will seek to interview you in due course concerning any knowledge you may have regarding the matters already testified to in court, as well as other specific matters of which we are aware." He then had the letter hand-delivered by one of his staff members to Ms. Freedman.

When Ms. Freedman received and read the letter, she made copies and released them to the press, stating that she was not satisfied with Merkle's reply. She stated, "I didn't do anything illegal or improper. I feel I was not treated fairly, and the bottom line is, I think I've done everything I can do."

I think she felt that Bowmer and Merkle were using this opportunity to run a smear campaign against her and other public officials whom Bowmer did not like or was trying to get even with. For a time, it was accusations back and forth, using the press to express their views.

The next day, Tuesday March 18, Bowmer was back on the stand to continue with his testimony. When asked by the prosecutor to further explain some of the other bribes he was involved with, Bowmer told the court that Tampa attorney Ted Taub had surprised him with $2,000 in 1982. Again, the courtroom was abuzz with this accusation. Mr. Taub had not been indicted on any wrongdoing, and this was the first time anyone was hearing about this incident. Mr. Taub was a well-respected lawyer in the Tampa Bay community, with strong family roots in Tampa, and he was the city attorney for the city of Temple Terrace and the former chairman of the Tampa Hillsborough Expressway Authority.

When asked what the money was for, Bowmer replied, "I felt like he was influencing me for future consideration." He stated that the payment took place a week or two after the commission approved Mr. Taub's zoning petition for an office complex on the eastern side of North Dale Mabry Highway and south of Ehrlich Road. He further explained to the court that Mr. Taub came into his office and closed the door and told him he appreciated his help. "He only paid me one time," he further stated.

Under cross-examination by attorney Patrick Doherty, Bowmer stated that the payment was unplanned, and he did not consider it a bribe. Then when another defense attorney got up to cross-examine Bowmer on this same matter, Bowmer said he felt that Mr. Taub was trying to buy future votes and that he had contributed to his 1980 reelection campaign but was unsure if his contribution exceeded the $500 limit.

When Ted Taub heard about Bowmer's testimony, he denied the accusations. Mr. Taub was never charged with any crime.

As Bowmer continued to testify, he brought up the name of A. G. Spicola, from another highly respected family in the Tampa Bay Area. He accused Mr. Spicola of offering him the use of a house his family owned on Clearwater Beach and contributing $500 to his reelection bid.

When defense lawyer Raymond LaPorte got up to cross-examine Bowmer about Mr. Spicola, he asked him, "Why do you think he offered you that?"

Bowmer replied, "I'm not sure. I assumed the beach house and the contribution would be to influence his applications that came before the commission."

I need to interject something here. Contributions—whether in cash or in kind—if accepted, by law, must be listed on the candidate's contributions list that he or she must file for the office they are running for. It is a common practice for attorneys to support an incumbent public official before whom they may appear in the hopes of getting a fair hearing. It is legal and done during every election throughout the country. The incumbent always has the advantage here, and Bowmer was no different than any other incumbent. But Merkle was trying to give the impression to the jury that this was some kind of secret under-the-table bribe.

Bowmer went on to explain how he met with Mr. Spicola and a man he assumed was Spicola's father, who was a former judge in 1980. He could not remember which Spicola handed him the money in cash. Again, the government could prove nothing here; they only had Bowmer's word. The Spicolas also were never charged with a crime or any wrongdoing.

Between the assistant prosecutors and the defense lawyers, the questions and arguments kept going back and forth in front of the jury. In the end, it always came down to the word of Jerry Bowmer.

During our trial on Friday, March 21, during the lunch break, one of my codefendants, John Demmi, received some wonderful news. In Mr. Demmi's first trial two years prior to this one, Robert Merkle had appealed the decision of federal judge Terrell Hodges to the federal appellate court in Atlanta after Judge Hodges threw out the charges against Demmi midway through that trial. The appellate court had ruled Wednesday that "the government attempts to appeal from clear judgment of acquittal. This cannot be done. The appeal is dismissed."

All the defense lawyers and codefendants gathered around Mr. Demmi to congratulate him. There were smiles, laughter, handshakes, and pats on the backs going around the room. The only ones not smiling were Merkle and his staff. Looking over to them, you could see Merkle's face turning red as he tried to keep his composure, angrily shaking his head while talking to Joe Magri and others at their table.

In dismissing all the charges against Mr. Demmi, Judge Hodges declared the government's case was based on "insufficient" circumstantial evidence and that the prosecutors had failed to produce enough evidence to warrant the case going to a jury. This lifted all of our spirits; we were happy for Mr. Demmi. But it made Merkle even more determined to get a conviction on Mr. Demmi since he had him bunched in with all of us. He now had a second chance to do what he could not do the first time.

That weekend, the press had a heyday with this news, and it was starting to take a different attitude toward our trial. Merkle was beginning to lose support from the media. Negative articles about his actions were starting to appear in the press. There was even a full-page editorial about Merkle, saying, "US Attorney Merkle Must Go" in *The Tampa Tribune*. The editorial staff of the paper was appalled at the tactics Merkle and his staff were using in our community. This editorial stated:

> Jerry Bowmer...told the jury that another defendant in the trial had told him that Tampa City Council Chairwoman Sandy Freedman was "on the take" for bribes. Bowmer's answer came in response to a question from one of Merkle's assistants.
>
> The other defendant, Michael Sierra, later that day said Bowmer fabricated the tale. "I think you'll find out this afternoon that he'll say the pope is his father," Sierra responded.
>
> Could Bowmer tell of any specific bribes involving Freedman? No. Did Bowmer have any knowledge other than hearsay that Freedman might have taken a bribe? No. Did Bowmer ever talk with Freedman about anything? No... Was Freedman a target of any investigation by Merkle? No [...].
>
> Due course, for Freedman and Martinez and all the others who have had a shadow cast across their reputations, has been three years.

When Bowmer was arrested by the FBI agents
in February 1983, he immediately was interrogated. He talked like a canary. Every conversation since then, inside and outside of Florida, has
been recorded by the FBI on its No. 302 forms.
Merkle, of course, has access to those documents
[…].

   If the FBI investigated and found no evidence of criminal activity, why then did Merkle
have admitted criminals associate the names of
Martinez and Freedman with criminal conduct?
If the FBI thought the charges of so little import
that it did not investigate, why did Merkle associate their names with criminal conduct? If the FBI
found evidence that Martinez and Freedman had
taken bribes, why hasn't he charged them?

   The answer must be that there was an
absence of corroboration. Merkle didn't have the
goods. His well-meaning intolerance of corruption has turned this man of zeal into a man without any understanding of fair play.

Then the editorial staff quoted other former federal prosecutors
and state attorneys who had things to say about Merkle's tactics:

Ed Austin is the Jacksonville state attorney whose
circuit falls within Merkle's 32-county district.
He says of Merkle: "He acts like he invented
integrity…He has abused the power of his office."

   A Miami defense attorney who was chief
of the criminal division of the U.S. Attorney's
office in South Florida, Neal R. Sonnett, has
seen Merkle's tactics firsthand: "People imbued
with the Holy War Syndrome want so badly to
go after corruption and illegal activity that they'll
do anything, trample anybody's rights, destroy
anybody's reputation. Merkle doesn't understand

that a prosecutor has to be concerned for individual rights."

The editorial went on like this throughout the article. It was a good insight to what was going on within our trial and in the community as a whole, and Merkle seemed to be getting away with it. It gave the defense a lot to talk about in the coming days when they would meet after court. The tide of public opinion was turning, but naturally, as always, I had to return to my cell at the county jail, without a clue to what was being said or being planned.

That same weekend at the county jail, one of the officers who had just been assigned to my cellblock was walking by, and he stopped by my cell. He opened the little window on my door and asked if I was doing OK. I got off my bunk and walked over to the door to get a better look at the young fellow. As I was standing next to the door, he said to me, "You don't remember me, but we met a while back in West Tampa. My dad is Fred Barksdale, and I'm his son Danny. I just wanted you to know my dad thinks you're a good guy and has a lot of good things to say about you."

"Well, you tell your dad I think he is a great guy also, and I appreciate the lift he gave me last year to help me get up to Maxwell prison camp. He's one man who can understand what I am going through. It's nice to see a friendly face here. How long have you been a deputy?"

"Oh, a couple of years now. I have to move on now and check the other cells, but if you have any problems or need anything, just let me know," he said to me before he turned and walked off.

I thanked him for his kindness as I watched him move along the cellblock, looking into each cell. Now I felt a little better and didn't feel so alone. Earlier, I had put in a request with the major who ran the jail if it would be possible to let any of us out of our cells for a few moments to have a little Bible study and fellowship. It seemed no chaplains came by that cellblock to hold any type of service. I guess they thought the men there were so bad that they would not be interested in any type of service.

During the time I had been here, I had taken a poll of the men in the cellblock with me during the breaks when they let some of us out to walk around a little. It seemed some of the men were interested in some type of service. Being Catholic and a Christian, I asked but hadn't gotten a reply back yet. It seemed like someone had to do something there; otherwise, no one would give a care. We may have been considered criminals by our jailers, but we were also human beings.

Bowmer was still testifying on the stand on Monday and Tuesday, making still wilder accusations, with both attorneys and prosecutors objecting to one another. I had to sit there and listen to it all day after day when most of the information being presented had no relation to my situation.

The jury was just taking it all in and making all kinds of notes. They had been taking notes since our trial started. The judge had informed them that this would be a long trial and that it would help them to refresh their memories.

When I got back to the jail on that Tuesday evening, I was informed by the deputy in charge of the cellblock that my request for fellowship and Bible study was approved for whoever wanted to come out of their cells and take part. But they still kept it to four inmates at a time, and we had to take turns coming out to fellowship.

It started out slowly, and with trust, the officers allowed more to come out to fellowship at one time. We built it up to about nine of us, more or less at times, having fellowship together. I remember a tall husky black fellow from one of the lower cells who always came out to fellowship with us. When he would speak, you could tell he was a little slow. He did not have much of an education and could hardly read. But he was a really nice person who was going to trial on murder charges.

During one of our prayer sessions, one of the other inmates asked him what happened. He told us that he was at a bar one night on Nebraska Avenue, and two men were making fun of him because of the way he talked. He was drinking and had gotten drunk, and the two men would not stop heckling him from outside the bar. So he left the bar and started home, but then decided to go back. He picked up a two-by-four and walked over to the two men who were still outside laughing at him. He then hit them with the two-by-four and kept hitting them.

When the police arrived, he was arrested and charged with murder. He said, had he been sober, he would never have done that. He was really sorry about it all, but it was too late now, and he was going to stand trial in state court when they set his date. Until then, he was being held here at the county jail.

We all got around him and prayed for him. No one had ever done this for him before. He cried, asking God to forgive him. We all felt for the man, but we knew it would be up to a jury to decide his fate.

As time went on, one of the officers told me that in all the years he had been in this jail and on this cellblock, he had never seen anything like this before, inmates in a maximum-security cellblock fellowshipping together. To them, these were the worst types of criminals.

It reminded me of something I had heard a long time ago. Even in the darkest crevasse, God's light can shine in. The cellblock had become friendlier now, and even the deputies assigned to the cellblock seemed to be a little more tolerant toward us. Then something that had never been done before in that institution started to happen. Many of the inmates there, myself included, started to share our canteen with others and helped those who had very little or nothing. This was a first; hardened and habitual prisoners just don't do things like that. I like to think I had some small part in this, but I know it was from a greater power. It made the time we spent there a little easier and more sociable.

Some will say it was just jailhouse religion, and maybe it was for most. But for me, it was real; and possibly for one or two of the others, it was also. For whatever reason, it made that cellblock less of a threat for everyone, and I know the deputies who had to work the area appreciated it. It eased a lot of the tension among the inmates in that cellblock. Over time, as inmates came and went, even the new ones, who were hesitant at first, would eventually join in and share.

Each day before someone would be taken to court, the night before, we would all gather around and pray for that person as our situation would allow. When they came back in the evening, we would share the events of the day and say a little prayer. It would go on like this while I stayed locked up in the county jail. This was a new experience both for the inmates and our jailers. Over time, the word would spread through the jail about what was going on in our area. From time to time, supervisors from different areas of the jail would stop by and look in on us to see how things were working out.

CHAPTER 29

The Secret List

March 1986

On Monday, March 24, Bowmer, the government's star witness was called to the stand to testify a number of times as the government kept introducing new "evidence," then bringing Bowmer back on the stand to explain it to the jury. The prosecutor would mention a name or a date; then Bowmer would elaborate on it. Then the defense attorneys would all take their turns discrediting his testimony.

There had been rumors of a secret list of names of people assumed to have been involved in bribes that the government had. The government had provided a partial list that it gave to all the defense counsels. The list was said to contain sixty-nine names and incidents that the government was looking into. But the copy the defense received from the government had about twenty of the names missing from this list.

The defense counsels knew the list they had could not be complete, and they were wondering who was left off the list that they were given. What was the government not telling them? Apparently, Mr. Magri felt they did not need to see the complete list. We heard motions and objections, statements and rebuttals, while the jury listened and took notes Monday into Tuesday.

On Tuesday morning, March 25, when I arrived in the courtroom, my mother, sister, and daughter were standing by the rail next to my table with Ray Harris, my attorney. They had brought some Dunkin' Donuts to court for me and the other defendants and their lawyers. You see, today was my birthday, and the marshals and bai-liffs let it slide, as long as we did not make a mess and cleaned up everything before the judge came in.

At that moment, it was a wonderful surprise for me and the others. My daughter knew I loved Dunkin' Donuts, and I hadn't had any since I started my prison sentence almost a year ago. Just about everyone wished me happy birthday on the defense side. As the pros-ecutors came into the courtroom and went by, they looked our way, some sneering and some just turning away as they walked to their tables. To them, we were just a joke that they were going to put away.

By the time we all finished the doughnuts and coffee, it was time for court to start, and the judge would be in any minute. My sister and daughter picked up all the empty boxes and cups and took them out of the courtroom, then came back while my mother sat on the bench behind me.

When court ended that day and I was sent back to my cell, I replayed the good parts of the day in my head. Alone again in my cell, I could feel the loneliness of being away from my family. I knew how hard this had been on my mother and my children. Seeing me like this was not easy, and spending a birthday like this was very hard on all of us. When some of the other men in my cellblock came by my cell, they would ask how my day went and what was bothering me. I mentioned what happened in court and that it was my birth-day. They wished me a happy birthday under the circumstances, then told me some jokes they knew to cheer me up.

Former County
Commissioner Bob Curry

By Wednesday morning, March 26, back in court, things started to heat up. Bowmer was back on the stand and was being questioned by Bob Curry, who was representing himself, since he too could not afford an attorney to defend him and he did not want a court-appointed attorney. He was being charged with racketeering, racketeering conspiracy, extortion, and two counts of mail fraud. Mr. Curry felt there were enough attorneys in this trial who could help him with advice if he needed it.

Mr. Curry got up from his chair and walked around the table he was sitting behind, then approached and greeted Mr. Bowmer, saying in a cordial manner, "Good morning."

We could all see as Bowmer looked at Mr. Curry and smirked for a moment before saying hello back to him. They once served together on the commission, until Mr. Curry lost his seat to Fred Anderson, who was also on trial with us.

Mr. Curry was holding a yellow writing pad in his hand containing the notes he had been keeping on Bowmer's testimony. As he stopped in front of Bowmer, he went over some of his notes on the statements Bowmer had made on February 28. As he recounted details of the meeting with Bowmer, he asked, "Was everything done properly?" and Bowmer answered, "Yes." Bowmer could never say for sure that Mr. Curry ever took a bribe.

When Mr. Curry finished with Bowmer and took his seat, John Demmi got up and approached Bowmer. He started questioning him about the secret list of names and the names that were missing. Attorney John Demmi, who was defending himself, asked Bowmer if he could remember some of the names on the list. The government had supplied all the defense lawyers with an incomplete copy of the list. Bowmer started to name names as all the attorneys looked down at their lists.

Mr. Demmi asked if Dick Greco was on the list, and Bowmer answered, "Yes." Dick Greco was a former mayor of Tampa. Then Mr. Demmi asked who else was on this list that he could remember. Bowmer then said, "I believe Gilmer Nix, Bruce Samson, and Donald Regar are also on that list."

The courtroom began to buzz. The names Bowmer had just mentioned were not on the list the government gave to the defense attorneys, nor were a number of other names that the government had kept secret from all the defense lawyers.

Bruce Samson at this time was a candidate running for mayor of Tampa. He was now the second candidate running for mayor whom Jerry Bowmer had mentioned in our trial; Sandy Freedman had already been mentioned.

John Demmi was doing a great job of cross-examining Bowmer and getting information from him that the government was withholding. He then asked Bowmer if he could remember all the sixty-nine acts on the list. Bowmer responded that he couldn't. "One moment, Your Honor," John Demmi said. Then he walked over to the table where he had been sitting and picked up some papers, then walked back over to Bowmer and started to read from a copy of the list the government had given him to refresh Bowmer's memory.

After Demmi had read a few names, assistant US attorney Joe Magri got up and objected and requested a sidebar before the bench. All the attorneys got up and approached the bench and spoke in whispers privately with the judge for several minutes. Then, on the record, Judge Carr ordered the government to release the complete list of sixty-nine acts to all the defense lawyers, citing their impeachment value to us defendants on trial. Copies of the list were kept secret from the public.

When they finished, everyone returned to their seats as John Demmi continued with his questioning. Demmi said he would refer back to the list at a later time. Mr. Demmi continued to question Bowmer on other matters that had come up, causing Bowmer to stumble on his answers, and Mr. Magri objected. It was getting late, so Judge Carr postponed any more questions until the next day, and the court was adjourned.

It was back to the Morgan Street Jail for me as everyone else headed home or to their offices for the evening. It had been a long day for everyone and, thanks to Mr. Demmi, a very productive one.

When Thursday came around, the defense had been given a copy of the full list of the so-called sixty-nine acts the night before.

Bowmer was called back to the stand, and Mr. Demmi was to continue with his questioning. But when Bowmer was walking over to his seat, he did not look too well. As he sat down in the witness box, he stated that he was feeling a little under the weather and that he might have a touch of the flu. Joe Magri approached him then asked him to continue with his statement about the bond issue. He then stated that he reorganized the selection of the investment banking firm for a county bond issue in 1980, but he was never paid money to do so.

He went on to claim that he had discussed the change with Bruce Samson and Donald Regar, whom he alleged had indicated that once they were approved on the bond issue, the monies for that particular project would be funneled to the Metropolitan Bank for the bond issue. Bowmer believed he would benefit from this deal by improving his ability to receive loans or whatever he would want from the Metropolitan Bank.

When Mr. Magri finished with Bowmer, Mr. Demmi approached Bowmer and asked him to explain how the list of bribes came about. Bowmer stated that he had compiled the list for the federal authorities after he was arrested for extortion back in 1983. He also said that some of the names on that list were only there to refresh his memory and were not considered to be involved in any wrongdoing.

During the questioning, Joe Magri had gotten up and objected to the characterization by the defense that this list of sixty-nine was a list of bribes. "It is not a list of bribes," he said.

As Mr. Demmi continued to question Bowmer, he said, "Do you see that number 14? Was that anything illegal?"

"It's questionable," Bowmer replied.

Bowmer then went on to describe a 1980 meeting attended by himself, Samson, and Regar at the Metropolitan Bank. He stated that he was called to the meeting by Dick Greco, whom he identified as the bank chairman. He said Greco met him at the door of the bank then took him to Regar's office. Bowmer never mentioned if Greco stayed for the meeting.

At the meeting, to his surprise, Bowmer said, were Becker, Samson, Nix, and Don Regar. One of them closed the door behind him and told him to have a seat. Then they began to tell him about the bond issue and that the recommendation that was received by the Board of County Commissioners wasn't exactly like it should be, with their names in the top.

Bowmer said, "Samson then handed me a piece of paper. It was something like a press release or a motion, you know, that would be made at the Board of County Commissioners, where his firm and Becker's firm would be picked for that particular issue back in 1980. E. F. Hutton had been recommended to the board as the top choice."

Then he told the court, "Someone in the room gave me the number of E. F. Hutton's representative, Les Hirsch. Then the group told me to get then-commissioners Robert Curry and Charles Bean to switch around, and all I would need to do is make the motions, you know, on the thing to reorganize the selection of those firms. The group informed me that they had talked already with Curry and Bean about the change."

Bob Curry got up and objected to Bowmer's testimony as hearsay but was overruled.

Bowmer continued and said that after the meeting, he had called Mr. Hirsch and told him that due to some problems that came up, he was going to have to take a backseat on this particular issue. His firm would be included in the bond issue, but not as the top firm. For the record, Dick Greco, Gilmer Nix, Donald Regar, and Bruce Samson were never charged with any wrongdoing, nor was there any evidence to that effect. It was all based on Jerry Bowmer's testimony that their names were even on that list with so many others.

When Mr. Demmi was finished with Bowmer for the moment, he went back to his seat. Mr. Magri got up and approached Bowmer, who seemed to be looking a little pale and appeared to be sweating a little by now. He asked him to explain to the jury, to the best of his knowledge, his dealings with Mr. Kotvas and Mr. Anderson. He then took a position to the side of the witness box so the jury could see Bowmer clearly as he gave his testimony.

With a slow Southern drawl, Bowmer began to tell the jury of the alleged bribes he was involved in with Mr. Anderson and myself. He began saying that he was paid a bribe by a construction company owned by John DeCarlucci for two rezonings. Then he split the money with Mr. Anderson and Kotvas.

Mr. Anderson's attorney got up and objected to the testimony but was overruled. I turned to Ray Harris, my attorney, and asked why he didn't get up to object. He just told me to be patient and that we would have our chance as we continued to listen to Bowmer's testimony. I was having a very uncomfortable feeling about all this as Ray wasn't looking too well himself.

John DeCarlucci had been indicted and was to stand trial with the rest of us at the beginning of this trial. Judge Carr had severed him from the trial and later dismissed the charges against him.

Bowmer went on to explain more alleged bribes. He stated that a farmer named Ronnie Fulwood made a deal to pay him for rezoning three zoning petitions. After they passed, Bowmer claimed he picked up the money from Fulwood, then split it with Anderson and Kotvas. More objections were overruled.

Then he named Richard Guagliardo, who was a fuel suppler in Tampa, as having paid him to vote to rezone two of his petitions before the county commission. Again, he claimed to have shared the money with Anderson and Kotvas. Again, more objections by all the defense attorneys for their clients as Judge Carr overruled them. Mr. Guagliardo and Mr. Fulwood were also defendants in this trial.

After this, Mr. Magri asked Bowmer, "What about Mr. Kotvas?"

Bowmer replied that a rezoning petition by Gourmet Food Holding Co. Inc. netted the three of us—Anderson, Kotvas, and himself—$1,000 apiece, and it was Mr. Kotvas who paid him the money. At this point, Ray Harris got up and objected to hearsay. Judge Carr overruled the objection and told Mr. Harris he would have his chance to cross-examine Mr. Bowmer. The Gourmet Food Company was never charged with a crime.

"And Mr. John Demmi?" Magri asked.

Again, Bowmer alleged that Mr. Demmi had paid him a bribe that he shared with Anderson and Kotvas for a borrow pit application that was approved by the commission.

"Objection, Your Honor," John Demmi said, standing next to his table as the other attorneys raised objections also. Again, the judge overruled the objections.

Then Bowmer got to a former classmate of his from high school, Mr. Marcellino Echevarria, who was a local builder, claiming he paid him to approve a rezoning. This time, Bowmer never said he shared the money with anyone.

It had been a long morning, and Judge Carr ordered a short break in the trial before the defense lawyers could cross-examine Bowmer. Bowmer left the witness box, and the jury left the room while the defense lawyers got together to discuss strategy during the break. I just sat at my table waiting for Ray to get back with me while he finished talking with the other attorneys. When Ray returned to our table, I told him that he needed to get into Bowmer and that all of this was an outright lie. If I was supposed to have done all this, then where was all the money? The government had gone through me with a fine-tooth comb and hadn't found anything. They had been through my bank account and my savings, what little I had. I was overextended in my bills and owned a used car at the time, which was broken down in my yard. The government even went to my accountant and reviewed all my tax returns and still found nothing. So if I did all Bowmer accused me of, why was I broke and in debt at the time?

I told Ray, "Why hasn't the government produced any of my holdings or where this money went? They can't, Ray. You need to do something!"

Ray just told me to settle down. He could see I was excited and upset about it all. Just then, the judge came back into the courtroom and called the court to order and asked the jury to come back in. The judge had been informed a few minutes earlier by the US marshals that Mr. Bowmer had taken ill and could not continue with his testimony at this time because of the flu.

Judge Carr informed the court of the situation and said the trial would continue on Monday at 8:30 a.m. As he dismissed the jury, he instructed them not to discuss the case with anyone. I was now going to have a miserable long weekend in the county jail while everyone else went home to their families.

Back in my cellblock at the county jail, I had made friends with most of the inmates, and we all got along well together, I'm happy to say. But I was still unaware of how unique our situation was until one of the officers assigned to our unit came by my cell over the weekend and told me, "Mr. Kotvas, because of the type of unit this is, I don't know what you did or how you did it. But I want you to know that since you have been in this unit, this has become one of the most orderly units in the county jail. We have not had one incident here when usually there are two or three a week. Even the major has taken notice.

"In all my years, I have never seen men the likes that are sent here be so well-behaved. The only thing different that we all noticed is you being here and your attitude toward the others."

The only thing I said to the officer was, "Thank you for saying that. But if you treat a man like an animal, he will act like an animal. But if you treat a man like a man, he will act like a man. All anyone wants is to be recognized with self-respect."

The officer then went about his duties, and I thought about what he had said. It kind of made me feel good to know I might have brought a little light to a dark place. But I could not see what I had done. All I really did was to be myself and try to show the other inmates there that by cooperating with one another and sharing what we had, things could be a little easier for all of us.

My sister and daughter came to visit on visiting day. They did not bring Steven. This had all been very hard for him, and every time he left the prison, he got very upset. Unless you and your family have been in a situation like this, you cannot understand what it was like for my children.

On Monday, March 31, Bowmer was back on the stand, feeling much better. Magri had finished with him, and it was the defense lawyers' turn to tear into him. Joe Bealer first, then John Demmi,

Ray LaPorte, and the others all took turns discrediting Bowmer's testimony.

When Ray Harris got up to cross-examine, he basically said the same things as the others; plus he asked Bowmer, "You knew Mr. Kotvas pretty well, didn't you?"

"Yes," was his reply.

"Isn't it true Mr. Kotvas never received any money from you and you kept it all for yourself? And that you made up the story that he gave you some money to make him look guilty?"

As Bowmer was answering, Joe Magri got up and objected, and the judge sustained the objection. But Bowmer answered, "No," while the objection was being made.

Ray then had no further questions at this time for Bowmer. It went on like this for the next couple of days until midday on Thursday, April 3, when a new witness would be called to the stand.

In all these weeks, Bowmer had testified to receiving more than seventy bribes from his time in office. He was finally excused from the stand by Judge Carr. As he got up to leave, he flashed a huge smile to the court and said, "Oh gosh." I could see the prosecutors cringing at that moment, and the jury also could see his demeanor.

CHAPTER 30

Charles Bean Takes the Stand

April 1986

Charles F. Bean III said a cable TV consultant was hired for "show" in the awarding of a county franchise.

On Thursday, April 3, assistant US attorney David Runyan called Charles F. Bean III to the stand as the prosecution's next witness, just a few moments after Jerry Bowmer finished his testimony. Bean had been a colleague of Bowmer's on the county commission back in the late '70s. Once Bean was sworn in, Mr. Runyan asked Bean to explain to the jury the sequence of bribes he was involved in.

Like Bowmer, he went through a list of alleged bribes he was involved in, from garbage-hauling contracts, rezonings, and apparent personal matters. He claimed to have accepted five cash bribes from

1978 to 1980. He claimed he considered them illegal campaign contributions to influence his vote on commission business.

On the stand, he accused one of the defendants on trial with us, a former county commissioner, Robert Curry, as being the middleman in a $1,000 illegal campaign donation from Bill Peterson, owner of a waste-hauling business.

Mr. Runyan asked, "Of course, at that time, you were aware it was illegal?"

"Yes," was Bean's reply.

The legal limit for campaign contributions at that time was $500. Mr. Peterson was never charged with a crime. Charlie Bean had been appointed to the county commission in April of 1978 by then-governor Rubin Askew to fill the vacated seat of Joel Koford, who resigned to be the city manager of Temple Terrace, Florida. In 1980, I defeated Bean in the general election and won his seat on the commission. He then went into business as a marketing services contractor.

When Mr. Runyan asked Bean to whom he credited his appointment to the county commission, Bean said, "It was Nelson Italiano, who was the chief of patronage in Hillsborough County for then-governor Askew."

Nelson Italiano was one of the defendants who was severed from this trial to be tried at a later date.

Then Mr. Runyan said, "Mr. Bean, tell us when you first started accepting bribes."

This was when Charlie Bean started going down his so-called list. He started his allegations off with, "I first accepted illegal campaign cash in the spring of 1978, just shortly after my appointment to the commission."

He alleged that the money came from Tampa zoning lawyer John Demmi. He said Mr. Demmi had three friends who were seeking approval of a zoning petition for a strip shopping center. Bean, sitting in the witness box, avoided looking at Demmi or any of us, instead staring at the floor as he talked. He claimed Mr. Demmi gave him $1000 cash after the county planning commission recommended denial of the project.

"I knew it was illegal," Bean said. "I knew it was to influence my vote on a pending petition. I knew it was wrong. I was apprehensive when Demmi told me the three developers didn't want their names reported on official campaign financial statements. I insisted that he provide me with other names to cover up the transaction. He came back with a list of ten people who supposedly contributed $100 apiece in order to satisfy state campaign laws limiting cash donations to that amount."

Then Bean went on to tell of another payment he received in 1978 from Commissioner Bob Curry, claiming he received a $1000 donation from Curry a week or two after a meeting with him to discuss commission politics. He told the court, "Curry had promised to help me in a couple of ways and gave me the cash on behalf of Bill Peterson. He told me that there were a number of garbage haulers, and they were all friends and that they looked after us. Curry also told me that the commission needed to take care of them when their waste contracts came up for renewal. That fall, I voted to renew Peterson's contract because of the payment."

Bean went on, "A few days after Curry paid me, I took another $1000 in cash from him. This time, he told me the money was from Mr. Eugene Thomason. I'm not sure what the money was for. It appeared to relate to a personal matter involving a friend of Thomason. I also accepted $1000 from real estate broker Wilbur Brantley, who had a zoning petition before the board. He came into my office and told me he had some money for my campaign. The money influenced my vote to approve the petition, although he didn't specify what application he was talking about."

(I have to take a moment to stop here and state for the record that neither Wilbur Brantley nor Bill Peterson were ever charged with any type of crime related to Merkle's ongoing investigation or this trial.)

As he continued to testify, Bean then said, "The largest cash payment I received was from Claude Tanner, president of Suburban Disposal Service. Mr. Tanner told me in 1980 that he and his associates were very happy with the commission, and they were going to raise money for his campaign. A couple of months later, Mr. Tanner hand-delivered an envelope from the people Mr. Tanner said were all my friends in the south part of the county. Inside the envelope was about $4,700 in cash. Then Mr. Tanner said to me that a large portion of the money had come from Buster Williams, president of Alafia Land Development Corp."

"And what was this cash for?" asked Mr. Runyan.

"This was cash for me to spend any way I wanted and to continue to influence my position on the board," Bean claimed.

When it was time for the cross-examination by the defense attorneys, Joe Bealer, representing Claude Tanner, got up and asked Bean, "When a person in office has to run for reelection, is it not normal for people to get together and help raise money for the incumbent to be reelected?"

"Yes, that's correct," Bean replied.

"Is it not a fact that incumbents usually raise more money than their opponents?" Bealer asked.

"Yes, I guess so," Bean said.

Bealer went on like this for a while to discredit Bean's testimony. Mr. Bealer was the highest-paid lawyer of all the defendants in our trial. Claude Tanner had mortgaged his property and taken out several loans to raise about a million dollars to get Joe Bealer to come up from Miami to represent him. Then Juliann Holt, representing Suburban Disposal Services, got up and asked, "Mr. Bean, according to the election laws of the State of Florida, isn't it legal for a corporation to donate to a person's political campaign?"

"Yes, it is," Bean said.

"If all this money was for campaign contributions, why didn't you just list them as such? Was it because you wanted to keep all the money for yourself and not declare it?" Ms. Holt demanded.

Objections came from the prosecution as Ms. Holt said, "I withdraw the question."

It was the same when Bob Curry crossed-examined Bean. By then, Bean looked nervous and appeared to be sweating. When John Demmi got up, he tore right into Bean, making good points over the objections from the prosecution.

Mr. Demmi underscored that Bean had made a deal with the government for a lighter sentence and that by testifying, Bean had been kept out of jail all this time. He told the jury that Bean would say and do anything to keep from going to jail.

It was getting late now, and the judge ordered a recess until tomorrow. Charlie Bean would be called back to the stand, and the questioning would go on. I turned to Ray and said, "You see, much of the testimony has nothing to do with me. How is the jury going to distinguish between who did what to whom? There are so many of us, and I had nothing to do with most of them."

Ray just said for me to be patent. He assured me that the jury knew what was going on, and they were taking notes. He also reminded me that we still had a long way to go before the trial would be over. I told my mother, who was sitting behind me, not to worry as the marshals came over to cuff me for my trip back to the Morgan Street Jail.

That night in my cell, my mind would not stop running and rerunning the day's events in my head. Why, why could I not be out working on my defense like the others? *Boy, the government really wants to break my chops to get me to lie for them. They don't care for the truth. All they are interested in is convictions*, I thought to myself. I wondered how many others were victims like myself, suffering in prisons around the country, caught up in situations just because someone said they were involved in something illegal. There had to be a way to get the truth out! All I could do was lie there and pray.

Friday morning came, and we were all back in court. I sat at my seat drinking my Cuban coffee while we all waited for the judge to enter. It was the only pleasure during the trial where I could enjoy feeling like a person. Once Judge Carr took his seat at the bench, he asked for the jury to come in. The trial was about to continue, and Charlie Bean would be the first to take the stand.

Charlie Bean had pleaded to one count of taking a bribe but admitted to accepting thirteen so-called bribes or payoffs between 1978 and the early 1980s, agreeing to testify along with Jerry Bowmer for a lenient sentence. Back on the stand, assistant US prosecutor Mr.

Runyan asked Charlie Bean to explain his involvement in the county cable television franchise.

Bean opened, saying that he had received $5,000 and that allegedly Bob Curry received $10,000 for their votes on the cable television franchise. He accused Nelson Italiano, who was severed from our trial, saying he was associated with Coaxial Communications and that they needed the county's cable business to improve their chances of getting the city's franchise. Bean said he met Italiano and Dennis McGillicuddy, the manager of Coaxial Communications, at the time to discuss the company's bid. He said Italiano told him that the city of Tampa franchise was what they were really after. They had the cable franchise for the city of Temple Terrace and were going to apply for the city of Tampa.

(I believe this is how Tampa mayor Bob Martinez and city council members Eddie Caballero and Tom Vann ended up on the so-called secret list the government had. The city of Tampa never awarded the franchise to Coaxial.)

Bean stated, "I think it was in the spring of 1980 when he, Italiano, and possibly Tampa businessman Eddie Perdomo, and others spent time at Italiano's Boca Grande beach house for some relaxation and swimming. Italiano took me outside and told me about the $10,000 payment to Curry. Italiano told me I would benefit personally if Coaxial was approved for the county.

"There were eight to ten such discussions regarding the cable franchise, and after we gave them a favorable vote, I received the money. In my parked car outside a restaurant, Italiano pulled out an envelope and said its contents were from Dennis, whom I presumed was Coaxial's McGillicuddy. There was $2,500 in the envelope, and another $2,500 came later."

Bean went on to say, "I have received amounts from $250 to $1,000 to buy my votes on various commission matters, mostly rezonings. The payments, which included general influence money, came mostly from lawyers and local businessmen."

Then Bean mentioned some new names in this circus of bribes. He recalled an incident with a fellow named Harvey Ryals (Mr. Ryals was not charged with any crime). He told the court that Mr. Ryals paid him $500 after a favorable 1980 rezoning vote. Back then, Commissioner Curry lobbied on Ryals's behalf, and state senator Malcolm Beard (D—Seffner, Florida), telephoned him to say that Ryals was a good friend. Bean then said Malcolm Beard did nothing improper.

Then Bean said that after leaving office, he had worked as a consultant; and in 1982, he bribed Commissioners Anderson, Kotvas, and Bowmer on a zoning petition. Bean claimed he gave Bowmer $500 and Anderson $1000, of which $500 was earmarked for Kotvas.

Ray Harris and Fred Anderson's attorney Robert Polli got up and objected to the statements but were overruled by the judge, who said we would have our chance to cross-examine.

When it came time for Mr. Harris to cross-examine Bean, he got up from his chair, walked slowly over to Bean, and said, "Mr. Bean, you said you gave Jerry Bowmer $500 and Mr. Anderson $1000, and he was to give Mr. Kotvas $500?"

"Yes."

Then Mr. Harris asked, "Did you see if Mr. Anderson gave Mr. Kotvas the money?"

"No," Bean replied.

"Do you know if Mr. Kotvas received any money?" Mr. Harris asked.

Again, "No" was the answer.

Then Mr. Harris asked, "So, to your knowledge, you have no idea if Mr. Kotvas ever received any money or was involved in this alleged bribe other than what Bowmer told you?"

"That is correct," Bean said.

"I have no further questions, Your Honor," Mr. Harris said as he walked back to his seat. Then he bent over toward me and whispered, "I think the jury got the point."

Then Mr. Polli, Anderson's attorney, got up and asked Bean if he had ever lied in the past. Bean responded that he had. "So you lied in the past, and you're lying now?" Mr. Polli said.

"No, that's not true," Bean answered.

"Tell us, Mr. Bean, did you accurately recount this event with Mr. Anderson?" Mr. Polli asked.

"That's exactly what happened," Bean said.

"How do we know you're not lying now? Tell us that you haven't lied to your wife and family, your community, your office," Polli demanded.

Then Bean admitted on the stand that he wasn't truthful with his mother when he falsified his campaign contribution reports, which she had to sign as treasurer for his campaign, and that he wasn't truthful when he had his wife sign a fraudulent tax return, which didn't reflect some of the bribes he took while on the commission. He then told the court he had dishonored a minister, who recommended that Governor Rubin Askew appoint him to a county commission vacancy in 1978.

Then he said, "I swore, so help me God, to uphold the laws of the nation but broke many of those laws during my term in office from 1978 to 1980."

At this point, Mr. Polli said to Bean, "So you have been a pretty good liar over the years. You've been lying all this time, and now you and Mr. Bowmer made a deal with the government for a lighter sentence. This is why you're lying about Mr. Anderson's involvement in this matter."

As the prosecutors objected, Mr. Polli withdrew the question.

Mr. Polli had the prosecutors jumping. The objections kept coming throughout his cross-examination. After all that, the court adjourned until the morning.

The next day was Tuesday. Charlie Bean was back on the stand, and John Demmi was taking his crack at him. Mr. Demmi would question Bean for most of the day. During his cross-examination, Mr. Demmi brought up a bribe that Bowmer had claimed earlier in the trial, saying that Bean paid Bowmer $20,000 to get an architectural firm the contract for the Hillsborough County Jail expansion.

When Demmi asked about it, Bean said, "Mr. Bowmer is absolutely mistaken. I was a consultant at the time, and I lobbied Bowmer hard about it. We never discussed a bribe."

Then Mr. Demmi said, "According to Bowmer's testimony a month ago, Mr. Bowmer had gotten the impression that you were offering him a bribe to get the architectural firm you represented the contract."

"No, Bowmer has to be mistaken," Bean repeated.

Then Mr. Demmi pointed out to Mr. Bean and to the jury that this particular bribe or attempted bribe was not on the sixty-nine racketeering acts alleged in our indictment. With that being said, Mr. Demmi then asked if Bean, "Do you consider Bowmer to be a wild man or a nut?"

"No, but I do think he is strange, different, inconsistent, and a man who has his own style," was Bean's response.

Mr. Demmi reminded Bean that they were once friends and that Bean was betraying that friendship to save himself from a long jail sentence. Mr. Demmi had demonstrated to the court that if this bribe was wrong, then the misdeeds of the other bribes could be wrong also. By the day's end, he gave the jury a lot to think about.

The way it looked to me, he was doing a better job on cross-examination of the witnesses than Joe Bealer, who was the lead attorney, and I told Ray Harris that when we adjourned for the night.

That night, when I was returned to my cell, the area had been on lockdown. We had a new guest in the cellblock. They placed the man in the empty cell on the second level just two cells to the right of my cell, so I would have to walk past it to get my cell.

As we walked up the stairs to where my cell was located, the officer escorting me informed me that the new inmate in our unit was the serial killer and rapist Bobby Joe Long. "He's transferred here from state prison to stand trial for the murder and rape of one of his victims. Then he will be returned to state prison to continue serving his time on death row till they execute him," the officer said.

As I walked past his cell, he was standing in front of the small opening in the cell door, just looking at us as we walked by. He was just staring out at us. I could see his eyes. They looked black and round like a shark. He had that dead, lifeless stare that you get if you see a shark up close. Maybe it was the way he looked at us, but it gave me the chills as I passed by. Everyone had heard of Bobby Joe Long.

He was national news, doing time on death row for the number of murders he was convicted of.

During the time he was locked up with us, I never saw much of him due to the fact I was in federal court most of the time, and he would go to circuit court. When back in the unit, he was never allowed to mix with us. He would get his hour break in the unit by himself, and they kept him in cuffs and chains to walk around in when he was out of his cell. He never showed any emotions during his time there, nor cared to say anything to anyone.

We all basically stayed away from his cell; we had enough problems of our own. Plus, he didn't care much for any of us. We could read about what was going on with him at court in the news. When he was there, he always seemed to give us the creeps. He stayed in our unit for a little more than a month before they took him back to prison in North Florida. To this day, I can never forget that first look on his face when I saw him.

It's funny—I later found out that Bobby Joe Long had worked at Tampa General Hospital as an x-ray technician before he was arrested for his crimes. Years later, I ended up working at Tampa General Hospital as an x-ray technician myself, and I would still hear some of the staff talking about him.

After dinner was served and all the trays collected, the officer in charge of the unit let me and a few others out to fellowship and have some recreation time. We huddled around one of the tables and held hands as we gave thanks for the day and prayed for those going to court in the morning, including myself. Then a couple of us played some cards while the others walked around the unit to get their exercise.

Bobby Joe Long would just stay by his door, always looking out and down at us when any of us were out of our cells. He was a no-contact inmate, which meant he was not allowed to have physical contact with anyone.

Except for Bobby Jo Long, over time, I had developed a kind of camaraderie with the other inmates in our cellblock. It didn't matter to any of us what we were charged with. I tried to show the men— and most of them realized it—that if we worked together, the time we had there would be a little easier on all of us. The officers working the unit appreciated it, but they were always on their guard for safety reasons. After all, this was still a high-security unit, full of men accused of murder, rape, grand larceny, and other crimes.

The word had gotten out among the officers working the Morgan Street Jail that this was a good unit to work because there had not been any incidents or problems in the unit for several months. Everyone seemed to notice the change, and sometimes the officers would allow us to have a little extra time out of our cells together for fellowship.

Most of the time, I would just stay in my cell and lie on my bunk, thinking about the day's events. When morning came, it was back to the same routine: cuffs and chains then off to court.

On Friday April 18, the government called more witnesses to the stand. This time, Dennis McGillicuddy, who was the brother of a Florida congressman and had been representing Coaxial Communications, told the court he had paid a $30,000 consulting fee to former Hillsborough County administrator Rudy Spoto on the word of Nelson Italiano that Mr. Spoto could help Coaxial with the county on them getting the franchise contract, but he never saw Mr. Spoto do anything for the cable company.

Then he said he had paid fees of up to $25,000 to Mr. Italiano to help get a franchise in the county near Temple Terrace. But he denied that he had any knowledge of any bribes. The prosecutors were alleging that part of these consulting fees were payments being passed on from Mr. Italiano and Mr. Spoto to Commissioners Charlie Bean and Bob Curry as bribes to vote in favor for the franchise to go to Coaxial.

Neither Mr. McGillicuddy nor Mr. Rudy Spoto had been charged with any crime. Only Mr. Italiano had been indicted, and he would be tried after this trial was over.

The next witness the government called was Harvey "Bo" Ryals, owner of Brandon Camperland, who claimed he knew Jerry Bowmer real well and had paid $1,000 to each of the three commissioners (Anderson, Kotvas, and Bowmer) for a zoning bribe, that he had been dealing with Bowmer for a long time and had been dealing also with

Charles Bean. The government had called Mr. Ryals to the stand to confirm Charlie Bean's earlier testimony. Mr. Ryals said he once paid Bean $500 for his vote. After that, he stated that one commissioner he never bribed was Robert Curry. Mr. Ryals was never charged with a crime and was given immunity for his testimony against us.

As the days came and went and the trial dragged on, more witnesses were called to the stand to testify. We could see the jury's reaction to some of the witnesses. Whether they believed them or not, only time would tell. Many of the jurors kept taking notes as each witness testified. Some only took notes every so often, but all made notes when they looked around the courtroom to see how we reacted to the testimonies. There was one older female juror who seemed to pay special attention to what was going on in the trial, especially when John Demmi got up to cross-examine a witness. I would say she was about five feet five tall, thin build, with silver-gray hair that she always wore pinned kind of up on her head, and was neatly dressed. She was always staring at us and watching the prosecutors as she took notes. It would be years before I would find out who she was.

Former commissioner Fran Davin was called to the stand but could only say she had her suspicions that something was going on between Charlie Bean and Jerry Bowmer but had no direct knowledge of any wrongdoing. Then a lawyer by the name of Charles Rambo took the stand and made the claim that I solicited a bribe from him, that he met with me about a zoning, and that I told him it would take some money if he really wants to get it done.

I turned to my attorney and said, "That is not the way it happened. He's lying."

Mr. Harris just said, "Let's hear him out."

Mr. Rambo went on to say that he later picked me up at the county courthouse and took me to lunch. Then after lunch, he gave me an envelope in his Vann as he drove me back to my office at the courthouse. He did say he never told me what was in the envelope because he said I knew. He then dropped me off and left, and the zoning passed 3–2. How the story had changed from what really happened! Mr. Rambo was also given immunity by Merkle for his testimony. Merkle needed something to try and put a nail in my coffin since there was very little evidence against me.

I explained to Mr. Harris what really happened. "Yes, I met with Rambo, and he asked me for help with his zoning petition. I didn't say it would take money. I told him he needed to make an appointment with all the commissioners and try and explain the situation just like he explained it to me."

Mr. Harris asked, "Did he meet with the other commissioners?"

"Yes, all but Jan Platt. She would not meet with him. And I know he had a long meeting with Jerry Bowmer because he told me, but he never informed me what was said." Then I said, "And yes, he later took me to lunch and afterward handed me a large envelope as he drove me back to my office, asking me to give it to Jerry Bowmer for him.

When we got back to the county building, I saw Jerry's car in its parking space and said to Rambo, 'Why don't you just go up to his office and give it to him? He's in his office right now.' He told me that he had to run. He had a meeting to go to, and he was running late and did not have time to go in. So I took the envelope and went up to Jerry Bowmer's office before walking over to mine and handed Jerry the envelope, saying it was from Mr. Rambo. That is how it all happened, not the way he just described it."

Mr. Harris wrote all this down and, on cross-examination, made the point that the payoff was between Mr. Rambo and Jerry Bowmer; that Jerry had used me as a pawn and go-between for Rambo and himself; that I was never aware he had made a deal with Bowmer nor what was in the envelope since he admitted he never told me the contents.

Of course, there were objections, but they were overruled. And the jury was taking all this down. We all could see how nervous and shaking Mr. Rambo was as he gave his testimony. He could not look anyone in the face, and he rushed off the witness stand when he was excused.

Mr. Harris was doing the best he could for me, but I could see that this trial was taking a toll on him. He was not looking well at all. He would fall asleep on me during the trial, and I don't know how much of this the jury could see. He didn't really stand up for me and object when the time for it came, and he did not present the whole picture to the jury for me.

By this time, I was very worried that I would be caught up in the other defendants' charges by confusion. The way the government conducted this trial, even I was confused, let alone the jury! It was too late to change attorneys, I thought, and the trial would be over in a few more weeks. I was scared, and I didn't know what to do. I really hadn't had much input in the defense like all the others. I had been locked away during the whole trial with limited attorney visits. It seemed Merkle had me where he wanted me.

CHAPTER 31

Fred Anderson Takes the Stand

May 1986

Late in May, Commissioner Rodney Colson was called to the stand. He claimed that one day, shortly after he was elected, Michael Sierra asked him to stop by his office, which was just down the street. When he did, Mr. Sierra asked him if he wanted a piece of the action without saying what it was.

"What was your reaction?" asked US assistant attorney David Runyan.

"I declined the offer, and Mr. Sierra then said to me, 'I thought you would say that.' Then I turned and left his office."

On cross-examination, Ray LaPorte asked Mr. Colson, "Could Mr. Sierra have been talking about an unspecified business deal? Since Mr. Sierra has many business interests?"

Mr. Colson answered, "Yes."

By now, the trial was starting to wind down, and it would be the defense's turn up at bat. The government was finishing up and getting ready to rest. By Wednesday, May 28, the government rested; and Robert Polli, Anderson's attorney, called Fred Anderson to take the stand. He was the first of the defendants to take the stand. Fred had been waiting since his first trial to take the stand and have his say. He knew his health was not good and that, at any moment, he could have a heart attack or stroke. He desperately wanted to get his side of the story out in case something should happen to him. He, like I, felt that if we had only said something in that first trial—anything—we would have never been convicted. Now Fred was going to get his chance.

His attorney Mr. Polli thought this was a bad idea for Fred, the way Merkle and his staff had piled together all these different cases into this trial, many of which had nothing to do with us. He felt this all could backfire on Fred if he failed to convince the jury and the judge. But Fred Anderson was going to have his say, and his time had finally come.

After Mr. Polli got up from his chair and approached the bench, he turned to the jury and said, "I call Fred Anderson to the stand."

Fred got up from his chair and walked around the table he was sitting at toward the witness box. He was wearing a dark suit with a white shirt and a black-and-white striped tie. Fred was a tall man, a little over six feet in height with a stocky build. His hair was salt and pepper, and his complexion did not look too good. His skin coloring was kind of grayish, and his eyes had dark shadows around them At the witness box, he raised his right hand and swore to tell the truth, then took his seat. Mr. Polli walked over to him and asked him how he felt.

Mr. Anderson answered him in his husky high-pitched voice, "Normally ill."

Then Mr. Polli asked him to explain to the jury exactly what went on when Jerry Bowmer came into his office.

Mr. Anderson declared that all these witnesses against him were liars. "If anybody says I took any money, it's a lie. Jerry Bowmer is crazy and a bold-faced liar, and Charlie Bean and Harvey Ryals are liars who cut a deal with the government to save themselves."

When Mr. Polli asked about the tapes that the government made when Bowmer entered his office, Fred told the jury that the tapes lied because the tapes contained unspecified omissions that the government conveniently filled in to say what they wanted them to say and not what was actually said.

The government had admitted earlier in the trial that they had their experts in Washington, DC, go over the five tapes and fill in the gaps to what was said. This was handed to the jury and defense to read while listening to the tapes.

I turned to my attorney Mr. Harris and said, "That's just the point I've been trying to make all this time. How could five tape recorders all malfunction at the same time and some of them not record when Bowmer came into my office? Yet the government is allowed to present their versions of the recordings to the jury!"

Ray just said, "It's OK. Anderson made the point for you."

Fred went on to say that Merkle and his staff—who were prosecuting him and the other defendants for racketeering, conspiracy involving bribery, extortion, mail fraud, and obstruction of justice—were telling lies.

When cross-examined by Joe Magri about some of the other witnesses, Mr. Anderson told the court he didn't recall the testimony of several of the other witnesses earlier in the trial who said they had heard bribe money they were putting up would be split with the other commissioners, including himself; that if they said it, then either they were lying or repeating lies.

He went on to say, "Everyone knows Jerry Bowmer is crazy, and he is always lying about something."

Then Mr. Magri asked him if he was familiar with or ever heard the term *family* used.

Mr. Anderson answered, "I had never heard of it until Crazy was up on the stand."

He then began telling about his ill health and the kind of medications he was taking since his three heart attacks during the Christmas holidays back in 1982, five weeks before his arrest. He seemed to be hoping some of the older jurors would understand the effects of his medications, should any of them have or know anyone who might have a heart condition.

He told the jury that these medications had left him befuddled when the bribe money was delivered to him on February 1, 1983. "I was in a complete fog, which made me an easy target for that crazy man. He set me up to take the fall for him."

Mr. Polli asked, "Would you explain to the jury how were you set up?"

Anderson said, "Bowmer had planted the wad of cash that he had by leaning over him in a strange manner and dropping it in an open desk drawer. He came to the desk. He reached over and dropped whatever he had in his hand. He lay right across me and put the money. I thought it was money—they said it was money—in the drawer. Had I had my normal faculties, I would have hit him. He was not acting like a man, what I would call a tutti-frutti. It was because of all the medications I was taking. When they arrested me and took me down the fire stairs, I was so sick I could barely walk."

Then Mr. Anderson went on to say, "Because of the medication I was taking, I bumped the drawer closed with my knee when some of the delegates from the Brandon Chamber of Commerce walked into my office as Bowmer was leaving."

His attorney Robert Polli continued to question Mr. Anderson for about four hours about some of the other alleged bribes, with Mr. Magri on cross.

It was getting late now. Mr. Harris and I had been watching the juries' reaction to Anderson's testimony. "I don't think the jury is buying all of this. I feel Fred might have hurt himself, taking the stand," Mr. Harris whispered to me.

"I know. I feel the same way. I just hope they understand how sick he is," I replied.

When Mr. Anderson was finished for the day, Judge Carr called for a recess till the morning, when Mr. Anderson would continue with his testimony. For me, it was back to the county jail.

Once back in my orange jumpsuit and in my cell, I started to reflect on the day's events and Fred's testimony. Over and over in my mind, I kept asking myself, *Was his testimony believable? Did the jury understand him, and did they believe him?*

Whatever the outcome, I knew it would have an impact on my case as well. I only hoped that the other defendants would come across a little better to put us all in a good light. At this point, after hearing Fred, I wasn't sure if I still wanted to take the stand. Ray, my attorney, was against it. And after hearing Fred, he now was even more against it. It would be a decision I would have to make, but only after I had heard some of the other defendants testify.

The next day, Thursday, May 29, we were back in court, and Fred Anderson would continue with his testimony. The court had reconvened, but while the jury was still out of the room, Judge Carr had to restrict some of the lines of cross-examination by the prosecution. He explained to assistant prosecutor Joe Magri not to pursue certain points because the evidence was already strong in the case, and the government didn't need to go any further.

Mr. Anderson was still under oath as he took his seat in the witness box, and his attorney Mr. Polli opened by asking if he had been offered any type of deal by the government. Mr. Magri objected and was overruled by the judge as Mr. Anderson explained the situation.

Then Mr. Anderson turned and said to Judge Carr, "Your Honor, Mr. Magri is asking questions just to irritate me." The judge told him that he needed to answer the questions.

Then he turned and faced Magri and said, "You know, and I know, Mr. Magri, if I don't get a heart transplant, I'm going to be dead before long. I want to give my side of the story. I only have a little time in this world."

The judge then turned and looked down toward Mr. Anderson and told him to get on with his testimony.

At that point, Mr. Anderson told the court that Robert Merkle personally offered him immunity from prosecution if he would come down there and testify to the truth as the government knew it. When he said that, the prosecutors and FBI agents in the courtroom looked surprised and confused, shaking their heads and whispering to one another. Robert Merkle was out of the courtroom on this day when Mr. Anderson made the accusation. He was said to have been at some meeting in Tampa giving a speech.

When I heard this, I turned to my attorney and said, "This is almost what happened to me after my first trial, back in Jim Caltagirone's office. But it wasn't Merkle. It was Joe Magri. He didn't offer me immunity since I had already been convicted in my first trial. He and an FBI agent met with me and Jim in Jim's office and told me that if I would cooperate like Jerry Bowmer, I would receive consideration for my cooperation and receive a reduced sentence, and I would see my son Steven grow up. He was indicating that if I cooperated, I could have a similar deal to the one they made with Bowmer. I wanted to tape the meeting, but Jim would not let me. I wish I had. Then we would have proof of the conversation and what really went on."

Mr. Harris was taking notes of what I had said and what Fred was saying. He then said to me, "Take it easy and let's just listen."

Fred was saying and bringing out many of the things I wanted to say.

When Joe Magri cross-examined Mr. Anderson on this alleged deal, Fred said to him, "If I had taken immunity, I would have been up here testifying against the rest of the Hillsborough County Commission bribery, racketeering defendants just like these other turkeys that you have up here."

The government had thrown a bunch of them at us during this trial and had given many of them immunity to testify. Others, like Bowmer and Bean, had pleaded guilty for a lighter sentence.

Mr. Magri had to ask repeatedly before Mr. Anderson would narrow down when this offer was made. He told the court that it was between the day he was arrested, back in February of 1983, and June of that same year, just before he went on trial for extortion, to the best of his knowledge.

Mr. Merkle, who was not in the courtroom, would later be asked by the press about the immunity offer, and all he would say about it was, "I really cannot comment. I really can't say anything about Mr. Anderson's claims. I'm under a gag order by US district judge George C. Carr and cannot comment." That was all he had to say to the press this day.

As Mr. Magri continued to question Mr. Anderson, suddenly he made a move that Mr. Anderson noticed. It seemed that Mr. Magri had tugged on his earlobe in what might have appeared to be an unconscious gesture, but Fred had noticed it. Since the government had made claims earlier in the trial that the commissioners used facial signals as signs to show when a fix was on, Fred leaned forward, his face very stern, and said in his husky voice, "Excuse me, is that a signal?"

Everyone couldn't help but look over at Fred and the prosecutor when Fred said that in his loud voice. Mr. Magri, taken slightly aback, looked a little baffled when Fred said that to him. Then he caught on and, with a grin on his face, asked Mr. Anderson when he had seen it before.

"The last time you did it," Mr. Anderson shot back.

Then Magri said, "How about this one?" laying a finger up beside his nose.

Again Mr. Anderson shot back, "I've seen this one," thumbing his nose at Magri for everyone to see.

As the cross-examination continued through the day, Mr. Anderson continued to deny the charges of bribes when the prosecutor asked about them. He called the array of witnesses against him everything from deliberate liars to dupes of an evil government that was out to persecute him.

Everyone, including the jury, was taking notes. I felt Fred had made some good points, but I also felt that he might have hurt our case. I couldn't tell what the jury was thinking, but the judge did not look too pleased with his testimony, nor did a number of the defendants.

Even though Mr. Anderson had made some good points during these two days, Mr. Magri had torn into his testimony and made him look kind of foolish at different times when being questioned. When Mr. Anderson was finished with his testimony, he left the stand and took his seat at the table next to mine. Joe Magri walked back to his table looking quite smug, with a silly smirk on his face. I could sense a feeling of overconfidence in his demeanor as he approached his colleagues.

While the trial continued with Joe Magri taking point as lead prosecutor, Robert Merkle was out of court most of the week. He was busy giving speeches to different organizations and taking care of personal business.

Merkle's office continued the witch hunt on his targeted public officials. By Friday, the May 29, the state legislature had adjourned for the summer, and all the legislators were getting ready to leave Tallahassee, including state representative Elvin Martinez. However, just the day before, Merkle had someone on his staff file a court document in Tampa regarding the case of a drug smuggler Pedro Jose

Leal, who once was a client of Representative Martinez from his law practice.

The document included allegations against Representative Martinez that Merkle claimed came from Leal. When Representative Martinez found out about the document by the press in his office in Tallahassee, he just said to the reporters that "US attorney Robert Merkle has sadistically renewed allegations of corruption against me. Mr. Merkle just can't stop scheming against me since I was acquitted of perjury charges last year, after Merkle's office had accused me of lying when I denied personal drug use."

According to the press, Merkle's allegations were that Representative Martinez had used cocaine with Leal and received marijuana from him, and that he had received money from former Hillsborough state attorney EJ Salcines from an informant fund. It was well-known in the legal community that Mad Dog Merkle hated to lose when he felt he was right about someone. He would continue to dig with a wild obsession.

According to the press at the time, Leal was freed from a thirty-year prison sentence in 1981 with the help of EJ Salcines, who stated that Leal had become a valuable informant. Merkle had been investigating the situation for much of that time since, and he was now accusing Leal of obstruction of justice and contempt of court for refusing to testify after he gave Leal immunity for any charges that might develop from the investigation.

I don't know, but this sounded to me like the pot calling the kettle black. Wasn't this exactly what Merkle was doing to us in our trial? Giving immunity to the witnesses who testified against us and making deals with the likes of Jerry Bowmer and Charlie Bean?

So what Merkle was saying was that it was all right for the federal government to make deals like this, but it's a possible crime if state and local officials do it. Yet deals of immunity and lighter sentences have been all too common throughout the justice system since time began.

Representative Martinez, from his Tallahassee office, released a one-page statement saying, "Mr. Leal was of tremendous assistance to the state. A state agent has testified that Leal's assistance led to the arrest of seventy-five other drug smugglers. The law provides for the reduction of a sentence in cases of this sort. That's the way the law is supposed to work. Robert Merkle simply cannot accept these simple facts. He has a preconceived script of what and whom he wants to believe, and he thinks anyone who does not agree with him is a liar. Once again, the prosecutors have shown their habitual disregard for the truth, for fairness, and for my rights." This was all Representative Martinez would say about the issue before he left his office to come home to Tampa and be with his family.

Merkle was elated that he had all of us in a barrel. Those who managed to get out of the barrel seemed to fare better. By this time, Merkle was starting to lose favor with the public. His witch hunt had hurt the reputations of many of Tampa's beloved political figures and well-respected community members based on rumors and innuendoes.

CHAPTER 32

The Defense Continues to Testify

June 1986

It was now June, and the trial was coming into its fifth month. Many of the other defendants were getting up one at a time to take the stand in their own defense, attempting to tell their side of the story. All were painting something of a Picasso picture of Bowmer, showing the many parts of his sick and cunning mind and hoping the jury could put the pieces together.

During this time, I started to notice something different about the jury. They did not seem to have the same distant, stern look as before when the prosecution was presenting its case. I think many of the other defendants noticed it too. It appeared that some of the jurors were even smiling at some of us defendants when we would enter the courtroom. They weren't looking as uptight as when the trial first started. At the time, no one could tell what it might mean, nor did I know if anything was being said about it after the day's end. Not being privileged to any information by being locked up in my cell every night after court, I always felt like the lone mushroom.

By the afternoon of June 4, Marcelo Echevarria was called to the stand by his attorney Claude Tison. Mr. Echevarria was a thirty-seven-year-old gentleman of average height and build with dark wavy hair, nice, clean-looking, with a genteel demeanor. He told the jury that he did not care much for politics and that he didn't even vote until he got into the real estate business in the '70s.

He said a lot of that changed in the late 1970s when he found himself trying to understand the political and legal complexities of land rezoning. He realized he needed to educate himself in these things. He had to come to know the political doings in the Hillsborough County courthouse. "This was when I started to make campaign contributions. I made contributions in the $50 to $300 range and met such politicians as county commissioners," he said.

When asked about the bribery allegation by his attorney, he just said, "No, sir, I have not. Ever."

The point was brought out by his attorney Mr. Tison that Bowmer had testified during the beginning of the trial that Mr. Echevarria had allegedly offered him $500 for one zoning and $1,000 for another. Mr. Tison asked him to explain to the jury what really happened.

"Until the corruption probe erupted, I was certain that it was my bright idea to put a buffer of roadside shops between a garbage haulers' headquarters garage and Linebaugh Avenue, which led to the commission's approval of the rezoning. If indeed there was bribe money paid to commissioners as Bowmer has testified, then I know nothing about it," he said.

Then he went on to say, "The $1,000 check that was apparently cashed at the time Bowmer said I paid a $1,000 bribe was an innocent intercompany transaction. The FBI never even bothered to ask me to explain the check. I did mistakenly serve as a front for two $1,000 campaign contributions, which were really from Allen Wolfson, one of Tampa's legendary wheeler-dealers."

Mr. Wolfson at the time was connected to the Metropolitan Bank, which was one of the largest banks to fail at the time. At that moment, I looked at my attorney and said, "You see, this too was like what happened to me. The FBI came to my office and never gave me a chance to explain the envelope that Bowmer left on my desk. They were in too much of a hurry to make a big arrest. When they got me back to their office, all they wanted to know was what I knew about Allen Wolfson. They weren't interested in the truth about what happened. All they were interested in was making arrests and getting convictions. It's just a numbers game to them."

"I understand," was all Mr. Harris said to me.

Then Mr. Echevarria said, "Wolfson asked me to help the Metropolitan Bank by using my name for the contributions so that Mr. Wolfson would not be seen to be exceeding the legal $1,000 limit."

Then Mr. Echevarria added, "I later turned down a third request from Wolfson to fund yet another $1,000 contribution. One of those contributions went to Charles Bean, a former commissioner, who pled guilty and is testifying for the government. On the check that went to Bean, my name was used as a convenience. I didn't even meet Bean until two weeks later, and thus I could not have used the contribution to influence Bean's vote on a rezoning."

It was getting late, and the judge called for a recess until the morning. Mr. Echevarria would then continue with his testimony. As I looked around and watched the jury when he was testifying, it appeared that some on the jury liked the way he testified. I saw some give an occasional smile every now and then. I just hoped tomorrow would bring the same kind of results.

Back in my cellblock at the county jail, some of the inmates would ask how things were going. I would just say, "As well as can be expected. Who knows what goes through a juror's mind during a trial."

The next morning, I was back in court, and my daughter and mother were sitting in the first row of benches behind me. They had brought me a bacon and egg sandwich on Cuban bread with Cuban coffee. What a blessing it was compared to the food in the county jail. I had to drink and shovel it down in a hurry before court got started again. By now, the court bailiffs and marshals were starting to frown on it, although they still kind of looked the other way.

When court reconvened, Mr. Echevarria retook the stand and continued his testimony. Bowmer had made the claim months earlier in the trial that Mr. Echevarria had offered him payoffs on previous zonings using a three-finger sign and a whisper.

When asked about it by attorney Claude Tison, Mr. Echevarria told the jury just the opposite: that it was Bowmer who was trying to extort cash from him.

Echevarria said, "At our first meeting at Frisch's restaurant in downtown Tampa, Bowmer advised me to forego the expensive engineering reports and legal advice and just rely on a payoff. Bowmer said to me, 'If you want to work something out with me, just go down and file a simplified rezoning request, and it will be approved.' Bowmer was lying when he described the bribes."

I told my lawyer, "I can believe that. Bowmer is a real schemer and good at doing things like that."

Then Mr. Echevarria said, "Mr. Bean was not wrong when he said we met, but he is grossly mistaken about when we met. It was not early in 1980 that I gave a $1,000 contribution to Mr. Bean as he had said, but much later in the year when I had nothing before the county commission."

Then assistant US attorney David Runyan asked him, "Didn't you tell an FBI agent in 1981 that you had taken the $1,000 campaign check to Bean's headquarters yourself?"

"No, I never said that. The FBI agent who interviewed me must have been mistaken," Echevarria told the jury.

Mr. Tison, questioning his client about the check, asked, "Was this the check where you were acting as the front man so the real source of the contribution could be disguised?"

"Yes," was Mr. Echevarria reply. He then told the jury that he paid Bean several hundred dollars, maybe $200 or $300, as campaign contributions that he gathered from others. He denied ever handing Bean a cash contribution of $500. Then he said that the only money he ever gave to Bowmer was in the form of a loan and not a bribe. He told the jury and court that Bowmer said he needed money to go on a hunting trip.

"He only had a couple of hundred dollars on him at the time, and to get Bowmer off my back, I gave it to him. I realize the prospects of getting paid back were remote. The ones who scare me to death are the ones who pay you back because they might come back for another loan."

The jury started to laugh at that statement.

"I just wrote him off as a panhandler," he finished.

Mr. Runyan then asked him, "Do you think it was unethical for a realtor and developer to lend or otherwise give money to a commissioner who votes on zoning cases?"

Mr. Echevarria just said, "I thought there was nothing wrong with it."

When he was finished and excused from the stand, we could see that a number of the jury seemed to be smiling at Mr. Echevarria as he took his seat.

The trial was moving along with defense lawyers presenting their evidence and witnesses. It would not be long before we would have our turn with the jury. I just prayed that Mr. Harris would be up to the task. By this time, the strain of the trial had taken a big toll on his health; and as the trial continued, I would have to shake him from time to time so he would pay attention to what was being said in the courtroom. I would find out later from Mr. Sierra that he had missed a number of the strategy meetings the attorneys held. But Mr. Harris would tell me that he wasn't invited or did not know of them all the time.

I didn't know what to believe, being locked up every night and not having any real input into what was going on. It just seemed like since I was already in jail, I was being made the sacrificial lamb who would be doing most of the time in prison with nobody to really defend me. I realized everyone had their own problems to deal with, but it just seemed to me that I was being left out in the cold. Ray Harris was all I had, and there would be no other help coming.

As far as Judge Carr was concerned, Mr. Harris was providing me an adequate defense, and he saw no need to make any changes.

By Friday afternoon, June 6, it was our turn to put on a defense. Mr. Harris only called two witnesses to the stand, one who had asked me to help him collect a fee on a zoning case. He told the jury that nothing illegal was involved, nor was he being charged with any crime or violation. The other was my accountant, who tried to present my bank records and financial statements. On the objection of the prosecutor, it was not allowed into evidence since the government never went into my finances during the trial.

Had it been allowed, it would have shown that there was no money trail and that I owed out more than I had in savings or checking, that I was just living and supporting my family within my means. So where was all this money Bowmer claimed he paid? I knew the government went over all my accounts and assets and found nothing to prove against me. This was why they were so careful to not bring up anything about my personal finances.

When Mr. Harris rested my case, I was shocked, and so were many of the other defendants. The whole defense did not last more than fifteen minutes, without making any further presentation. Most of the other defendants' lawyers took hours or days pleading the defense of their clients before resting.

I asked Mr. Harris, "What are you doing? Why have you rested our case without presenting more evidence or witnesses? Why didn't you call me to the stand?" I was really upset now and worried.

He just said to me, "Don't worry, we got our point across. Most of the other defendants have said what needed to be said, and I would only be repeating what the jury already knows. I did not call you because I did not want you to come off like Mr. Anderson after Merkle gets through with you. Believe me, the key will be in our closing arguments. That is where it all matters, and I am preparing us for that."

We had rested our case. All my hopes rested on his closing arguments and the closing arguments of the others. Although I trusted Mr. Harris, I was never more scared than during this part of the trial. There were still a few more defendants to testify before closing arguments. I figured it would all be over in the next few weeks, depending on how much time the judge gave everyone for their closing remarks.

That weekend, back in my cell, I was still upset with it all. When my sister and daughter came to visit me, they asked me what had happened. "Why didn't Mr. Harris go into this or that?" I just told them that he knew what he was doing, and he was holding it all for closing arguments (I prayed I would be right).

Back in the county jail, we held our nightly prayer session between us inmates while Bobby Joe Long watched us from the open viewport on his door. He would never say a word to anyone, just stared out the viewport with those cold eyes of his. He was never allowed to mingle with us, always eating alone, and he was only allowed to walk around the lower part of the cellblock by himself after we were all locked in. He was being held there for trial for the ten murders he had committed that the state knew of.

On the morning of June 9, city councilwoman Sandy Freedman was called to the stand to testify. Mrs. Freedman was an announced candidate for mayor since Mayor Bob Martinez had resigned to run for governor of Florida. She had been upset for some time at the way Mr. Merkle handled the Bowmer testimony.

Bowmer had made accusations about Mrs. Freedman and Michael Sierra in some of his earlier testimony, claiming that he had told some intimate friends that he was planning to retire from local politics and move to South Carolina. He claimed Sierra told him that Mrs. Freedman might run for his seat on the commission and that he had worked with Mrs. Freedman on a bribe before, saying that she was on the take on the city council.

On the stand, Mrs. Freedman said Bowmer's testimony was garbage, and she denied ever receiving a bribe or bribe offer from Mr. Sierra as Bowmer stated. She declared that she had no knowledge of any improprieties or illegal behavior. She was then excused from the stand. I felt at the time that she came off quite well, and I think the jury could see her sincerity in her testimony. The way I felt about it all was that Merkle was trying to tear our local government apart with his witch hunt.

By Monday afternoon, it was John Demmi's turn to put on his defense. He had been defending himself throughout the trial, but this time, he was going to take the stand, and he asked for assistance from Attorney Arnold Levine, who had successfully defended him in a prior trial a couple of years earlier when Merkle was trying to convict him of drug violations, racketeering, and bribery of local prosecutors. Judge Carr had dismissed the charges and thrown out the case against him.

When asked by Mr. Levine to explain his side of the allegations against him, Mr. Demmi explained that he was a political groupie, very vulnerable, and an easy target for the lies of Bowmer and Bean.

He told the jury that he had innocently violated election laws by giving Bean $300 in cash back in 1978 (the time limit on prosecution for that offense had passed three years previous), along with three names to whom he could attribute the funds so that the $100 legal cash limit would seemingly be complied with.

He went on to explain that he legitimately raised another $400 for Bean during that time. He said that Mr. Bean was wrong about the $1,000 figure and the idea that a bribe was involved. But he did say he collected $1,000 apiece for Bowmer and Bean in late 1982 from a car dealer and a banker who were seeking a rezoning vote. Again, he denied that any bribe was involved. He told the jury that the money was a campaign contribution for Bowmer to move to South Carolina and run for sheriff there.

I remember that back then, Bowmer would make all kinds of crazy statements on what he would be running for. The man would talk out of his hat.

The jury were taking all this down as he continued talking, saying that he was a trusting, naive person and had served as a county juvenile court prosecutor and, for a decade, as an assistant county attorney. When asked about certain bribes, he would say over and over that he was not involved in any bribery deals. He gestured emphatically as he tried to explain certain incidents, sometimes talking rapidly in a tone of hurt and indignation but making a wisecrack every now and then, making the jury and others in court laugh.

When Mr. Levine asked another question about his background, Mr. Demmi said, "I'm like my dad. My dad is really a great guy. He is innocent. He is a giver, always a giving person. He loves people, and they love him. I saw him do it, and I did it. It just came naturally. I have always reveled in politics from the old days of Mayor Nick Nuccio when Tampa was small. I realized soon after meeting Bowmer back in 1976 that I did not like him. I didn't trust him. The commissioner was paranoid, suspicious, and deceitful. Now Mr. Bean, he was smoother, more intelligent, and cooler. He fooled me like he fooled all his friends. He is a user and a taker. I have nothing to hide."

When Mr. Levine asked him, "Mr. Demmi, why were you indicted?"

He replied, "Because I'm vulnerable. Stupidly, I dropped my guard. That's why I feel so stupid because I knew Bowmer might do what he did and level accusations. Mr. Bean just sucked me in and would pump me about the corruption investigation before the indictment. Neither one of them wants to go to jail."

Then Mr. Levine rested the case for Mr. Demmi. We were all studying the jury while Mr. Demmi testified. There were smiles, laughter, and friendly expressions on their faces. Here too, it seemed that the jury liked his presentation. Only time would tell the outcome. It had been another long day, and more was still to come.

CHAPTER 33

The Court Turns to Laughter

June 1986

Early on Wednesday, June 11, Ray LaPorte, attorney for Michael Sierra, began calling witnesses on his client's behalf. Over a dozen witnesses were called and took the stand to testify throughout the day. Most of them testified to their lack of knowledge of any payoffs, even though they knew Sierra well or had been involved in projects Sierra was accused of fixing.

Mr. Magri, for the government, had earlier presented a witness against Mr. Sierra by the name of Andrew Argintar. Mr. Argintar was an attorney who was appointed as a zoning hearing officer back in the early '80s. He had been given a grant of immunity by the government for his testimony. His earlier testimony back in mid-April to the jury stated that in 1980, Sierra offered him a bribe, and he declined it.

He claimed Sierra invited him for a spin in Sierra's Mercedes Benz, then dropped a wad of bills in his lap in an attempt to set up a fix on two zoning petitions pending before him. He made the claim that Sierra told him there was $2,500 in the wad of bills he was just offered and that $2,500 more would be coming if he would keep an open mind on the rezonings involving a site for a CDB Pizza off east Fletcher Avenue and an eight-unit Oak Ramble townhouse complex in northeast Hillsborough County.

He stated that he tossed the wad back and declined to hear the rezonings. They were heard by another hearing officer and approved.

He admitted that he failed to report any such bribe attempt, but he declined to testify before the special federal grand jury investigating local public corruption by invoking his Fifth Amendment guarantee against forced self-incrimination.

Today, to counter this testimony, Mr. LaPorte called a longtime secretary of Mr. Sierra to testify. By now, it was getting late, and the judge wanted the trial to move on.

Margie Lashley was called to the witness box. After she was sworn in, she took her seat, and Mr. LaPorte proceeded to question her on what happened on that day of the alleged bribe to Mr. Argintar. She told the jury she remembered that, on that day, Mr. Sierra had just stepped out of the office after receiving a phone call from the hearing officer, Andrew Argintar. When he returned to the office a little while later, he seemed upset and agitated. He then exclaimed that a zoning hearing officer had just tried to shake him down for a bribe.

She continued that Mr. Sierra said to her that Mr. Argintar had tried to shake him down and that if Mr. Argintar did not excuse himself from ruling on his rezonings, he would report him to the Florida Bar Association, which initiates disciplinary actions against lawyers.

At this point, I whispered into Mr. Harris's ear and said, "I see why Argintar took the Fifth and refused to testify until he was given immunity and not charged with anything. Everybody wants to make deals to hurt the other fellow to get out from under their problems."

Mr. Harris just said to me, "Just keep listening, Joe, and take notes." I sensed the jury felt the same way I did about Mr. Argintar's testimony. I felt that Ms. Lashley came across as a believable witness.

When Ms. Margie Lashley was finished with her testimony, she was excused from the witness box. As she was departing the box, Judge Carr, who wanted the trial to move along because it was close to adjournment time for the day, leaned forward from his bench and said to Mr. LaPorte, "Do you have any short witnesses?"

When everyone in the court heard that, the room broke out with laughter. Ms. Lashley was four feet eleven inches tall, and the judge's comment stopped her in her tracks. She threw up her arms in a kind of mock indignation. Everyone was still laughing as she walked out of the courtroom.

At first, the judge didn't get what all the laughing was about, but then he realized what he had said and quickly recovered, delivering the punch line, "About four feet two?" The moment had awakened everyone in the room, and the jury looked like they were in a good mood as we were adjourned for the day. After what had happened, the judge wanted to end the day on a jovial note.

Over the next few days, more witnesses were called on Mr. Sierra's behalf to rebut the testimonies of his accusers. Some of the witnesses testifying stayed on the stand a short while, while others would take up much of the day. When Nicholas Geraci was called to the stand by the defense, Judge Carr, on a sidebar, prohibited the federal prosecutors from asking about an alleged cocaine deal to finance a zoning bribe for the Galleria project from our first trial back in 1983.

In his ruling, the judge said, "Any mention of the cocaine deal in this trial might unfairly prejudice jurors against defendants who are not even charged with having anything to do with the Galleria rezoning."

All the defendants and defense lawyers were happy about this ruling as this is a normal trick the government uses to get a large group of people on trial convicted. By introducing alleged evidence that many of the defendants had nothing to do with, they could have made it seem to the jury that all were involved, and we could all be found guilty of something we had no part in. Magri and his staff did not agree with the judge's ruling, but the judge made it clear, and they all understood.

Neither Mr. Geraci nor any member of his family were ever charged with a crime or indicted for any wrongdoing. Mr. Merkle attempted in our first trial to present the theory that the Geracis, in denying any knowledge of a bribe, were lying to prevent forfeiture of the Galleria, which might occur if it became known the property may have been connected with a drug deal. If allowed, it would definitely have had a very adverse effect on our trial in favor of the prosecution.

When Mr. Geraci was asked by Mr. LaPorte about Mr. Sierra's involvement with his zoning, Mr. Geraci informed the court that Mr. Sierra had no involvement on his rezoning and that his name had only been mentioned in passing.

When Mr. LaPorte was with the witness, my attorney Ray Harris got up to ask one question. "Mr. Geraci, before the zoning came before the county commission, were you aware that Mr. Kotvas was going to vote against the zoning? And did you and Steve Reynolds meet with Mr. Kotvas about it?"

"Yes, I was aware that Mr. Kotvas was not in favor of our zoning. Mr. Reynolds arranged a lunch meeting a month or two before the zoning to discuss the matter," he said.

"Did any mention or indication of a bribe come up?" Mr. Harris asked.

"No, he told us he could not approve the zoning but would keep an open mind about it. There was no indication or mention of a bribe."

"No further questions, Your Honor," Mr. Harris said, then walked back to our table and sat down. He had made the point to the jury and the court that I was not going to support that zoning and had not, as the county records reflected.

"Redirect, Your Honor," Mr. Magri said as he was getting up.

"Proceed," Judge Carr said.

"Mr. Geraci, is it possible that Mr. Kotvas was stalling to get a bribe?" Magri asked.

"It's possible, but he never approached me on the matter," he answered.

"No further questions, Your Honor." Then Magri took his seat.

Soon it would be Mr. Sierra's turn to tell his side of the story to the jury.

That moment came on Monday, June 16. The time had finally come for Michael Sierra to take the stand. After being sworn in, he took his seat in the witness box as his attorney Ray LaPorte approached him and asked about the claim Bowmer had made about his conversation with him with regard to Sandy Freedman.

316

"I have never stated to Bowmer or anyone else that Tampa City councilwoman Sandy Freedman was on the take. I have never said such a thing, and I don't believe that's the case. As far as I know, Mrs. Freedman is absolutely ethical and a diligent city council member," he told the jury.

As Mr. LaPorte continued to question his client on the witnesses who testified against him, Mr. Sierra answered the questions with what appeared to be an air of confidence and truthfulness. I think the jury could pick this up from his testimony, for many of them seemed busy taking notes.

He explained how Bowmer had ripped him off for $600 in cash, which Bowmer allegedly snatched out of his hand as a purported loan that he never paid back. Then he said, "Otherwise, he got nothing of value from me and certainly no bribes for rezonings or alcoholic beverage permits as he claims."

When asked about the client he advised to take the Fifth, he simply said, "I advised a man involved in a zoning bribe to take the Fifth Amendment against self-incrimination and refuse to testify before the special federal grand jury investigating local public corruption. I deny that giving the advice was an attempt to obstruct justice. I was acting as any lawyer would in giving legal advice to a client."

He went on to say, "I am not guilty of anything, and I am offended by it, with the lack of evidence the government has presented and only on the word of Bowmer, a person I think is worthless. I also wish now that I had reported Andrew Argintar for demanding a $2,500 referral fee on each of my zoning cases he handled."

It had been another intense, long day, with both the defense and prosecution going back and forth on his testimony, so the judge called an adjournment until the morning, when Mr. Sierra would continue with his testimony.

I don't know, maybe it was just me, but the jury seemed a lot friendlier than when the trial first started. I think the other defendants noticed it too. They seemed to be paying more attention to what was going on and taking down a lot more notes. Some of them would even smile toward us when they were seated in the morning or before leaving in the evening. Obviously, they seemed to like a number of the defendants who had testified, which would anger Magri and his crew. I know they must have sensed the same thing I did. But the trial was still going on, and anything could change at any time; plus, we hadn't gotten to closing arguments yet.

Back in my cell at the county jail that evening, some of the other inmates would ask how it went in court that day before we would begin our nightly prayer circle. I would just tell them that it was hard to tell, and things seemed to be going all right. I wouldn't elaborate on it.

Mr. Sierra denied ever trying to recruit Commissioner Colson into a corrupt majority of commissioners who were willing to sell their votes for cash. He also said, "If there was a reference to getting Colson a piece of the action, as Colson has testified, it regarded a legitimate business deal. I did call Colson over to my law office in late 1982 or early 1983. But the subject of our brief conversation was to see if Colson was interested in an $80,000 borrow-pit deal that was suggested by Jerry Bowmer."

Mr. Sierra went on to say, "The subject definitely was not Colson's willingness to join the long-running, self-perpetrating wholesale bribe scheme that Bowmer has depicted in this trial. If I remember correctly, when asked if he wanted a piece of the action, Mr. Colson said no, and I said, 'Commissioner, I thought that's what you'd say.' Neither he nor I wanted to have anything to do with Bowmer.

"The reason our conversation was hurried was because I was late leaving for Tampa Bay Downs where, as a horse owner, I spend most afternoons to see what is running at the track. It was Bowmer who first tried to interest me in investing $80,000 for a one-third interest in a property near Oldsmar that had a potential borrow pit on it from which valuable construction fill could be scooped. I turned Bowmer down but agreed to contact Colson when Bowmer asked me. Remember, Colson also said in his testimony that my proposition might indeed have been about a legitimate business deal."

I thought Mr. Sierra was doing well. I felt he had explained himself, showing that the government only had circumstantial evidence and hearsay evidence against him. It also appeared that the jury was taking it all in.

Mr. Magri and a couple of his associates were handling most of the cross-examinations of the defendants. Robert Merkle was absent from the courtroom quite a bit, taking care of other government business and giving speeches or continuing his witch hunt.

During the next week, the trial moved right along, with the government making some good points against the witnesses the defense presented, and the defense also making excellent points against the evidence and witnesses presented by the government.

By Tuesday, June 24, Robert Cannella took the stand in his own defense. He told the jury that he denied any involvement in any bribery attempt. Assistant US prosecutor David Runyan questioned Mr. Canella about a $2,333 cut he received of a $7,000 fee paid by a businessman named Ronnie Fulwood to get over 1,075 acres in eastern Hillsborough County redesignated for residential development.

Mr. Cannella answered, "I more than earned that money. I share an office with John Demmi and Larry Goodrich, and we all worked together to put the petition together. Besides putting in a good number of hours working on the petition during the week, because of the time limit to get the petition ready, we took the extraordinary step of working most of the weekend on the case. Contrary to what you might think or what Bowmer has said, this was a legitimate petition. When you put in this much time on a matter, you expect to be paid for that time, and this was a legitimate legal fee."

"What did Demmi do to earn his $2,333 from the $7,000 Fulwood paid?" Runyan asked.

"He worked with us on the legal description. You are totally incorrect when you implied we lawyers had only worked on the case that one weekend. I have worked very hard on these cases. It was not window dressing," Mr. Cannella said.

When he was asked by Runyan if he had paid any monies to Bowmer of any other corrupt act involving members of the county commission, Mr. Cannella replied, "No, I have never paid any monies to Jerry Bowmer or anyone else for that matter."

I felt he had proven it was common sense that attorneys expect to get paid for their work and that they charge according to the time they put in on a case. All they had was Bowmer's testimony. I felt bad for Mr. Cannella. In my opinion, he shouldn't have even been in our trial. All the times I had seen him come before the board of commissioners on any matter, he was always very soft-spoken and professional. Like many of us, Robert was a man who did not need any of this in his life. He was on trial with us, trying also to take care of his family and a terminally ill wife.

I knew he had to be going out of his mind with all of this. His wife had not been doing too well. I'm sure the trial must have affected her health. I know from my own personal experience with my late wife.

Mr. Fulwood, who had been charged in this case and was one of the defendants along with the rest of us, had his charges dismissed very early in our trial on what the judge referred to as a legal technicality. The government did not have enough evidence against him, nor could they prove he was actually involved in a bribe. The majority of our trial was based primarily on Bowmer's word. Whether the jury would believe him was yet to be seen.

Merkle, like most prosecutors, didn't seem to care whom he hurt. For him and his staff, it was all a numbers game—get as many as you can indicted and try them all together, then see how many wins you get. It seemed that, to them, innocence or guilt didn't matter. It was convictions that counted, so they would go ahead after all they could. It didn't matter whom they destroyed as long as they won their convictions.

By midafternoon, when Mr. Cannella had finished testifying, word was buzzing around the courtroom that Mayor Bob Martinez would be officially announcing his candidacy for governor of Florida and would be resigning from office sometime soon. That would mean that Sandy Freedman, who was the Chairman of the city council at the time, would become mayor. Both of these politicians were still under Merkle's sphere of suspicion from his unsubstantiated which hunts.

On this same afternoon, in another part of the courthouse in US district judge William Castagna's courtroom, Judge Castagna was ordering assistant US attorney John Fitzgibbons to drop one of the charges against state representative Elvin Martinez, who was also part of Merkle's countywide which hunt and who would be tried at a later date during the year.

The next day, councilwoman Sandy Freedman was called back to the witness stand by Ray LaPorte on behalf of Mr. Sierra. Mr. LaPorte asked Mrs. Freedman twice in different ways if she had ever received a bribe offer or a payoff from his client, Michael Sierra.

Mrs. Freedman replied no both times to the question.

Making his point to the jury for both his client and Mrs. Freedman, Mr. LaPorte had no further questions. When Mr. Magri attempted to cross-examine Mrs. Freedman on whether she was present at any conversations between commissioners and Sierra about herself, he was cut short by Judge Carr, who said that the question was asked and answered and that he should move on. With no further questions, Mrs. Freedman was excused.

After Mrs. Freedman left the stand, defendant Richard Guagliardo took the stand and said he was not guilty of any wrongdoing and that it was all hearsay from Bowmer without any proof, then rested his case. His closing remarks were short, but not as short as the next defendant who took the stand.

Next was Caesar Rodriquez, defending himself, who stepped up to the podium with a yellow notepad in his hand and spoke to the jury. Mr. Rodriquez was a tall, stocky middle-aged gentleman with thinning dark hair and a ruddy complexion. On that day, he was wearing a light-blue pinstripe suit with a light-blue shirt and tie.

When he reached the podium, he placed the notepad on it, looked at it, then raised his head up and looked at the jury, saying, "I'm Caesar Rodriquez." Reading from the notepad, he continued, "Since the government has not proven a case against me, I rest my case. Thank you." He then turned and walked back to his seat. I think that must have been one of the shortest closing speeches of the whole trial.

By Friday, June 27, the trial was in its final phase, and the lawyers and the prosecutors were arguing the final points of the case to the jury. I am sure there was more that could have been said by both sides, but those were trying months for all of us. I was wondering what must have been going through the minds of the jurors. My attorney had advised me not to say anything since many of the defense witnesses had already said what needed to be said on my behalf. He felt it would all get lost in the mountain of information that the jury had to go over on who said what and when. The majority of the case rested on whether the jury believed Bowmer and Bean.

CHAPTER 34

The Trial Comes to an End

July 1986

On the morning of Tuesday, July 1, assistant US attorney Joseph Magri gave the closing remarks of the trial for the government. He started off with, "Good old-fashioned bribery is what the Hillsborough County Commission bribery racketeering case boils down to. It's been a long trial," he told the jury. "This is not a complicated case. In its essence, it's straightforward. In its essence, it's good old-fashioned bribery. As you all have been listening, weeks after weeks, of all the testimony and evidence, it is clear that there was something terribly wrong in the Board of Hillsborough County Commissioners, which, beginning at least a decade ago, has been plagued by bribery and corruption."

Standing there at the podium, he was very passionate in his delivery to the jury. He was a fairly good-looking man of medium build, neatly dressed wearing a dark suit with a white shirt, dark tie, and black shoes. His dark hair was combed neatly to one side.

"I submit," he said, "that not one of these defendants will be able to stand up and tell you that petitions were not being bought. Too many witnesses have taken the stand and admitted to bribery. What you will hear from the defense, in turn, is that this defendant or that defendant was not involved. I tell you, ladies and gentlemen, that this was a systematic public corruption engineered by a self-perpetuating partnership in crime—that the public trust in Hillsborough County was being run over by a corruption train, and bribes are the fuel for the train. Some of the defendants in this trial had private cars on it. The train traveled around for the mutual benefit of all these corrupt commissioners on trial here, plus Jerry Bowmer and Charles Bean as the engineers."

Magri continued, "Even though commissioners were in the driver's seat, the real power for the train fueled by bribes belongs to those people who own the cars, to the wholesale fixers such as Tanner, Sierra, and Williams are alleged to be. There were at least two corrupt majorities of commissioners, one following the other until February 1, 1983," he told the jury.

As I listened to Magri's closing arguments, my attorney could tell I was upset by the way Magri was making his case for the government. It seemed he was doing a good job of putting nails in my coffin. Mr. Harris reached over and put his hand on my forearm and gave it a little squeeze and, whispering to me, said, "It's not over yet. A lot of good points were made by all."

Magri went on to say, "February 1, 1983 was the day the FBI, with the cooperation of Bowmer, who had been caught red-handed the night before, taped Anderson and Kotvas pocketing their share of a down payment on a zoning bribe. Two different majorities—the continuity of the train along the tracks is captured in that fact."

When I heard this, I turned and whispered to Mr. Harris, "There was no red-handed catch. I was trying to get ahold of Albert Tosca in the state attorney's office about the matter when they arrested me. All the information on the tapes was garbled when he walked into my office. It was the government who filled in the missing pieces to make me look guilty because they had no idea what was being said between Bowmer and me."

Mr. Harris just told me to relax and listen; the point was made to the jury during the defense about the tapes.

I listened as Magri continued, "It's not just Jerry Bowmer. Bowmer, who is a thoroughly corrupted insider, is indeed the government's star witness, but far from the only one. Jerry Bowmer was a crooked politician just like Fred Anderson and just like Joe Kotvas. But Jerry Bowmer is no master deceiver, no master con artist. I submit that no one was smart enough to make up all you have heard about in these five months. Besides Bowmer, there was Bean, another grafting insider who has confessed his guilt and testified for the government. There are the dozens of bribes payers who described their dealings with Bowmer, with Bean, and with various defendants, men whose stories tally in all but insignificant detail with one another and with those of Bowmer and Bean."

Then Magri got to the tapes again. Since he and Merkle had such good success with the tapes in my first trial to get everyone convicted, he was going to push the tape issue in this trial to try and convict everyone again.

Magri explained to the jury, "And of course, there is the tape recording made as Bowmer delivered the stacks of $20 bills totaling nearly $5,000 to Anderson and Kotvas in their courthouse offices on February 1, 1983, a tape recording that contains cryptic remarks that Bowmer has testified referred to yet other payoffs still owed for commission votes already bought and sold."

"On that tape," he told the jury. "Bowmer and the FBI were able to bring back a conversation like those that have been occurring for years in lawyers' offices, in hallways, in dark restaurants. Whatever you think of Jerry Bowmer, he came out of those offices with those conversations on tape. The tape does not lie. This is not looking for immunity, ladies and gentlemen."

I could see by the way he conducted himself throughout this trial that he really believed everyone here on trial was guilty of a crime.

"Although the government's case is not perfect, it doesn't have to be. There may be a couple of little warps in those windows of the corruption train that the government promised to open when the trial began. But the requirements of finding guilt beyond a reasonable doubt does not make your job impossible. Just render a verdict that speaks the truth," Magri finished. He would get one final opportunity to make his case once all the defense lawyers had finished their closing arguments on rebuttal.

I watched the jury as Magri gave his closing arguments, and I could see that they were not smiling anymore. They were busy taking notes on what he was saying.

Magri went on for most of the day, taking up over seven hours with his closing arguments. When he finished, Judge Carr called it a day. As everyone was getting up to leave, I felt sick to my stomach. Although I disagreed with Magri's interpretation of events, I felt he had given a very persuasive narrative in his closing arguments. As the jury got up and started to leave, none of them were smiling like before. They just walked out of the courtroom, most of them not even looking our way.

My personal feeling was that the prosecutors and agents had manipulated a lot of the evidence and threatened a number of the witnesses over the past year, such as attorney Steve Reynolds, to make them twist their statements to fit their agenda.

The next day, July 2, because of the number of defense lawyers and defendants, Judge Carr had to instruct all the defense lawyers to keep their closing arguments to around ninety minutes each so the trial could move along.

First up, attacking Bowmer's credibility, was Mr. Richard Lazzara, attorney for Richard Guagliardo, who only had two federal charges against him for alleged bribes. With a strong voice, Mr. Lazzara said, "Bowmer is a master con artist, master extortionist, and master manipulator. He is a man with a basic character flaw that affects his personality. Above all, he is a liar."

He pointed out to the jury time and time again that the only witness to testify against his client was Bowmer. Then Mr. Lazzara went on to produce documents for the jury to show that nothing had changed since his Bowmer's arrest. He demonstrated how Bowmer had violated his various oaths of office by his corrupt deeds, his filings of various inaccurate financial disclosure documents, and his own admitted falsification of his income tax returns.

Then Mr. Lazzara brought out Bowmer's most recent business activities dealing with his family corporation, particularly his company minutes and officer designations, that could have been backdated during the trial. He said to the jury, "This is a most pathetic attempt to cover up previous lies on the witness stand."

He then produced a number of personal financial statements made by Bowmer to acquire loans since February 1, 1983, the date that he came to the county courthouse and set Fred Anderson and myself up to be arrested by the FBI. Mr. Lazzara said, "Those financial statements show deceit that amounts to criminal fraud, and the revelations of Bowmer's recent conduct presents the government with a dilemma in that it's clear that Bowmer may have committed federal crimes for which prosecutors should, in justice, prosecute their own star witness."

That being said, he then asked the jury, "I call upon you to free Richard Guagliardo from this web of deception created by Jerry Merle Bowmer—this web of deception and corruption in which Mr. Bowmer has trapped him. The list of Jerry Bowmer's victims goes on and on. I'm asking you not to add Richard Guagliardo's name to the list. Thank you, ladies and gentlemen."

Mr. Lazzara finished then walked to his seat as the next defense lawyer got up to give his closing arguments. For the next few days, much of what was already said would be repeated by all, exposing Bowmer as a master con artist, extortionist, and manipulator. Each lawyer attempted to derail the government's alleged corruption train. By late Thursday afternoon, Judge Carr called for a recess till Monday morning. He thanked the jury and reminded them not to discuss the trial with anyone, not even the press. The jury and everyone involved in the trial (except me) got to enjoy the Fourth of July weekend so they could come back to court refreshed.

For me, it was back to my cell at the county jail while everyone else could enjoy this time with their families. It is very difficult to try and explain how something like this affects you both mentally and physically. Seeing everyone smiling day after day, going home to their families and friends after the day's trial, while I had to return to a lonely cell, takes its toll on a person.

The holiday weekend in my cell was like every other weekend I spent there. I talked to some of the other inmates in our cellblock, but I spent most of the time lying on my cot, looking up at the walls and ceiling, daydreaming of a life long past. My mother, daughter, and sister came to visit me for an hour, which only hurt more after they left. I just wished I could reach out and hold them for even a moment. But this is what it is like when you're locked up.

On the evening of the Fourth, I could see from my small window people setting off fireworks from the projects across the street from the jail. Oh, how I wished I was out there with them. At times, I could see the night sky light up with all the fireworks and the sound of the explosions vibrating through the cellblock. It was a long weekend for me.

On Monday, July 7, back in the courtroom, Bob Curry got up to give his closing remarks. In a passionate plea to the jury, he said, "Bowmer, the admittedly crooked commissioner, was willing to tell falsehoods. Bowmer's own girlfriend, who testified earlier, said that Bowmer confided in her that his commission colleague Bean was a crook, that his commission colleague Curry was dumb but honest. It hurts my feelings a little bit. I knew he knew I was honest. I didn't know he knew I was dumb."

Everyone in the courtroom, including the judge, chuckled at that statement. He then went on to say, "Not one witness said I conspired with them to extort money. Not one person, except for Mr. Bean, said I delivered money. Not one witness testified that I took money as a bribe. Not one. Not one. Show me one witness who testified I was guilty of all these things. All kidding aside, I'd rather carry the stigma all my life of being dumb but honest rather than smart but crooked. Please keep my reputation dumb but honest and not, with a conviction, change it to smart but crooked."

I could see the jury was taking notes as Mr. Curry was speaking. The trial was coming to an end, and everyone was winding down. Soon it would be time for the judge to instruct the jury. Just a few more closing remarks by both sides, and the trial would be over.

The trial came to an end for the defense on Tuesday, July 8, with attorney Lee Fugate, representing Cullen H. (Buster) Williams, giving his closing arguments on behalf of his client. Mr. Williams was a large, overweight rough-looking gentleman who kept his hair in a crew cut. He was once a buddy of Jerry Bowmer, and he ran a dirt-hauling business, as well as working as a land developer.

Cullen H. "Buster" Williams, 47-year-old Riverview dirt hauler and developer.

Mr. Fugate said, "I accuse Bowmer of treachery in the way he used his friendship with Buster Williams. Bowmer was such a master manipulator, master extortionist, that he tricked federal agents and tried to trick the jury with a tape he made from a hidden board in an attempt to frame such erstwhile companions as Williams and to protect people who can help him."

The majority of the defense lawyers' focus was on Bowmer. The defense constantly reminded the jury of the necessity of going beyond a reasonable doubt if they were to find any defendant guilty.

At the end of this long day, Judge Carr announced to the jury that on the following day, the prosecution would have a chance to rebut the defense. Then he informed the nine women and three men of the jury that they would soon need to pack a suitcase. "Don't forget your toothbrush when the case is turned over to you for deliberation."

He then added, "At that time, I will instruct you on the legal issues involved, including the legal standards for assessing the credibility of some of the witnesses and most especially the burden of proof that the government must have met before any of the fifteen defendants may be convicted.

You will then be sent out to deliberate until you come back with a unanimous verdict on each count against each of the defendants on trial, or until you declare yourselves hopelessly deadlocked. You will need to pack for at least a week, and you will be sequestered during your deliberations under the eyes of the deputy US marshals. You will be spending your nights and eating your meals in a hotel."

With all that said, he dismissed the jury for the night to hear the government's rebuttal in the morning.

On Wednesday morning, July 9, the honor of rebuttal from the government went to assistant US attorney David Runyan. I was surprised it wasn't Robert Merkle (who I believe was out giving speeches to different civic clubs at the time) or even Joe Magri, who had done a good job in trying to prove the government's case against us. For a while there during the trial, he even had me almost believing I might have committed a crime.

Unlike Joe Magri, who alleged there was a train of corruption in Hillsborough County in his closing arguments, Mr. Runyan described Jerry Bowmer as a cancer, saying, "Jerry Merle Bowmer is like a cancerous mole that is itself a potentially deadly disease but can serve the good purpose of warning a person to look for a growing fatal tumor within the body. You can disbelieve everything Bowmer testified to and still have evidence to convict all but one of the fifteen defendants on most of the charges. But even that defendant, Richard Guagliardo, the evidence might suggest he paid zoning bribes as charged. It isn't just Jerry Bowmer anymore but the dozens of witnesses whom we maintain corroborated one or more of Bowmer's accusations," he explained to the jury.

He then told the jury, "Bowmer, after being arrested on January 31, 1983, admitted extorting around one hundred bribes between 1979 and his arrest. He has been the target of orchestrated defense vilification because his testimony implicates every one of the defendants to some degree or another in what the government alleges was a long-running, self-perpetrating crime family involving scores of greedy businessmen, crooked lawyers, and grafting politicians who systematically stole honest government from the residents of Hillsborough County."

I guess it was a feather in Runyan's hat to have the final word in the closing arguments, pointing out to the jury the more than two hundred witnesses and the bales of exhibits that the government had produced. He spent the whole day in front of the jury giving his rebuttal.

When Mr. Runyan finally rested the government's case, it was getting late, about 5:15 p.m. At this point in the trial, Judge Carr turned to the jury to give instructions for deliberation. He dismissed four of the alternate jurors and thanked them for their time and patience during these long months of the trial. He then instructed the remaining jurors to go back to the jury room and pick one from their group to act as foreman for the jury before he dismissed them for the night.

He advised them, "You will then go home and pack enough belongings for several days of deliberation. Then you will return in the morning to the jury room to start your deliberation. When you return in the morning, you will be sequestered for the duration of your deliberation and will be required to stay in your hotel rooms where your meals will be served when not in court, and not to have any contact with any outside influence, under the security of the US marshal's office."

The jurors then recessed to the jury room and selected a foreman for the group. He was an older gentleman who lived in Pinellas County. In fact, most of the jurors were from Pinellas County. There were eight from Pinellas, two from Hillsborough, and two from Sarasota County, whose ages ranged from their midthirties to their mideighties. When they informed the judge that they had selected a foreman, he released them to return home and to come back in the morning with their bags packed for a long stay.

We were all dismissed to go about our business until the jury came back with a verdict. There was nothing more anyone could do but wait. What it all came down to was that the whole trial, along with our lives and reputations, were now in the jury's hands. This was the most nerve-racking part of the trial for us all.

Everyone had mixed emotions regarding the outcome. When the jury left the room, some of the jurors looked very stern in their expressions, but a few of the others seemed to smile our way as they walked out. The government prosecutors and their staff were all smiling as they packed up their belongings. I think they thought they had put the final nail on our coffins with Runyan's closing remarks. In contrast, as I watched all the defendants and defense lawyers collect their belongings, they all looked very somber as they talked among themselves.

As for me, the long wait till the jury came back with the verdict meant that I would stay locked up in the county jail the entire time. No more seeing my family in court where I could hold and hug them. No more Cuban coffee or good snacks during the day. No more seeing anyone until we were called back into the courtroom for the final verdict. For me, the isolation and loneliness while I waited was the hardest.

Before the marshals took me back to the jail, my attorney Mr. Harris informed me that this would not be like my first trial. It might take the jury a number of weeks before they came back with a verdict because of all the evidence they had to go over. The one thing nobody on the defense wanted was for the jury to come back with a quick verdict of guilt.

It was now in the hands of God and the jury. For all of us, it was finally over until the jury came back with their verdict. As for me, I was cuffed and chained, then escorted out of the courtroom that late afternoon to a holding cell in the federal building until I could be transported back to the county jail.

It was midevening when I arrived back at my cellblock and was locked in for the night. I could see Bobby Joe Long standing inside his cell staring out at me with those cold, dark eyes of his as I entered my cell. Like me, he was waiting for a decision to be made in his case for the eleven murders he had committed. Just about everyone in the block was charged with one type of capital crime or another. I guess the government felt this was a fitting experience for me.

One of the prisoners in the next cell asked me how it went in court. I explained that the trial was over and it was in the hands of the jury now to come up with a verdict for the judge. He just said, "I'll pray for you, brother. Like you've been telling us all this time, we just have to have faith in times like these."

I just said, "Yes, we must keep our faith." Still feeling depressed, I rested on my bunk.

On the bright side, I was able to get along with everyone in there without any incident. Most of the other inmates seemed to like me; there was sort of a way about me that made everyone around me feel comfortable—except for Bobby Joe Long, whom no one was allowed to be around and was kept in extreme isolation.

During the months I was with these men, I got to know some of them pretty well. In our free time together, we would talk about what our lives used to be like and how we ended up in trouble. We discussed what we would do if we had a second chance and hoped for the best in our trials. These were men just like any other men, caught in the wrong place at the wrong time, who made a mistake and were now paying for it.

On the next day, July 10, as I sat in my cell, the strangest thing happened. Something unheard of—or at least that probably never happens or very rarely ever happens in a jail or prison—one of the older prisoners in my cellblock named Riley Lee wrote a letter to Judge Carr with a petition from all the inmates in our cellblock (except Bobby Joe Long) signing it, asking the judge to keep an open mind and a merciful and compassionate heart in my case.

Here is a true copy of the letter and petition verbatim:

> To: The Honorable Judge Carr
> From: The Undersigned of cell-block 200 c/1
> (H.C.J.)
> Date: July 10, 1986
>
> RE: Joseph Kotvas
>
> I'm writing this letter in regards to Joseph Kotvas, Jr. But first something about myself.
>   I am 48 years of age. I was introduced to prison life at the age of 19 yrs. I've been in jails in and outside the United States. During those times in jails and prisons, I have known Trespassers, Doctors, Lawyers, Judges (Judge Peel at Florida State Prison), murderers, but never a politician, until I met Mr. Kotvas. Sir during these times

(of incarceration) I have watched and observed many men. For my own benefit and survival. When I form an opinion of one's character, I find that I am right more often than not.

Your Honor, Joe Kotvas, is one of the finest men I have ever met. Every man housed in 200 c/1 maximum security feels the same as I do.

Five (5) months ago when Joe was moved to this cell, it wasn't a nice place to live. Only four (4) men at any given time was allowed out their cell for a period of two hours, twice a day. Still, there was stealing, fighting and arguments among the four (4). Certain men weren't allowed out with the others. Judge Carr, Joe, with God's help has changed all that. Now every morning at 6:45 a.m., all doors are unlocked, so we can hold fellowship and worship God.

Your Honor, we have seen prayers answered and miracles worked in this cell. We pray for another miracle to happen. For we know that it will take one to set Joe free.

Joe started me on the right track to God. My whole life has been turned around. So, what I'm about to write comes from a Christin's heart.

I was at visitation when his daughter came to visit him. We were almost shoulder to shoulder, so I inadvertently overheard most of his conversation. And believe me, it would have touched anyone's heart. His daughter is 22 years old, has the responsibility of caring for his 13 year old son. She's not only his sister, but his son's mother and father, as well. She has *no* social life, the house is falling apart at the present time, and the plumbing is the big problem. There is *no* money to correct this problem.

Joe Kotvas does not *deny* doing favors we all know that goes with politics. Joe was known as the "Poor Man's" commissioner. Joe does not own a ranch in Tennessee, or any other State. If he has *all* the money he allegedly made on all those so-called deals, not favors; would he burden his daughter and son with all the hardships they are going through? I believe not. Your Honor, Joe needs his family. His son and daughter desperately need him.

Judge Carr, we, the men of 200 c/1 have prayed for you to hear Joe's case with an open mind and a merciful and compassionate heart. We pray Joe will be found not guilty of the crimes he's charged with. We pray he can soon be reunited with his family. We pray, when he is free, he can continue his career in politics. We pray, he will someday be the Mayor of this great City of Tampa. We need good men in our local city government. Amen!

Thank you kindly for your consideration and attention concerning the contents of this letter. May the Heavenly Father bless and keep you.

Respectfully yours,
Riley Lee

Petition from men of cell-block 200 c/1

Cell A – Don E. Gorbrough
Cell B – Calvin Harris
Cell C – Eunice Moore
Cell D – Tim R. McAfee
Cell E – Steve Chapman
Cell F – occupied by…Joseph Kotvas
Cell G – Riley Lee
Cell H – David Clark

Cell I – Terry L Smith

Cell J – Joseph G. Brown Jr.

Cell K – Unoccupied (Bobby Joe Long was in court at the time of the petition.)

Cell L – Unoccupied

Cell M – Timothy S. Wiseman

Cell N – Clayborn L. Shepard III

Cell O – James D Hill

Cell P – Timothy Hudson

I was totally shocked. I have never heard of anything like this happening before, nor had any of the officers in the cellblock. They could not believe it. Mr. Lee had given the letter and the signed petition to the officer of the day to go out in the mail to Judge Carr's office. I shed tears of joy when they told me about it. By what strange miracle did I deserve this from these men, who had much bigger problems of their own?

That night, I gave thanks for the blessing I received, for these men, and for the time I was there in that dark place.

On that same day, the jury was back in court, ready to begin deliberation on the trial. The piles of evidence used in the trial had all had been crammed into the little jury room on the first floor of the federal courthouse for them to review.

I would find out later from a visit by my attorney that on this first day, the jury had asked the judge for a clarification on the racketeering law. This is a law that requires that the prosecution prove a defendant guilty of two separate criminal acts for that defendant to be convicted.

This is one of those laws that prosecutors use as a catch-22 when they want to get mass convictions on large groups of people on trial. It seemed they wanted to know what happened if they could not agree in any individual case on two racketeering acts. It was clear that if they decided unanimously that an individual did not commit a certain act, bringing the number below two, they must acquit. It was also clear that if they decided unanimously that an individual did commit two or more acts, they must find the individual guilty of racketeering.

It seemed they were not sure of the middle ground. What if they could not decide? Would they become a hung jury on that particular racketeering count for that particular defendant? Or should they acquit that defendant of that act?

Mr. Harris told me that Judge Carr had to refer the jurors to the instructions on the law that he gave them before handing the case over to them on Wednesday. It was up to them to decide on the evidence that was presented. When I asked Mr. Harris what it all meant, he just said that there were a lot of theories going around from both the defense lawyers and the prosecutors. Who knew what the jury was looking for. There were fifteen defendants, some charged with multiple charges and some with just a few. There was a lot of information they need to take in and consider. Only time would tell what it all meant.

Changing the subject, I then asked him how he was feeling, for he looked all tuckered out. He just said he was going home to rest until we heard from the jury, for there was nothing more any of us could do. He was right about that. I felt so helpless at this point. I returned to my cell with nothing more to do but sit and wait, looking at the four walls or out through the narrow window.

By early Monday morning, July 14, I heard a commotion outside my cell. I got up from my bunk and looked outside into the cellblock through the meal hatch from my steel door. I could see some deputies over at Bobby Joe Long's cell, getting him ready to go back to criminal court. They had him chained pretty good as he waddled out of his cell down the catwalk. Being in court most of the time for all these months, I never really got to see any of the men here coming or going to the county court to answer for their charges.

I would find out later that one of his lawyers, Mark Rubin, was trying to delay his trial, saying that their client could not get a fair trial in Hillsborough County because of all the publicity about serial killers. Bobby Joe Long had already pled guilty on one count of murder under a plea agreement with the state attorney's office. The trial he was having was to see if a jury would recommend the death penalty or a life sentence for his crimes.

According to the news media and jailhouse scuttlebutt, Bobby Joe had already been given twenty-six life sentences the year before after admitting to a series of rapes, kidnappings, and murders back in 1984. He was presently serving a death sentence for another murder he committed in Pasco County, Florida. His attorneys were trying to delay the trial for as long as they could.

Between Bobby Joe Long's trial and my trial, we were one of the top news stories in Hillsborough County and throughout the state, and possibly the nation, at the time. I know the news media was having a field day with all of us, which did not make things any easier for me. Still, for the moment, they had someone else to villainize while we all waited for the jury to return with their verdict.

Then on Tuesday, the fifteenth, things took a turn in the jury deliberation. It seemed Mrs. Florence Corbin, the oldest juror on the jury, wanted to be excused from the deliberation in our case. All the attorneys were called to Judge Carr's chambers to hear what was said between Mrs. Corbin and the judge.

Mrs. Corbin was from Seminole, Florida, which was just across the bay from Tampa. We all learned that she was the national executive secretary and Florida aide-de-camp of the Disabled American Veterans. She was asking to be excused to fly to Reno, Nevada, on Thursday evening to attend the national convention of the veterans group. She told the judge that she could not comprehend that we had not been moving faster. She had felt a quick verdict of guilty or not guilty would be reached so she would be able to attend her meeting. She said she had no idea that putting an end to the marathon case would take so long.

Judge Carr also told the defense lawyers that Mrs. Corbin, who was in her seventies, had complained of ill health; that at her age with one kidney and heart disease requiring medication, she didn't need any more stress. But her main reason to get off was to attend the convention since she had already paid for the plane fare and put a deposit on a hotel room.

The judge let the court stenographer read verbatim to the defense lawyers the conversation he had with Mrs. Corbin. He informed her that he would help her in getting her money back for the plane ticket. She then agreed to stay on and finish with the deliberation of the trial. She was then excused to return to the jury room to continue working with the other jurors on a verdict.

Had she been excused, there might have been a mistrial called, and we all would have to go through another long and expensive trial. This was something that neither the government nor the defense wanted to see happen.

At the time, I thought it might not have been a bad idea to have a mistrial. It might have meant that Fred Anderson would be able to stay longer with his family and get good medical care. I might also be able to stay in Tampa and be near my family and be able to get out of jail when I had to be in court. At the moment, I only had prison to look forward to. Michael Sierra already had his sentence reduced to be served at a halfway house in Tampa.

CHAPTER 35

The Verdicts Come In

July 1986

On Friday morning, the eighteenth of July, I was summoned from my jail cell to report to the federal courthouse. It seemed that the jury had come back with some of the verdicts but were deadlocked on others. All the defendants, defense lawyers, and prosecutors were called to report to Judge Carr's court to hear what was going on.

It appeared that the jury had agreed on the guilt or innocence of some of us but could not agree on all of us on all counts. When I arrived at the courthouse, just about everyone was there speculating on what was going on. My attorney Ray Harris greeted me and tried to tell me what he and the others had learned. The judge had been addressing the jury on continuing deliberation on all counts until a verdict could be reached.

The news of a deadlock on some of the thirty-eight counts against the fifteen of us was buzzing around the courthouse. The judge had received the note about the deadlock late in the morning. Judge Carr then called all the jurors back into his courtroom to admonish them to go back to work on all the charges. He explained to them the expense of the five-month trial in time and effort, money, and emotional strain to both the defense and the prosecution.

The judge urged the jurors to strive for an agreement so that some counts against some of the defendants would not have to be tried again. He stated to them, "If a substantial majority of your number is in favor of a conviction, those of you who disagree should reconsider whether your doubt is a reasonable one. On the other hand, if a majority or even a lesser number of you are in favor of an acquittal, the rest of you should accept the weight and sufficiency of evidence that fails to convince your fellow jurors beyond a reasonable doubt."

He then asked them to keep trying but also told them that if they honestly could not change their minds to reach agreement, that was all right too. There was no hurry to see that justice is done. He told them, "You may be as leisurely in your deliberations as the occasion may require, and you should take all the time that you may feel is necessary."

At around 1:00 p.m., Judge Carr convened all of the lawyers and defendants to his courtroom. He explained to us, "I have received the following message: 'We the jury are at a point where we cannot reach any more unanimous decisions.' It is signed by the foreman, Marvin Gillis. I have instructed the jury this morning to continue with their deliberation and try to come to a unanimous decision on the remaining counts."

He then dismissed us all to go about our business until the jury returned with the final verdict. Many of the lawyers and prosecutors hung around the courthouse, talking and drinking coffee in the courthouse lobby. I was sent to a holding cell in the marshal's office upstairs in the courthouse.

The jury recessed for the night sometime after 5:30 p.m., so I was also taken back to the county jail for the night. All the coming and going and the long, lonely waiting were become a little nerve-racking. I have to say, that evening, I did not get much sleep. All the thoughts of what the jury must be thinking were going through my mind. How much of Bowmer did they believe? Did we put on a good defense? How many of us would be found guilty? Questions upon questions kept running through my mind.

In my heart, I felt that many of the defendants should never have been on trial with us. To me, it was the government's way of grabbing all it could, throwing it out, and seeing where it all landed. Like my first trial, it was guilt by association.

Saturday morning came, the nineteenth of July, and I was still awake. They came by with the breakfast trays early. I just sat on my bunk eating, knowing the jury would be back at it within the hour. It was about 7:30 a.m. I knew the jury had mountains of material to review. They had been going over it all for the past week. How much longer they would take, no one knew. I could see it was a bright, sunny day outside my cell, with children playing in the park across the street from the jail and very light traffic flowing on the streets below me for a Saturday morning.

By midday, I received word that the jury had returned with a full verdict on all thirty-eight counts of the indictment. I was to return to court immediately for the verdict. I was escorted down to the loading area where I changed out of my orange jumpsuit and into my civilian suit for court, as two US marshals put me in a van and drove me to the federal courthouse to stand with all the rest of the defendants.

All the defendants, lawyers, prosecutors, family members, spectators, and reporters packed into courtroom number 1 on the first floor of the federal courthouse. Because of the large number of people expected to attend the hearing, it was felt that a bigger courtroom was needed, so they moved everyone to courtroom number 1 on the first floor.

US attorney Robert Merkle stood with the crowd that was jamming the entranceway. He had an air of confidence about him. His staff was at the other end of the courtroom, smiling and talking to one another, feeling good about what was going to happen. At this point, I think they felt we were all going to be convicted on most, if not all, of the charges against us.

As for us defendants and our attorneys, it was a little more somber. Many of us had worried looks about us as we talked with one another. Some of us had over twenty-five different counts against us while others only had a few. How do you overcome those odds? Yesterday the jury could not decide on all the counts; today they were ready to give their verdict. Was that good, or was that bad? We would all find out soon.

When everyone had arrived in courtroom number 1, it was around 5:00 p.m. The bailiff notified the judge that he could begin with the proceedings. Judge Carr entered the courtroom, and we all stood and watched him as he took his seat behind his bench. Then all sat down and waited for the jury to enter. The judge ordered the bailiff to seat the jury.

A very strange thing happened as the jury entered the room. Along with the rest of the courtroom, I watched the jury as they entered and took their seats. Many of the jurors were looking our way, and they seemed to be smiling at some of us. Marvin Gillis (the jury foreman) and Florence Corbin (one of the older jurors) were whispering and smiling as they sat down in their places next to each other. Now Ray and I were totally confused, as I'm sure many of the others were also. What could it all mean? In a few moments, we would all find out.

When the jury was seated, the judge called the court to order then asked the jury foreman if they had reached a unanimous decision on all the counts against all the defendants. The jury foreman, Mr. Gillis, got up and said, "We have, Your Honor," then leaned over and handed the clerk a number of envelopes to be presented to the judge.

The whole courtroom was jam-packed with people. Every seat was taken, every space was being used, and people were standing crammed together all around the walls of the courtroom in anticipation of the verdicts. The whole room turned silent as Judge Carr opened the sealed envelopes and started reading the verdicts.

"In the government's case against Fred Arthur Anderson, the jury finds the defendant *not* guilty of all the charges, except conspiracy, one count of mail fraud, and racketeering, and acquitted of all other charges."

The government had charged Fred with twenty-four counts in the indictment but was found guilty of only three.

"In the government's case against Robert A. Cannella, the jury finds the defendant *not* guilty and acquitted of all charges."

I was so happy for Robert. Here was a good man who did not belong in this trial. The government had four counts against him.

Now he could spend his time taking care of his sick wife and getting his life back together.

"In the government's case against Robert E. Curry, with five counts against him, the jury finds him *not* guilty and acquitted of all counts.

"In the government's case against John DeCarlucci, with only three counts against him, the jury finds him *not* guilty and acquitted of all counts."

John David Demmi was also found not guilty and acquitted of all counts. He was one man whom Merkle really wanted to stick it to, but he could only come up with six charges against him and not one conviction. This was the second time that Mr. Demmi won over Merkle and his staff.

As the verdicts were being read, US attorney Robert Merkle, standing in the crowded courtroom, could be heard by a number of the people around him, muttering, "Jesus Christ...Jesus Christ," under his breath. He could not believe what he was hearing, nor did he like it one bit. His face turned red with silent anger as the verdicts continued.

"In the government's case against Marcelino 'Marcelo' Echevarria, with only three counts against him, the jury finds the defendant *not* guilty and acquitted of all counts.

"As to the defendant LeRoy R. Gonzalez Jr., with six counts against him, the jury finds the defendant *not* guilty and acquitted on all counts.

"As to defendant Richard D. Guagliardo, with just two counts against him, the jury finds the defendant *not* guilty and acquitted of all charges."

Merkle could be seen making faces and muttering in the back, his face beaming red. Some of the other federal agents and prosecutors were also muttering to themselves or whispering to one other in total disbelief.

"In the case against Joseph Henry Kotvas Jr..."

The government had piled on the charges against me in the hopes that I would cooperate with them against the other defendants, just like Bowmer and Bean had done, for an easier sentence. I was charged with twenty-three counts in the indictment.

"The jury finds him *not* guilty and acquitted of all counts except for three: guilty of conspiracy, one count of mail fraud, and racketeering."

To be convicted of the racketeering charge (RICO Act), you need two predicate acts. The conspiracy and mail fraud charges were the two acts, so I was also found guilty of the RICO Act. There were so many charges against Fred Anderson and myself that basically the jury found us guilty on the evidence that was used in the first trial, with the tape recordings and transcripts.

"In the case against Cesar Augustus Rodriguez, with five counts against him, the jury finds the defendant *not* guilty and acquitted of all charges.

"With defendant Harold 'Hap' L. Rossiter, with only two counts against him, the jury finds the defendant *not* guilty and acquitted of all charges.

Claude Tanner, 56-year-old

"In the case against Claude Tanner, with a number of counts against him, the jury found him guilty of conspiracy and acquitted him of all other counts.

"In the case against Eugene Thomason, with four counts against him, the jury finds the defendant *not* guilty and acquitted of all counts."

"In the case against Cullen H. 'Buster' Williams, with seven counts against him, the jury found him guilty of conspiracy, one count of extortion, two counts of mail fraud, and racketeering. They found him *not* guilty of two additional counts of mail fraud and acquitted him of those charges."

To make the government look even more foolish and to add insult to injury, the jury acquitted all three corporations that were accused of being part and parcel of the alleged racketeering enterprise.

After hearing all of the verdicts, with a disgusted look on his face, US assistant attorney Joe Magri approached the bench and withdrew the ninety-one forfeiture counts against all the defendants. When Judge Carr asked, "Is that all?" Mr. Magri just said, "At this time, we'll dismiss that one forfeiture." Then he walked back to his table and sat down.

The last one he mentioned was against Fred Anderson, and I think he felt there was no good reason to pursue the issue in light of what had just happened in court.

With all the verdicts read, the trial was over, and Judge Carr thanked the jury for their patience and time, then dismissed them. As the jury was leaving the courtroom, Florence Corbin turned, smiled at us, and waved at Robert Polli, Anderson's attorney. Mr. Polli, who looked surprised, smiled then waved back.

Judge Carr then called the court back to order and said, "On the four defendants found guilty, I will hold a sentencing hearing on September 25 for all the defendants. If there is no further business to come before this court," he pronounced as he looked over the court-room, "this court is adjourned." He struck his gavel on his desk, then got up and walked back to his chambers.

At that point, the courtroom bustled out with excitement. There were crying, talking, smiling, shaking of hands, and hugging every-where on the defense side—not so on the prosecution side, where the attorneys were gathering up all their evidence and belongings.

Robert Butler, who was the special agent in charge of the Tampa office of the FBI, was in the courtroom at the time. All he could say was, "Amazing, astounding, I'm at a loss for words."

Reporters were all around everyone, trying to get as many statements as they could from both us and the prosecutors. They were like hungry wolves looking for anything that would give them a good lead.

When they asked me how I felt about the trial, all I could say was, "It could've been a lot worse. I guess there were so many charges against me that we could not win them all. I was found *not* guilty on twenty-two of the charges. That should say a lot about my situation. The other three counts were only affirming my earlier conviction, which I feel the jury knew I was already serving time for."

As much as I was hurting inside, I was very happy for all the others, many of whom I did not know till this trial started. For Michael Sierra, much of the evidence used in this trial was from our first trial. This time, he was found *not* guilty of all counts. This tells me that he must have been innocent of the charges from our first trial and was found guilty in that trial only by association with us. I think this was one of the reasons why the judge reduced his sentence. I believe even the judge thought he might be innocent and was convicted unfairly.

With my family in the courtroom, the marshals allowed me to hug them before I was taken back to the county jail. My mother, sister, and daughter were crying. Even my father, who came to hear the verdict, had tears in his eyes. It was a very emotional moment for all of us. We could not win a total not-guilty verdict, and now there would be another sentencing hearing for me and the others.

A lady friend of mine named Susan Eldrige, whom I knew as a fine Christian woman, came over to us and said she had been praying for me throughout the trial. She had been attending the trial off and on when she was not working. She said to me, "You have to be strong, Joe. God is not through with you yet. I believe he has great plans for you. Just hang in there." Then she gave me a hug and left the courtroom. My sister just said, "That was real nice of her."

For myself, Fred Anderson, Mr. Tanner, and Williams, we had yet to see what lay ahead. For Mr. Merkle and his staff, this was an embarrassing defeat. They gained nothing, no big convictions. All he did was ruin the reputation of good people and tear families apart while costing the US taxpayers probably millions of dollars in manpower, time, and court costs—and all for what? To satisfy his growing ego?

To one of the reporters, Claud Tison Jr., defense lawyer for Marcelo Echevarria, said, "This is a massive indictment of the US attorney Robert Merkle and his office."

Mr. John Demmi, when asked by reporters, said, "I think they sent out a loud, loud message to the US attorney's office and, hopefully, to US senator Paula Hawkins and Lawton Chiles. Let's go after the bad guys."

When stopped by a reporter as he was leaving the courtroom, Caesar Rodriguez, being Caesar Rodriguez, just said, "I had a fool for a client, but it turned out all right."

Robert Curry, when also asked by reporters, said, "It's entirely too easy to indict American people today. What's a probable cause? The prosecutor doesn't like you. I certainly look forward to going home, cooking me a steak, relaxing, and going to bed. It was like living in a daze for five months."

Patrick Doherty, attorney for Robert Cannella, when asked what he thought, just said, "We came in here *not* guilty. We walked out of here *not* guilty."

This was another devastating legal defeat for Robert Merkle and his office, which had been conducting a witch hunt on public corruption at full speed ahead since the Bowmer arrest back in 1983. He was relying heavily on the likes of Bowmer, and he came up with egg on his face.

Like most government cover-ups after a disaster, Merkle had to save face on this embarrassment. So he immediately capitalized on the very small victory he received from the four remaining defendants' guilty convictions. Downplaying his humiliating defeat, he told reporters that the trial was the best-prosecuted case he had seen in his considerable experience as a prosecutor. He also insisted as he said, "The guilty verdicts, though few, did demonstrate that the corruption that was epidemic in this town for ten years has been laid open."

By this time, I was being taken back to the county jail to wait out the time till my next hearing. It was around 8:00 or 9:00 p.m.

when I returned to my cellblock, and a number of the inmates were curious as to what happened in court. Still a little upset by the guilty verdict, I tried to explain to them how the jury found eleven of the fifteen of us not guilty of all charges and how the three corporations charged were found not guilty also.

I said, "Only I and three others were found guilty of any wrongdoing, and even then, we were found not guilty on most of the charges. The government had about twenty-five counts against me, and the jury could only find three to convict me on, but those were basically the same charges I was found guilty of in my first trial. In a way, this was a big victory for me also."

With all that said, I walked to my cell and turned in for the night. I didn't feel like talking anymore, and I just wanted to rest. My body was so drained from all that had happened. It was all finally over for now. All that was left was the sentencing, then the long road back to prison.

The next day Sunday, there was nothing much to do but sit around my cell and stare out the narrow window, watching the world go by. By the early afternoon, my mother, sister, and daughter came to visit me. We talked about how they would take care of my son Steven and how my daughter Julie's work was going and how she had been taking care of our house. They also shared how they thought the trial went. None of us knew how long I would be held in the county jail after the judge resentenced me. It was so hard on me knowing it was just as hard on them, with everything that happened and me in this situation, helpless to do anything for them.

When they left, I was alone again. With nothing more to do, I would just have to wait in my cell till September, when I would learn my fate. The days would go by slowly for all of us in that cellblock. All the excitement of going to trial for the past five and a half months was gone. We were now yesterday's news, and everyone was trying to get on with their lives. The media frenzy had died down, with only bits and pieces popping up in the back pages of the news every now and then.

Fred Anderson was still allowed to stay with his family on house arrest till the next hearing. The judge allowed this because of his medical condition. Claude Tanner and Buster Williams were also allowed to stay out of jail on bond till the next hearing. As for me, home sweet home at the Morgan Street Jail.

Early Friday morning on July 25, deputies came to our cellblock to take Bobby Joe Long back to county criminal court for sentencing. Late that afternoon, he was returned to his cell. Nothing much was said, for he never really talked with any of us while he was there.

The next day, one of the deputies in our cellblock was kind enough to share his newspaper with me. I read in the Saturday *Tampa Tribune* that circuit judge John P. Griffin had sentenced Bobby Joe Long to death. This was his second death sentence, and he showed no emotion in court when the sentence was passed. I could believe this, for he was a cold fish the length of time he was with us at the county jail.

The judge said in passing the sentence, "There is no question in this court's mind that the defendant, Robert Joe Long, had various mental and/or emotional problems. However, the outrageously wicked nature of the murder, its cold and premeditated manner, the fact it occurred during a kidnapping, and Long's prior record outweighed any reasons for mercy."

The state prosecutor in the case, Mr. Michael L. Benito, had this to say about Long: "He was a rabid dog as far as I was concerned. You have to destroy the rabid dog. That's exactly what the judge did."

A few days later, they came for Long and transferred him back to state prison to finish out his time till they executed him. His cell would remain empty the rest of my stay at the county jail.

Days turned into weeks, and it was now the middle of August. Bobby Joe Long was gone, but most of the other men in our cellblock were still there, and we continued with our little prayer sessions and the sharing of our canteen supplies with some of the less-fortunate men among us. The short visits on the weekends with my family were the only thing I had to look forward to.

On Thursday, August 21, came another slap in the face for Robert Merkle and his staff. State representative Elvin Martinez was under a federal indictment by Merkle's office for allegedly lying to a federal grand jury back in a time when Merkle's witch hunt was going hot and heavy. Representative Martinez was scheduled to go on trial for perjury sometime in October.

But on this day, Representative Martinez was named an honorary agent of the Florida Department of Law Enforcement. This was an honor from one of Florida's top law enforcement agencies. Representative Martinez also happened to be the chairman of the Criminal Justice Committee in Tallahassee, where he had worked tirelessly over the years to help the FDLE and law enforcement agencies throughout the state. This said a lot about this Tampa native who was just another victim to Merkle's wild accusations.

When I heard about the award, all I could think of from my cell was, *Way to go, Elvin. You're a better man than Merkle will ever be.*

After that, things seem to get quieter around town. There was nothing going on in the news anymore about the trial or any of the defendants. For the moment, I guess all of us were just yesterday's news. Nothing more to do but sit in my cell each day, waiting for my sentence.

CHAPTER 36

The Day of Sentencing

September 1986

The day of sentencing finally came. On the morning of Thursday, September 25, I was taken from my cell, dressed out, and escorted back to the federal courthouse for sentencing. The whole courtroom was filled with spectators and reporters. My attorney Ray Harris and my family were there waiting for me, as were the three other defendants with their families and their attorneys all standing around talking. Fred Anderson was sitting in a wheelchair with his wife, Pat, standing next to him. The prosecutor Joe Magri and his staff were at the other side of the courtroom, going over some files, I guess to be presented to the judge.

When Judge Carr entered the courtroom and took his seat for the proceedings to begin, a silence came over the room. You could have heard a pin drop from the stillness in the air. He opened the hearing, asking if any of the defendants had anything to say to the court before he passed sentence, calling Fred Anderson to the stand first. Fred's attorney moved his wheelchair to the front of the podium facing the judge as both of them looked up at Judge Carr. Fred did not look well at all. He looked gray and pale, suffering from chronic heart disease.

"Would you like to say anything to this court before I pass sentencing?" Judge Carr asked.

Fred looked at the judge and said, "The fact that I'm in prison is not teaching me anything, except how to run coke and marijuana.

I am not getting anything out of prison because of the low characters with whom I am surrounded with. I ask the court to please consider my condition. I am not getting the proper medical care that I need." This was all that he had to say.

The judge then asked if the prosecution had anything to say. Assistant US attorney Joe Magri stepped forward and said, "Your Honor, the defendants Anderson and Kotvas had shown no remorse, no acknowledgement of guilt, and no intention of cooperating to root out other corruption in the area. I ask this court to send the public and would-be corrupt officials a message that public corruption doesn't pay."

The judge answered Magri, saying, "I agree that the public needs to know that prison sentences await those who breach the trust put in them by the voters."

As I watched and listened to what was going on, I could see that the judge was not giving any consideration to Anderson's plea. Judge Carr said in a condescending voice, "I believe you have gotten and would get fine care in a prison hospital. I am convinced you lied under oath to this court when you took the stand and called the prosecution liars. For this, I feel you deserve an especially stiff sentence. I am sentencing you to seventeen years in prison to run concurrent with your first sentence. You will be returned to the prison hospital in Lexington, Kentucky, to continue serving out your sentence."

Next, I was called up before the judge for sentencing and was also asked if I had anything to say. I was so nervous after hearing what Fred's sentence was that everything was a blur. All I can remember was that I mumbled a few words to the court about the government's misconduct in my case. When I finished, Joe Magri just said, "This is just one more instance of an unrepentant defendant caught red-handed, trying to blame the government."

The judge scolded me for refusing to come to terms with my crimes then sentenced me to twelve years in prison to run concurrent with my first sentence. I guess it would have been much worse if I had taken the stand like Fred.

I may be guilty of a lot of things in my life. I think we all are guilty of one thing or another sometime during our lives. But I was not guilty of the charges of my first trial for a zoning I had voted against. The tapes and the government-prepared transcripts of those tapes and my not speaking up at my first trial were what got me convicted. The jury in this trial cleared me of most of what the government was trying to prove against me. I guess I will just have to live with the results of my first trial.

The next person to stand before the judge was Cullen (Buster) H. Williams. He sobbed as he walked up to the bench and faced the judge. He said, "I was a victim of extortion and not a corrupter. I was too dumb. I did what I did, and I'm sorry. I never made a dime off nobody." Williams bowed his head as he finished speaking, standing before the judge.

Judge Carr said to him, "I sentence you to eight years in prison and fine you $25,000. You may remain free on bail pending your appeal."

Wiping the tears from his eyes, Williams walked back to his seat and sat down.

The last man to appear before the judge was Claude Tanner. His attorney Joe Bealer spoke for him, telling the judge what a fine member of the community Claude was, having done good works for others, and what a good family man he was. There were many supporters from the community for Claude in the courtroom.

When Mr. Bealer finished with his presentation, Judge Carr looked at Mr. Tanner and said, "I agree that Mr. Tanner was not as responsible for corrupting local government as prosecutors had made him out to be."

While the judge was talking, a smile came upon Claude's face, but it changed quickly to a frown when the judge said, "I sentence you to four years in prison and fine you $25,000. You may remain free on bail pending your appeal." Claude walked back to his seat and sat down.

Judge Carr then said, "If there is no other business to come before this court, then I declare these proceedings closed, and court is adjourned."

The marshals took Fred and me back into custody to serve out our sentences. We were allowed a few moments with our families before being taken away. They would be moving Fred to a medical facility right away. I would return to the county jail till I could be transferred back to Maxwell Prison Camp.

Buster Williams, whenever he started his prison time, would have to serve about four years of the eight-year sentence before he could be released on parole. Claude Tanner would have to serve about two years of his four-year sentence before he could be released on parole. Of course, their sentences would only be served if they did not win their respective appeals.

For Fred Anderson, now with seventeen years concurrent with the twelve years he was already serving, the federal parole guidelines required that he serve a total of six years before becoming eligible for parole. As for me, with the twelve years added to my eight years—meaning I was now doing twelve years all together—I would have to serve five years before I could be considered for parole.

As everyone was leaving, we all said good-bye to each other and shook hands or hugged one another. Ray Harris, my attorney, said to me that he would keep an eye on my family for me and try to see what he could do for them. I appreciated that, for I knew that things were not all right with them. The marshals then escorted me back to the Morgan Street Jail.

When I returned to my cellblock, all the men were eager to know how things had gone for me. I just explained to them what had happened in court, then went to my cell to lie down. When they asked me about the petition they sent to the judge, I just said that he never mentioned it. The guys felt kind of bad for me; they were aware of how I must be feeling about it all and left me to myself.

Jerry Bowmer and Charlie Bean had yet to be sentenced for their crimes. It would still be some time before they would go before a judge for sentencing. They were still free and out and about, available for court appearances to testify against those who had been severed from the big trial that just ended.

I would stay in the county jail another week before being transported back to Maxwell. When it was time for me to leave, my cellmates all wished me well. We had created a strange sort of bond during the many months I was held at the jail. I told them that they

355

JOE KOTVAS

should continue with the fellowship and pray for one another after I left. This was the last time I saw any of them. We would never meet again.

It would take the Marshals Service almost two months to get me back to Maxwell, stopping and dropping me off in jails and prisons in little towns and cities along the way. I would be left at these places for days or weeks at a time, till we got to our final destination.

After about a week of stopping at one jail after another along the way, I was dropped off at a rural county jail somewhere in North Florida. It looked as though a few manufactured houses had been put together to make the sheriff's office and jail. I was given a jumpsuit and some clean linen, then escorted to an area where they had detention cells that were attached to the main building. The place was long and narrow, with the open cells running on one side and an open walkway on the other. The unit had three separate cells, all open so you could see everything that was going on in any of the cells. Each cell had two bunk beds on each side and could hold four inmates. The iron beds were bolted to the floor. There was a stainless steel commode and sink all in one against the back wall of each cell, with the bunk beds on each side of it.

This place had no privacy whatsoever for the men who were housed here. This was also the same area where visitors could come along the outside of the cells and stand in front of the cell to visit an inmate. If someone was on the commode when a visitor was present, they could see everything. There was no partition in front of the commode for privacy. It was very humiliating and embarrassing for everyone, especially if there were children visiting. I was placed in the middle cell with three other men who had been convicted in federal court and were waiting to be transferred to their locations. In the next cell over was a local man who was being held by the county. The cell on our opposite side was empty. It seemed we federal prisoners were locked in together, which filled the cell.

The food was not very good. Each day we would receive our meals cold and in Styrofoam containers. I have to say, I never believed that story about *Green Eggs and Ham*. Well, we didn't get the ham, but we sure did get green-looking cold eggs in the mornings. This

356

county must have had a small budget for their sheriff's department, for it seemed the place would blow away with a good hurricane. They rented out jail space to the federal marshal's office to house federal prisoners in transit to bring in extra income for the department.

The men I was housed with for the week were all convicted of bank robbery, but not all together; each one had committed his own crime. It was strange that they all ended up there together like myself, to be transported to some prison somewhere in the country.

We talked and got to know a little about one another to help pass the time. There was nothing to do in the place but sit or walk around in the tight little cell. Sometimes one of them would talk about his trial and how he ended up there. Other times we just kept to ourselves. When someone had to take a dump, we would all turn away and cover our noses so as not to gag from the smell. It wasn't pleasant for any of us, but when you have to go, you have to go. We felt like caged animals in a circus.

One night, while we all were sitting on our bunks talking, one of the men opened up on what he had done and what his sentence was. He told us that he had robbed a number of banks in Florida and gotten away with it. Sometimes, he said, he would rob one bank, then go a few blocks down the street while all the police cars from around the area were at the first bank. He would rob the second bank that was down the street because all the cops were busy at the first bank, and he would get away clean.

So we asked him, "What happened? How did you end up here?"

He told us that when the money ran out, he was feeling bad about it all, so he turned himself in. We all said, "What?" He said yes, he walked into a police station and turned himself in and confessed to robbing the banks. Then he told us he also copped out to about ten others he had robbed. Thinking he would get a break for turning himself in and copping out to all those crimes and closing their cases, was he in for a surprise. He said he didn't think of making a deal with the government before they charged him with all the robberies. He was sentenced to twenty years in prison. When we all heard that, we busted out in laughter. We could not stop laughing for almost ten minutes.

We all just looked at him. I couldn't help but feel sorry for him. Here was a real genius. He robs banks, doesn't get caught, no one knows what he did, and then he turns himself in without making a deal. Real smart. And now he would be doing twenty years. What could any of us say after that but, *What an idiot?* Of course, I would not say that to him, but some of the others were not so polite. The people you meet along the way.

After that, I was back on the road to Maxwell. A few more stopovers on the way, then I finally made it back to the prison camp.

While I was gone for over a half a year, some changes were made to the camp. The new dorms they were building were almost ready. New two-story brick dorms were being built to replace most of the old wooden one-story buildings in order to house more of the inmates who were coming into the system. Once finished, most of the old dorms would be torn down as the men moved out of them.

I was again placed in a temporary dorm until I could be assigned to a permanent one. On the whole, the camp looked pretty much the same. The chow hall was still down the path from the control room between the dorms, and all the inmates and officers were going about their business like any other normal day. By now, it was the beginning of November. I kept my eyes open to see if any of the men I knew before I left were still there.

Settling in was a lot easier for me this time since I was already familiar with the routine. A number of the men I had met during my first stay had been either paroled and sent home or transferred to another location. It would not be long before I would be assigned to a permanent work detail, now that I would be serving out most of my time there.

It did not take long for the loneliness of missing my family to set in. How I missed the weekly visits that I had at the county jail—and the Cuban coffee and snacks that I received when I was in court. Being up in Montgomery, Alabama, made it almost impossible for me to have visits from my family. This was a costly and long way to travel for them. The holidays would soon arrive, and that made it even more depressing. I attended prayer meetings in the evening during the week and mass on Sundays. It helped my morale to fellowship with the civilian volunteers who offered their services to us through the prison ministry. Not many of the men took advantage of it, but I felt it was doing some good.

Toward the end of November, I was assigned to the base laundry as my work assignment. The base laundry was operated by UNICOR under the Department of Justice, Federal Prison Industries Inc. This was a way to help inmates learn a trade and earn a few cents more than what a normal inmate would make. For some men, this was all the money they could make while in prison. Depending on the job, an inmate could earn anywhere from ten cents an hour all the way up to a dollar an hour. I was being started at twenty-five cents an hour, which there at Maxwell was not bad. This gave me some spending money for the things I needed from the commissary. It meant I would not have to burden my family for money every month.

During this time, I received a letter from the federal court stating that I was being assigned a new attorney to handle my appeal and that he would be getting in touch with me sometime soon. I would find out later that Ray Harris was too ill to continue with my case and had asked the court to be relieved on medical issues.

By early December, I received a letter from my daughter, Julie, explaining how things were going for her and the family. She enclosed a news article from *The Tampa Tribune* that she thought would interest me. It explained that Governor-elect Bob Martinez and two Tampa city councilmen, Tom Vann and Eddie Caballero, had been subpoenaed to testify in federal court on bribery allegations involving them and Nelson Italiano relating to a cable television franchise for the city of Tampa.

Nelson A. Italiano is accused

The subpoena was issued by attorney Arnold Levine on behalf of his client, Nelson Italiano. Italiano was one of the defendants who had been severed from my second trial. It seemed that their names had surfaced earlier that year while my trial was going on, and that their names were contained in a sealed document filed by prosecutors with a federal judge that recounted the statements of an Italiano associate alleging that the city cable bribe had been paid.

They had all denied the allegation, and none of the three had been charged with a crime. Mr. Levine wanted the governor-elect and the two city councilmen to testify on Mr. Italiano's behalf. He hoped the governor-elect would come down from Tallahassee to clear the air about the matter.

I felt this should be very interesting. I wished I was back in Tampa to see it all. My daughter said in her letter that she would keep me informed on the situation, and she and my sister, Rose, would send me all the news articles on the trial. After reading my mail, I thought to myself, *How many more good names in Tampa are Merkle and his staff trying to destroy?*

I was unaware of this at the time, but the outcome of this trial would have a significant bearing on my conviction. Over the next few days, I received a number of news articles about what was going on back in Tampa; and when I was able to make phone calls to my family, they kept me up to date.

I read in one of the articles sent to me that Robert Merkle was planning to handle the Italiano case personally. The only charge against Mr. Italiano was one count of mail fraud, which, if he was convicted, would carry a maximum penalty of five years in prison. Mr. Italiano was represented by one of the best attorneys in Tampa, Arnold Levine.

By personally going after Mr. Italiano on the mail fraud charge, Mr. Merkle was trying to tie together the allegations of bribe taking that extended from the Hillsborough County Commission to the Tampa city council, all the way to then-mayor Bob Martinez, who was now the governor-elect of Florida.

The article from *The Tampa Tribune* stated that Mr. Levine planned to have the governor-elect deny any knowledge of an alleged 1979 bribe for the city cable franchise, a bribe that federal witness Eddie Perdomo would presumably testified that he paid. Mr. Perdomo was once in business with Mr. Italiano sometime back in the late '70s.

Mr. Perdomo was claiming that he used the money not only to pay off Martinez but also city councilmen Tom Vann and Eddie Caballero. None of these men had been charged with a crime, and they all denied the allegations. Mr. Merkle was trying to create a pattern.

It seemed that things were getting hot in the political arena in Tampa again. As for me, unless I got a break on my appeal, it would be a long time before I saw home again. When I finished reading the material, it was time for the daily count. If it came out correct, all of us in our dorms would get ready to be called out for dinner.

After dinner, a little later in the evening, I was walking back to my dorm from the camp library, where they had a few old DOS computers for the inmates to use to work on motions or type letters. I heard a voice call out, "Kotvas!"

I turned around to see who called my name, but there were a lot of fellows hanging around the area, and I did not see anyone I recognized. Then the voice called out again, "Joe Kotvas!" I looked over to where the sound came from, and I saw an inmate walking over to me. I did not recognize him at first because he had a full beard and a bushy head of hair. As he kept coming toward me, he started to smile.

"Alan Wolfson," he said as he greeted me. I was shocked but happy to see a familiar face from Tampa.

"What are you doing in Maxwell?" I asked.

He told me he had been transferred from a maximum-security prison where he had been incarcerated for some time, and he would finish out the remainder of his time at Maxwell. He had been sentenced to prison a few years back for securities fraud. He heard I was back at the camp, and he wanted to know what was going on back in Tampa.

I explained the situation to him and what happened at my trial. I talked about what Merkle was up to and how there were still more defendants to stand trial from my case. He did not have anything nice to say about Merkle or the federal government. I explained what had happened when I was arrested and how the first thing they had wanted to know before they asked anything about my situation was about him and what I could tell them.

I said none of it made any sense to me. "They seemed to think I might have known or had some information about you that they could use. Of course, I could not tell them anything because I didn't know anything."

We talked for a while, and he showed me what dorm he was in, and then we both turned and walked away. I knew we would be seeing each other while at this camp. It was nice to have someone from home whom I could talk to. Boy, how he had changed. He looked a lot heavier now than he had been when I knew him before, and so different with the bushy hair and beard. He used to be so clean-cut, always wearing nice suits, well-groomed, and clean-shaven. This Alan Wolfson looked so different from the man I knew back in Tampa. He would later tell me that he wanted to stay looking like this to keep a low profile and stay out of sight so no one would recognize him while he was in prison.

Besides the government, he felt that there might be some others who might have it in for him. Here was a once prominent and powerful man in Tampa, now just another inmate at Maxwell. Places like this housed many a man who had tried to beat the system.

Maxwell, like all prison camps, was designed to house nonviolent and short-term inmates, as well as inmates who had served most their time in upper-level prisons and kept their noses clean, now sent to the camps to finish out their time.

However, because of overcrowding in the prison system, a good number of hardened criminals were being transferred to the camps also. What used to be a place for white-collar offenders and those who had committed crimes now housed a good number of drug dealers, bank robbers, thieves, and smugglers—you name it. They were there finishing up their time so they could go home.

We still had a good number of white-collar offenders, but the number of drug offenders in the camp was growing. Over time, you couldn't help but get to know a number of them. Many of them were Vietnam veterans who got hooked on drugs while in the service. Some were former servicemen who had worked for the government or the CIA, then got greedy. Some were members of the Cuban or Columbian cartels or independent dealers trying to make a big score. Then you had the small-time mules who got caught trying to bring in a few pounds of coke or pot to make a few quick bucks. You could say we were a melting pot of the wrong type of society.

When I got back, I found out that we even had a US district judge there at Maxwell doing time for income tax evasion. This was something of a real situation to have a federal judge doing time. He was the Honorable Harry E. Claiborne from Las Vegas, Nevada. It seems that he had made a number of enemies in the Justice Department over the years for dismissing their cases because of lack of evidence and sloppy investigation. Federal prosecutors and the FBI in his district wanted him off the bench, so it seems that they investigated the poor man for a long time, and all they could come up with were trumped-up charges of tax evasion. His case is an example of how the federal prosecutors, if they are out to get you, will do anything, including circumventing the law, to get a conviction on you.

His case makes very interesting reading on how the government can twist the truth. I was able to get a copy of a special report on his impeachment titled "The Impeachment of Judge Harry Claiborne." I was shocked to read what the government had done to this man because he believed, according to the letter and spirit of the law, that each defendant is entitled to justice under the law. I was also shocked to read how the federal prosecutors manipulated the law to serve their advantage.

Judge Claiborne kept to himself most of the time and stayed away from most of the men at the camp. For the most part, he was a loner, although a number of inmates from time to time would try and talk to him about their cases. Most of the time, he would just tell them he could not help them or that he didn't have time, for he was working on his own case at the moment.

He was a very distinguished gentleman with gray hair, thin build, and average height. I did have the honor to be able to speak to him for a little while about my situation. He was kind enough to take a quick review of some of the information from my first trial. He told me that he was sorry, but I got screwed. Based on the information I showed him, he told me he would have thrown out the transcript that the government filled in and supplied to the jury, but he would have allowed the tapes to be heard. Other than that, he would not say anything more without knowing the whole story from both sides.

I did not bother the man anymore after that, but when we met on the compound or at meals, we would smile or nod as we passed. He just wanted to do his time so he could get back to his family. His case only goes to show you that no one is safe from zealous prosecutors.

As time went on, I got to know a few of the other men there at the camp, and I was able to build a trust among us. I could see a lot of changes going on in the camp with the population expanding. There were a number of social cliques in the camp. Most of the Cubans hung out together. The same went for the Columbians and the blacks; each had their own social group. The white Anglos in the camp didn't really have any organized group. The nonviolent white-collar inmates mostly kept to themselves. The others who had been involved in the drug business also kept to themselves.

Nobody would bother or mess with any of the groups; they all had their own free space around the camp during their free time. A lot of the men used their time working out at the weight shack or jogging around the perimeter of the camp to keep in shape. Many of the men knew they would become short-timers soon and would be leaving in a year or two, so they were not going to mess up and be sent back to a higher institution.

The government offered Pell grants to inmates who wanted to improve their education. We were allowed to attend Troy University in Montgomery, Alabama, in the evening, wearing civilian clothes, as long as we returned to the camp by lights-out. The camp provided a bus with an officer who took the men to the university and picked them up when their classes were over. Allen Wolfson was one who took full advantage of the program. I was able to take a few classes there also. This was one of the things that made us feel normal again, even if only for a few hours. I was surprised that more men from the camp didn't take advantage of this program. A lot of the men just sat around the camp and vegetated or hung out with their so-called friends.

Allen and I were not really friends, just men from the same hometown doing time at the same institution. He was the type of person who had a superior attitude about himself, and he still thought he was better than most of the men there at the camp. Except for occasional social chats, we never really spent any time together. He stayed over in his dorm, and I stayed over at mine. He was kind of a standoffish cold fish. Unless he wanted something from you or wanted you to do something for him, he wouldn't bother with you. In fact, for the whole time he was there at Maxwell, he was basically a loner. He kept to himself and did not really connect with anyone. He was also like that back in Tampa when I first met him, so prison life really didn't change him. But he did use his time to do a lot of studying while he was there.

CHAPTER 37

Bowmer and Bean

December 1986

Jerry Bowmer was the government's star witness

Former County Commissioner Charles F. Bean III pleaded guilty last year to racketeering...

By the middle of December, I finally received word on the status of Jerry Bowmer and Charlie Bean. It seemed that on Monday, December 15, Jerry Bowmer appeared before Judge George C. Carr to finally plead guilty to his charges. Even though things were starting to level off, he was still an active witness for the government against those who had been severed from the big trial. The judge gave him only three years for his crimes because of his plea bargain and cooperation with the government. This was time to be served at the Eglin Air Force Base prison camp whenever the government was finished with him. He would actually end up only doing several months and then probation.

Mr. Merkle would say on Bowmer's behalf, "This man was heroic for standing up for his crimes and helping the government to clean out corruption in this community."

The next day, Charlie Bean entered his guilty plea; and the following day, Judge Carr sentenced him to four years in prison but, because of his plea bargain, suspended the sentence to six months also at Eglin Air Force prison camp with four years of probation and ordered to perform four hundred hours of community service. Again, Mr. Merkle told the judge that Bean was also a hero for pleading guilty and cooperating with the government and that he was still being used as a witness for the government in the upcoming trials. Because of this, they were both allowed to be free on bail until the government concluded all its business with the remaining defendants. The Italiano trial was still going forward at the time.

From what I could find out from family and friends, as well as from the news articles that were sent to me, things were still heating up back in Tampa. Right after his guilty plea and sentencing, Bean was on the stand testifying against Italiano with regard to the Coaxial cable franchise and how cash was being paid out.

Another person who was going to testify for the government was Dennis McGillicuddy, the CEO of Coaxial Cable at the time and brother to US representative Connie Mack. Merkle gave him immunity for his testimony at the trial. Merkle was attempting to tie together the campaign contributions that Governor-elect Martinez received from Coaxial when he was running for mayor of Tampa back in 1979, claiming they were actually bribes. These contributions had been funneled to the mayor's campaign by Mr. Italiano and Eddie Perdomo (who was a witness for the prosecution) and also to the campaigns of city councilmen Tom Vann and Eddie Caballero. None of these men had been indicted or charged with a crime.

Mr. Levine, representing Italiano, whose only charge in the matter was mail fraud, subpoenaed the governor-elect to testify at the trial and did not expect the governor to take the stand till after the holidays and into the New Year.

Sitting on my bunk back in my dorm, I read the articles from *The Tampa Tribune*. Mr. McGillicuddy claimed he gave $10,500 of cable money to be distributed toward the campaigns of these men. He said, "Mr. Italiano was a man of high status in the city of Tampa. My company hired Mr. Italiano to give advice and to lend his name to the franchise efforts."

As I continued to read, I caught the part where US attorney Robert Merkle was questioning Mr. McGillicuddy on paying a bribe to Martinez to get the cable franchise. Mr. McGillicuddy denied having an arrangement to win Martinez's support through financial remuneration.

It seemed from what I could read that Merkle was really trying to hit this issue home and make the new governor look guilty of a crime in the eyes of the public. This was another example of Merkle's tactics to try and destroy the reputation of good leaders in our community.

From what I had been hearing from home, Merkle and his staff were starting to make enemies in high places. He was no longer the golden boy of *The Tampa Tribune*, and people were starting to question his motives. The once savior from corruption now appeared to be the demon of innuendos. It was just a little too late for me. I was sure I would be hearing a lot more of Merkle's shenanigans in the coming months.

Toward the end of December, I received word that outgoing Governor Bob Graham, who had won a US senate seat and would take office in Washington, DC, the first week of January 1987, was asked by prominent members of the Tampa community to look into the affairs of the US attorney's office for the Middle District of Florida and how Mr. Merkle was conducting his office in the investigation of state representative Elvin Martinez and other state and local officials.

Because of the change in offices and the upcoming holiday season, the senator-elect would make no comment about the issue one way or the other. At the moment, he had other pressing issues that needed attending to. He would look into the matter at his earliest convenience.

It seemed to me at the time that waves were starting to form into a storm for Mr. Merkle. He was not looking so clean and innocent anymore. He had been bullying and stepping on too many toes in his quest for recognition and power.

As the holidays came and went and 1986 turned into 1987, there wasn't much to celebrate around the camp, unless you were being released. Just as they are everywhere in the prison system, the holidays at Maxwell were some of the worst times for the inmates. Many of the men suffered from a depression we called the *holiday blues*. Even when the civilians who came to fellowship with us brought us little goodies that the warden would allow them to give us, it didn't change the sense of loneliness we felt not being with our families. The warden of the prison camp tried to decorate the camp and put up a Christmas tree for the holidays, but it only added to the depression of some of the men. Others like myself tried to make the most of the situation and worked to cheer some of the others up while holding our real feelings inside of us. In the camp, we did not control our lives; that was for the government to do. Some of us had to stand suicide watch over some of the men so they wouldn't do something to harm themselves. You get a few attempts at times like these.

By the beginning of January 1987, I received a news clipping from my sister, Rose, that had been cut out of *The Tampa Tribune*, stating that Merkle was accusing US senators Lawton Chiles and Bob Graham of meddling in his affairs, claiming he was asked by Senator Chiles to ignore rumors of corruption in Hillsborough County.

As I read, I could not believe that Merkle was now on the defensive and was attacking the reputations of two highly respected US senators from Florida. It appeared battle lines were being drawn all over the state of Florida and all the way to Washington against Merkle's conduct. The article was written by *Tribune* staff writer Bentley Orrick and began with the declaration, "US attorney Robert Merkle has charged that Florida's senior Democratic US senator pressured him to ignore any rumors of public corruption in Hillsborough County."

Mr. Merkle, who is a Republican appointee of President Reagan, in an open letter, alleged that Sen. Lawton Chiles made the suggestion at a brief one-on-one meeting before the Senate voted on his nomination back in 1982. That Chiles stated to him that any such malicious rumors about Hillsborough or Tampa corruption were unfounded and the subjects of those rumors were known to the senator to be men of integrity.

That Chiles continued, saying to him, "He expected, were I to be confirmed by the Senate vote as United States attorney, that I would ignore such rumors." When Chiles was asked if he made such a statement to Merkle, his response was that he remembers no such conversation and the gist of the charge that he attempted to pressure Merkle against combatting public corruption in Hillsborough is totally wrong.

This was a Christmas Eve letter to the outgoing Governor Bob Graham, also a Democrat, who was soon to join Chiles in the U.S. Senate. This letter was written in response to Graham's remarks to a Tribune reporter that he would be taking a hard look at Merkle's methods and results once he got to the Senate. Merkle also accuses Graham of politically motivated meddling in federal investigation.

In Merkle's letter to Sen.-elect Graham he writes, "I assure you as I assured Senator Chiles over four years ago, that the decisions of this office have never been made for political reasons, nor will they ever be daunted by political concerns."

It appeared that Graham's chief of staff Jay Hakes had something to say about the letter from his office in Tallahassee. He tells this reporter who is interviewing him that Merkle's letter was one of the most incredible pieces of mail we've ever received. That there seems to be a lot of innuendos in it. It's hard to deal with innuendos.

When Senator Chiles was asked about the meeting with Merkle, he said he doesn't even remember specifically meeting Merkle but thought he must have because he always sees such nominees before he would blue-slip them with a yes vote. He also stated that he does have a standard refrain with candidates for the federal prosecutor's post that Merkle might have heard and misinterpreted. That standard refrain with candidates is a warning not to take the entrenched opinions of law enforcement officers at face value, but to find out for yourself.

According to the article, Senator Chiles also said that Merkle himself said their meeting ended cordially, if coolly. I don't think he'd be worth his salt if he ended a meeting cordially after someone had tried to pressure him in the manner he related.

It seems Mr. Merkle has led major investigations of local public corruption in almost every major city in his federal district. Politicians and law enforcement officers in Jacksonville, Orlando, and Fort Myers have been among the targets. But most thoroughly probed, however, have been politicians, officeholders, and power brokers in Tampa and Hillsborough County. Most of the targets were identified with the dominant Democratic organizations in the area.

The article also indicated that EJ Salcines said Merkle's investigation was a politically motivated attempt to destroy Hillsborough's most successful Hispanic vote getter. Plus, Hillsborough County's Sheriff Walter Heinrich complained that several of his deputies had allegedly been abused by Merkle in the secret confines of the grand jury.

Merkle's final remarks in his letter to Graham were, "Take your best shot in any future investigation. If you decide to launch yet another inquiry, I would request that it be conducted entirely in the public eye so that a full and fair accounting may be assured."

Wow, what was going on in Tampa? It appeared that the tables of popularity for Merkle were turning around. Maybe it was time for someone to look at the real reasons that were motivating Merkle.

I read and r-read the article several times, then put it away with the other articles that were sent to me, wondering what more would be developing in the days to come back home. It was hard not being able to say or do anything from where I was. I had settled into my life at Maxwell. In prison, you really don't make friends; you make acquaintances. These are people you talk with or hang out with, but you're never really friends, and you really don't want to be. It's not good to let other inmates know too much about you; it could cause problems later on in your life. You just try and get along with everyone, keep your nose clean, and move on with your life.

Life at Maxwell was starting to become routine. I got up in the morning for count, then walked over to the mess hall for breakfast, and reported to the inmate bus stop to be taken to my work assignment. I rode the bus that took the men to the base laundry. Most out-of-camp work details started between 8:30 a.m. and 3:30 p.m. The buses would be at our pickup points at 3:30 p.m., and we all had to be on time or get written up. It was mandatory to be back in camp for the four-o'clock count. We all worked five days a week and had the weekends to ourselves. The evenings during the week after work were our free time also. Some men would go to the weight area and work out, and others would hang out in the cardrooms that each dorm had and play cards or board games. Others who were able to get grants to attend Troy State University would attend college at night while working for a degree or extra credit. These men could use this to help with their records with the parole board.

Others used the camp library where volunteer instructors would come in and teach classes like basic computing, acting, arts and crafts, or they would just take out one of the many books to read. We all had to follow the basic rules of the camp, but we did not have the high-security pressure that inmates get in the higher or maximum institutions. This was a far cry from some of the institutions I had been kept in during my travels. You were on an honor system there, and if you screwed up, they would transfer you to a maximum-security prison to finish out your time. You might never get a chance to be sent back to a camp.

Governor Bob Martinez

Things continued to develop in Tampa. Merkle was still on the warpath, attempting to prove his theories of corruption from Tampa to Tallahassee. Governor Martinez was in Tampa on January 8 and 9 to testify at the trial of Nelson Italiano. He had been subpoenaed by Italiano's attorney Arnold Levine. On both those days, Merkle attacked the governor, accusing him of taking illegal campaign contributions and bribes because of some inconstancies in his campaign reports back in 1979. Merkle referred to testimony from a witness named Eddie Perdomo, who claimed he gave Martinez $4,000 in checks from Coaxial Cablevision for his support, then another $4,000 in cash to his 1979 mayoral campaign.

Also, Merkle questioned a $1,000 check contribution from Mr. Italiano on his campaign report, which stated that $500 was from Italiano and $500 was from Italiano's wife. The governor denied the accusations by Merkle and repeatedly denied that any bribe was made or cash given him by the witness Perdomo. According to the article I read, things got pretty heated in the courtroom. Merkle kept going back to the checks and alleged cash throughout his questioning of the governor. Martinez said he signed and initialed the campaign reports but never really looked at each and every item on it. He said he left that to his campaign treasurer.

From my own experience as a candidate running for office, I knew that it is not uncommon for the candidate during his busy day just to sign and initial his contribution reports without taking a closer look at them. You have to trust the person keeping track and filling the forms for you. Still, Merkle was trying to make it look like something illegal was going on. An ambitious prosecutor can always find a way to turn something simple and innocent into some type of criminal activity, even if there are no grounds or cause.

This was the new governor of Florida, for goodness sake, and the first Hispanic governor of the state since the time when Spain ruled Florida. Mad Dog Merkle was doing everything he could to discredit him, and the two city councilmen who also took the stand after the governor was excused.

While on the stand, Martinez called Perdomo an unmitigated liar. When Martinez was finished testifying, both Tom Vann and Eddie Caballero took the stand and denied that they ever received any illegal campaign contributions from Eddie Perdomo. In spite of all his efforts, Merkle was never able to prove anything against these men, and none of them were ever indicted or charged with a crime.

While Governor Martinez was testifying in Tampa, I read that one of his aides in Tallahassee leaked to the press that the governor would seek to remove Mr. Merkle from office. It appeared that his initial four-year term had run out some ten months prior, and he needed to be reappointed by the president for another four years or have another appointed to his position by the president of the United States and the US Senate nominating committee. Governor Martinez was going to use his influence, with the help of Florida's two US senators, to push the issue in Washington, possibly discussing the matter with the president himself.

Merkle's response to these rumors was, "I won't let politicians impede my job performance."

All of this that was going on at the time had, in an indirect way, some effect on my situation. I couldn't allow the anger that I felt for Merkle, Bowmer, or anyone from court to fester inside me. I knew that if I allowed my anger to get the better of me, it would eat me up with bitterness. I could see what hate and anger did to one in that place, for it was all around me. I didn't want to be like them. I had my children to go home to and a life to rebuild. I refused to let my situation get the better of me. I was not going to become an empty shell of a man who only had his anger and bitterness to keep him going. When the hurt and anger would start to build inside me, I would silently pray for the seeds of bitterness to be removed from my heart so I could go on thinking clearly. It seemed to help, for I was able to face each day with a better outlook.

The next articles I received from my family stated that the trial of Italiano was in closing arguments and would be going to the jury very soon for deliberation. Even in closing arguments, accusations went back and forth between the defense and the prosecutor. Merkle would not give up on the governor. In his closing remarks he said, "Among those lying to continue the cover-up is Governor Bob Martinez. Another liar is the defendant himself, Nelson Italiano, a politically prominent banker and insurance man."

He continued maintaining to the jury that the governor took an $8,000 bribe in cash and campaign contributions that were part of the alleged Italiano scheme. It was obvious, by all the information being reported, that Merkle believed the governor was a crook, and he was gunning for him. On the afternoon of January 13, the Italiano case was turned over to the jury for deliberation.

The next day, back in Tallahassee, Governor Martinez called the White House, urging the president to replace Robert Merkle as federal prosecutor in Tampa. There was a new war going on in the political background of Tampa, with a swell of anti-Merkle sentiment coming forth.

The next article I received and read stated that the jury came back with a guilty verdict in the Italiano mail fraud case and that this verdict was a victory for US attorney Robert Merkle, who had cross-examined Governor Martinez and told the jury the governor had lied. The article went on to say that this was particularly sweet for Merkle because Martinez had gone to the White House seeking to have Merkle fired, based on allegations that the federal prosecutor was reckless and abusive.

Merkle said to the press, "I intend to stay right here. I perceive no threat to my job here."

In a hastily called meeting in Tallahassee, Governor Martinez declared that the verdict was no sign that the jury disbelieved him. US district judge Terrell Hodges would hold a sentencing hearing on Italiano in the near future, pending a background investigation and recommendations.

So the only charge against Mr. Italiano was one count of mail fraud. That whole circus of events with the governor was more for show for Merkle's benefit than anything else. He was able to get his digs in on the governor, hurting the reputation of another good man. Yes, there was a war brewing between Merkle and the political powers that be, and as always, the press was joining in.

A few days later, I received a copy of an editorial from *The Tampa Tribune* saying in big headlines, "No Homer for Merkle—He Fanned Against Martinez." The editorial pointed out that Merkle had tried to implicate Governor Martinez of a crime during the Italiano trial. The governor was not named in the May 1983 federal indictments charging twenty-five individuals with racketeering, bribery, or corruption when he was mayor of Tampa.

The governor of Florida was brought into the case when federal judge W. Terrell Hodges permitted Merkle to introduce similar act testimony, which is allowed in federal racketeering trials, to bolster his case against Italiano and injure the reputation of Governor Martinez.

Governor Martinez, who took the stand as a defense witness at the Italiano trial, stating he had done nothing wrong or illegal, was crossed-examined by Merkle about an alleged fourth $1,000 check and $4,000 in cash he supposedly received during his campaign when he was running for mayor of the City of Tampa based on testimony from Eddie Perdomo.

Only three checks were reported on Martinez's campaign finance records, leaving the implication he pocketed the fourth. But Merkle never proved there was a fourth check. Mr. Perdomo could not even produce any of the alleged checks. Instead, Merkle showed the jury enlarged copies of the three checks reported in the campaign records that Merkle obtained from microfilm records of Perdomo's bank account. Merkle claimed the negative where the fourth check might have been being said to be fogged.

There was no proof that the fourth check existed, and no proof of the $4,000 cash other than Perdomo's hearsay testimony. The editorial ended with, "Merkle hit no home run off the governor. He struck out."

As I read into the editorial, I found quite interesting much of what they were saying about Merkle and how, although he attempted to try and show that Governor Martinez had committed a crime, the governor had never been charged with a crime nor indicted on any charges. The way Merkle handled this situation was a lot like the way he handled my trial, with a lot of innuendos and hearsay. In my case, however, I was tried with a group of defendants rather than by myself.

It now seemed that Merkle was on the defensive. He called a news conference and lashed out at the press and editorial staff, ripping his press coverage and saying that the news media reporters were confused in their trial coverage and the editorial writers inaccurate in their criticisms.

Governor Martinez was saying he had suffered abuse at Merkle's hands and had gone to the White House in an effort to get Merkle fired or at least subjected to US Senate scrutiny.

Another article seemed to show that Merkle's actions angered Hispanics. Right after the Italiano trial and the way the governor was treated, the Latin community throughout Tampa was upset with Merkle. Merkle's vendetta against Latins reads like a who's who in the Hispanic community—EJ Salcines, Elvin Martinez, Bob Martinez, and the majority of the twenty-five defendants from the corruption trials were of Latin heritage. Now there was a public outcry against the way Merkle conducted his office, compounded by the mistrust from the Hispanic community.

At Maxwell, I could only watch from the sidelines. There was nothing more I could do or prove to help my situation. I was going to be there for quite a while. When not working at the laundry and on my free time, I did some research in the prison library to help with my appeal.

By the end of the month, I received a visit from the new attorney who was appointed by the court to handle my appeal. His name was Arthur Addess, and he was from South Florida. He was about my height but a bit stocky in frame, with dark wavy hair and a round face with a short nose. He wore a light suit. He seemed to be a nice-enough fellow, and we hit it right off. He had been going over the transcripts from my trial, and he asked me why my other attorney did not sever me from the other defendants in my trial as some of the others were.

I explained that my attorney Mr. Harris did make an oral motion to sever, but it was denied. He then asked me why he didn't follow it up with a motion to appeal the judge's ruling. "I don't know," I told him. I explained that Mr. Harris was not a well man, that he was very sick during the trial, trying to do the best that he could.

Then Mr. Addess went on to inform me that if Mr. Harris would have taken the time to file a motion to appeal the judge's ruling with the Court of Appeals, they would have had to sever me from the trial or hold the trial up till a ruling was made on the motion, and that could have taken months. The government and the judge were not going to wait months on a ruling that was going to hold up a trial of this magnitude. They would have had to sever me in order to go on with the trial and try me at another time by myself.

From what he had read from the transcripts so far, he believed the government would have had a hard time getting a second conviction against me. At that moment, my heart sunk in my chest. It all made sense to me now, the way Mr. Addess explained it all to me. Because Ray Harris was taking so many medications for his condition, he had missed a golden opportunity to have me removed from the big trial. An alert attorney would have followed up the oral motion with a written one to the Court of Appeals, and that would have put the trial on hold till it was heard. "I hate to say this, Mr. Kotvas, but I feel you got a royal screwing out of this trial," he said to me.

Mr. Addess promised he would try to do everything he could to help me with my appeal. It would take time as there was a mountain of material he had to review and motions he needed to make for discovery before he could draw up my appeal. He said I needed to be patient and he would keep me informed of his progress all along the way.

This was a good first meeting, and I felt I finally had an attorney who knew what he was doing. We talked for a while; then he told me he had to drive back to Tampa to pick up some more records and talk with a few people. After he left, when I left the visiting area, I had a good feeling about this man. Now I would see what he really could do for me as I went about my business in the camp.

By the end of the month, I was transferred to the dry cleaning section of the laundry, which gave me a twenty-five-cent increase in my work pay. I was now making fifty cents an hour. This was a big help for me, although the work was a little more physical, for at times we had to move and empty fifty-gallon steel drums full of chemicals from the dry cleaning machines. I was working with a couple of Columbians who used to live in the Miami, Florida, area before being sentenced to prison for drug trafficking. These guys liked to joke around with me when we worked. It seemed they didn't much care to have a gringo working with them. They would have preferred another Latino in my place, but we still seemed to get along.

Back in Tampa, the feud between Merkle and Governor Bob Martinez was heating up. The governor submitted a letter of support to the White House for Ray Gill, the Republican state attorney in Marion County, to replace Merkle. Hearing of this, Merkle's only comment was, "I'm too busy right now to worry about this. If people think Mr. Gill or Mickey Mouse can do a better job, then let them do it."

When Ray Gill heard that his name had been submitted to Washington with an endorsement from the governor for the position of US prosecutor for the Middle District of Florida, he said he was honored to be considered as a possible replacement for US attorney Robert Merkle, but he had some mixed emotions about leaving the elected post he had held since 1984. Still, he said that if it came down to it, he would accept the appointment. He stated, "If the president thought I could best serve the criminal justice system in the US Attorney's Office, it would be very hard to turn down."

Things were getting a little stormy in the Middle District of Florida. I found out the situation was now getting national attention when I received an article from *The New York Times* written by a Phil Gailey. I found the article to be very interesting as I read it.

> To his supporters, Robert W. Merkle is a folk hero, a combative Federal prosecutor who is undaunted by political pressure as he pursues corrupt officeholders and illegal drug traffickers, a colorful troubadour whose ballads and comical impressions have added a satirical edge to his battle with the legal and political establishments.
>
> But to his critics, who include the State's new Republican Governor, its two Democratic Senators, prominent lawyers and major newspapers, he is a reckless zealot who has abused the powers of his office and smeared the reputation of innocent people.
>
> Mr. Merkle, a Republican who has been U.S. Attorney in Florida's Middle District since 1983, is at the center of a political controversy that has reached the White House, where officials are considering whether to replace him to appease Gov. Bob Martinez, whose political allies include Jeb Bush, son of the Vice President. Mr. Merkle's term expired last April and since then he has served at the pleasure of the president.
>
> The furor over the conduct of Mr. Merkle, whose nick name is Mad Dog Merkle, crested earlier this month: Mr. Martinez, two days after

his inauguration, found himself confronting Mr. Merkle in a Federal courtroom as a defense witness for Nelson Italiano, a prominent Tampa Democrat accused of mail fraud involving a cable television bribery scheme. Mr. Italiano was convicted.

The Governor was on the witness stand for almost five hours, yet the Governor, who was not charged with a crime, defended himself against the allegations of a Government witness, Eddie Perdomo, who said he had given Mr. Martinez $8,000 in campaign contributions and cash gifts in 1979, when Mr. Martinez was a candidate for mayor of Tampa, as part of an attempt to buy favors for the cable television company.

While the Governor was testifying, his chief of staff, J. M. Stipanovich, said Mr. Martinez had called Mitch Daniels, the White House political director, to ask that President Reagan replace Mr. Merkle, a move that heightened the political drama surrounding the case. "There's nothing partisan about him," Mr. Stipanovich said in this interview. "This man believes he was commissioned by God to smite politicians."

Some critics contend that Mr. Merkle, whatever his legal skills, is temperamentally unsuited for his job, that he goes out of his way to personalize his battle with elected officials and lawyers.

"How can he not be popular with a lot of people?" asked one lawyer here. "He goes out of his way to show his contempt for lawyers and politicians."

The St. Petersburg Times, a critic of Merkle, published two editorials this month calling for his dismissal, saying in one that Mr. Merkle "has built a record of prosecuting people without evi-

dence to convict and smearing those he lacked
evidence to indict.

Now they saw what I had to contend with back in 1983. How
this last paragraph of this article summed up my situation to a T! I
wondered where all these reporters and editorial writers were during
my trial. Now everyone was beginning to realize what type of person
Merkle really was. But for my situation, it was too late. No one could
really see what this man was doing or how he was doing it to me; at
the time, he was a big hero.

After everything that had happened to me since my arrest back
in 1983, one cannot imagine the anger and hate I felt inside of me
for Merkle and his staff—all the lockdowns and institutions I had
been in, the way I was transported all over the country and the isolation of it all, what it all was doing to my family back home, and being
so far away from them. Of all the defendants in my trial, I couldn't
even get a little break to be placed on house arrest while the second
trial was going on. Merkle knew I had no money. I was not a flight
risk nor a danger to society. Still, he kept a tight rein on me, and
he seemed to enjoy it because I would not cooperate for him. The
hatred I was feeling was starting to eat at me as I went about my daily
chores. I just kept everything inside me, for at the moment, there was
nothing I could do.

In March, my daughter, Julie, came up to visit me. It was a
big blessing being able to see and give her a big hug. We talked and
walked around the visiting area, and she brought me up to date on
everything that was going on in Tampa and with the family. She
explained how hard it was on my son Steven with me being away like
this, which only fueled the anger in me. She said that my mother and
the family were all right, and they all missed me.

As we talked, she showed me an article from *The Tampa Tribune*
with the headline, "Sheriffs Say Merkle Must Be Ousted." Now the
movement against Merkle seemed to be spreading statewide. The
article indicated that the Florida Sheriffs Association had endorsed
Governor Bob Martinez's effort to dump US attorney Robert Merkle.
Some of the members said that Merkle had abused the power of his
office. (No kidding, tonto—look at me).

The sheriffs felt it was appropriate to make a motion that Mr. Merkle should find other employment. The article stated that two sheriffs in Merkle's district accused the US attorney of being abusive. The offices of both were scrutinized by the federal prosecutor. These men were Hillsborough County sheriff Walter Heinrich and Lee County sheriff Frank Wanika. Both were present at the associations meeting the article stated.

I thought it would be interesting if anything came from all this. But I know politics, and all this was just a lot of saber rattling. Nothing would be done until the president stepped in and made a decision. The visit I had with my daughter was great. When she left to drive back to Tampa, I was left empty inside as I made my way back to my dorm. I don't know which was worse, the pain of not seeing them at all or seeing them for a short time once or twice a year. For me, time just seemed to move slowly at the prison camp.

By the end of April, we had a new guest to join us at Maxwell. It seemed that Nelson Italiano had been sentenced to two years for mail fraud, and the Justice Department had sent him there to Maxwell where he was to do his time. After he had been processed at the camp and assigned to a dorm, I ran into him on the compound grounds talking with Allen Wolfson. It seemed he was assigned to the same dorm Wolfson was in. I was surprised to see him there. I thought he was still out on appeal. We all talked for a while, and he brought us up to date on what was happening back home and what jerks he thought Merkle and Magri were. I could see he was very bitter about his situation and all that had happened to him. He had lost his appeal on his conviction; then he had received a notice by the Justice Department to report to Maxwell and start serving his time.

It was strange seeing him standing before me and listening to what he was telling us. Here was a man who once was one of the most politically powerful behind-the-scenes men in Hillsborough County. Now he was just another number, like me.

There were three of us here at Maxwell now who were the victims of Merkle's witch hunt. With their contacts back in Tampa and my own family and friends, I was able to keep abreast of everything that was happening at home. From time to time, whenever any of us received news of what Merkle and his staff were up to or something that pertained to our situation, we would share it with each other. We never really hung out together except to exchange information. Everyone mostly kept to himself and did his own thing here at the camp.

CHAPTER 38

A Plea for Anderson

May 1987

By early May, I received word that there was a move going on back in Tampa to try and get Fred Anderson an early release, possibly as early as the next April. Mr. Anderson had been very ill for some time, with his heart condition and poor health. His wife and their attorney were appealing for help from Senators Chiles and Graham on humanitarian reasons due to his medical condition.

I also was informed that Merkle and Magri were out to try and stop any move to get Anderson an early release. Merkle told the press, "An early release is inappropriate for an egregious felon like Anderson."

The commission approved Anderson's early parole for medical reasons, but a news article from *The Tampa Tribune* by Bentley Orrick that was sent to me stated that Merkle was giving the US Parole Commission decision serious review and would probably push for a reconsideration.

Tampa attorney Robert Polli, who represented Anderson during his second trial but had not represented Anderson during his parole hearing on this matter, said that he did know that Anderson "suffered a heart attack on January 8 that was so severe that he had to be moved temporarily from the Kentucky prison to a private hospital."

US district judge Carr, during Anderson's September 25 sentencing, had made a provision for early release if Anderson's health warranted it. But the judge had warned Parole Commission members they should not interpret the special provision as a suggestion of leniency or anything else.

I was happy to hear that Fred Anderson was given an expected parole date of April 25, 1988. It seemed that two hearing examiners had traveled to the Federal Correctional Institution at Lexington, Kentucky, in February for Mr. Anderson's parole hearing and that the final recommendation to release him next April was made in March.

Officials said the Federal Privacy Act prevented them from disclosing matters in Anderson's file and that they could not comment whether there were any letters or reports of phone calls for or against Anderson's release.

Of course, Merkle was going to look into this matter personally. I think he felt this was another mark against him for the way he conducted his office during the big trial. He didn't have much to show for his efforts after losing the majority of the cases he was after when he thought that this trial would have been the crowning glory of his career. So he was going to make sure that Fred and I would do as much time as possible to satisfy his hurt ego. To him, it did not matter how sick Mr. Anderson was or how poor his condition. As far as he was concerned, he was going to get his pound of flesh.

Merkle said, "It's basically giving Anderson no sentence at all for the major crime of racketeering, much less his concomitant perjury that the judge pointed out when he sentenced him."

I guess Merkle had forgotten all the hard time we had done up to this point and all the hardships we had been put through. I knew Fred was a very sick man, and I wished I could do something for him. He did not deserve the poor treatment he was getting from the so-called justice system.

If anyone has ever seen a picture or a statue of Justice, she is a tall lady standing and holding up a scale that is supposed to mean the balance of justice, and she is blindfolded so she cannot see what is going on around her. To me, this indicates that she can be led by the hand and manipulated any way the prosecutors want the scales to tip. Justice is truly blind.

I had a very bad feeling that Merkle was not going to let go of this. His reputation was already injured from all the not-guilty verdicts he got from our trial. He needed somebody to pay for all his efforts to get convictions, and I guess that somebody was us.

Due to the impact this had on all of us, I was kept informed by friends and family on what was going on back in Tampa. As time went on, it seemed that Senator Chiles had intervened on Anderson's behalf, which helped with the early April 26, 1988 release. Mrs. Pat Anderson had visited his Lakeland office a number of times, seeking Senator Chiles's help with her husband due to his medical condition, supplying all his medical records that explained his condition.

By no means was Merkle going to take this lying down. He was out to stop the early release any way he could. As far as he was concerned, Anderson was an egregious criminal who did not deserve consideration. By the end of May, I was shocked to learn that Merkle had succeeded in stopping Fred from getting his early release. It seems the early release date had been voided and set for reconsideration after Robert Merkle called Anderson an egregious felon and requested serious reconsideration of the matter.

All anyone could find out about the matter came from a Mr. Tom Kowaiski, regional administrator of the Parole Commission, whose branch office was in Atlanta. He said that the revised decision was based on new information presented to the commission, information that was confidential by law.

As I remember it, I received a letter from a friend telling me that it seemed Merkle had made a personal appeal to the commission on the Anderson matter. He apparently claimed that Anderson was not as sick as he pretended to be and was using this as an excuse to get an early release (thank you, Dr. Merkle!). Oh, how angry I was after reading that letter. Who was Merkle to take a person's health in his hands and say how sick they were or weren't only to satisfy the ego of his office and his future ambitions? One can only speculate on what went on at that meeting.

A few days later, I was informed from home that Merkle was requesting a new special grand jury to replace the one that had just finished its term of service. Merkle claimed that the investigation into alleged criminal conduct by public officials was not complete. I guess he needed a new grand jury to continue his witch hunt throughout his district.

It was still eating me up inside what Merkle had done to Fred. In my heart, I knew this was not right. I knew how sick Fred was and that it would only be a matter of time before something really bad would happen to him.

One evening toward the end of May, a thought hit me on what I possibly could do. I had no clue if it would possible, nor did I know what the judge might think about it. But that evening after the four-o'clock count and meal callout, I walked over to the camp library, sat at an empty table, and wrote a personal letter to Judge Carr on Fred Anderson's behalf. Since I could already see the writing on the wall, the way Merkle was and how he had it in for us, I knew there would be no help for me in getting any type of early release, no matter how hard Mr. Addess worked on my case. I knew Merkle would see to it that I did the maximum amount of time for my refusal to cooperate with him and his office. So what did I have to lose? It was clear I would never see my son Steven grow up. They had already had seen to that. I knew I would be spending the better years of my life here or wherever they sent me.

At this point, I was so depressed that I really didn't care. If I couldn't help myself, maybe, just maybe, I could do something for Fred. I sat there and composed a letter to the judge, asking him to intervene on behalf of Fred Anderson for an early release. I implored the judge to find it in his heart to help Mr. Anderson get out of prison early so he could receive the proper medical care that he needed. In that letter, I told the judge that I didn't know if it is possible but I would be willing to take the time Fred had left on his sentence and add it to mine, that I was more than willing to do the time for Mr. Anderson, and that should still satisfy the letter of the law. I told him that I was truly sincere in this plea, and young enough and healthy enough to do the time for both of us. I told him I knew what I was asking, and I took full responsibility for this action.

I ended the letter with, "I appreciate you giving this matter your utmost attention." Then I signed it, placed it in an envelope, and addressed it to Judge Carr's office at the federal courthouse in Tampa. It would go out with the next mail delivery.

I really meant what I said in that letter. I could only imagine what Merkle would say or do when he got wind of the letter. I realized I wasn't going to get any breaks, and my family would still have to get along without me. I had no doubt that my family would be upset about this request, but I could not stand by and just do nothing. I just hoped they would understand. I felt at this point that, except for my children, I really didn't have anything to go home to, so whatever anyone thought, it really didn't matter to me. I just felt that I might be able to do just one last good thing for someone from there in prison.

That night, lying on my bunk, I prayed that the judge would consider my request and that my children would understand. I also prayed that the Lord would remove all the hate and anger that was burning inside me, for I really would have liked to have put my fists into Merkle's face.

I started to realize that as long as I kept feeling this way, the hate would consume me and turn me into something I did not like. I wasn't going to walk out of this prison when the time came as a hateful, angry person looking for revenge. That was not me. I've seen others leave like that, and it ruined their lives, their families, and their marriages, and bringing more troubles down upon them.

I didn't want to be like that. I had to get these bad feelings for Merkle and his staff, for Bowmer, for the court, and for all others who had hurt me during my trials out of my system. I felt I couldn't go through life trying to get even with them. I couldn't hold a grudge forever. What good would come out of trying to take revenge? You hold on to who you are, and I have always been a person who tries to help others, not hurt them. So I prayed on it every night. It couldn't hurt, and I needed to do something to let it all go. I knew it wasn't going to be easy. I had so much anger and hate bottled up inside me, and every time I received bad news on my situation, it only drove the nails of hate deeper into my heart. At that point in my life, I didn't even know if God would be listening.

By the beginning of June, I received another news article from home concerning Merkle. It seemed that state representative Elvin Martinez was lashing out at Merkle publicly. The article by Howard Troxler stated that state Representative Martinez said Robert Merkle had sadistically renewed allegations of corruption against him.

"Mr. Merkle just can't stop scheming against me. He simply cannot accept these simple facts. He has a preconceived script of what and whom he wants to believe, and he thinks anyone who does not agree with him is a liar. Once again, the prosecutors have shown their habitual disregard for the truth, for fairness, and for my rights," said Martinez.

I could see things were not getting any better in Tampa. At Maxwell, all I wanted to do was keep my nose clean, do my work, and one day walk out of the place, God willing.

Time moved on slowly for me as things at the camp became routine. Every time there was some type of prayer service, I would try to attend. I attended Catholic services, Baptist services, and even Jewish services. I found it very interesting and also found that there were a lot of similarities between the different religions. I met a lot of nice people who came through the prison ministry to fellowship with us. Still, I never could find the answer to why all these bad things were happening to me. All I would hear was, "Have faith, pray on it. God has a plan for you." Statements like that didn't seem like much at the time. Still, no matter what service or fellowship I attended, I always seemed to leave when it was over feeling a little better. None of this was going to change my situation, but it did make my time a little more bearable.

By the beginning of July, we heard that one of the defendants who had been severed from my trial was starting his trial that month. He was Paul Johnson, one of Tampa's most prominent attorneys and a nationally known trial lawyer. It seemed his time to face Merkle had come. Merkle had charged him with extortion and perjury and two counts of mail fraud. Johnson's attorney made a motion to dismiss the mail fraud counts based on a recent US Supreme Court decision that had been passed just the week before.

Paul B. Johnson is accused of

I wouldn't find out till some time later that this decision by the US Supreme Court would have a big bearing on all the defendants who were indicted or incarcerated from our indictments, and a personal bearing on my present situation.

It seemed that the chief witness against Mr. Johnson would be Jerry Bowmer, who alleged that Mr. Johnson paid him a bribe on behalf of one of his clients. I also learned from the media that I was being subpoenaed by the defense to testify on Mr. Johnson's behalf, but I had not received any word about it as of yet.

I thought that this was very interesting since Fred Anderson and I were both found not guilty by the jury at my trial of the charges that Merkle was trying to pin on Mr. Johnson. The federal grand jury that indicted Mr. Johnson never heard any testimony from Bowmer in relation to Mr. Johnson. It had been only our trial jury that heard any testimony from Bowmer with regard to Mr. Johnson, and they had rejected it.

Even though we were found not guilty of those charges, Mr. Merkle was going to use his office to ramrod these allegations and use them against Mr. Johnson, allegations that I felt should have been dropped. It did not matter to Merkle that we were found innocent of the charges, which meant Mr. Johnson must have been innocent also. Merkle was going to try and get something to stick to the defendants who were left from the big indictment, and although Mr. Johnson might have been innocent, he was going after him regardless.

By this point, Mr. Merkle was not looking to good in Tampa, and he was out for blood. Nothing was going to stop him from using all the power he had and all the government's money at his disposal to get as many convictions as he could to improve his stature in the community. He had declared war on the who's who of Tampa and Hillsborough County, and thus far, it had not been going too well for him.

I received word from my sister, Rose, when I called her (very expensive reverse charges, of course) to find out how everyone was. She informed me that Mr. Johnson had his two mail fraud charges dismissed by Judge Carr, who would be hearing the case against him, and that his trial might be held up till September if Merkle appealed the discussion.

She read me some statements from the news article she had on the matter saying that Merkle said to the judge that "the Johnson case involved tangible things of value, such as the borrow pit permit and the bribe money, which still could be prosecuted under the mail fraud statute despite the Supreme Court ruling."

The judge responded, "I disagree. You've got some problems. It's a different story now, a different situation."

She also said that the judge warned Merkle that without the mail fraud counts, some of the evidence that he wished to present might be excluded from the trial. Merkle's response to the judge was, "I have a very strong argument, and I feel I have a right and duty to appeal your ruling. I feel the government's argument gives it a pretty good shot at winning an appeal."

When my sister finished with the article, I told her I thought Merkle was losing it. I thought Merkle was a little off his rocker, going against the judge's decision and holding up the trial. I told her, "This only proves what a mad dog he is. He will stop at nothing and do anything to get his way. He's like a spoiled little boy."

After that, we talked about my children and how hard things were for my daughter and how my mother was doing everything she could to help out. At the end of our conversation, I told her to give my love to all and that we would talk more at a later time. I knew how expensive those calls were, so I would only call maybe once or twice a month, unless there was something very important I needed to know.

A few days later, I received some articles about the Johnson trial from my sister stating that there might be a big delay in the trial. They also mentioned that Mr. Johnson was being represented by the famous lawyer F. Lee Bailey, a onetime partner and good friend of Mr. Johnson.

Wow, Merkle was now going against some of the biggest lawyers in the country. I felt that this was becoming very personal with Merkle, and I knew this was going to cost the American taxpayers a small fortune to satisfy Merkle's ego as he pushed ahead with his blind determination to destroy our community politically.

While all this was going on in Tampa, back at Maxwell, Mr. Italiano was getting ready to be released, pending his appeal on his mail fraud conviction. It seems that his lawyer John R. Lawson Jr. had filed a motion to appeal Mr. Italiano's conviction on mail fraud and asked the court that he be released from incarceration pending the appeal due to the recent US Supreme Court's ruling on mail fraud.

US district judge Terrell Hodges signed the order for Mr. Italiano's release from Maxwell Prison Camp. He was now a happy and free man on appeal. I walked over to him as he was leaving to wish him well. He could not wait to get out of there, and I couldn't blame him. His family had sent him a ticket to fly home, waiting for him at the Montgomery airport. I was glad for him as I watched him get into the prison van that would take him to the airport; he was wearing his civilian clothes. He had only spent a few months at Maxwell, but I think he understood that this was no Boy Scout camp or country club. It was now all up to the Federal Court of Appeals whether he would return or remain free.

By August, I found out that a federal judge had indefinitely postponed the extortion trial of Paul Johnson. This was to allow the federal appeals court time to consider the judge's dismissal of the two counts of mail fraud. For the time being, everything was on hold.

CHAPTER 39

"Oh, the Pain"

September 1987

Life and work went on as usual as the leaves in the area turned all sorts of colors with the approach of fall. Judge Claiborne was now a real short-timer. Word was that he had served his time and was scheduled for release sometime in October. I couldn't be happier for the man; he would be back in Nevada with his family soon. After what the government had done to him, I wondered what he must have been thinking and how he would rebuild his life.

I always felt good for the men who would be going home soon, but it always left a sad and depressing feeling inside me because I knew I still had a long way to go before my turn would come.

For me, there was still a long way to go before I would see the outside world again. By now, I had adjusted to prison life. It all started out as quite an education for me because of all the different institutions I had been housed in. Now, all this had become the norm for me. I was just another number locked away in the system.

On the afternoon of September 7, as I was working in the dry cleaning section of the laundry, one of the Columbians and I needed to move a five-hundred-gallon drum of chemicals over to one of the dry cleaning machines so we could fill the chemical tank on the machine. The other Columbian working with us was standing by the machine waiting for the chemicals.

It wasn't an easy job, moving those drums. We had to lift the drum onto a dolly to be able to move it over. The Columbian working with me asked me to bend down and lift one end as he tilted the drum to get under the dolly. As the drum was tilted, for some reason, the man let go of the drum as I was holding on to it to keep it from crushing my hands and turning over onto me. I felt a sharp pain and a snap in my lower back as I let the drum slide its side to the ground. When I straightened up, I felt some pain in my lower back but thought nothing of it at the time.

The man claimed it was an accident and that he didn't realize I was still holding on to the drum when he let it go. I didn't say anything to anyone at the time because I felt I was all right and it was just another one of their little jokes on me, and I did not want any trouble. Since there were no other witnesses to the incident, it would be my word against the two of them, and you know how that goes.

For the rest of the day and evening, my lower back was very sore, so I walked around the compound for a little while, hoping the pain would ease up. Everything seemed to be all right when I turned in for the night and lay down on my bunk.

Then it happened. Sometime late that night, I woke up with the most terrible pain in my back and running down my left leg. The pain was unbearable; I could not move in any direction without it getting worse. My left leg was like one unbelievable charley horse. It was so bad that tears were coming out of my eyes, and the other men in my dorm could hear my cries of pain. The men came over to see what was going on and what they could do to help. It was now about three-thirty to four o'clock in the morning. A couple of officers came over to see what all the commotion was about. When they saw my condition and how much pain I was in, and that I could not stand nor walk, they got permission to transport me to the air force base hospital emergency room. Four or five of the men from my dorm carried me to the van that would take me to the hospital. I had never felt so much pain in my life, and it was getting worse. Once they got me into the back of the van, an officer got into the passenger side and told the driver to take us to the hospital emergency room.

I arrived at the emergency room around five-thirty in the morning. It was now the eighth of September. After being examined by both the emergency room doctors and the neurosurgeon on duty, I was admitted into the base hospital. No matter what they gave me at the time, nothing would ease the pain. The pain in my back was getting worse, running down my leg and causing some numbness and weakness in my lower left side. The contractions of my leg muscles made it even worse.

When I was finally taken to a room, I was transferred to a hospital bed, and my right leg was cuffed to the bed. Due to all the pain I was having, I was unable to get any rest and kept moving around in the bed, trying to get comfortable. After a long while, I finally dozed in and out of some type of sleep.

During my stay at the base hospital, I was made to feel like a human being. The air force staff of doctors and nurses who attended to me gave me very good care. I was a patient, not a number to them; and for that, I was very grateful. After a while, the pain subsided to a dull painful feeling in my lower back. My left hip and my left leg were getting very numb as I seemed to be losing the feeling in that leg off and on.

During the next few days, they ran all sorts of tests on me, taking x-rays that showed my disc spaces narrowing at L5-S1. On September 16, 1987, I was taken to an outside diagnostic imaging center for a CAT scan. Most of the tests done came back negative, but the scan of my lower spine showed that I had a large ruptured disc at L5-S1.

I was then referred to an outside neurosurgeon for further evaluation. On October 5, 1987, I was transported to the office of Dr. Joseph Keith in Montgomery. He gave me a thorough examination and reviewed the x-rays and CAT scans of my lower back, which indicated I had a large ruptured disc at L5 left. After the evaluation in his office, he informed me that I would need surgery on my back as soon as possible to relieve the pressure on my nerves and spine, or I might lose the ability to walk. He sent a copy of his report to the doctors at the hospital and to the warden at the prison camp, wherein he stated, "In view of the fact that Mr. Kotvas has a large ruptured disc and continues with pain, I think surgery is indicated."

Later on that same day, after receiving the recommendation from Dr. Keith, Mr. Jose L. Acebal, PA, sent a memo to the warden of the prison camp, stating:

> This is to notify you that patient Joseph Kotvas 03026-018 was seen by Dr. Keith, neurosurgeon, in his office in Montgomery. Dr. Keith strongly recommended that patient Kotvas have surgery as soon as possible to correct a herniated disk in his lower spine. He has stated that due to the size and nature of the herniation, he does not feel that it's feasible to pursuit corrective surgery locally and recommends transfer to a Federal Prison Medical Center for definitive therapy.

My transfer to a Federal Prison Medical Center was approved by the warden and the prison system. But which one would I be sent to? I had heard rumors from a lot of the inmates there that the prison hospital in Springfield, Missouri, was a nightmare, with poor medical services for the inmates. At this point, I was very nervous, for it looked like this was where I was going to be transferred to.

On October 15, I was discharged from the hospital, going back to the prison camp on complete bed rest till my transfer. Once back at the camp, I prayed that I would be sent to some other facility other than Springfield. I was still in a lot of pain, but not as much as before. A day or two later, I was informed that I would be transferred to a new medical facility in Rochester, Minnesota, which was connected with the Mayo Clinic there. My prayers had been answered.

CHAPTER 40

Mad Dog Merkle Can't Let Go

October 1987

At times, it seemed that time would just stand still for me, now that I was confined to my bunk. Being so far from home, an occasional phone call once or twice a week was all I had to look forward to, except for when there was mail call. I looked forward to receiving letters from home from family members or friends who would write occasionally and send me news articles on what was happening back home. It was all I had to keep my spirits up. At times, the place could get pretty depressing.

By the middle of October, the weather at Maxwell was getting cold. The leaves on the trees had changed colors from green to orange and yellow to brown, and they were starting to fall off the trees onto the ground. The ground crews were going to have their hands full this fall season. I was glad I wasn't working outside with the ground crews. I hated the cold weather, and there at Maxwell, it was a damp, wet penetrating type of cold.

The next day, I was informed by the medical officer at the camp to get all my stuff packed. I would be flown to the FMC (federal medical facility) in Rochester, Minnesota, in the morning. A couple of the inmates whom I knew from my dorm helped box up all my belongings for transfer. At this point, I really could not be of much help to anyone.

My airlift authorization to FMC Rochester had been approved. I would be flying out early in the morning on October 20 from

Montgomery's commercial airport and should arrive sometime after noon in Rochester, Minnesota. I had a restless sleep that night, in and out of intermitting pain on my lower left side.

When morning came, I was put into a wheelchair and taken to the processing center where I changed out of my prison uniform. I was surprised that I was given my civilian clothes to wear. Most of my belongings were put into storage for me. The rest would be sent on ahead and would get there after I had already arrived. As for my medical records and x-rays, the officer escorting me would carry them. I was also given an overcoat. They told me it would be very cold in Rochester that time of year.

This time, when they transported me by van to the airport, they only handcuffed me as I sat in the wheelchair. When we arrived at the airport, I was assisted onto the plane by the officer. This time, I was not flying Jail Air. They sent me on a direct flight to Rochester on a commercial chartered plane that carried about twenty or thirty passengers. What a relief. I still remembered well the nightmare of my last trip with the Air Marshals Service. I guess the doctors must have made it clear how important it was to get me to a proper medical facility as soon as possible.

Even though I was in a lot of pain in the cramped seats during the flight, I did not complain. It was a nonstop flight, and the flight attendant was very nice to me even though she saw my handcuffs, which we attempted to cover with my jacket. At that moment, pain and all, it was heaven; and in a few hours, we would be landing in Rochester, Minnesota.

When we landed sometime in the early afternoon, there was a van waiting to take us to the federal medical facility. I could see snow on the ground everywhere. The rush of cold air as we got out of the plane was freezing as the officers assisted me into the van. As we drove through the city to our destination, I could see a number of the nice homes on the way decorated for Halloween. I could not believe how much snow there was on the ground. It was a beautiful sight, something out of a Norman Rockwell painting.

When we arrived at the medical facility, I could see that the place was fairly new. It appeared to be spread out over a large area, with barbed-wire fencing all around it. The buildings all looked new, but like everything I had seen so far, all the grounds outside were covered in snow. As we drove into the compound, I could see men shoveling snow from a number of the buildings and putting down sand or salt on the pathways so they would be passable. I was driven to the intake center for processing and evaluation. There I would be assigned to a medical unit in the facility.

After processing, they admitted me to building 9, where I was placed into a medical two-man cell. It was more like a dorm room with what looked like a regular door that had a window toward one side so officers and staff could look into the room to make sure everything was all right and to make the regular daily counts. The door handle had a lock that was secured for evening lockdowns. It had a two-man bunk bed along one wall. Of course, I had been assigned the bottom bunk because of my back. A stainless steel sink and commode were situated at the back wall of the room, and there was a nice-sized window a foot or two above the commode that looked out onto the compound.

Standing in front of the window and looking out into the compound, one could see the chain-link fence that ran around the facility and the nice residential homes on the other side. The room also had a desk with a lamp and chair along the other wall. Everything appeared to be very clean and new. I was informed that there would be another inmate assigned to this room to help me get in and out of bed and to help me get around the unit in my wheelchair. I was assigned to no duty of any kind while in this unit.

I was amazed to find out that this place had a maze of underground tunnels. About an hour after I settled in, an orderly came by and transported me over to the medical building that was about two buildings from where I was by wheelchair for a medical workup. But instead of going outside and using the icy walkways, he took me to an elevator that took us down to the basement, where there were a series of underground tunnels that connected to all the buildings throughout the compound. A person using the tunnels could travel to any part of this medical facility and prison compound without ever stepping out onto the surface. As the orderly rolled me along, I could see others moving along in the tunnel passageways. Some were walking; others were riding in little golf carts to wherever they were going. The place was a beehive of activity underground.

The young man informed me that the snow and ice on the ground sometimes got as high as the second level, with the snowdrifts getting even higher. They needed the tunnels to move staff and patients safely between the buildings. The place was like nothing I had ever seen before in the prison system. The tunnels were nice and warm, as were all the buildings. They kept the place well lit and heated, and also extremely neat and clean. All the buildings had elevators that took you down into the tunnels, plus walkways and ramps to move heavy equipment or small vehicles around.

When we arrived under the medical building, we took an elevator up to one of the floors, and I was wheeled into a doctor's office for an evaluation of my condition. After being asked a barrage of medical questions and examined, I was referred for an appointment at the Mayo Clinic the next day for further examinations.

When I was returned to my cell (which I will call my room, for it felt more like a dorm room than a cell), there was a nice-looking, clean-shaven young blond man in his late twenties—he was of medium build, and I would say about five feet nine inches tall—in the room, sitting at the desk. His name was Eddy, and he had been assigned to the room to help get me around the place to wherever I needed to go and to assist me if I needed help. When he wasn't helping me or on another assignment, Eddy would spend his time reading or listening to his portable Walkman cassette that he was allowed to have.

We seem to hit it off well as he helped me into my bunk, for I was exhausted from all the traveling and moving around I had been put through during the day. My back and left leg were killing me, and I would have to wait for the nurse to come around with the medications before I would get anything for the pain.

The building to which I was assigned was a medical and surgical building for inmates who needed constant medical attention. All the men in the building would have their meals brought over from the main dining hall and served in an area on the main floor that was used as a recreation and TV room and doubled as a mess hall. Those who were not able to go to the rec area for their meals would receive their food trays in their rooms. The showers were down the hall from us, and when I needed to take my shower, I would be taken to them by wheelchair. Then a chair would be placed in the shower for me to sit on as I showered. The medical staff did not want me standing or moving around too much for fear I would hurt myself. In the beginning, this was kind of rough on me, but I managed.

Due to my limited movement, my food trays were delivered to our room, where I would take all my meals until I was able to move a little better. That first night was one of the roughest for me, even with the pain medication. I think my lower back area was inflamed and sore from all the movement of the day. Tomorrow I would be examined by the Mayo Clinic doctors for my upcoming surgery. This would determine how they were going to do my surgery. I knew they would also be ordering more tests and x-rays to compare with the ones taken in Montgomery before making their decision.

The next day, I was transported over to the Mayo Clinic by van. We drove through residential neighborhoods till we arrived downtown at the clinic hospital. There, I was examined by two physicians, one of whom was a neurosurgeon. They looked at all the medical records and x-rays that came with me, then ordered more tests on me, which meant I would have to come back and forth for the next few days. I have to say that both physicians seemed earnestly concerned for my condition and were very sensitive to my fears. They treated me like a human being, not an inmate. They also informed me of everything that would be happening to me and promised to let me know more when all the test results came back. Some of the tests would be done at the prison medical facility and others at the clinic. They informed me that my surgery would probably be scheduled for a week or two from then, after my final evaluation.

When I arrived at the Mayo clinic, I had time to look around and at all the people coming and going. The place was extremely busy. One thing that stood out there was the fact that a majority of the staff and people working and walking around there were blonds or redheads with fair skin. I had never seen so many blonds or redheads in one place like that in my life. I guess it had to do with a lot of Scandinavians settling their back in the 1800s. This was something you didn't see back in Tampa, with its high Latin and Italian community.

CHAPTER 41

"God, Can You Hear Me?"

October 1987

Back at the medical prison, I was returned to my bunk for a much-needed rest. The pain was killing me from all the movement. I felt a little better after taking my meds, so Eddy filled me in on what was going on there and who was who in the place. He told me that there was a sick old man there who was a Mafia kingpin from Chicago. He even had his own inmate bodyguard who attended to his every need and saw to it that nobody could approach him without permission. As long as he followed the rules, even the guards would not bother him. Eddy told me that the man liked to keep to himself, and except for his age and medical condition, he seemed to fare a little better than the rest of us. You never know whom you might meet in a place like that.

I would have days when the pain became so unbearable that even the medications could not help much. There was even a time when the pain was so bad that I was almost ready to throw the towel in and confess to anything the government wanted me to. Whatever Merkle wanted to hear, I would have confessed to it. I would even have said I was part of the Kennedy conspiracy if that would have gotten me help to get out of there. Now I understood how people could say or sign anything when in such pain. There is only so much the human body can take. But then I realized, even with all the pain and isolation from all my loved ones, I couldn't hurt people I did not know, whether they had committed a crime or not. It was just not me.

After lights-out, the officers in the building came around, took count, and locked all the doors. As I lay in my bunk thinking and staring up at the ceiling, I began to pray. You cannot imagine how scared I was, with no one around for moral support. This was 1987, and I had heard that having spine surgery could be very risky; that mistakes could happen, and one could be paralyzed for life or end up as a cripple. No matter how good an institution might be, mistakes do happen. I didn't want to just trust in the surgeons; I felt the need to trust in God also. Between the pain in my lower back and lower leg and all the fearful thoughts going through my mind, I opened myself up to the Lord like I had never done before. For the second time since my arrest, I called out to the Lord.

During my many travels through the prison system so far, I had time to do a lot of reading along the way. Back when I was in one of the solitary lockdown cells for a spell, I read a book called *When Bad Things Happen to Good People* by Harold Kushner & Harold J. Kushner. It was one of the many books that were left by the prison "holy joes" who came around the jails. It basically said that God has a way of testing our faith. I wondered if maybe that was why some of these things were happening to me. When my wife had died of cancer a few years before, I had turned my back on God, the church, and a lot of things I cared about. One only knows the kinds of things that go through one's mind in situations like this.

I had a lot of time to read the King James Version of the Bible, especially the story of Job, which I read over and over many times. I picked this particular book in the Bible because, in a way, I could see a lot of comparisons between myself and Job. Here was a good man who once had everything; then the Lord allowed the devil to take it all away from him. He lost all his possessions, his wife and family, his position in life; plus, his friends and neighbors accused or believed he had done something wrong to earn such punishment. But in the end, he stayed faithful, and the Lord restored to him all that was lost and more.

I guess you could say Jerry Bowmer was my devil, and Merkle and the justice system his helpers. They, like many others including the media, were blind to what really went on during that zoning meeting. I was once a shining star in the community. Now I was just a forgotten number, hidden away in a faraway place in unbelievable pain.

In my prayers that night, I explained to the Lord that I was not comparing myself to Job but just pointing out the similarities between us and thinking maybe that was why all these bad things seemed to be happening to me. My cellmate Eddy was sound asleep and could not hear my whispered prayers nor see the tears running down my face as I continued.

I explained to the Lord that I was a sinner; I knew that. Throughout my life, I could have been a better person in a lot of ways—a better father, a better husband, a better son, and being not so busy, always running off to help somebody that I couldn't spend more time with my family. I'm no angel, and I'm sure there may be a number of things I might be found guilty of. But what I was found guilty of in my first trial, I had no part in, and you are aware of that, Lord.

As I continued praying, I could feel the pain stirring in my lower back. My meds must be wearing off, I thought to myself. I said to the Lord, *I know I have to let go of all the hate that has built up inside of me—my hatred for Merkle and his staff for the way they handled my case, my hate against Jerry Bowmer for what he has done to my life, plus all those who wanted to hurt me to save themselves, the bad feelings I have for Jan Platt for the way she voted, whatever her reasons may have been; plus, her goody-two-shoes attitude and innuendos about the whole situation. She, without any real knowledge of what really went on, just made statements to make herself look good in the public eye. Yes, I would forgive her also. I would forgive them all for what has been done to me and my family. I would leave the matter in your hands.*

It was time for me to let it all go. I told the Lord that I was very scared and felt alone, but whatever was His will, I would accept it. I had walked into prison on my own two legs, without any help. All

I could ask the Lord was that I would like to be able to walk out of prison the same way, when that time came.

While I continued to pray that night, I said, *Let it be your will, not mine, Lord. If you want me to have this surgery, whatever happens, I place myself in your hands. I feel I can't go on much longer with this pain. Father in Heaven, I will accept whatever happens. Let thy will be done.*

I prayed through most of the night, with all the pain in my lower back and leg, till I finally fell asleep. The next morning, I was still having a lot of pain, and my lower left leg was pretty much numb. As I tried to get up from the bed with Eddie's help, I wondered if my prayers were ever heard. Knowing that there was a world full of troubles and millions of people praying daily for their own needs, did I have a right to ask for help? It was now time for me to get ready for some of those tests I needed to take.

On October 29, all the tests had been completed, and I was again taken back to the Mayo Clinic for my final evaluation. This would be my final examination by the doctors who would be doing the surgery. They had already scheduled it for two days from then. When my escorting officer and I arrived at the hospital, I was wheeled into an office where there were three doctors sitting around the room, already waiting for me.

One of them was the neurosurgeon with two of his associates. As I sat in my wheelchair facing them, the neurosurgeon said to me, "Mr. Kotvas, your recent test results came back to us, and your neurological test shows signs of improvements. It seems that you are starting to get feelings back in your left leg and lower back. Because of this, it appears that your situation has now changed. You now have the option of two choices to make.

"We can go ahead with your surgery as planned, or you could opt out for physical therapy and see how that goes. Either way, you will be at a point where you would be in two years with the therapy or the surgery. If you choose the therapy, the facility you're at can provide all the necessary physical therapy and training you need to get you up and walking again."

When I heard that, my heart skipped a beat. My feelings were coming back. I could choose therapy instead of surgery, and in two years, I should be recovered from my injury as if I had the surgery. I could not believe it; once again, my prayers were answered. I could only believe that God heard my prayer and sent me an answer. A feeling that all was well came over me. Of course, I chose the therapy. They told me it would not be easy and that, in the beginning, it would be very stressful and painful, but they expected good results. I really did not care. I was given a new chance, and I felt this would be better than surgery—plus, I was willing to do whatever it took to get back on my feet.

When I was finally returned to my dorm at the medical prison, I told Eddy the good news. By this time, the Mayo doctors had sent over to the prison doctors a regiment of exercises for me to start on. I'm happy to say that the facility there had an excellent physical therapy department, where I would receive very good care. The next day, it all began; and like they said, it was very painful to move around and do the exercise for the next few weeks. But little by little, I was able to get up from my wheelchair and finally walk around using the aid of a walker.

It was now November, and the holidays were fast approaching. From time to time, I would look out my window. I could see the snow piled several feet high from the ground. As I looked out toward the residential homes across from the prison fence, I could see all the holiday lights decorating them. It looked beautiful but depressing from where I was. Although every night I would give thanks to the Lord for all he had done for me while asking him to look after my children, I also asked him to remove the seeds of hate from my heart. I even thanked him for the pain I was feeling, knowing he was taking care of me. I felt I no longer had anything to fear while I was in prison. That everything was going to be all right.

At this point in my life, I did a complete turnaround. Instead of complaining at every little thing that was happening to me, I would just give thanks for it. No matter what it was, bad or good, I would give thanks for it. As time went on, it seemed that the more I gave thanks for the bad things, the more I noticed that they never seemed to last as long.

As time moved along, I was now able to get around with a walker. Of course, I moved very slowly at first, and I would feel a stinging sensation every now and then in my lower back as I walked. But each day, I was getting stronger, and I walked around the inside of the building and up and down steps to build up my strength. Now I was also allowed to eat my meals in the recreation area with the other inmates from my building. There were people there from all over who had been found guilty of all types of crimes, both major and minor, who needed medical attention.

Hanging out in the recreation area, on occasion, I was able to observe the big man from Chicago about whom Eddy had told me. Usually, when I saw him, he was sitting in a wheelchair with an oxygen tank on the side. He looked very old and overweight, partially bald with limited gray receding hair. He was always accompanied by this big burly guy in white hospital clothes who stood by his side. This man would take care of anything the old man needed. I really did not know what his true story or situation was, nor if he would be living out his life there in that prison hospital. By the looks of things that was probably what would happen.

Everyone I asked about him would only say he was once the head of one of the biggest crime families in Chicago and that he was one who should not be messed with. Even the officers watching us never messed with him. He would often take his meals in his room and stay away from the rest of us. His bodyguard would make sure of that.

I would wonder about Fred Anderson every now and then, and I added him to my prayers at night. I still had not heard a word from Judge Carr on the letter I sent him on behalf of Fred. I only wished that Fred could have been transferred here. I know he would have received excellent medical attention in this place. I could only wonder how he was doing. I heard stories from many of the inmates I met along the way, and none of them had anything good to say about the institution he was in. As for me, I had to get better so I could walk out of this place.

Every day I would go to therapy, and every day my body would get a little stronger. By mid-December, I did not need the walker anymore; I was steady enough to be able to walk with a cane. At first it was hard, and I was a little wobbly on my feet, but I got the hang of it. I still had a low numbing pain and occasional stinging sensation in my lower back when I would try to twist my body, but not as bad as it had been. I just gave thanks to the Lord every time I felt it.

When the mail came, I looked forward to the letters and news articles from home. I kept my family informed of my progress, since there was no way any of them could afford to come up to my icebox for a visit.

Once I was walking, Eddy was soon transferred out of my unit to another building since I no longer needed his assistance. It felt good to be able to manage on my own after all that time. I thanked God each morning when I got up for giving me this opportunity. For the moment, I had the room all to myself. It was a very good feeling getting some of my independence back. For the time being, they still recommended that I shower sitting in a chair to prevent me from slipping in the shower stall.

By mid-December, I was allowed to walk outside on the cleared-off walkways around the compound. I had to be very careful. Even though they put sand and rock salt down, the walkway at some points was very slippery with ice, forcing me to take very small steps as I walked. I have to admit, when it's cold up there, it's really cold! The temperature can drop below zero sometimes, and the wind makes it even worse. I did slip and fall a couple of times, but thank God no damage was done. Just a little more back pain and more therapy.

The holidays came and went, and the beginning of January 1988 came around. I wondered what the New Year would hold for me. Everything was white on the ground as it snowed a lot up there, and the snow stayed on the ground for long periods of time. Outside the fence area, people still had all their holiday lights up. I would be needing my cane for some time to come to assist me in getting around. I didn't mind; at least I was able to walk again. Soon I was allowed to eat in the main mess hall building with all the other inmates who were doing time there.

The walk from my building to the mess hall would be good exercise for me since it was some distance of a walk for me. I had not realized it, but I was lucky to be in the building I was in because even though the place was a fairly new facility, many of the other buildings were already overcrowded.

On January 11, the intake officer informed me that I was being discharged from the medical facility and would be sent back to Maxwell as soon as transportation was arranged. This time, I would not have the luxury of traveling by commercial air; I would be returning by the US Marshals Service.

Again, the long trip back by the Silver Bullet bus was an experience. Once on the road again, I would be dropped off at different institutions for a time till another bus would pick me up. Most of the time, the institutions I was dropped off at would take their time in sending my medical report to their medical staff, so I would go without any of my needed medications until the medical officer saw me. All this was a far cry from the treatment I had received in Rochester. It would be several weeks before I would reach Maxwell.

CHAPTER 42

The Good News

February 1988

I finally made it back to Maxwell Prison Camp by mid-February. The new dorms that had been under construction when I left were now open and occupied. Most of the old wooden buildings had been torn down, but they left a few standing for other needs. It felt good to be back, but I noticed the population of the camp had grown considerably. I was placed on limited light duty until my condition improved, which gave me plenty of time to get the feel of the place again.

I informed my family that I was back at Maxwell, and before too long, my oldest son, Joseph, came up to visit me. He was still in the navy, serving on the USS *Nimitz*, whose home port was Jacksonville, Florida. He was on liberty for a few days and took time to come up and see me. I cannot tell you how good it was to see him. We had a wonderful visit as he informed me that he was engaged to be married to a nice young Christian girl named Lisa, whom he had met while attending Trinity Baptist Church in Jacksonville, Florida. My son, who was brought up as a Catholic, had switched over to become a Baptist. I was happy for him, but not so much for the switch. But God is God, and however we showed our love for him was all right with me. I have to remember that Christ never created religion; this was man's doing. And like it says somewhere in the Bible, "Love the Lord your God with all your heart." It doesn't ask what religion you are.

I could see he was very happy with what he was doing and very much in love with the young lady who would soon become his wife. He told me that when he was not on duty with the navy, he spent a lot of time doing volunteer work for the church. The church people were like a family away from home to him.

He had been at boot camp in San Diego, California, when I was first arrested and tried back in 1983, so he never got to see what went on during my trials. As we talked, he asked me how they could find me guilty of soliciting bribes on a zoning I did not vote for. I tried to explain it as best as possible. I just said, "It's politics. Everyone was caught up in the frenzy, and they were not looking for the truth. All the prosecutors were looking for was how many people they could get convictions on. Plus, I failed to take the stand in my own defense, a big mistake that did not help matters. So I was basically found guilty by association. You have to remember how people think. If one is guilty, then they all must be guilty, or why would they be arrested? I guess this was the general consensus."

It was hard for him to understand, but my son knew how dirty politics could be. We just left it at that. What was done was done, and I told him that I had put the matter in God's hands.

We had a wonderful visit, talking and walking around the visitor area. I had not seen my son for a number of years since he left home to join the navy. When it was time for him to leave, I could feel pain inside me, wanting him to stay a little longer. You always get a feeling of loneliness when your children have to leave.

The days moved slowly for me as I got around the camp doing my exercise. I could feel my back and legs getting stronger. I was walking much better now, and I did not need to use the cane that much. By the end of February, I received word from my attorney Mr. Addess that the US Court of Appeals would be overturning the convictions of mail fraud for all the defendants indicted and convicted of the charge associated with our trial.

Mr. Italiano's attorney had successfully appealed his mail fraud indictment, and the favorable ruling by the Court of Appeals was a binding precedent applicable to all the defendants who had been indicted by Merkle on mail fraud. The mail fraud charge would be vacated from our convictions as well.

Mr. Italiano, who was now out on bond, was a free man from this conviction. I could not have been happier for him. Thanks to the efforts of his attorneys, his case would have a big effect on all our cases. Mr. Addess sent me a copy of the court's February 22, 1988 decision, which stated in its conclusion:

> We emphasize that at the time the grand jury returned this indictment, several courts of appeals had held that public officials could be success-fully prosecuted under the mail fraud statute for depriving citizens of good government; unfortu-nately, the law changed after the return of this indictment. It is too late now for the government to claim that its indictment was returned by a grand jury cognizant of and acting in accordance with the new teachings of the Supreme Court.

We hold that the district court erred by denying Italiano's motion to dismiss the indictment where it failed to allege that either the county or state was defrauded of money or property by the alleged scheme. Accordingly, Italiano's conviction of mail fraud in violation of section 1341 is reversed and the judgment is vacated.

The Court of Appeals pointed out that the single count of mail fraud was fatally flawed. This was another major setback and black eye for Robert Merkle. It showed how he could manipulate the grand jury to get his indictments. His credibility was starting to tarnish, and he was losing favor in many sectors of the community.

Over the next few weeks, I received a number of letters and articles about the Italiano victory. My attorney and the attorneys of the other defendants all moved to have our mail fraud convictions reversed and vacated, and in due course, they were.

Mr. Addess put me in good spirits with the news. He informed me that without the mail fraud conviction against me, the govern-ment had no RICO case against me. The government needed two predicate acts to get a RICO conviction, and the mail fraud was one of them. Now they no longer had two predicate acts, so Mr. Addess was going to file a new appeal on my behalf to have the RICO conviction vacated. This was great news for me, for this would clear me of my second trial. I couldn't wait to tell my family. That evening, I called home and gave my daughter, Julie, the good news on what Mr. Addess had said. I told her to let my sister, Rose, and my mother know about it. This would take time, but Mr. Addess felt pretty good about it. That night, I thanked God for the good news. I had let go of my problems and had put them in his hands. Maybe this was his way of sending me a message? Whatever the reasons, I was feeling pretty good for the moment.

By March, I was fit enough to be assigned to the Air Force War College at Maxwell AFB in the research section. It was light duty, and I was out of the prison camp during the workday. My job was to help find articles and reports that the officers attending the war collage needed for their research. It was a fortuitous assignment. I had always had an interest in history, and this gave me an opportunity to do some of my own research.

This was also where I found the inspiration to research the book that I would write years later called *Men of the Invisible War*. A wealth of history and information was stored in the basement of the building I was working in. I was allowed access to everything, classified and unclassified. Most of the information was locked away in file cabinets and old boxes stacked around the place and on dusty shelves in the basement. As I worked my way through much of this stored information, I realized that most of the people there had no idea what all they had down there.

When I wasn't looking up something for one of the officers, I would use my free time to go through many of the old boxes and files. My air force supervisor did not mind as long as I did not break any of the rules. Inmates assigned to the war college pretty much had freedom of movement around the place. We provided a much-needed service for the military, which otherwise would have had to hire more civilian personnel to handle the workload.

For me, it was a blessing. If only for a little while, I felt like a real person working around others who were not judgmental of who

I was or what I had been accused of. At the end of the day, we would all get on the prison bus that came at around 3:30 p.m. to take us back to the prison camp for our four-o'clock count and then dinner.

After the count, and when I was finished with my dinner, I would work on my back exercises to keep my back and legs in shape. Things seemed to be going a little better for me, and I now had some hope about my situation. It was all the waiting that was frustrating.

By the end of March, I received word that Michael Sierra had been disbarred by the Florida State Bar Association and banned from practicing law for a period of five years. The ban took effect on May 23, 1985, so he was not allowed to apply for readmission until after five years from that date. I felt that that after the five years, he would have a good chance of getting his right to practice law reinstated. This was another good man who was paying for someone else's crimes.

Things were not going so well back in Tampa for Robert Merkle. He and his staff still had some ongoing cases related to my trial. There were also rumors going around that Mr. Merkle was planning to run for the US Senate seat that was opening up and that he was planning to resign from his current office.

In May of 1988, my son Joseph sent me word that he had gotten married in Jacksonville. I cannot explain the hurt and sadness I felt, locked up and unable to attend his wedding. He told me it was a nice small family wedding and that they all missed me. I was happy for them, and I knew he would be a good husband to the young lady. My son had become a young man now, starting out with a new life of his own. I guessed I would have to stop thinking of him as the little boy who always wanted to tag along with me whenever I wanted to go somewhere. I am so proud of the man he has become.

Life in prison went on as usual, working and trying to keep my nose clean. Even with the expansion of the camp and the new dorm buildings that opened to house more inmates, the place was still getting overcrowded with more and more inmates being sent there every week. We were well over capacity for what the air force base said we should have, but no one did anything about it.

I received word from my sister, Rose, toward the end of May that my mother was very sick and not doing well. She was having a lot of cardiac issues and not eating well. My sister was busy taking her back and forth to the hospital because of her condition. She informed me that her health seemed to be deteriorating rapidly. There was nothing I could do for her from where I was. I knew a lot of her condition had been brought on by what had happened to me and all that I had gone through. I knew my mother was worried sick from all that had happened to me. Over time, all of this was having a negative effect, taking a heavy toll on her health and mental state.

Even my daughter, Julie, was very worried about her. There was little anyone could do but hope she would improve. I felt so helpless in that place. My mother needed me, and there was no way I could be there for her. All I could do was pray for her and hope she would start to get better.

This has always been a big problem for families with the federal prison system. It is like a double punishment, always sending the convicted to a prison or camp far away so it puts a burden on the families and loved ones, even though there are institutions that are much closer to their homes. Regardless of the situation in which we find ourselves, we have to make do with where we're at and what we have.

Time is our keeper. It moves slowly in a prison camp while you're always counting the years, the months, and the days. During the day, you try not to think of it; but at night, when you're all alone in your bunk after lights-out, it all hits you. You just lie there staring at the ceiling till you're able to fall asleep.

Toward the end of June, I received word that Robert Merkle had resigned from office. I had been hearing rumors about it for some time, but it was finally official. I received a number of news articles from my family about his resignation and his bid for the US Senate race.

Merkle resigned from office on Monday, June 28, 1988, holding a news conference in the conference room of his US Attorney's Office in Tampa. The article stated his wife and nine children were standing at his side. I have to admit, as much as I disliked the man and the way he ran his office, I always respected him as a good family man. This was the one area I could not find fault with.

From the information I had received, it seemed he was starting his campaign on a shoestring budget. It seemed the man was so self-centered that he felt donations to his campaign would just flow in once he announced and got started on the campaign trail. He would be running against US congressman Connie Mack, who, up to that time, had no Republican opposition.

Many of the political experts were saying that he was too late, and the Republican Party did not want him in the race. They felt he would just muddy up the waters within the party. A great many party leaders were also angry that Merkle had joined the race just days before President Ronald Reagan's appearance at a fund-raising luncheon in Miami for Connie Mack and other Florida Republicans.

From what I was reading, it seems they felt Merkle would embarrass the president. I know as a fact that Merkle had created a number of enemies throughout the State of Florida. Even from prison, I could see the writing on the wall. Merkle was opening himself up for payback from many of the people whom he had stepped on as a prosecutor. Regardless of the odds, Merkle was going to bully his way into the senate race just as he had done as a federal prosecutor going after whatever corruption he thought he could find.

His chief assistant Joe Magri would temporarily take over as chief prosecutor for the Middle District of Florida until he received the full appointment, or a new prosecutor was appointed. There were still a number of cases left unfinished that needed to be tried from the list of those indicted from my trial. Magri was now responsible for bringing these cases to a close.

Would any of this help my situation? Only time would tell—for the moment, out of sight, out of mind. It seemed I had been forgotten by everyone. My world was gone; prison life had become my reality.

CHAPTER 43

The President of the United States

July 1988

President Ronald Reagan

A couple of weeks into July, I received some news articles about Merkle's campaign. One of them reported that on Wednesday, June 29, at a Republican luncheon fund-raiser in Miami for US representative Connie Mack, President Ronald Reagan came out and endorsed Connie Mack for US senator over Robert Merkle. The president said, "That's why I'm here today, to campaign for the next United States senator from Florida, Congressman Connie Mack."

I'm guessing this had to be a big blow to Merkle's ego when he heard the news. Merkle reacted by attacking the president's endorsement, saying, "I consider Reagan's endorsement of Mack a violation of the eleventh commandment for the Republicans, the party's unwritten law against infighting."

I could see from what I was hearing and reading that the month of July would be a very busy month for Merkle, who now was on the defensive against the Republican Party. He had entered the race late, without giving any of the GOP leadership the courtesy of discussing his intentions. The majority of them had to find out from the news media. By announcing, Merkle had now forced a September 6 Republican primary with US representative Connie Mack, who had no other GOP opposition in the race.

As far as the GOP was concerned, Merkle was the underdog who was mudding up the waters for the party with no chance of actually winning. Merkle was running a shoestring campaign with no money, no headquarters, and no real staff to help him.

Ironically, Merkle's bid reminded me of my own story and how I was first elected to public office. Back in 1972, I did pretty much the same thing. Starting out, I had no money, no campaign headquarters, and no real staff but my family and a few friends who helped me. I was the dark horse in that race, and all the know-it-alls believed I didn't have a chance against a twelve-year incumbent who had a lot of influence from Tampa to Washington. Plus, I was in a six-man race at the time. No one was more surprised than I was when I won.

As much as I disliked Merkle, I had to admire the man. It took guts to do what he was doing, going against the establishment. I also had been accused of that in the past. That was part of the reason why I was in this mess to begin with. I wondered if Merkle would be as reckless and self-centered in this race as he was as a federal prosecutor.

US representative Connie Mack

By Wednesday, the thirteenth of July, it was official that Robert Merkle had entered the Republican primary race for US senator against US representative Connie Mack. He wasn't winning any brownie points by attacking the president of the United States for endorsing Connie Mack, or by labeling Mack a "political chameleon."

Merkle was making claims that party leaders told him not to get into the race because they had already picked Mack as their candidate. I guess he knew he would be bucking both the odds and the Republican Party when he decided to run in that race. Part of his opening remarks after his announcement were to criticize Connie Mack for agreeing to appear with retired Marine Lieutenant Colonel Oliver North, who was being charged with fraud and obstruction of justice in the diversion of money to Nicaraguan contra rebels from American arms sales to Iran. According to Merkle, Mr. North would receive $37,000 to stump for Connie Mack at Republican fund-raisers in Orlando and Fort Lauderdale in August.

Merkle, in his usual snide manner, said to the press, "While I presume Mr. North innocent of any charges, I find it curious that Mr. Mack, in a state that has the worst crime problem in the nation, would ask parents to put him in the Senate while espousing that the end justifies the means. I don't need to import courage or the appearance of courage for the voters to make an informed choice about me. I'm running on my credentials and my abilities." He also said that he did not feel threatened by President Reagan's endorsement of Mack for the Senate seat, which he felt was given under pressure from the Republican Party leaders in Florida.

I had to admire the man's guts, but I felt he was going at it all wrong. I could see now that he would be the same as he was as a prosecutor, presenting a case before a jury. Now, in a totally different arena, he would be presenting his bid for office to the public in his same mad-dog fashion. There was no doubt in my mind that Merkle was utterly self-centered, with an ego bigger than his own head. By all appearances, I can only think that Merkle believed he was God's gift to the political field. I think he and Jerry Bowmer would make nice matching bookends.

As much as I missed my family, being so far away from home, I always enjoyed mail call. I cannot begin to tell you how much a letter or a card from home meant to all of us who were incarcerated. Most of the time, it was the only spark of happiness we got around there. For me, it helped to know what was happening to my family and what was going on back in Tampa. It helped keep me apprised of the political system back home and what was going on with the other defendants still waiting for trial.

Rose wrote saying that she had been taking our mother to the doctors every week but that her health still seemed to be deteriorating. This was starting to worry me. Before I left for prison, she was doing fine. Now, with all this time away and the stress of the two trials, trying to help my children, and worrying about me was taking its toll on her. There was nothing I could do for her but pray she would get better. I still hadn't heard anything about my situation or my appeal, which my attorney was still working on.

One day by the middle of July, I received an article in the mail about Merkle blaming one of the jurors for the loss of his big bribery case. I could not believe it. Had the man gone mad? He was picking on a little gray-haired widowed lady who had been one of the twelve jurors in my second trial. This was insane! I wondered whether Merkle was losing his mind as I continued to read.

The article was written by Todd C. Smith, a staff writer for *The Tampa Tribune*. The article stated that a few days after Merkle became an official candidate for the office of US senator for Florida, he broke his silence on perhaps his most embarrassing loss as a US attorney: the 1986 Hillsborough County Commission bribery-racketeering trial in which jurors acquitted eleven of the fifteen defendants.

Merkle claimed that his watertight case became undone because of one juror. He said, "There was a renegade juror on that jury," claiming that senior citizen Florence Corbin, a little gray-haired widowed lady from Seminole, Florida, had the power to sway a mixed panel of eleven other jurors. A good number of the other jurors were much younger and probably better educated than her, but somehow Merkle thought she was able to sway them to vote her way.

Please, give me a break. It was bad enough that he and his staff were taking out their loss on Fred and me. But to now come forward and make statements like this, to put the blame on others because he was running for office? How low could he go?

He was claiming to the press that Florence Corbin befriended some of the defendants and then swayed the jury to acquit them. When contacted at her Seminole home, Florence Corbin, who had since remarried and was now Florence Brennan, denied Merkle's accusation. Her remarks to the press were, "Ah, come on. No way, why is he after me? It's kind of tacky for Merkle to name me when eleven others had their opinions too."

The article stated that Mrs. Brennan was reluctant to discuss the case but said, "The jury felt the people who should have been on trial were the ones who were given immunity and plea agreements."

Mrs. Brennan said she did not know or befriend any of the defendants. She added, "I almost forgot I was on that jury."

By the time I finished reading and digesting the article, I could see that Merkle's attitude was that he could do no wrong and it was the other guy's mistake that caused the problem. What an egomaniac he was. Was this the way he was going to run his campaign, by attacking everyone who was opposed to him? Since I had nothing but time on my hands, it was going to be very interesting to see how this all turned out.

About a week later, I received some news articles from home stating that the nominating committee for the replacement of the US attorney for the Middle District of Florida had sent three names to Washington for review. Bypassed from the list was Joseph Magri, Merkle's chief aide, who had been serving as the acting US attorney since Merkle's resignation the previous month.

Merkle, infuriated by the move, said, "I am outraged by the secret and under-the-table maneuver and predict it would fail. I have the personal assurance of Attorney General Meese that my former first assistant Joseph D. Magri would get the job. But for that assurance, I would not have resigned because I was very concerned lest that office be compromised by hidden political agendas."

When asked about the situation and if he would like to keep the post, Magri replied, "I find it curious that I wasn't talked to by anybody. It would be impossible for someone who has been part of a six-year effort to create an independent, honest, vigorous, and effective US Attorney's Office not to be interested. I do not want to drag our office into a political controversy. I have a job to do, and I'm just going to do it."

The way Merkle and his staff conducted their office and investigation during my trial and all the people they had stepped on trying to get cooperation and convictions were finally coming back to bite them. Would any of this affect my situation? I could only pray that I would receive some type of break from all this.

Soon I received another article by *Tribune* staff writer Todd Smith titled "Juror Demands Merkle Apologize for Remarks." The article said that the woman former US attorney Robert W. Merkle last week called a "renegade juror" had demanded that Merkle publicly apologize for his remarks.

> Florence Corbin Brennan, a member of the jury that acquitted 11 of the 15 defendants in the 1986 Hillsborough County Commission racketeering-bribery trial, befriended several defen-

dants and swayed other jurors to find them not guilty, Merkle said.

In a letter mailed Tuesday to Merkle, Brennan wrote, "You owe me and the entire jury of your favorite case a public apology after labeling me a renegade. You implied they were all simpletons with no minds of their own."

She added, "Your accusations that I knew any of the defendants is wrong. I never saw, met or heard of any of the jurors, defendants, or their lawyers until the trial."

Mr. Smith wrote in his article that Mrs. Brennan did not address Merkle's claim that she befriended the defendants during the six-month trial, but she did say that she talked to the defendants.

"When you see people for six months day after day after day in the same predicament, you say, 'Good morning,' 'How are you?'" She would not elaborate any more.

Merkle claimed and quoted another juror as saying the jury caved in to Brennan, but it is not known who. Mrs. Brennan praised the integrity of the other jurors and said, "Merkle had a childish attitude."

I think everyone could see that by the way he conducted himself. *Go girl, my hat is off to you,* I said to myself. What a jerk, going after a juror just to make headlines to get free press. I guess when you don't have money for your campaign, you have to take desperate steps to get your name in the papers by bullying the helpless.

It was his intimidation and bullying of the witnesses that got them to change their stories about me and helped to convict me. As I mentioned in an earlier chapter, a number of the witnesses apologized to me after the trial, saying they were intimidated by Merkle to testify the way they did. There was nothing I could do about it now. Still, Merkle's true colors were starting to show for everyone to see.

It appears that part of Merkle's campaign strategy to get media attention without having to pay for it was to attack and make public accusations against law-abiding citizens or public figures wherever he could find them. Starting off the week of July 25 in Clearwater,

Florida, Mr. Merkle again set his sights on Governor Bob Martinez, accusing the governor of improperly trying to control the selection process for his successor as US attorney. He claimed, "Martinez's responsibilities do not include dictating who the US attorney will be in the Middle District." If you can't buy political ads, then that was apparently how you made the news and got free press. It sold newspapers.

As the government expanded the population at Maxwell, more and more inmates were transferred in from other institutions. As soon as the new dorms opened for housing, they were already full to capacity. As the new men came in and many of the short-timers left, I was becoming one of the more senior inmates here with still a lot of time to serve. Most of the men I knew when I first arrived at this place had already gone home. Now the camp was full with hundreds of new faces that replaced the old.

The small circle of friends I had made when I first arrived there was getting smaller and smaller. Every day, when I was not on assignment or occupied with other duties, I continued my exercises for my lower back to help improve my walking and movements. I could feel the improvements the more I exercised. I still took the meds I needed for the pain that kept coming and going.

I couldn't wait to get the latest news from home. The month of August was a real circus on the political scene. It was like a living soap opera, and I didn't want to miss the next episode. Within the first week of August, the fireworks hit the fan.

It seems US attorney general Edwin Meese nominated Robert W. Genzman to replace Merkle as chief federal prosecutor for Central Florida. Merkle was in a wild frenzy and fuming over the appointment. This appointment of a man whom Merkle felt did not even come close to matching Joe Magri's credentials was a stab in the back. Magri had no comment to make about the appointment and would remain in charge of the district until the appointment was confirmed.

In a heat of anger, Merkle called a news conference from his Clearwater office to express his opinions on the matter. In a strident voice, he called the attorney general of the United States Edwin Meese III a liar.

In a news article by Bentley Orrick, *Tribune* Staff writer, Merkle was then quoted lashing out at US representative Connie Mack and Governor Bob Martinez, billing them a "dynamic duo of sleaze."

I was amazed at what I was reading. *This guy is starting to lose it,* I thought. *Because he didn't get his way, he goes off on a tantrum like a spoiled little boy.*

Merkle accused the Cape Coral congressman, his Republican primary election opponent for the Senate, of joining the governor in orchestrating a "tawdry" act of "political vengeance" in bypassing his friend and chief aide Joseph D. Magri. In almost the same breath, Merkle went on to accuse Martinez of having taken the bribes detailed in the testimony of a bagman for a cable-television consortium headed by Mack's brother, and he chided Vice President George Bush for having Martinez in the largely honorary post of national cochairman for the Bush presidential campaign.

Merkle went on to say, "The actions of Martinez, a former Democratic restaurateur who took cash payments intended to influence his actions as a public official, bring little credit to the Bush campaign."

In response to the allegation of Meese being a liar, Justice Department spokesman Patrick Korten denied that Meese had welshed on a commitment to appoint Magri. All Meese agreed to, Korten said, was to name Magri the acting US attorney, which was done.

"However," Korten added, "at no time did Mr. Meese promise to recommend Mr. Magri's name to the president as a candidate to replace Mr. Merkle on a permanent basis. It's a pity Mr. Merkle should choose to use such virulent language. We can only conclude it's a ploy to attract attention."

Martinez's spokesman Jon Peck said, "Mr. Merkle's comments are completely without foundation. He tried to brand the governor with those unfounded allegations a year and a half ago. It didn't wash then, and it doesn't wash now. If there was any proof to what he says, he would have brought it to a grand jury when he was US attorney. He didn't because there's no substance to it."

Connie Mack's press secretary Mark Mills called Merkle's statements "completely ludicrous."

"I think it is mean. It is vicious. It is a sign of a very bitter, frustrated candidate who is doing badly in the polls and will say anything and do anything to try to get a little attention. Mack did nothing behind the scenes to scuttle Magri's chances for the US attorney's job. Merkle's comments are ludicrous, and Mad Dog Merkle obviously is very bitter and a frustrated candidate," Mills said.

Alixe Glen, a spokesman for Bush, said, "The vice president and the Bush campaign have total confidence and respect for Governor Martinez and are tremendously pleased with his efforts."

Merkle would answer no questions from reporters after his news conference. The very next day, it was reported in the press that one of Florida's top Republican leaders urged Merkle to withdraw from the US Senate race and possibly from the GOP in the wake of his attack on fellow Republicans.

According to reporter Joe Brown of *The Tampa Tribune*, in a fiery speech to the Pasco County Republican Executive Committee, L.E. "Tommy" Thomas, former state party chairman and now a state committeeman, said, "It made me sick when I read of Merkle's attacks on Governor Bob Martinez, Vice President Bush, former attorney general Edwin Meese III, and Merkle's primary opponent, US representative Connie Mack."

He went on to say, "Merkle is all wrong. We should not have a candidate from our own party making accusations like this just to get his name in the paper. Mad Dog Merkle's barking up the wrong tree."

The big guns were now lining up against Merkle. Where was all this when I needed a little help with my defense on how Mad Dog Merkle had won his conviction against me? Now the man's true colors could be seen by the whole world.

No more than a week later, Merkle took a jab at reporters, claiming he was being ignored on the issues. Speaking to a small crowd at the Harbor House family restaurant in west Pasco County, Merkle said, "All I want you guys to do is report facts. If I can't come in with $1 million to put into television commercials, it's critical the press report my issues."

Boy, I wish I was back in Tampa to get into the issues with them, I thought to myself. Being far away and on the sidelines, I could only imagine what must have been going on back home. As much as I was hurting for being in my situation, a small part of me could not help but feel sorry for the sap. The man was too blind to see what was going on, and I felt for his family because of all they had to put up with.

As things continued, news from home was not good. My mother took a turn for the worse and was placed in a rehab center across the street from St. Joseph Hospital. The family was hoping that she might regain her strength and come home soon. There was nothing I could do from where I was. The last time I had seen my mother, she appeared to be in good health, but her spirits seemed down because of my situation. That had been a couple of years back when I was in the county jail on Morgan Street in Tampa. I had not seen her since, although we talked on the phone whenever we had a chance during all my travels in the system.

Every so often, Allen Wolfson would come by and ask to borrow the articles I received from home. He too was interested in keeping up with everything going on in Tampa. He still had some time to do on his sentence, and he spent much of it studying in the library or in his dorm. He didn't shave. He had a bushy beard, and he let his curly hair grow out like an Afro. He looked more like one of those bushy, hairy-faced guys you see from the Middle East. How he had changed from the clean-cut, well-manicured, well-dressed man I had once met in Tampa!

This was August, and the Republican National Convention was being held in New Orleans. All the Republican state delegates and candidates, plus anyone who wanted to be noticed, would be there, as well as all the major news outlets from around the country. This was going to be a very big affair, and Merkle was going to make sure he showed up for it.

Soon I received an article written by Bruce Dudley of the *Tribune*. He headlined his article "Merkle's Out, Mack's In with GOP Leaders." He reported,

> The Republican hierarchy leveled a seemingly well-orchestrated assault Monday the 15th of August, on renegade U.S. Senate candidate Robert W. Merkle on the eve of the former U.S. attorney's scheduled arrival at the Republican National Convention.
>
> Merkle's primary opponent, U.S. Rep. Connie Mack, at the same time was receiving promotions and plaudits from Republican leaders.
>
> 1. Mack's staff released a letter that former state party Chairman L.E. "Tommy" Thomas sent to Merkle accusing him of running a reckless campaign and being just plane nasty toward Republicans.
> 2. The National Republican Senatorial Committee, a GOP panel assembling Republican banners, had a news conference in New Orleans to promote Mack, while ignoring Merkle.
> 3. The senatorial committee's staff helped Mack land a speaking role during the convention proceedings today, while again snubbing Merkle.
> 4. Merkle's name was left off a report on Florida's Senate race that was released by the senatorial committee.
>
> Merkle's campaign manager, Jan Halisky, in turn said the ex-prosecutor has made "factual statements" about Mack and other Republican leaders and has not run a negative campaign, as claimed by Thomas.

"If that's un-Republican or un-American, then they're talking about another system of government," Halisky said.

Halisky also said he assumed the Republican leadership would afford Merkle equal treatment upon his arrival and arrange a convention appearance for him.

But Jann Olsten, the executive director of the senatorial committee, said Merkle will get no help from his group.

Olsten said Mack secured the national Republican organization's help before he had a primary opponent and before U.S. Sen. Lawton Chiles, decided not to seek re-election late last year.

"Connie Mack took the chance when it was a real risk and we made a commitment to him and you cannot recruit good candidates and make commitments unless you stick by them," Olsten said.

Then the next day, Tuesday, before leaving for New Orleans at the Suncoast Tiger Bay Club, Merkle reiterated his claim that Governor Bob Martinez took a bribe. He had made the allegation just hours before Governor Martinez was scheduled to address the Republican National Convention.

Of the many times Merkle had stated that Governor Martinez had received illegal money contributions, this was the first time he actually referred to it publicly as a bribe. Merkle claimed he had been too busy prosecuting drug kingpin Carlos Enrique Lehder Rivas to seek a perjury indictment against the governor. (Sure, a man like Merkle, with his reputation on corruption, would let something as big as that go by the wayside. I don't think so.)

Martinez's spokesman Jan Peck responded, "The reason he didn't seek perjury charges is because there was no perjury. Merkle wants to be US senator, and he doesn't have time to get around to something like this? I mean, come on."

In New Orleans, Merkle felt the full weight of the Florida Republicans making a point of shunning him, as the news media reported. Merkle came to town to shake GOP hands, but some Republicans treated him like a leper. Florida lieutenant governor Bobby Brantley even refused to shake Merkle's hand at a cocktail party that Wednesday.

Tribune reporter Bill Osinski, who was at the convention, wrote in another article that the Florida Republicans made a point of shunning Merkle. But he pointed out that not all Florida Republicans refused to shake his hand. Jeb Bush, the son of the vice president, didn't seem to mind shaking Merkle's hand. It was one of the very few greetings he received from the attendees at the convention.

At least one good thing was coming out of all this. Now that Merkle was out of office and spending most of his time campaigning, it only left his chief assistant Joe Magri to clean up the unfinished mess he left behind. There would be no more attacks on the good reputations of men like EJ Salcines, Elvin Martinez, and others without grounds of any wrongdoing.

CHAPTER 44

The Loss of a Mother

August 1988

One sunny morning toward the end of August, as I was working at the Air War College, an officer from the camp came by the office where I was working and told me I needed to report back to the camp and that he was there to escort me back. He would not tell me the reason I was being called back. Usually, when you were pulled from your work detail and escorted back to the camp, it was because of some infraction you might have committed, or because some type of contraband was found in your belongings at your bunk area, and it meant they were taking you to the hole till your disciplined. Or it could be an unscheduled attorney visit or medical recall.

I knew I hadn't done anything wrong, but around there, anything was possible. Someone could have planted something in my bunk area so they would not get caught with it, or it could have been just about anything. The officer escorting me was quiet all the way back to camp, hardly saying two words, which made me think something was very wrong and that I was in some kind of trouble.

When we arrived back at the camp, I was escorted to the warden's office and asked to wait in the outer hall. After a few moments, I was called into his office and asked to take a seat, wondering what this was all about.

The warden said to me, "Mr. Kotvas, there's no easy way to put this. Earlier today, we received word from your attorney that your mother had passed away. I'm very sorry for your loss."

I was numb. I couldn't say anything at the moment. The pain of the thought of losing my mother, after everything I had been through, was a little more than I could handle. They say strong men don't cry and that you should never show your emotions in prison, for it is a sign of weakness. But after a few moments, I could not hold back the tears.

The last time I had talked with my sister a while back, she had said our mother was starting to feel a little better. How did this happen? I was not able to be there for her. Hundreds of miles away from home, there was nothing I could do. I just sat in that warden's office in a partial daze as he told me that my attorney was filing a motion with the court for me to go on emergency leave for the funeral and that my family would pay for my round-trip transportation to Tampa for the funeral and back to the camp. The funeral was scheduled for some time the next week.

The warden told me that when the order came through, he would approve an emergency leave for me. I would be given a four- or five-day unescorted leave, depending on how long the travel time would take. I was to be sure to return to Maxwell on time. Then I was told I could return to my barracks, and I would be notified if and when the paperwork came through.

As I got up from the chair, I thanked the warden for his kindness then walked out back toward my building. As I was walking back, some of the buses were bringing the men back to camp from their work details. A few of those who knew me came and asked me why I was taken off my work detail that day. They seemed honestly concerned. I just told them that my mother had passed away, and I was going over to my bunk to lie down for a little bit. I could see they felt bad for me. They understood what it was to lose someone you loved when you're in a place like this.

When I walked into my building and got to my bunk, I just lay down and stared at the ceiling, thinking. I was still numb inside from the news. Tears flowed down my face off and on as memories came to mind.

My mind wandered back to my early childhood, then back to the present, and back again. My mother was seventy-seven years old when she passed away, and I was not there to say how much I loved her. Then I sat up on my bunk as anger started building up inside me. *It is my fault*, I thought to myself. If I wasn't so stubborn and self-righteous, I could have made a deal with the government and been home with my family, and maybe my mother would be alive today.

I don't know, all kinds of thoughts were going through my mind, and I was very angry—angry at myself, at the government, at Jerry Bowmer and Merkle, at the whole justice system. What more could they do to me that hadn't already been done? *How much more must I suffer, Lord?* I cried inside me. I was hurt and angry, and there was no one and nothing I could take it out on. I knew my daughter was trying to keep what little we still had together. God, how hard things must have been for her, taking care of our home and her little brother. My sister and her family were doing all they could to help out. Now with the death of my mother, it seemed like my whole world was coming apart. I was not home to comfort my family, nor was there anyone here to comfort me.

Once word got out in the barracks that my mother had passed away, a number of the men stopped by to give their condolences. Some of them even took turns watching me through the night to make sure I didn't do anything crazy. It happened sometimes when a man got bad or depressing news from home.

Two days later, I was called to the administration building and told that my emergency furlough was approved and I was to dress out in civilian clothes. I would be leaving for the Greyhound bus station in two hours, where a round-trip ticket was waiting for me. I rushed back to the dorm to change out then reported back to the control area to be picked up by the prison driver. About forty-five minutes later, the prison camp car pulled up, and I was taken to the Greyhound bus station and dropped off.

It was a long ride back to Tampa on the bus, with several stops along the way. It wasn't until about nineteen hours later that I arrived in Tampa. My sister met me at the bus terminal with my daughter and my son Joey, who came down from Jacksonville, Florida, with his wife, Lisa. It was a very emotional reunion. We all hugged and kissed one another and cried in one another's arms. They drove me home so I could rest and clean up for the funeral, which would be the next day. My sister had held everything up till I was able to get there. My brother, Frank, and his wife, Charlotte, were down from New Jersey for the funeral, staying at my sister's house in Ybor City. My son Joey and his wife were staying with us at our house.

It felt good to be home even for a short while, to be with my children. One thing I noticed right away was that my dog, Molly, was missing from the picture. She had died some time back while I was in prison. I sure missed her too. She had so much love in her, and we all loved that dog. There was so much I wanted to say, but it was very late, and we needed to get up early for the wake and mass, which would be held at Our Lady of Perpetual Help Church in Ybor City, where my mother attended mass just about every day.

The next day, my daughter drove us to my sister's house where we all had a good breakfast before the services. I was able to talk with everyone face-to-face for the first time in years. It was good to see my brother and our whole family together. Who knew when I would be able to see them all again.

The priest gave a good eulogy for my mother before we left for the cemetery. My brother and I, my brother-in-law and his two sons Frankie and Evalio Jr., plus my son Joey and my niece's husband, Frank, acted as pallbearers. After we left the cemetery, we all drove over to my sister's house, where I was able to spend some time with all the family. Everyone wanted to know how I was holding up and whether I was being treated right by the prison system.

What could I tell them? I could see it was hard on all of us. I just said, "I'm holding up all right." I knew my brother-in-law would understand. It was great to see all my loved ones and spend some quality time with them, even though I had to leave in the morning to get back to Maxwell on time. I knew that once I left, now that my mother was gone, nothing would be the same anymore for any of us. The anger and bitterness of it all was still festering inside me.

The next morning, I got up and had a nice breakfast with my children and said good-bye to my youngest son, Steven, as I gave him a big hug and told him he needed to be strong and help his sister.

They didn't have my mother anymore to help them out. My sister, Rose, my daughter, Julie, and my older son, Joey, drove with me to the bus station to see me off. My sister and daughter had tears in their eyes as I boarded the bus back to Montgomery. It was going to be a long and lonely ride back to the prison camp.

The ride back to Maxwell gave me a lot of time to think about everything as the bus drove along. I was reliving my life from the time I was a child to the present in my mind. I reminisced on growing up in Manhattan and the Bronx when we moved back there from Tampa when I was very small. I tried to remember all the things I had done with my mother and brother when we lived in a cold tenement building in Manhattan before moving to the Bronx. Then the many memories of my wife and our wedding, the birth of our children Julie and Joey, and our lives together flashed through my mind. I remembered our move to Tampa, the police department, the city council, the birth of my son Steven, and her illness with cancer till her death.

There was so much going through my mind on that trip back to the camp—the thoughts of my life after my wife's death, the commission race, and me taking office. What had happened? How did I end up in this situation? How did I not see it happening? What could I have done differently to avoid this situation? All these thoughts crossed my mind. It didn't matter now. It was done, and I would have to live with it.

Late in the afternoon on the next day, I arrived back in Montgomery, Alabama. From the bus station, I had to take a cab back to the prison camp. It was getting close to my time limit for being out, and I wanted to make sure I got back in time so I would not have any problems with the prison system. The last thing I needed was to be placed on report for showing up late.

Back at the camp after I was processed in, I walked over to my dorm to change back into my prison greens. A number of the men asked about my trip and expressed sympathy about my mother. I didn't say much. After that, I don't think I was the same. I felt a big void inside me, and I kept mainly to myself for a long while. Life there for me became routine again, getting up in the morning and reporting for work, then coming back and getting ready for the late afternoon count, then hanging around the dorms till lights-out. It seemed that time was moving even slower now than before. It felt like I was never going to get out of that place, no matter how promising my attorney said my appeal was going.

By that time, I really didn't care what Merkle was up to with his campaign. I was in prison, and he was out there, traipsing around the state trying to make a name for himself. Although I still received articles from home about the election, none of it seemed to matter anymore. I just wanted to do my time, and I hoped that someday I would get out of that place.

The Florida primaries for Republicans and Democrats were held on September 6, 1988; and when the results came in, Connie Mack had won the Republican primary, giving Robert Merkle a sound defeat and winning with 62 percent of the vote to Merkle's 38 percent. Although, I have to say, for a first timer with little money and not much of a campaign organization, Merkle didn't do too poorly. I figured that now that the campaign was over, like so many other lawyers, Merkle would probably fade into private practice with some law firm or open his own office someplace in the Tampa Bay Area.

After his election loss, I figured that would be the last I heard of Merkle. How wrong I was! Toward the end of September, the Bahamian government asked the Justice Department to investigate former US attorney Robert Merkle for misuse of unsubstantiated allegations of bribery against Prime Minister Lynden Pindling of the Bahamas.

It appeared that during one of Merkle's trials of the drug lord Carlos Lehder, the prime minister's name came up, and Merkle started an investigation into the prime minister and his family for allowing drug smuggling from South America through remote Bahamian islands into the United States.

Again, the evidence was based on hearsay and could not be substantiated against the prime minister. Here again, Merkle, without proof, had released statements attacking a government official as he had done against Governor Martinez and EJ Salcines. Independent federal investigations into the allegations against those men found no basis of truth. This time, it was against a head of state of a foreign country. I could see where their government would be a little upset about the whole thing.

When Merkle was asked about the request by the Bahamian government, all he said was, "In a nutshell, Sir Lynden is full of hot air."

It was allegations like this that got me here in the first place. But I did not have the luxury of overcoming his or Jerry Bowmer's allegations that placed me in two trials with so many others. This was where Mad Dog Merkle stood out. Using his position of power as chief federal prosecutor for the Middle District of Florida, he could hurt anyone's reputation with just innuendos and hearsay allegations. He built his reputation on that, hoping something would stick so he could prosecute. That was the Merkle way, and he was very good at it.

In spite all of Merkle's allegations and an investigation of the Bahamian prime minister by the US Justice Department, nothing would come of it, and no charges were filed. This beloved prime minister, a hero to his people, would continue to serve as prime minister of the Bahamas until August of 1992.

After all this, things seem to quiet down back home. I continued exercising for my back problem, and I was walking a lot better. I had become used to life at Maxwell, and for me, it started to seem the norm. Everything else in the world was just a memory. Rarely did anything ever change around there, except the rules. As more men were sent there and the place got even more crowded, the justice system tightened the rules that governed us, giving us even less freedom than we had before.

By December of 1988, the face of Maxwell had changed a great deal from when I first arrived back in 1985. We had new brick two-story dorms that replaced the old wooden dorms, yet we were still over maximum capacity. There were so many new faces coming and going that you didn't really know anyone. The few of the longtimers like myself, we kept mostly to ourselves. We really didn't care for a lot of the new men coming in. Many of them were Columbian or Cuban smugglers; others were from the hood or street gangs finishing up their time here before being released. The place had changed while we all tried to get along in harmony.

By December, I heard that Merkle had gone into private practice over in Clearwater, Florida, just across from Tampa. He had opened his small office in the hopes of having a big first-class law firm sometime in the future. He claimed he was very busy and doing well and now would be looking for partners to expand his practice.

During this same month back in Tampa, Joe Magri was being replaced as first assistant prosecutor by the new US attorney for the Middle District of Florida, Robert W. Genzman. Magri would be reassigned to the civil division early next year, and Gregory W. Kehoe from Fort Lauderdale would be replacing him as first assistant prosecutor. I think this might have upset Magri a little bit since he was still in trial trying to get a conviction in the bribery trial of one of my codefendants Nelson Italiano, who was now dealing with a new trial after overturning his mail fraud conviction.

The dismal holidays were approaching for those of us serving time. These were always depressing times for most of us. The new trial for Italiano back in Tampa was coming to a close. It wouldn't be till the beginning of January 1989 before the jury would be selected for the trial of Paul B. Johnson, a distinguished attorney from Tampa. US attorney Robert Genzman was letting Magri finish up the trial cases he had been working on during the Merkle witch hunts before he moved into the civil division.

By the beginning of 1989, the trial for bribery and extortion against Attorney Paul Johnson was well underway. Johnson was a former Hillsborough state attorney and high office holder in the American Bar Association. Another codefendant who had been severed from my big trial was finally getting his day in court after all this time.

Throughout all this time, Mr. Johnson had maintained his innocence, claiming the changes were the results of vendettas by the government's chief witness Jerry Bowmer and by former US attorney Robert "Mad Dog" Merkle.

It seems one of Johnson's clients had implicated Bowmer in drug dealing, so Johnson felt Bowmer had invented the bribery allegations against him out of spite. Plus, Mr. Johnson was accusing Merkle of being out to get him for refusing to testify a few years back against former state attorney EJ Salcines, who was the target of a grand jury investigation at that time. Mr. Johnson also said he told EJ Salcines and Hillsborough sheriff Walter C. Heinrich that one of his clients had information linking Bowmer with a Belize-based marijuana smuggling ring. This is why Bowmer made up the bribe story—as a way to get revenge.

On a positive note, I came to find out that Mr. Johnson was being represented by the famous defense attorney F. Lee Bailey of Miami. His opposition on the prosecution's side would be assistant US attorney Joe Magri, who had handled most of the county corruption prosecutions. The big guns were coming out to join the fight for Mr. Johnson's defense. The only real witness the government had was Jerry Bowmer.

I had a special interest in this case because I was implicated in it and had been found not guilty of these charges back in '86. The question on my mind now was, *Would this jury believe Bowmer, who was an admitted liar?* Now he claimed to the jury that he was telling the truth—good luck with that one, Mr. Magri.

During Mr. Bailey's cross-examination of Bowmer, he was able to catch Bowmer in a number of discrepancies between his earlier testimony and his account at this trial. Bowmer admitted that he lied in 1974 about being a college graduate when he applied to be a Hillsborough sheriff's deputy, that he lied during his 1980 divorce to reduce his alimony payments, and that he lied in a letter to a federal judge seeking leniency before his sentence in 1986. Even so, he denied lying in this trial against Paul Johnson.

As Mr. Bailey continued to question Bowmer, the jury found out that Bowmer, who was the mastermind of all these corruption allegations, had only served eight months in a minimum-security faculty and was now living in Lake City, Florida, doing some farming.

As days turned into weeks, the trial against Paul Johnson continued. Toward the end of January, I was receiving articles about the trial just about every other day. To verify Johnson's claim that he had gone to the authorities about Bowmer's connection to the marijuana smugglers, the defense called both Sheriff Walter Heinrich and former state attorney EJ Salcines to the stand to testify on Mr. Johnson's behalf.

When Sheriff Heinrich was on the stand, he said he was told by Mr. Johnson in December of 1982 that one of Johnson's clients, Charles Rex, had seen Bowmer with a drug smuggler in the Central America nation of Belize in July of 1982.

Previous testimony in this trial had established that Rex had been convicted of drug trafficking and was attempting to reduce his sentence by cooperating with the state police. Sheriff Heinrich also testified that he and Johnson met with Salcines about Rex's accusation and that the sheriff's office opened an investigation. When Salcines was on the witness stand, he told the jury that he could remember little about the meeting other than that Johnson was willing to do anything to help the investigation.

Sheriff Heinrich also testified that his office closed the matter on February 1, 1983, the day after Bowmer was arrested in a federal bribery sting, because Rex was unable to provide any substantial information to support his allegations.

During this same time, I received a letter from the United States Courts Office of Probation in Tampa, telling me that US district judge George C. Carr had received the petition that was sent back on July 10, 1986 from the men of cellblock 200 C/1 from the Hillsborough County Jail on my behalf. The judge had forwarded it to the probation office in Tampa for review. I was now being informed by Clatyon T. Godfrey, US probation officer, that they had it on file. It only took them two and a half years to send me acknowledgment that they had received the petition. I guess they were not going to do anything with it but file it away since no action was taken upon it up to this time. At least now, I know what happened to it and where it ended up.

It made me feel good about those men who took the time to write a petition on my behalf when they had problems of their own. It brought back fond memories of our fellowship together. I felt that maybe, in all this madness I might have done a little good.

By the end of January, I received the article that said Paul Johnson had been acquitted of his extortion and bribery charges. Another slap in the face and defeat for Merkle and Magri. Even this jury did not believe the key witness Bowmer.

As Judge George C. Carr read the four innocent verdicts to the packed courtroom, applause and tears of joy greeted the defendant. The jury also cleared Mr. Johnson of two counts of perjury for denying during a voluntary grand jury appearance in May of 1985 that he had paid bribes. There was only one charge of perjury that the jury was deadlocked on, and Johnson's attorney F. Lee Bailey said he would file a motion to have Judge Carr acquit Mr. Johnson on the remaining charge. At the same time, he called the government "sore losers" for not dismissing it, saying, "It would be a laughingstock to try that case by itself."

Mr. Richard Gerstein, another of Mr. Johnson's defense attorneys said, "The innocent verdicts should answer all the charges. The jury has said that Paul Johnson did not pay a bribe, and that was what the case was all about."

Mr. Bailey told reporters that Merkle's revenge didn't work, for a change. Mr. Johnson, ever a gentleman, said, "I don't keep grudges, and what has happened in the trial is over. I want to get along with my life and my law practice."

It appeared that in the final arguments to the jury, Mr. Bailey lambasted the government for believing Bowmer, saying that the charges against his client were the result of a mindless government agency and a known pathological liar, and that anyone with a shred of honesty knew Bowmer's story was false on its face and it couldn't be true."

Mr. Magri had also agreed during his final argument to the jury that Bowmer was not the most truthful witness, calling him a "venal, corrupt crook."

I was very happy for Mr. Johnson and his family. It was another victory over the county witch hunt that Merkle had started. It was also a good example of why it pays to be severed from a large trial with multiple defendants. The government has a hard time proving its case against a single defendant because the evidence used to convict the majority is not always the same for the individual.

When you try a large number of individuals, should one or two be guilty, it usually will also stick to the others. On the other hand, when you are tried by yourself, the government has to show the evidence pertaining only to you. This way, you have a better chance of defending yourself. This was one of the reasons why I was unable to get severed from my trials. If I had, I would have had a better chance of defending myself and possibly could have been acquitted.

CHAPTER 45

Heartbreaking News

February 1989

As February rolled around, I didn't think I would be hearing as much from home since everything seemed to be quieting down after the Johnson trial. The losses had been piling up against Magri and Merkle. After years of hard work and millions of taxpayers' dollars, the government had little to show for it in the way of convictions. I think the US attorney for the Middle District of Florida thought it was time to send Magri back to the minor leagues in the civil division.

By the second week of February, while I was calling home, I received the sad news from my daughter, Julie, that Fred Anderson had passed away. I was shocked and numb when I heard it. I just held the phone to my ear and stood there for a few moments to let it all sink in. It was like a sharp, dull pain went through my body with the news, just like I felt when my mother had passed away. My daughter said she sent me the article about his death and I should get it in a few days. I didn't say much after that except for a little small talk, finding out how she and the rest of the family were doing.

When I hung up the phone and started walking back to my dorm, I was burning up inside with anger. How could the government let this happen? They knew how sick he was. Why couldn't they have gotten him a break and sent him home where he could have gotten good medical care? Again, I was angry at Merkle and Magri for doing this to Fred. I blamed them for his death. To me, it was the same as if they had taken a gun and shot him. I had heard all the horror stories about the care in maximum prison hospitals. It was nothing like what I received up at Rochester, Minnesota, at the Mayo Clinic. That was where he should have been transferred.

His poor family. I could only imagine what they must be going through, his wife and daughter not being there for him in his final hours. He was so far away from his family that it was almost impossible for them to visit him on any regular basis. The cost would be prohibitive.

I felt at the moment that Merkle and Magri must have been real proud of themselves, knowing that they had helped to perpetuate his heart condition. They needed somebody to beat on with all their losses and embarrassment with the court system. The only ones they really could take it out on were Fred and me, and they did a good job on Fred. But I was still kicking. They hadn't gotten me down yet, and I was not ready to give up.

Like my daughter said, a few days later, I received the article on Fred's death. As I read it, I could see that the press was not very kind as they reported his death. Even in death, they had to bring up all the negative things that happened to him. I guess it was a preview of what they would say about me when the time came for me to kick the bucket. Hopefully, not for a long time.

As far as I was concerned, I held Robert Merkle and Joe Magri responsible for this tragedy. They didn't have to fight Fred's petition for early medical release. There was nothing more to gain by it, except to heal their shattered egos. They had gotten their convictions and their pound of flesh from us, even though it was a small victory for them. I guess a little mercy or compassion was not in their way of doing things. They had us where they wanted us. They had put us down, and they would keep us down just to show off their power. Human decency means nothing to an ambitious prosecutor. To understand mercy, you have to have a heart.

I find that this is something lacking in our justice system. All it understands is punishment, punishment, and punishment. It doesn't matter how many families it destroys. For every inmate they can keep in the system, it means more money for the prison system.

That night, back in my bunk, I could not help but think of the man I knew who had the office next to mine at the county courthouse. You could say he was a big teddy bear on the inside, even though on the outside, he looked like a rough-and-tumble guy. I remember the tears I shed for him as I prayed for his soul that evening.

His prison time was finally over. I had to believe he was in a better place. I also prayed for his family. I felt bad for them, wondering what would happen to them now. This was an unnecessary tragedy. As I reviewed the article again, I read Merkle's callous, cold, and unfeeling response. Even the reporter who wrote the article, Bentley Orrick of the *Tribune*, was very condescending and harsh toward Fred. He could have been a little more sympathetic to the man and his family, considering all the good things that Fred did for our community to make it safe, both as a firefighter and a county commissioner.

Orrick headlined the article, "Convicted Ex-Commissioner Dies in Prison at 60." I guess it's headlines like this that sell newspapers. The article quotes Anderson's attorney Robert Polli speaking on the family's behalf, stating that Mrs. Pat Anderson had received a telegram from the prison system telling them that Fred Anderson had died of a heart disease involving an irregular heartbeat.

Evidence that had been presented in court during our trials showed that Fred suffered his first heart attack less than five weeks before he was arrested in his office at the courthouse back in 1983. During our trial, when Fred suffered a heart attack in court and while the paramedics were working on him in the courtroom, just before transferring him to Tampa General Hospital, I and a couple of other defendants and defense lawyers overheard someone from the prosecution's side say to his colleagues, "The guy's faking it." This was the type of contempt they had for us.

An effort was pushed forward by his family and friends to help Fred get an early release due to his medical condition, but Merkle and Magri succeeded in blocking his early release. Mr. Polli said, "I think the prosecution was very aware that Fred was not faking his heart disease."

Mr. Merkle, so he would not look like the bad guy, said, "It's a tragedy for his family, obviously, and God rest his soul. Our office insisted that he be treated like any other convicted felon. We left it totally up to the doctors."

When Fred started serving his sentence, he was sent to the federal correctional institution in Lexington, Kentucky. Then sometime last year, he was transferred to the Federal Prison Medical Center in Springfield, Missouri.

To this day, I do not understand why he wasn't sent to the one in Rochester, Minnesota, where he would have gotten the best of care from the Mayo Clinic doctors, who were better equipped to handle his type of condition.

After this, I did not hear much more about Fred. My daughter told me by phone that the family had a private funeral for Fred and wanted to keep everything out of the news. His wife and daughter just wanted to be left alone by everyone, especially the media. They stayed in their home most of the time, not really going anywhere unless they had to. She wanted to know how I was holding up, and I just told her I was holding up. There was not much more I could say as time moved on.

Sometime during the second week of March, I received word that the remaining charges were dropped against Paul Johnson. It seems that Judge Carr had dismissed the remaining charges against Mr. Johnson, ending the four-year-old allegation that he was involved in the commission of bribery.

Again, I was happy for one of my codefendants, for Mr. Johnson and his family; their part of this nightmare was finally over. Now he could get on with his life and practice. Another loss from the witch hunt.

From this point on at the Maxwell prison camp, things were just about routine. Allen Wolfson's turn came up for him to be paroled from Maxwell, and he couldn't wait to get out of there. We said our good-byes, and I think he told me he was moving out west someplace to start over. Wherever he was leaving to, I wished him well. The next day he was gone, and that was the last time I had any contact with him.

I was starting to get close also. I still had a little over a year to go on my sentence before I would be eligible for parole, but there was a federal rule that stated if an inmate had a job waiting for them, they could get released from prison six months earlier to be placed on parole six months sooner. The inmate had to have a letter from the employer promising that he had a job waiting for him, then submit the letter with an application for early parole to the parole board. If approved, then you would have six months cut from your sentence and added to your parole.

With that information, I immediately asked my daughter to contact some of the people we knew to see if any of them would give me any type of job and a letter to that fact that I could submit to the parole board. My daughter and family started contacting many of the friends we had who owned businesses. It seemed like many of them were afraid to give such a letter for fear that the government might come looking into their affairs.

At the moment, it seemed no one wanted to get involved with the government, and my prospects did not look good. But then, one friend said he would write a letter on my behalf and give me a job, which was what I needed to be granted an early parole. His name was Gene Olstine, a man I had met during my early campaigns a number of years ago. He was in the liquor business and owned a number of liquor stores and bars in the Tampa Bay Area. He was the only one who came through for me.

When my lawyer Arthur Addess received the letter, he immediately sent the letter and the petition off to the Federal Parole Commission for review. Now there was nothing to do but wait and see if I would be approved. I had no idea how long these things took, nor if the federal prosecutor in Tampa would block it. All anyone could do was hope and pray for the best.

By the time the end of November came around, the charges against Nelson Italiano, who was still out on bond pending his appeal, the statute of limitations had run out and barred the prosecution from retrying him. Mr. Italiano's attorney John Lawson Jr. would be arguing before a three-judge panel of the Eleventh US Circuit Court of Appeals that federal law prohibits such charges more than five years after the alleged crime was committed. It now appeared that it was all over for Mr. Italiano, and he too could move on with his life. It was clear now to almost everyone that Merkle's bag of dirty threats, innuendos, and hearsay evidence was no longer holding up. I'm sure he and Magri must have been ticked off about all this.

The winds had changed since 1983, when Merkle had made headlines with his corruption witch hunt. Now he was out of the picture in private practice. As for Joe Magri, he left the federal prosecutor's office to join Merkle in private practice. I have to admit, from what I know of them, the two of them were excellent lawyers, or they could not have accomplished all they did. I just didn't care for the way they went about it. Now they were just Merkle and Magri, partners in law, building a foundation for their law practice in the Tampa Bay Area.

It was now almost the end of another year. I still had not received any word on my petition for early work release. For the moment it looked like the government was taking their sweet time on the matter since I wasn't going anywhere for a while. Just another year to look forward to. But I also had my blessings to count. As bad as some of the things I had gone through were, throughout this ordeal, I still had a lot to be thankful for. I still had the respect and love of my family. Thanks to the Lord, I was able to survive some of the darkest moments in my life; plus, he gave me back the use of my legs without surgery. I was now able to walk without a cane or any assistance. I was still alive and well, and I felt I could now stand up to just about anything that would come against me.

I had not given up on my dreams; I just needed to take a different road from the one I had been on. One thing you learn quickly in prison is that you don't need a lot of things to survive. You just need the basic necessities; everything else is just icing on the cake.

Things were finally quieting down back in Tampa. The community was getting back to normal now that the witch hunts were finally over. People were more at ease with their local politicians. After all had been said and done, what had it all come down to?

Over eight years, the prosecutors and federal government had spent millions upon millions of dollars of taxpayers' money on investigations, depositions, man hours, grand juries and jury's costs, court trial costs, and expenses for witness and witness protection, plus transportation costs—and for what? To gain the convictions of less than a handful of defendants, the majority of whom doing less than eighteen months in prison or probation, with only Fred Anderson and myself doing most of the long, hard time? The majority of the other defendants from all the trials were found not guilty, with no real justification for their indictments. It was all just to satisfy the ego of an overzealous prosecutor out to make a name for himself. It's allowed Bowmer and Bean out in the world after doing just a few months of prison time.

So a man died in prison and is forgotten (or some would say was legally murdered, depending on how you wish to look at it, thanks to the federal prosecutors of Tampa, who lacked compassion for a sick man). Did anyone really care except the family and close friends? Meanwhile, another man was waiting out the years in prison so he could one day rejoin his children and try to rebuild his life. Who were the real winners here? I guess you could say they were Bowmer and Bean, who played the government well, leading them in all different directions while the government was handing out indictments on their say-so just to stay out of jail. Now they were able to move on with their lives.

For me, life went on no matter where I am. I was not ready to throw the towel in. I still had a lot of life left in me, and I was going to put it to some good use, there in prison and when I got out. Sure, mistakes were made, but we can't look back. All I could do was either pick myself up and move on, or wallow in self-pity. I've never been one for self-pity, and I couldn't allow myself to be eaten up with bitterness. I needed to be practical, so I guessed I'd just move on and keep looking ahead. Nobody said life would be fair, and that is how I must accept it. I had now come to a fork in the road with my life. There were two directions in which I could choose to go. I have never been one for the easy road, like Bowmer or Bean. If I had been, I wouldn't have been there in prison. For me, I'll take the road less traveled and accept wherever it leads me to.

CHAPTER 46

The Day of Jubilation

January 1990

It was the start of another year for me, and I had been in the prison system nearly five years. I checked with my sister, Rose, to see if her husband, Evalio, could find out anything from Gene Olstine, if he had been contacted by the parole board. I told her I would call back in a week to see if he was able to find out anything for me.

Just under a week later, I made another collect call to my sister, and she told me that Evalio said Gene had received some forms to fill out from the government and that he had filled them out and sent them back well over a month or two ago. No one had heard anything back since. We talked for a little while longer, but not too long as these calls are very expensive when you have to reverse the charges.

After I hung up, I thought to myself, *They probably turned it down.* I knew the Tampa federal prosecutor's office had a say in this matter also, so I figured they would probably block the petition. They hadn't done me any favors in all those years, and they certainly didn't do Fred Anderson any favors when he applied for a medical parole, which was more needed than mine.

If it was disapproved, I wondered when I would receive the notice. I knew they liked to take their time in matters like this. By that point, it didn't really matter; I was used to disappointments. I had been in the system so long that it had started to change me. Even though I kept a positive outlook on things, I knew I could survive in the system. It had become a way of life for me. It was my home, and I made the most of it.

By the third week of January, I was called to the control center for a phone call from my attorney Arthur Addess. He called to inform me that my petition for parole work release had been approved, that the Tampa federal prosecutor's office had no objections, and that they now had to go through the prison system for approval. This was great news; now it would be up to the warden to give the final sign-off. Mr. Addess didn't know how much longer the process would take, but he felt sure I would be getting out very soon.

When I hung up the phone and left to get back to my dorm, I was on cloud nine. For once in all these years in the system, something had gone right. But it was not over yet. Anything could happen before the orders came down. I had to be doubly alert not to get any infractions that would jeopardize my situation. For the moment, I didn't say anything to anyone about it, just in case someone wanted to screw around with me to cause a problem.

Around the thirtieth or the thirty-first of January, I made a collect call home to my daughter, Julie, who had already received the good news from my attorney over a week prior. She and everyone in the family could hardly wait till I came home. Even my son Steven was excited and couldn't wait to see me again.

Then she told me the news. Judge George C. Carr had passed away the other day. He was the trial judge who had sentenced me and Fred to prison. She informed me that he had died of a brain tumor that he had had for several years. He was sixty years old, and she thought he had looked much older during the trial. He had stayed on the bench right up till his death, she said. There were rumors going around in the courthouse that, that might have had an effect on his decisions in the cases he had tried. Who really knows, there are always rumors going around the courthouses.

I told my daughter I hoped to see her soon and hung up the phone. *So Judge Carr is dead*, I said to myself as I walked back down the walkway to my dorm. I didn't feel satisfied or happy about it. I know how most inmates feel about their judges, but I kind of felt sorry for the man that he died that way. That night, I even said a prayer for him. I didn't blame him for what happened to me. He sentenced me on the evidence presented and Bowmer's statements. He could have been a little easier on us, but he was who he was, and he had a job to do. I didn't care what others might have thought of the man; I felt no animosity toward him, just pity.

On the morning of February 4, I was called to the warden's office and informed that my parole had come through and that I needed to report to the central processing center, where five years previous I had been processed in, to be processed out. He said my parole would start the next day on February 5, and a cab would pick me up at the front of the building very early in the morning. I was to have all my belongings packed and ready to go with me and to turn in all my prison uniforms and anything that belonged to the institution.

I had to fill out and sign a number of forms then return to my dorm and pack everything up. They gave me boxes to put everything in and take back to central processing for inspection and then to be sealed. You never saw anyone move as fast as I did on that day. After everything had been returned and all my personal belongings were packed and ready to be shipped out, they would ship all my belongings to my home in Tampa so I would have nothing to carry on my trip home. I would wear my civilian clothes for the rest of the day till it was time for me to leave.

That night, it was hard for me to sleep. My heart was pounding with anticipation, and my mind was going a mile a minute with thoughts of my children and what I would see and find when I got home. The next morning, after the 4:00 a.m. count, I was allowed to proceed to central processing to be signed out. It was only a matter of a few hours before I would be out of there.

Standing in front of the desk of the officer who was processing me out, I had to sign more papers for my release. I was given $96.00 for bus and taxi fares, $100.00 for gratuity, and the $4.81 that was left in my canteen account. This gave me a total of $200.81 to cover my trip home. Now all I had to do was wait for the cab to pick me up and take me to the Greyhound bus station.

At 7:15 a.m. on February 5, 1990, I was officially signed out of prison and officially on parole, waiting for the cab. I had been informed by the officer who discharged me that I was to immediately report to the Federal Probation Office in downtown Tampa at 500 Zack Street the next day after my arrival. They were expecting me to report promptly the morning of the sixth for my orientation.

By 8:30 a.m., the cab finally arrived to take me to the bus station. It was a strange and elated feeling to leave the camp. This had been my home off and on for the past five years. All the men I met along the way who came and went and all the stories I had heard about their situations and adventures were now behind me.

As we approached the gate to freedom, I asked the driver to stop. I told him I would meet him on the other side of the gate; then we could continue on to the bus station. He gave me a strange look but complied. I got out of the cab and waited for him to drive through the gate and stop. At that point, I walked out of the gate and across the line to freedom on my own two legs as I had said I would a few years back.

This was my day of jubilation; I had been set free. I imagine my elation must have been similar to how the slaves of the South must have felt when they were set free from their taskmasters by the Union solders over a hundred years ago. I couldn't help but do a little dance once on the other side while the cab driver waited for me to get back into his cab. He must have thought I was some kind of nutcase. I don't think he could understand what this all meant to me as we drove off toward the bus terminal.

Timing was perfect. At the terminal, I paid the cab driver for the ride; then I walked into the terminal and purchased my ticket to Tampa. I didn't have to wait too long; the bus pulled out within the hour. I had taken a seat near the back of the bus so I could watch the people get on and off. It was a long ride home with a number of stops, but I enjoyed every minute of it.

As the bus drove along, I looked around at the other people riding with me. I could see the bus was a little more than half full. There was an old couple sitting across from me, a young woman with a child just down the aisle in front of me, and there were a couple of young adults across from her. A Mexican family took up a number of the seats toward the front, and another older man was sitting just behind the driver. The beginning of the ride was a little noisy because of the kids from the Mexican family, but after a while, they settled down.

I sat back and just enjoyed the view from the window as we headed south. While resting and staring out the window, my mind started to drift. I started to reminisce about the past five years of my life, thinking about all that had happened to me. My trial, my sentencing, the many journeys through the prison system and marshals services. All the people I came into contact with during my travels. My stay at the air force hospital at Maxwell and the prison hospital in Rochester, Minnesota. All the doctors and my back pain. Sadness came over me when I thought of my mother and Fred Anderson. I wondered how Pat Anderson was handling it all. So much was being filtered through my mind, like I could see it all as if it were yesterday. I was brought back to reality every time the bus stopped to pick up new passengers or let off the ones who reached their stop.

It wouldn't be till after 1:00 a.m. the next day that I would arrive in Tampa. My sister, brother-in-law, son, and daughter met me at the station as I pulled in. It was a very emotional time for us all. I had to get home and get some rest because I had to be at the probation office early in the morning, so we hugged one last time that night as we walked over to my sister's car. They had all come in one car to meet me. My sister, Rose, would drive us to her house in Ybor City, where my daughter had her car to drive us home.

Then next morning, I reported to the US Probation Office at the federal building at 501 East Polk Street in downtown Tampa. I reported to room 900 where I was met by a Ms. Linda Crutchfield, who explained the rules of my probation and gave me more papers to sign. I was told that for the next fifty-nine days, I would be on curfew parole, from February 5, 1990 to April 4, 1990. I was to remain in the confines of my home between the hours of 9:00 p.m. to 6:00 a.m., seven days a week, except when excused by my probation officer. The probation officer assigned to me was named Larry Gibbs.

He would drop by sometime during the week to introduce himself, and he would check up on me from time to time.

After about an hour of questions and answers and signing all sorts of forms, I was allowed to go home and start rebuilding my life. Ms. Crutchfield told me as I was leaving that Mr. Gibbs would be coming by to see me sometime that week and to make sure I did not violate my curfew.

Is she kidding? I thought to myself. *All I want now is to stay home with my children and just enjoy being back—to sleep in my own bed, cook in my own kitchen, and walk out onto the patio and smell the sweet smell of freedom.*

When I got back to my house, I called Gene Olstine to find out when he wanted me to start work and told him my restrictions. He understood, and he told me to take the rest of the week off to be with my family and settle back in; then we would get together next week and talk about the job.

The week went by fairly fast. During the day, my daughter left for work and my son Steven went off to school. I would just relax around the house till they came home since I didn't have a car to get around in. At times, my brother-in-law, Evalio, would come by and take me around to different places to see old friends.

I was starting to see that things were not going to be the same. As we traveled around town, stopping at different coffee shops where we knew a lot of our old friends hanged out, the reception was kind of cold. Many were polite, but a few would turn their back toward me when we approached. Some wouldn't even shake my hand. A few had some harsh words to say to my face, and others just talked behind our backs.

It was all right, though. My brother-in-law would get pissed off, but I just told him it didn't matter anymore. People will believe what they want to believe on what they read or heard. They really didn't have a clue what really went on, and trying to explain would only make things worse.

So we would leave and go someplace else, where the atmosphere was friendlier. A lot of my good close friends were happy to see me. They didn't seem to care about what had happened. They were sincerely happy to see me back. Many of them knew I had been through hell, so it was a very mixed Tampa that I came home to. A number of people suggested that I should take my family and move to start my life over where no one knows me. But this was the Tampa I was determined to rebuild my life in. I'm no coward nor a quitter. I had no reason to run and hide in shame. Like so many, I too was a victim, and now I was ready to stand up against anyone.

When I met Gene, he turned out to be a great guy. I had met him a number of times when I was in office, but this was the first time I really got to know him. Over time, we would become good friends. He started me out working at one of his liquor stores and even loaned me one of his daughter's cars so I could get around.

This same week, Mr. Gibbs, my probation officer, came by my house after 9:00 p.m. to check up on me. He had to fill out an evaluation report on me and needed to look over my home and situation. He seemed like a nice guy, asking me how I was doing and getting along. He asked whether I was having any problems and that I could call him any time if I had a problem or just needed to talk. He talked with both my son and my daughter on how they were getting along having me back home; and when he finished, he just said to me that if there was anything he could do to help me, just let him know. Then he left.

He would come by in the evenings just about every other week to check up on me and see how I was getting along. Those first few weeks for me were the hardest. After I was away for so long, everyone had their own agenda, and I didn't seem to fit in well with it. This period of adjustment was extremely hard on all of us. I seemed to be crowding everyone around me. My daughter loved me, but she had her own life to live. Now that I was home, she wanted to move on and get on with it and not worry about Steven or the house anymore.

For my son Steven, he thought that once I was home, things would be like they were before I left. He couldn't understand that things would never be the same again for us. I guess I seemed to be a disappointment to him, not being able to do a lot of the things we used to do. He started hanging out with the wrong crowd.

My oldest son, Joey, was living in Jacksonville, and he had his own life and family to worry about. He knew he was not in a position to help me, and I didn't want to bother him with what was going on here at home. So I kept a lot of my depression inside me and tried to keep a happy face.

My father would come by to visit every now and then. He was happy that I was home. We were never really close, but it was nice to see him every so often. He was in no position to help me as he was living on a pension in a retirement apartment complex in South Tampa. My whole world had turned upside down at this point, and it was hard to figure out where I would go from there. Gene was very good to me. He knew my situation, but there wasn't too much more he could do for me. He knew I needed more income to be able to get along without my daughter's help.

I wasn't prepared for this homecoming. I wanted to come home so badly, but I didn't realize what I would be facing when I came home. What was supposed to be a happy time was turning into a human tragedy. During my first two months, the tension and disappointments around the house were taking their toll.

My son Steven, who was now seventeen at this time, got into trouble with the law because of the crowd he was hanging out with. They were all sent to prison for a spell. There was nothing I or my daughter could do for him. It was too late; he never came to me for advice or help. He broke my heart. At this point, I felt like a total failure. This was a very low point in my life.

This might not have happened if he had a father around to help guide him. Being away for five years changes a family, especially one that does not have a father or mother at home to guide them. In my absence, Steven had bounced around from relative to relative. It was hard for my daughter to control him with no man in the house, so in his younger years after I was sent away, he was sent to live for a while with my brother, Frank, in New Jersey, then with my son Joey in Jacksonville and back again to my daughter in Tampa.

This is what happens to families that are caught up in the system and there is no help available for them. As far as the courts or the justice system are concerned, it's not their problem. The system doesn't really do much to help families of convicted felons. They are laying the seeds of more discontent. It is a system that fails society by foresting more crime. This is one of the reasons why our jails are full of young offenders.

Had I been afforded house arrest or a shorter sentence, then maybe this situation would never have happened. I could have been there for my son to guide him and redirect his energy and education to something positive. But it became too late for us; I no longer had his attention. I had lost the ability to reach my son at this point.

After his arrest, he realized it was too late to undo what he and his friends had done. He was tried as an adult, and for the next couple of years, he would experience a lot of what I went through. I had been home less than two months, and we never had enough time to get to know each other better. I felt like a failure and was totally depressed.

One night, when my probation officer came by the house, he could see I was not myself. I explained my problems and what had been going on while he listened patiently. I tried to explain to him that I felt I didn't belong there anymore, that I didn't fit in, that I would be better off if he sent me back to prison. I understood prison, that I had a life there, that life and everything was simple and regimented for me. At least there, I wasn't an outcast, and I could get along with everyone. I wanted him to know that this new world I was in was not my world. I felt I no longer belonged in it. It seemed I had become what they called "institutionalized," and I felt more comfortable in prison than in my own house.

When I finished, he looked at me and said, "Joe, give it time. You just got out after five years. The world has changed in that time, and you still need time to adjust to it. I know things look tough now, but that will change. Just give it time. You've been doing so well. You really don't need supervision. You need to get out and find your place. You're already making something of yourself. Remember who you are and all the things you are capable of. I read your file, and if you're anything like the man I read about, you will overcome this just as you have overcome every obstacle in your life. Please, just give it a chance. You're out now. It's up to you to make the best of it, and there still are a lot of people who want to help you.

"You're not the only one to feel this way. Why, everyone who is released after serving a long sentence feels just like you. It's hard on them, and it's hard on their families. That's why it's called the period of adjustment. You have to give it a chance to work, and that takes a little more time."

I listened and understood what he was trying to tell me. He could see that I had been very depressed, and he didn't want me to do anything foolish. We talked for a little while longer; then he left when he saw I was starting to feel a little better.

He was right. A few weeks later, I was starting to feel like I belonged. By April 5, I was off curfew parole. I now had more freedom of movement, and I felt like my chains had been removed. Mr. Gibbs would come by from time to time to see how I was doing for the reports he was required to turn in. I was still working for Gene, being able to work at nights now. He would have me manage one of his lounges from time to time to see if anyone might be stealing from him.

On one occasion, I was working out on Highway 98, out in Seffner, Florida, just east of Tampa, at a place called Billy Jack's. It was kind of a redneck bar with entertainment on the weekends. On certain nights on the weekend, there was a $5 admission fee to get in, so he would have me work the door and collect the money to see if the other fellow who worked the door was skimming off some of the funds. After the first two weeks, he told me he had made more money with me at the door in two weeks than he had made in a month. He fixed the problem, and I moved on to run a new liquor store that he had bought in North Tampa.

One night at work, I received a call from my sister, saying that our father had passed away in his apartment in South Tampa. When I arrived, I was informed that my father had died of a heart attack the night before, and they found him the next day when he did not come down to check at the front desk like he did every day. He was a veteran, so we buried him at the military cemetery in Bushnell, Florida.

Now both my parents were gone, may they rest in peace. I guess I was sorry that we were never that close. I also regret that I never really told him that I loved him. I have to live with that.

I stayed working with Gene for over a year while still trying to better myself. Everywhere I tried, it was the same thing. Once I wrote that I was a convicted felon on the application, no one would hire me. It didn't matter where I went—big corporations that claimed to be equal-opportunity employers, or little mom-and-pop shops. No matter how many times I tried, I never got a call back, or they just filled the job, or someone was more qualified, or I was overqualified. It was the same story everywhere I went.

Being a former public official, I was a hot potato. No one wanted any press or heat brought down on them. I could see how it was; the writing was on the wall. When I was in office, everyone wanted something from me. Now no one wanted to know me. All the people and companies that I had gone out of my way to help now forgot about all that. It was up to me to change things around. So I went back to school, taking some refresher night courses on radiology.

Years ago, I had started out as an x-ray technician back in 1962 and continued in the field throughout my careers as a police officer and city councilman, moonlighting as one on occasion. This was something I knew, something I had trained for and done throughout my life. So why not?

Toward the end of 1990, Gene helped me get a position with a security camera company as a salesman. The owner was a good friend of Gene's, and he was willing to give me a chance because he was looking for some good salesmen. The position gave me free movement around parts of the state, and the commissions were decent when I was able to make a sale.

I worked during the day and took courses at night to get ready to take the state's exams on radiology. I still had an active New York state license in radiology, but I needed a Florida state license to work in a hospital or clinic in Tampa. This was a position I knew how to do and enjoyed doing. It's what I always had enjoyed, being able to help people.

Most of 1991 was spent selling security cameras and studying at night. On weekends, I would try and drive up to North Florida toward the panhandle to see my son Steven, who was serving time up there. My daughter, Julie, had moved out of the house about six months earlier to have her own space. She got herself a nice little apartment in the Hyde Park district of Tampa and was working for a new real estate office at the time. She had been doing really well for herself.

As I promised the Lord when I was in prison, I would attend church every chance I got and give him the thanks for getting me this far. For a while, when I came home from Maxwell, I got in contact with Bennie Backer, the chaplain for the Hillsborough County Sheriff's Office. I told him I wanted to volunteer to see what I could do to help others who were in need of guidance and remind them that their lives were not over, and they could turn it around if they would only try.

He signed me up as a lay minister after taking a chaplain's course through the sheriff's department. Bennie and I became good friends. He was not judgmental, and he knew what I had been through. He even told me that he voted for me way back when, and he was happy to see what I was doing with my life. This was something I felt I needed to do. By trying to help some of these men and women, I was also helping myself. I stayed with the service for about two years, doing what little good I could in the county jails. You also run into a lot of negative people in the system. Not all were incarcerated; some were the officers whom we had to deal with.

It was strange at times, seeing some of the officers who had worked at the Morgan Street Jail where I was locked up. They could not figure me out now coming back to try and help others find their way to the Lord and back to society. I guess they thought I would want to stay away from places like this. It made me feel good when some of the officers who knew me would come over and shake my hand, telling me they appreciated what I was trying to do. They remembered what it was like for me when I was on the other side.

By September of 1991, I had finished with my studies and took the Florida exam for radiology. I passed and received a general radiographer's license, which limited me in the type of work I could do. I then started to make the rounds of all the hospitals in Tampa. Again, it was the same old story. As soon as I put down that I had been convicted of a crime on the application, I would receive a polite negative response. In the past, when I was a city councilman, I had moonlighted as an x-ray technician at St. Joseph Hospital and University Hospital in Tampa. Now they wouldn't even consider me.

In this same month, I received a letter from my attorney Arthur Addess, who was still handling my appeal. It basically said that Court of Appeals dismissed my appeal without an opinion. At this point, he was discharged by the court as my attorney unless I wanted to proceed further. The letter went on to say that any further appeals are rarely successful. I wrote him back and thanked him for all his effort and the time he had spent on my case. I saw no need to drag this out anymore. I was out and trying to rebuild my life. There was nothing more the courts could give back to me except vindication, which now seemed out of the question.

By the time the end of November came around, it seemed that no matter where I applied, it was the same old story. I was still working for the security company at the time but wanted to better myself and help people. This is what I had done all my life, helping and serving others. I had a wealth of knowledge and experience inside me and felt somebody could use it. But it seemed I was still too much of a hot potato for anyone to touch.

As usual, when you're depressed and everything seems hopeless because you ran out of places to turn to for help, there is always one place we can turn to—that is, to the Lord, where I should have gone in the first place.

When I got home one evening after being rejected again, I put my problems in his hands as I had done so many times before. I figured by now he must be tired of hearing my problems. Although things were rough for me at the moment, they weren't as bad as for some others who were less fortunate than me. I was home. I had a job, food on the table, and my family. There are those who have nothing and are living on the street. So what right did I have to ask the Lord for help when there were so many who were in need more than I was? Still, I asked, and he answered.

There was still one last place I hadn't tried, and that was Tampa General Hospital on Davis Islands in downtown Tampa. I figured there was no use in trying there since all the other big hospitals had already turned me down. What would make Tampa General any different? I thought they were all interconnected with the same hiring policies.

Like I did every night, I gave thanks to the Lord for the day he had given me, no matter how it had turned out, and asked for a blessing for the next day. I explained my needs and situation, although I knew he already knew about it. I just asked him, "You got me here, Lord. We came this far. Where do you want me to go from here?"

Again, I was all alone in the house. I missed my dog, Molly, who passed away when I was in prison. She would come over and stay by my side at night and put her head on my lap when I was blue. It would be a while before my son Steven would be able to come home and live with me again. Then I would need to be here for him when he got out to help him adjust back to a meaningful life. I turned off the lights and went to sleep. I had sales that I needed to make to make ends meet.

The next morning after I got up, I dressed and had breakfast. Sitting at the table, staring out my window and wondering how my day would go, a strange thought entered my head. It kept repeating itself over and over, *Go try Tampa General. Go try Tampa General.* I couldn't get the thought out of my head. Then I said to myself, *Oh, what do I have to lose? I've been rejected everyplace else. so why not one final time?*

At this point, I really didn't think I had a chance, but I'm not one to give up. I knew in my heart that there was someplace, somewhere, that could use a person like me. So I called my boss at the security company and told him I needed to take a personal day off. It really didn't matter much to him as I was a contract employee who worked on commission only and not a salary. So I only got paid for what I was able to sell.

That morning, I drove over to the hospital and asked to see the director of radiology. The information desk directed me to the second floor of the hospital's main building. There I walked over to the receptionist, who was sitting behind a glass enclosure, and I asked to speak with the director of radiology. The young lady said, "That would be Mr. Dick Barcia. I'll see if he is in."

She picked up the phone and dialed his office, which was down the hall from us, and informed his secretary that I wished to see him. A few moments later, his secretary came out and told me to follow her to Mr. Barcia's office and have a seat. Mr. Barcia was in a meeting and would be with me shortly.

After waiting about a half hour, Mr. Barcia came walking into his office. He was a stocky man well over six feet tall and casually dressed. "Joe Kotvas," he said as he entered and greeted me. "Take a seat. And how can I help you?"

His demeanor made me feel at ease as we talked. I started to explain my situation to him. He already knew who I was and where I was coming from. I explained I used to be an x-ray technician and would like to get back into the field, that I was qualified and registry eligible.

After some lengthy conversation, he gave me a confused look on his face and said, "Joe, do you mean to tell me that after all the people you helped in this town, no one would give you a decent job?"

I told him, "Yes. It seems I've been blacklisted, and everyone seems afraid to give me a chance to prove myself, except a few loyal friends."

He then reached over his desk and picked up the phone, calling the chief of the x-ray department into his office. A moment later, the man entered his office and said, "You wanted to see me, Dick?"

His name was Dave Vallejo, and he was in charge of the main radiology department. Mr. Barcia said, "You know Mr. Kotvas? He used to be an x-ray technician and is looking for a position with us. Let's see where we can put him to start."

Then he said to me, "Joe, you need to go to personnel and fill out an application, then come back here."

I couldn't believe it—again, a prayer had been answered! I didn't know what to say. Here were two men I hardly knew, yet they knew all about me and were willing to give me a chance. I rushed over to human resources and filled out the application. Because of the incident with my back a few years earlier in prison, I was subject to a two-day rigid physical exam, which I passed. The hospital was worried I would not be able to perform my duties. It took almost two weeks for me to get through everything, but I passed every obstacle.

When I was finally approved, I was to report back to Mr. Barcia's office for the final interview. He and David Vallejo were in his office when I arrived. They told me that since I was not yet a registered technician but only registry eligible, they could not put me to work as a full x-ray tech until I got my registry, which I would have to study for. So Davie Vallejo said that, under the law, he could put me on and pay me at the same rate of pay as a coop worker till I passed the registry. Once I passed the exam, then he could move my pay up to full rad tech.

I had the job! My first day of work was on December 23, 1991. I now had a position that meant something, in which I could prove myself and rebuild my reputation in the community. I owe a lot to those two gentlemen. They were willing to take a chance on me when most people refused to do so. It was the start of a new future.

After a year of studying and taking the registry twice, I finally passed and was moved to permanent technician status. By then, it was around November of 1992. On November 12, 1992, I received a letter from the US Probation Office, telling me that my supervision was officially terminated. As of November 12, 1992, I had no further obligation to the probation office or the government. I could now apply to have my civil rights restored by the State of Florida.

Now that I was off parole, I applied to the state to have my rights restored, filling out all the paperwork and going through a six-month waiting period. It wasn't until December 7, 1993 that I officially received my civil rights back. I was now truly free and a voting citizen again.

Dick Barcia and David Vallejo and I would become good friends over time. I have had a wonderful working relationship with

Tampa General Hospital and all its staff and doctors. From this point in my life, things started to get a lot better for me. My community as a whole started to take a different look at me, and people were no longer afraid to associate with me.

On occasion, when I would run into Charlie Bean or Jan Platt at different functions, I would put the past behind me and be cordial toward them. I guess the pain and scars of it all will always be with me, but forgiving makes it easier to face tomorrow and start living again. I found the best way is by helping others again. I was now a much happier person, for I always had the love and respect of my family and friends.

There is one thing I've always said to my children, "You're never a loser until you quit. I've never been one for quitting. If they knock me down, I'll keep getting up till they quit and give up."

Like the phoenix, I have emerged from the ashes of shame and despair to soar ahead with my life. Over time, I was able to rebuild my life. I now work in a position of trust and have held the position of weekend supervisor for the main radiology department at Tampa General for a good number of years.

My daughter had gotten married to a great guy and now has a son and a fine career in real estate. My son Steven finally came home and, with my help, has started to rebuild his life. These were difficult years for both of us. My son Joseph also got married, left the navy, graduated from Trinity Christian Collage in Jacksonville, and became an associate pastor in a Baptist Church in Fort Myers, Florida. He was also working as a full-time deputy sheriff for Lee County. He would later receive a calling to serve the Lord full-time and give up his position with the sheriff's department to dedicate his life to do missionary work with the deaf at a deaf school and church in Lima, Peru, where he and his wife and my ten grandchildren live and work today.

Like Job, for all that I had lost and all that was taken away from me, I believe the Lord returned it all to me over time. My true treasure is the love of my family and the many grandchildren I have been blessed with, plus all the people I've been trying to help along the way.

EPILOGUE

Today

Avenge not yourselves, but rather give place unto wrath: for it is written, Vengeance is mine; I will repay, saith the Lord.

—Romans 12:9 (KJV)

So where is everybody today? Most moved on with their lives, rebuilding their reputations or businesses. Others just seemed to fade away out of the limelight. The 1980's took their toll on the Tampa Bay Area, but our community has since bounced back.

I think if all this would have taken place today, the jury and the court might have taken a different attitude toward the way our trial went. Back then, the federal prosecutors, the FBI, and the justice system had an air of honesty about them that the public believed in.

Today you can pick up the newspapers or listen to the news on radio or TV and see how some prosecutors or FBI agents have manipulated evidence and threatened witnesses to get a conviction, and their cases are being overturned or looked into. In some minds, in the legal circles, it is no longer the Department of Justice but the department of injustices. To them, it is not a matter of innocent until proven guilty but guilty until proven innocent. Today, thanks to an alert media, we see so much prosecutorial misconduct in every level of government, something that had been going on for years without being noticed. A lot of this is changing today with more public awareness and private watchdog agencies.

Jerry Bowmer was the
government's star witness

As for Jerry Bowmer, after all his accusations and finger-point-ing, he served a total of eight months off and on in the federal prison system. He then went on to later be charged with cattle rustling in North Florida in 1992. He pleaded guilty and was sentenced to twelve years in prison. Bowmer was released in 1998, and from there, he opened a company called Buccaneer Property Services Inc. out of Lutz, Florida, where he was selling swampy land and property in areas that were inaccessible or undevelopable. Because of this, he was investigated by the attorney general's office for unfair and deceptive trade practices related to land sales on eBay. He claimed the land had a certain appraised value, which was greatly inflated.

So this was the man Robert Merkle called a hero to our com-munity, the man who initiated the great witch hunt of the '80s. Now the world could see him for what he really was. Nothing in all that Bowmer has been through has changed him one bit from what and who he really is (buyers beware).

Former County Commissioner Charles F. Bean III pleaded guilty last year to racketeering

Charles Bean ended up serving only four months because of his cooperation with the federal government. Unlike Bowmer, he quietly slipped back into private life here in Tampa, attempting to put his life back together and put the past behind him. He would no longer have anything to do with Bowmer or his scams.

I was no longer looking for any type of payback. I had already made a promise while in prison to let it all go. Still, as strange as it might seem, by some mysterious power, many of those from the prosecutor's side who had testified against us, judged us, or tried to make things difficult for us, within a few short years, met with some type of unfortunate situation or tragedy in their lives.

U.S. District Judge George C. Carr is presiding over the County Commission bribery trial

In 1990, US district judge George C. Carr, who was the trial judge at both my trials, died at the age of sixty of a brain tumor. He had served on the bench till the very end. I always wondered if that might have had some slight effect on his attitude toward us and the outcome of my trial.

Robert Merkle, after losing his senatorial bid, went into private practice and partnership with Joe Magri, opening the law firm of Merkle & Magri PA in Tampa. Although I disliked the man for what had happen to Fred Anderson and myself, I have never wished ill of him. Nevertheless, in 2003, he died of cancer at the age of fifty-eight, leaving behind a wife and nine children.

U.S. Attorney Robert W. Merkle is under fire from the

I was rebuilding my life when I heard of his death, and my heart went out to his family. I remembered how hard it was for me and my children when I lost my wife to cancer. I could feel their pain, for I really never got over the pain of losing my wife. Merkle and I had our differences. I realize he had a job to do, and he did it very well. To him, I was the bad guy, and he never took the time to see who I really was.

Nor did I want to take the time to see the type of man he really was. But I will never wish harm or cancer on anyone. By the grace of God, it took me a while to forgive him and his staff for all I and my family went through, and to let go of the hate and pain we were all going through. Unless you have experienced someone suffering from cancer, you have no real understanding what that person must be going through or their family. May God rest his soul.

There were others also who met with misfortune. Charles Rambo, who testified at my second trial, was the real estate attorney who claimed he had paid a bribe to the three commissioners on the word of Jerry Bowmer. A couple of years later, he was indicted for stealing money from his client's escrow accounts. He lost his license to practice and was sent to prison for his crime.

Allen Wolfson, whom the government had an interest in and who was serving time for the collapse and defrauding of the Key Bank of Florida and the Metropolitan Bank and Trust of Tampa, was released from prison in 1990, when he moved to Salt Lake City, Utah, to start all over. By 1997, he again was in trouble with the government and the Securities and Exchange Commission for running a stock manipulation scheme, securities fraud, and wire fraud.

As for Joseph Magri, he left the federal prosecutor's office after not receiving the appointment of chief prosecutor for the Middle District of Florida. He went into partnership with Robert Merkle, and they took on a third partner named Ward Meythaler. Today they still keep the name of their firm as Merkle, Magri & Meythaler PA in Tampa.

Many of the defendants whom Merkle had accused, successfully or unsuccessfully, of wrongdoing, rebuilt their reputations and went on to be very successful.

Mr. Robert Cannella, after his wife passed away with cancer, continued to take care of his family and go on with his law practice, which is doing very well today.

Robert E. Curry, a 55-year-

Former Hillsborough county commissioner Robert "Bob" Curry was found not guilty of all charges. After the trial, he retreated with his family to a quiet life in the community till his death at the age of seventy-eight in 2010.

Nelson A. Italiano is accused of arranging bribes.

Mr. Nelson Italiano, after winning his appeals, rejoined his family in Tampa. He continued working with his family in the family insurance business of Italiano Insurance, which is still in business to this day. Mr. Italiano passed away peacefully in his sleep in 2013 at the age of eighty-five. He is still well respected in our community.

Sandra Freedman, whom Robert Merkle attempted to implicate without foundation as having participated in illegal activity while serving on the Tampa city council, became the first female mayor of Tampa, serving three outstanding terms as mayor. Because of her efforts, in 1990, Tampa was designated as the "All-American City."

Former State Representative Elvin Martinez overcame Robert Merkle's unfounded accusations. He finished an outstanding career in the Florida House of Representatives, then was appointed by Governor Lawton Chiles as judge for Hillsborough County. He served and was reelected for many years on the bench till his formal retirement. He now enjoys his life with his family and grandchildren.

To further prove the faith and love for all his hard work for the people of Florida and the Tampa Bay community, as well as the faith the Florida legislature had for the man, in 2012, the Florida legislature designated Tampa Bay Boulevard as Elvin Martinez Road, placing a large sign at the intersection of Tampa Bay Boulevard and Himes Avenue, commemorating the sight in West Tampa where he represented his constituents.

Former mayor and Florida governor Bob Martinez was constantly accused by Robert Merkle of taking a political bribe, but Merkle could never prove it. Throughout his senatorial campaign, he kept making those accusations, attempting to hurt the governor's reputation.

Governor Martinez served the people of Florida with distinction, being the first Hispanic American to hold that office. When the governor left office, he was appointed to the position of director of the Office of National Drug Control Policy (also known as the Drug Czar) by President George H. W. Bush. Now he lives in Tampa as a very successful businessman.

The Honorable EJ Salcines, one of the most honorable men in our community, was persecuted by Robert Merkle for more than three years. His good reputation was ruined for a while, but in the end, Merkle's investigation came up empty. Neither he nor any of his investigators could find one thing wrong with Mr. Salcines. It was too late though; the damage to Mr. Salcines's reputation was already done. To Merkle's satisfaction, the honorable Mr. Salcines lost his bid for reelection.

This was not the end for EJ Salcines. Beloved by his community, he emerged as the Hispanic Man of the Year. Very active and knowledgeable about the history of Tampa's Hispanic culture, he would be invited by many groups and organizations to give talks on the subject. He would later be appointed by Governor Lawton Chiles to a judgeship on the Second District Court of Appeals in Florida, where he served for a good number of years with distinction until he had to retire upon reaching age seventy.

This man, whom Merkle tried to destroy, overcame all the obstacles thrown in his path to become one of Tampa's most honored citizens. He now lectures at Stetson University's law school here in Tampa and for the Tampa Bay History Center. He has been recognized by the Florida Prosecuting Attorneys Association, which just recently awarded him the Lifetime Achievement Award and gave him a standing ovation. This is a man whom Merkle could not destroy. Mr. Salcines came through the ordeal and was resurrected from the ashes to become one of Tampa's most beloved and honorable citizens.

Michal Sierra finished his sentence at the halfway house, and after five years, he was able to get his law license reinstated. Today he is still a well-respected attorney in the community. With his family at his side through all his hardships, he was able to rebuild an excellent law practice. His son Christopher and his daughter, Monica, both became lawyers. His other son Timothy works in promotions for the family's automotive business, which helped to support them through the hard times.

↑ Tampa lawyer Sierra was among the acquitted.

Mr. Sierra's daughter, Monica, ran for circuit judge in Hillsborough County and won the seat on the bench. She was the youngest circuit judge at the time. The Sierra name is a well-respected name in the Tampa community, and the community came out in support of them. The family has always done a lot of community service for the area.

Cullen H. "Buster" Williams, 47-year-old Riverview dirt hauler and developer.

Both Cullen H. Williams and Claud Tanner served their time and retired to private life in our community. They have since rebuilt their lives and prefer to stay out of the limelight.

Claude Tanner, 56-year-old

Juliann Holt, who represented Mr. Tanner's business during the trial, a few years later, went on to run for the Office of the Public Defender here in Hillsborough County. She won a resounding victory and has been reelected a number of times, holding the office to this very day.

Joe Bealer, the lead attorney for the defense, returned to a flourishing law practice in Miami.

Fred Anderson, as you know, passed away in prison. His wife and daughter are living a simple, quiet life away from the limelight here in Tampa, Florida. I can only hope and pray that the scars and pain they suffered will one day heal.

As for my attorney Ray Harris, his condition continued to get worse from his illness. After my trial, he never really practiced any law. For my own defense, because of his condition, I should have asked the court to appoint a new attorney to represent me. Due to my ignorance on procedures and feeling sorry for the man, I took no action; this cost me the loss of a good opportunity to get my side of the story out.

There was a lot of confusion going on during that time. As the only one incarcerated during the whole trial, I had no real access to advice or information on what I should do. When they would take me to the courthouse, everyone was busy with their own clients, and the trial would be starting within a few minutes. They would all meet after court and go over the day's events, but when the trial ended each day, I would be whisked away back to the county jail. But most of this, you have already read.

A few years after I was released from prison, Mr. Harris passed away due to his illness. We kept in contact when I came home because I was worried about him. After his death, his daughter told me that her father had been suffering from this illness ever since he had been in the service. The VA could never understand what it was. They believed it might have been a type of Legionnaires' disease. He had been fighting the condition since she could remember, and it had worsened over the years. She couldn't understand how he managed to do all he did as sick as he was. But he always had a keen mind and would try to work whenever he was feeling a little better.

You may think of me as you will, but as you have already read, I didn't quit or give up on my life. Maybe there was a reason for all these things happening to me. Maybe God was finding a way to use me so I would able to touch the lives of some of the people I met along the way and give them some sort of encouragement. All I know is, this all must have happened for a reason. By the power of prayer, maybe someday I will find out.

I do believe that with the Lord's help, I was able to turn my life around and rebuild a better future for my children and myself. To this day, I still work at Tampa General Hospital, trying to help others and giving comfort to those who are suffering with pain. By doing this, I have regained the trust and respect of the Tampa Bay community.

If one believes in God and the power of prayer, then life has a way of turning a situation around. As time goes on, we learn we can make a difference in our situation by not giving in to adversity. In all things, we should give thanks to the Lord, whether good or bad. We should try and look forward and not back. By always thinking positive and making the best out of a bad situation, life does go on, and so will I. Our future is not written yet. It is a blank page for us to fill. How it will read depends on what road in life we choose to take. We should make the most of it.

This brings me to a poem that my late wife, Catherine, wrote a few months before she passed away. I have recited this poem to myself often ever since I came home from prison, and I try to abide by it:

> I have paused along life's way,
> To share a feeling now and then,
> To help a sad and troubled heart,
> To smile and laugh again.
> I need to leave no tales of greatness,
> nor glory, wealth, or fame,
> It's enough that someone warmly smiles,
> When remembering my name.

For those of us who survived and moved forward, to God goes the glory.

All photos are from public domain, or courtesy of the State Archives of Florida, or from news articles from *The Tampa Tribune* newspaper, or were taken by Tony Zappone or the author. The drawing of the trial is courtesy of Jim Caltagirone.

ABOUT THE AUTHOR

Joe H. Kotvas was born in New York City in 1943. He has a brother, Frank, of New Jersey and a sister, now deceased, who made Tampa her lifetime home. Joe grew up in New York and Tampa and was raised solely by his mother, who worked in a shrimp processing plant and a laundry for minimum wage.

His mother had only a third grade education and could neither read nor write, but she did her best to raise her two sons under adverse conditions. Joe, unable to get study help from his mother and being pushed through the New York school system, did not learn how to read or write until he was ten. It was then that a fifth grade teacher saw something in him and took an interest in his education. He was put in a special remedial reading class, and by the time he got to the eighth grade, he was reading at college level.

As a small boy, he had an interest in history and loved to tell stories. As he grew older, history became his hobby. Joe attended high school at night so he could work and help his mother.

His work life started with a messenger service, learning how to get around the Big Apple. At seventeen, he went to school to become an x-ray technician and worked in major hospitals in New York. He was married at nineteen to Catherine LaCalamito, and they have three children: Julia, Joseph, and Steven. At twenty-one, Joe became a New York City transit patrolman.

While still in New York, at age eighteen, he founded the Triton Cadets Inc., a youth community service organization he would eventually introduce to the city of Tampa.

When Joe was twenty-five, he moved his family to Tampa to become a police officer. Three years later, he was elected to the Tampa city council. He ran for mayor of Tampa in 1973 and missed becoming chief executive of a giant Southern city by about 158 votes. His wife passed away from metastatic cancer in 1978, leaving him devastated and alone to raise his three small children. That same year, he was elected to continue serving on the city council. In 1980, voters gave Joe the nod to become a Hillsborough county commissioner.

In 1983, Joe was implicated in one of the county's biggest corruption scandals and charged with racketeering. Although there was no evidence that he had ever committed any crime, he was found guilty by association. He served five years in federal prison. Eventually, he was sent to a minimum-security facility at Maxwell Air Force Base in Montgomery, Alabama, where he started his research on the war in the Aleutians, which culminated in his recent book *Men of the Invisible War.*

When Joe was released in 1990, he had a difficult time putting his life back together; but within a year, he had regained his civil rights so he could move on. After several years, he reacquired his license as an x-ray technician. Joe had spent most of his life in public service, and he wasn't going to let this setback stop him from continuing.

Because of his record, trying to find someone willing to give him a chance at employment was not easy. After some time, it finally happened. He found a position in a first-class major trauma center at Tampa General Hospital, where he holds a position of trust as a team leader. Joe currently lives in Tampa with his youngest son, Thomas.

CPSIA information can be obtained
at www.ICGtesting.com
Printed in the USA
FSOW01n0105200117
29752FS